THE COMMON CORE OF EUROPEAN ADMINISTRATIVE LAWS

General Editors

GIACINTO DELLA CANANEA

MAURO BUSSANI

Administrative Rulemaking and Planning in European Laws

THE COMMON CORE OF EUROPEAN ADMINISTRATIVE LAWS

General Editors:

Giacinto della Cananea, Professor of Administrative Law at Bocconi University; and Mauro Bussani, Professor of Comparative Law at the University of Trieste and Adjunct Professor of Comparative Law at the University of Macau

OTHER TITLES IN THE SERIES:

Tort Liability of Public Authorities in European Laws
Edited by Giacinto della Cananea and Roberto Caranta

Administrative Justice Fin de siècle
Early Judicial Standards of Administrative Conduct in Europe (1890–1910)
Edited by Giacinto della Cananea and Stefano Mannoni

Judicial Review of Administration in Europe
Procedural Fairness and Propriety
Edited by Giacinto della Cananea and Mads Andenas

Procedural Requirements for Administrative Limits to Property Rights
Edited by Martina Conticelli and Thomas Perroud

The Austrian Codification of Administrative Procedure
Diffusion and Oblivion (1920-1970)
Edited by Giacinto della Cananea, Angela Ferrari Zumbini, and Otto Pfersmann

General Principles and Sector-Specific Rules in European Administrative Laws
Edited by Giacinto della Cananea and Jean-Bernard Auby

European Research Council
Established by the European Commission

The Common Core of European Administrative Law (CoCEAL) project has received funding from the European Research Council (ERC) under the Horizon 2020 Research and Innovation Programme 'Advanced Grant' Excellent Science (Grant Agreement No 694697).

Administrative Rulemaking and Planning in European Laws

Edited by
GIACINTO DELLA CANANEA
and
ANGELA FERRARI ZUMBINI

OXFORD
UNIVERSITY PRESS

OXFORD
UNIVERSITY PRESS

Great Clarendon Street, Oxford, OX2 6DP,
United Kingdom

Oxford University Press is a department of the University of Oxford.
It furthers the University's objective of excellence in research, scholarship,
and education by publishing worldwide. Oxford is a registered trade mark of
Oxford University Press in the UK and in certain other countries

Published in the United States of America by Oxford University Press
198 Madison Avenue, New York, NY 10016, United States of America

British Library Cataloguing in Publication Data
Data available

Library of Congress Control Number: 2024951459

ISBN 978–0–19–886761–6

DOI: 10.1093/oso/9780198867616.001.0001

Printed and bound by
CPI Group (UK) Ltd, Croydon, CR0 4YY

MIX
Paper | Supporting responsible forestry
FSC® C013604

The manufacturer's authorised representative in the EU for product safety is
Oxford University Press España S.A. of El Parque Empresarial San Fernando de Henares, Avenida de Castilla, 2 – 28830 Madrid (www.oup.es/en or
product.safety@oup.com). OUP España S.A. also acts as importer into Spain
of products made by the manufacturer.

General Editors' Preface

This is a new book in the series entitled *The Common Core of European Administrative Laws* (CoCEAL), based on a comparative research for which the European Research Council has awarded us an Advanced Grant. From the outset, it was decided that this research would have two major themes. The first concerns the methodology of comparative analysis. Our intent is to compare a plurality of legal systems, going beyond the mainstream scrutiny of the more influential ones and seeking to understand the role of various legal formants therein. Secondly, and more importantly, this comparison has a particular end in view. Our intent is to launch a large-scale debate not only on commonalities and diversities within the European legal space but also, and more importantly, on how commonality and diversity have extended and interact with one another, within and across legal systems, both diachronically and synchronically, in the past and today.

From the first point of view, the methodology adopted in our research owes a great deal to the pioneering seminars held at Cornell Law School during the 1960s and to the 'Common Core of European Private Law' project, launched in 1993. This methodology is based on a factual analysis insofar as it is based on hypothetical cases that are first subjected to scrutiny during workshops with experts from the legal systems selected for comparison in order to ascertain whether the proposed cases are plausible and meaningful. Only at a later stage are these cases forwarded to the experts, who formulate their responses based on all the pertinent legal formants. A further step consists in comparing the answers obtained, with a view to understanding the relevance and significance of both the commonalities and the diversity that emerge.

From the second point of view, this new research focuses heavily on administrative procedure and thus examines various types of administrative action, including adjudication and rulemaking, without overlooking the importance of traditional sets of issues, such as those relating to judicial review and government liability in tort, which are considered both 'classic' and important. Collectively, these topics allow us to duly acknowledge the contributions of those who have gone before, using legal comparison as a means to various ends. They enable us to call for increased attention to what is new and original in the European legal space, where national legal systems interact with one another and with the two regional organisations, namely the European Union and the Council of Europe.

The website dedicated to our comparative research, www.coceal.it, provides information on both the results of the research and the next steps to be taken.

Giacinto della Cananea and Mauro Bussani

Editors' Preface

This book marks a new stage in our comparative enquiry into administrative law in Europe. It addresses an area of administration that is, in the functional sense, both under-studied and under-theorized: administrative rulemaking and planning. Most comparative studies focus on administrative adjudication, whose rationale—according to Lon Fuller—is to confer a distinct form of involvement in the decision-making process on affected parties. However, this is neither the only, nor necessarily the most important, form of administration. Indeed, in an increasing number of cases, the content of individual decisions is pre-determined by administrative rules and plans. In other instances, rules and plans shape the balance of interests the decision-maker seeks to achieve. The issues that arise from this are undeniably significant, as they touch upon matters such as the separation of powers, legality, and transparency, among other things.

The comparative perspective adopted here, though limited to a selected number of legal systems, is a privileged one as it allows a better understanding of how these forms of administrative action are structured in modern societies and how the issues they raise are approached by public institutions, including parliaments and courts. As in the previous books in this series, we undertake a comparative examination of problems and their solutions, aiming to identify their commonalities and differences. Attention to both aspects is an essential feature of our research. Another essential feature of our study is the use of hypothetical cases. Some of these have already been discussed in earlier public law scholarship, while others relate to new challenges and scenarios. In both cases, our research aims to determine whether the same problems would have similar—if not identical—solutions or different responses, exploring the underlying reasons for the outcomes.

The book is structured as follows. Part I sets out the purposes and scope of our analysis, and Part II describes some general characteristics of the legal systems included in our comparative inquiry. Part III presents the responses given by the national experts regarding the hypothetical cases central to our 'factual' analysis. Part IV analyses these responses from the comparative perspective, with the specific goal of ascertaining not so much whether a 'common core' exists but how it is shaped and evolves.

It is necessary, at this point, to mention briefly the jurisdictions and problems examined in this study. Although our research primarily focuses on Europe, we have also explored other regions of the world to gain a deeper understanding of the commonalities and differences found among modern legal systems, incorporating the United States and China into our selection. We recognize, of course, that other legal systems are equally important and might yield different results, so further examination will be necessary in the future.

Lastly, we owe a considerable debt of gratitude to a large number of people. The CoCEAL research team, including Mads Andenas, Mauro Bussani, Roberto Caranta,

Martina Conticelli, and Marta Infantino, contributed to the design of the questionnaire. Some of the hypothetical cases were revised during the workshop held at Bocconi University in October 2022, and a new case was added following a suggestion by Josephine van den Brink. Adrian Bedford and Paola Monaco reviewed all the chapters for English language usage and compliance with the OUP guidelines, respectively. We also thank Bocconi University (and especially Paola Calogero) for their support in managing the project as a whole.

Giacinto della Cananea and Angela Ferrari Zumbini

Contents

PART III CASES

PART IV COMPARATIVE ANALYSIS

Detailed Table of Contents

Table of Cases

(Chronological order except where otherwise specified)

AUSTRIA

Constitutional Court (*Verfassungsgerichtshof*)

CZECH REPUBLIC

Constitutional Court

Supreme Administrative Court

Resolution

CHINA

Supreme People's Court

Intermediate People's Court

Other Courts

EUROPEAN UNION

GERMANY

HUNGARY

Constitutional Court

Curia of Hungary

ITALY

Constitutional Court (*Corte Costituzionale*)

Council of State (*Consiglio di Stato*)

NETHERLANDS

Supreme Court of the Netherlands (*Hoge Raad der Nederlanden)*

Administrative Jurisdiction Division of the Council of State (*Afdeling bestuursrechtspraak van de Raad van State* - **ABRVS**).

PORTUGAL

Constitutional Court (*Tribunal Constitucional*)

Supreme Administrative Court *(Supremo Tribunal Administrativo)*

Central Administrative Court (*Tribunal Central Administrativo Sul*)

SWEDEN

Supreme Administrative Court (*Regeringsrätten* **– up to 2020)**

Supreme Administrative Court (*Högsta förvaltningsdomstolen* **– from 2020)**

Land and Environment Court of Appeal *(Mark - och miljööverdomstolen)*

Parliamentary Ombudsman (*Riksdagens ombudsmän*)

UNITED KINGDOM

UNITED STATES OF AMERICA

Table of Legislation

CHINA

EUROPEAN UNION

GERMANY

HUNGARY

ITALY

NETHERLANDS

NORWAY

PORTUGAL

SWEDEN

UNITED KINGDOM

UNITED STATES OF AMERICA

List of Abbreviations

ABRvS	*Afdeling bestuursrechtspraak van de Raad van State* (The Netherlands)
AC	Law Reports, Appeal Cases (Third Series)
Admin L Rev	Administrative Law Review
AIA	Environmental Impact Assessment (Portugal)
All ER	All England Law Reports
Am Bar Ass J	American Bar Association Journal
Admin L Rev	Administrative Law Review
AJCL	American Journal of Comparative Law
AHG	*Amtshaftungsgesetz*
Am J Int L	American Journal of International Law
Am Pol Sc Rev	American Political Science Review
Am Univ L Rev	American University Law Review
APA	Administrative Procesure Act (Germany, Norway, Portugal, United States)
APA	Code of Administrative Procedure (Hungary)
art/arts	Article/Articles
AVG	*Allgemeines Verwaltungsverfahrensgesetz* (General Administrative Procedure Act) (Austria)
AWG	*Abfallwirtschaftsgesetz* (Austria)
BGBl	*Bundesgesetzblatt* (Austria)
BGBlG	*Bundesgesetzblattgesetz* (Austria)
BVergGKonz	*Bundesvergabegesetz Konzessionen* (Federal Concessions Award Act) (Austria)
B-VG	*Bundes-Verfassungsgesetz* (Federal Constitutional Law—Austria)
CAP	Code of Administrative Process (Italy)
Capital UL Rev	Capital University Law Review
CBA	cost-benefit analysis
CBb	*College van Beroep voor het bedrijfsleven* (High Administrative Court for Trade and Industry, Netherlands)
CEA	Cost-Effectiveness Analysis (EU)
Colum J Eur L	Columbia Journal of European Law
Columbia L Rev	Columbia Law Review
Cornell L R	Cornell Law Review
CPA	Code of Administrative Procedure (Portugal)
CPTA	Portuguese Code of Process in the Administrative Courts of Law
CRP	Portuguese Constitution
CUP	Cambridge University Press
dPCM	Decreto del Presidente del Consiglio dei Ministri

EAA	Environmental Appeals Act (Germany)
EAG	*Erneuerbaren-Ausbau-Gesetz* (Austria)
EASA	European Aviation Safety Agency
EC	European Commission
ECHR	European Convention on Human Rights
ECJ	European Court of Justice
ECSC	European Coal and Steel Community
ECT	European Community Treaty
ECtHR	European Court of Human Rights
EEC	European Economic Community
EIA	Environmental Impact Assessment
EMA	European Medicines Agency
EWHC	England and Wales High Court
ed(s)	editor(s)
edn	edition
eg	exampli gratia
EWCA	England and Wales Court of Appeal
Food, Drug & Cosm J	Food, Drug, Cosmetic Law Journal
ff	following
GALA	Dutch General Administrative Law Act (*Algemene wet bestuursrecht*) (The Netherlands)
GATT	General Agreement on Tariffs and Trade
GG	*Grundgesetz* (The Basic Law, Germany)
GISTI	Groupe d'information et de soutien des immigres
Harvard L Rev	Harvard Law Review
IA	Impact Assessment (EU)
ibid	ibidem
ICC	Interstate Commerce Commission (United States)
ie	that is
IG-L	*Bundesgesetz zum Schutz vor Immissionen durch Luftschadstoffe* (*Immissionsschutzgesetz – Luft* (Austria)
INS	Immigration and Naturalization Service (United States)
Int J Const L	International Journal of Constitutional Law
It J Publ L	Italian Journal of Public Law
J Contemp Legal Issues	Journal of Contemporary Legal Issues
J European Public Pol	Journal of European Public Policy,
J of Int Ec L	Journal of International Economics
JO	*Justitieombudsmannen* (Sweden)
Law & Cont Probl	Law and Contemporary Problems
LPPSPU	Law of Public Policy for Land, Planning and Urban Planning (Portugal)
LPIL	Land Planning Instruments Law (Portugal)
MB	*Miljöbalken* (Environmental Code, Sweden)
Modern L Rev	Modern Law Review
NEPA	National Environmental Policy Act
NGO	non-governmental organization

no(s)	number(s)
NS	*Nationale Spoorwegen* (Dutch Railways, Netherlands)
OUP	Oxford University Press
p	page
para(s)	paragraph(s)
PBL	Plan and Building Act (Sweden)
Pol Sc Quart	Political Science Quarterly
PSO	Public Service Obligation (Netherlands)
PvE	*Programma van Eisen* (Program of Requirements, Netherlands)
QB	Law Reports, Queen's Bench
ReNEUAL	Research Network on EU Administrative Law
Riv trim dir pub	*Rivista trimestrale di diritto pubblico*
s/ss	Section/Sections
SEA	Single European Act
SPG	*Bundesgesetz über die Organisation der Sicherheitsverwaltung und die Ausübung der Sicherheitspolizei* (*Sicherheitspolizeigesetz*) (Austria)
S Tex L Rev	Southern Texas Law Review
StROG	*Steiermärkisches Raumordnungsgesetz* (Styrian Regional Planning Act) (Austria)
StVO	*Straßenverkehrsordnung* (Austria)
TFEU	Treaty on the Functioning of the European Union
Univ Chicago L Rev	University of Chicago Law Review
UK	United Kingdom
UKHL	United Kingdom House of Lords
UKSC	United Kingdom Supreme Court
UmwRG	*Umwelt-Rechtsbehelfsgesetz* (Environmental Appeals Act) (Germany)
US	United States
Yale L J	Yale Law Journal
Yale UP	Yale University Press
VfSlg	*Sammlung der Erkenntnisse und wichtigsten Beschlüsse des Verfassungsgerichtshofes* (Austria)
VwGH	*Verwaltungsgerichtshof* (Supreme Administrative Court) (Austria)
WTO	World Trade Organization

List of Contributors

Lilla Berkes
PhD, Associate Professor, Pázmány Péter Catholic University, Faculty of Law and Political Sciences, Department of Administrative Law, Budapest (Hungary)

Gabriela Blahoudková
PhD, Faculty of Law of Charles University in Prague, Department of Administrative Law and Administrative Science

Jacobine van den Brink
Professor of Administrative Law, University of Amsterdam (The Netherlands)

Daniel Burda
Faculty of Law of Charles University in Prague, Department of Administrative Law and Administrative Science

Roberto Caranta
Professor of Administrative Law, University of Turin (Italy)

Edoardo Chiti
Professor of Administrative law, Sant'Anna School of Advanced Studies—Pisa (Italy)

Giacinto della Cananea
Professor of Administrative Law, Bocconi University (Italy), Principal Investigator of the CoCEAL project

Angela Ferrari Zumbini
Professor of Administrative Law, University of Naples Federico II (Italy)

Björn Forssén
Doctor of Laws and Member of the Swedish Bar Association

Balázs Szabolcs Gerencsér
PhD Habil, Director of Ereky Public Law Research Center, Associate professor at Pázmány Péter Catholic University, Faculty of Law and Political Sciences, Department of Administrative Law, Budapest (Hungary)

Rui Guerra da Fonseca
Associate Professor, University of Lisbon Faculty of Law; Justice of the Constitutional Court of Portugal; Researcher, Lisbon Public Law Research Center (Portugal)

Patricia Jonason
Associate Professor, University of Södertörn (Sweden)

Jeffrey Lubbers
Professor of Practice in Administrative Law, American University, Washington College of Law (United States of America)

Marco Lunardelli
Contract Professor of Civil Protection Legislation, University of Pisa (Italy)

David Mark
PhD, Queen's University Belfast (United Kingdom)

John Morison
Professor of Law, Queen's University Belfast (United Kingdom)

Leonardo Parona
Assistant Professor of Administrative Law, Law Department of Roma Tre University (Italy)

Sophie Praniess
Advisor for Sustainable Finance and Just Transition, Federal Ministry for Climate Action, Environment, Energy, Mobility, Innovation and Technology (Austria)

Jiří Rajchl
PhD, Faculty of Law of Charles University in Prague, Department of Administrative Law and Administrative Science

Eivind Smith
Professor of Public Law, Faculty of Law, University of Oslo (Norway)

Stefan Storr
Professor of Public Law and Public Economic Law, Department of Public Law and Political Science, University of Graz (Austria)

Xiaowei Sun
Associate Professor of Public Law, Centre de Recherches Juridiques de Franche-Comté (CRJFC), Université de Franche-Comté (France)

Louise Verboeket
Lecturer and Researcher, University of Amsterdam (The Netherlands)

Veerle van Waarde
PhD Candidate, University of Amsterdam (The Netherlands)

Lilly Weidemann
Dr, Judge of the Administrative Court Bremen (Germany)

PART I
GENERAL PRINCIPLES AND COMPARATIVE STUDIES

Part I discusses the main themes of this book and the methodological issues concerning our comparative research on European administrative laws.

1
Introduction

Giacinto della Cananea

I. The Main Themes of this Book

This book is about administrative and public law, and it focuses in particular on two main themes. The overarching topic, established at the outset of this comparative inquiry,[1] is that if we aim to improve our understanding of how administrative functions and powers are discharged by public authorities (and private bodies), we cannot focus exclusively, or mainly, on formal procedures and judicial review. The second, and more specific, theme that will be explored here is the need for greater attention to administrative rulemaking and planning. Both themes will be examined more fully in the following pages. It should also be noted straight away that this volume presents the findings of comparative research, which looks mainly at administrative law in Europe but also takes into account the legal systems of the United States and China.

This introductory chapter is divided into four parts. Sections II and III discuss the two themes just mentioned. Section IV examines some issues in methodology, including the nature of our 'factual analysis' and the choice of the legal systems selected for our comparative inquiry. Lastly, Section V outlines the overall structure of the volume.

II. Background: The Many Faces of Administration

As indicated earlier, this book has two main themes. The first concerns the little attention that has been devoted to the many administrative activities other than adjudication. The second is the area of administrative rulemaking and planning. Both themes will be addressed in the next two sections. After this, the international and supranational dimensions of administrative rulemaking and planning will be discussed.

[1] This point was initially made in an article: G della Cananea and M Bussani, 'The Common Core of European Administrative Laws: A Framework for Analysis' (2019) 21 Maastricht Journal of European and Comparative Law 217. It has been developed more fully in a recent monograph: G della Cananea, *The Common Core of European Administrative Laws: Retrospective and Prospective* (Brill 2023), https://brill.com/display/title/63447 accessed 20 November 2024.

Giacinto della Cananea, *Introduction* In: *Administrative Rulemaking and Planning in European Laws*. Edited by: Giacinto della Cananea and Angela Ferrari Zumbini, Oxford University Press. © Giacinto della Cananea 2025.
DOI: 10.1093/oso/9780198867616.003.0001

A. Beyond Formalized Procedures and Judicial Review

It is axiomatic that the meaning and significance accorded to central themes in administrative law—and the very definition of those central themes—will inevitably depend on both the structure of a given legal system and on the more (or less) generally accepted conceptual frameworks (or 'paradigms', to borrow Kuhn's terminology)[2] within which jurists and judges seek to solve all manner of problems. In particular, the emphasis legal scholars and practitioners—in both civil law and common law systems—give to legislatively defined administrative procedures and judicial review has cast a shadow over various aspects of administrative action. At the beginning of his detailed and comprehensive study on the exercise of discretion by administrators and prosecutors, Kenneth Culp Davis, an American public lawyer, observed that:

> Administrative law literature is devoted mainly to the 10 or 20 percent of administrative action that involves either formal proceedings or judicial review, and it largely neglects the 80 or 90 percent that escapes both formal proceedings and judicial review. . . .[3]

A similar opinion was expressed twenty years later by two French public lawyers, Georges Vedel (who at that time had just left the *Conseil Constitutionnel*, or Constitutional Court) and Pierre Delvolvé.[4] They observed that judicial remedies against administrative action were regarded as the natural form of protection. However, the importance of such remedies was exaggerated, as individuals could only have recourse to them after administrative authorities had acted. As a consequence, those remedies were used late, and in any case, they could prove unhelpful vis-à-vis some aspects of administrative action.

To borrow Davis' words again, there are many things within that 80 or 90 per cent that are seldom considered in administrative law scholarship. Within what public lawyers used to call 'active administration' there is, first, the elaboration and adjustment of public policies. Earlier theories of administrative law were based on the assumption that the administration was a sort of machinery and described its functioning according to the 'model transmission belt'.[5] On the other hand, contemporary public law and political science scholarship acknowledges that government officials make policies, in particular by drafting the agendas of political bodies.[6] In addition to producing the draft policy statements eventually adopted by political bodies, they publish a wide range of documents, including 'white' or 'green' papers proposing policy

[2] T Kuhn, *The Structure of Scientific Revolutions* (2nd edn, University of Chicago Press 1967) 10, <https://folk.ntnu.no/krill/bioko-references/Kuhn%201962.pdf> accessed 20 November 2024.

[3] KC Davis, *Discretionary Justice. A Preliminary Inquiry* (Greenwood Press 1971) vi.

[4] G Vedel and P Delvolvé, *Le système français de protection des administrés contre l'administration* (Sirey 1991) 125.

[5] RB Stewart, 'The Reformation of American Administrative Law' (1974–1975) 88 Harvard L Rev 1583.

[6] M Shapiro, 'Administrative Discretion: the Next Stage' (1983) 92 Yale L J 1487. See also S Cassese, 'New Paths for Administrative Law: A Manifesto' (2012) 10 Int J Const L 603 at 608 (arguing that administrative bodies are involved in policy-making in more than one way) and BG Peters, 'Agenda-Setting in the European Community' (1994) 1 J European Public Pol 9 (noticing that the European Commission makes the agenda for EU political institutions).

changes and setting targets for public policies, such as air pollution or welfare benefits.[7] The use of indicators as a governance technique is also rapidly increasing beyond the United States in the context of global regulatory frameworks.[8]

Secondly, there are a wide array of circulars, guidelines, instructions, and similar documents used to provide guidance for government officials. The terminology is neither consistent nor reliable, as a circular may contain either a statement about policy or about interpretative rules concerning new primary legislation (adopted by parliamentary institutions). These diverse regulations have a huge impact on administrative discretion. On one hand, public authorities often have broad discretion in their decision-making. On the other, precisely because these documents crystallize the objectives to be achieved and the required courses of action, they are—at least partially—binding upon their activities.

There is yet another important aspect of administrative action that can be termed informal as it involves activities where agencies negotiate with stakeholders before entering into transactions or adopting acts.[9] Thus, for example, public authorities dealing with environmental issues often negotiate agreements with corporations to reduce pollution.[10] More broadly, as another American administrative lawyer, Alfred J. Aman, has recently observed, there are several actions taken by public authorities 'which are addressed directly to citizens but are not legally binding on them', including advice and declarations.[11] Similarly, in her chapter on the Swedish legal system in this book, Patricia Jonason underlines the existence of non-binding acts, such as recommendations.[12]

Interestingly, Vedel and Delvolvé made another critical observation about legal scholarship. While they argued that the importance of judicial review was overemphasized, they noted that other means of addressing complaints about public administration existed but were under-studied and under-theorized. Other measures to protect citizens in the event of official mistakes, misuse, or even abuse of powers, included parliamentary oversight, ombudsmen (public authorities without judicial powers), public enquiries, and consultations.[13]

In connection with this, a non-negligible portion of administrative activity is dedicated to processes that assist public authorities in achieving their objectives. These include audits, rectification (identifying and addressing existing problems), and monitoring post-audit actions. Legal scholarship often overlooks these activities, which is a mistake. One may conclude that while audits do not entail adopting acts with binding effects like courts do, they still hold legal significance because they impose obligations to review conduct or amend actions.

[7] See E Page, *Governing by Numbers* (2001 Hart).

[8] See K Davis and others (eds), *Governance by Indicators: Global Power through Quantification and Rankings* (OUP 2012).

[9] Cassese (n 6) 609 (observing that administrative activities are increasingly being negotiated).

[10] See, with regard to France, P Lascoume, 'Negocier le droit: forms et conditions d'une activité gouvernamentale conventionelle' (1993) 11 Politiques et management public 47.

[11] AJ Aman, 'Informal Agency Action and US Administrative Law—Informal Procedure in a Global Era' (1994) 42 AJCL 665. For an earlier account, see KC Davis, 'Informal Administrative Action: Another View' (1977) 26 Am Univ L Rev 836.

[12] P Jonason and B Forssén 'Sweden', Part II in this book.

[13] Vedel and Delvolvé (n 4) 130–35.

Although this book does not cover all these sub-topics, as its focus is on administrative rulemaking and planning, I hope it can contribute (i) to a better understanding of the many facets of administration that are not fully addressed by either legislation or judicial review, (ii) to raise awareness of problems that merit further research and consideration, and (iii) to develop a framework for further comparative studies in this fundamental area of modern governance.

B. Administrative Rulemaking and Planning

The second, and more specific, theme of this book concerns administrative rulemaking and planning. Each of these sub-topics will now be addressed in turn.

In the past, it was assumed that a fundamental division existed—and had to be maintained—between rules and decisions as a consequence of the separation of powers. Rules were both general and abstract, defining standards of conduct for a predetermined class or category of individuals or legal entities, and for various legal relationships. Moreover, they had to be adopted by parliamentary bodies, which, in the early twentieth century, were seen as broadly representative of all parts of society, even if the term 'representative democracy' connoted very different realities. An individual decision, on the other hand, affected a specific individual or a predefined class of individuals or legal entities, for example in cases of expropriation and police powers, and had to be made by the executive. Establishing what the law is for a particular person; this was Otto Mayer's influential notion of the *Verwaltungsakt.*[14] This institutional framework did not exclude executive rulemaking, but it required authorization through delegation and was subject to limitations.

With the expansion of government, this once-clear division blurred somewhat. The two World Wars, along with the great economic depression in the interwar period and the widespread introduction of social security after 1945, all contributed to the emergence of what is often referred to as the 'administrative state', governed by massive bureaucracies. In the United States, the New Deal provided an important boost to administrative activities,[15] leading to the prominence of 'bureaucrats of rules and standards', to the point that the adoption of the Federal Administrative Procedure Act (1946) was a reaction to what was perceived as a sort of administrative despotism.[16] Interestingly, the more innovative part of the APA concerned rulemaking. Similarly, in many European nations, administrative authorities also began to adopt more and more rules. This practice was condemned in the more traditional legal scholarship, including by German public lawyer Ernst Forsthoff, on the grounds that it undermined the principle of *Rechtsstaat.*[17]

[14] O Mayer, *Deutsches Verwaltungsrecht* (1895), French translation by the author, *Droit administratif allemande* (Giard et Brière 1903) 121.

[15] Shapiro (n 6) 1487. See also D Kennedy, 'What the New Deal Did' (2009) 124 Pol Sc Quart 251, at 253 (arguing that the New Deal has a unifying pattern: security).

[16] For this argument, see Lord Hewart, *The New Despotism* (Benn 1929).

[17] E Forsthoff, *Rechtsstaat im Wandel: Verfassungsrechtliche Abhandlungen, 1950–1964* (Kohlhammer 1964).

The other sub-topic is planning. It concerns state authorities, which define national plans, for example, for the development of railway infrastructure and electronic communications networks. It also concerns local authorities. They do not confine themselves to promulgating by-laws and to adopting individual decisions. There are other acts with a broad scope of application in the nature of local government policymaking, in particular urban plans and zoning ordinances. These acts are an important factor of the way cities develop.[18] They thus impinge on both collective and individual interests, deciding where and to what extent urban development will be allowed or encouraged.

C. Theoretical and Institutional Foundations

For all their importance in modern administrative systems, there are several issues surrounding the theoretical and institutional foundations of administrative rules and plans. First among these is how they can be identified. Various elements appear to be relevant from the public law perspective, including the general applicability of a precept and its future effects.[19]

A precept is considered general when it applies to a predefined class of persons or legal entities, although such instances are still relatively rare. It must also be prospective, applying not only to existing legal relationships or situations at the time of the enactment but also to those that arise later. Rules, under this definition, become integrated into the legal system, although their effects vary. At times, they will have to be applied on a case-by-case basis, but they will often 'be determinative of the result and will strongly influence the outcome'.[20] In other cases, they are directly binding, like regulations.[21]

Similarly, a plan first specifies the goals and objectives and then establishes some kind of hierarchy between them. Thirdly, it indicates the means for achieving those goals. Normally, a plan is not directly binding, but it will influence the content of individual decisions.

A second issue concerns whether administrative institutions wield such powers legitimately. This issue relates to the separation of powers, in the sense that—as Montesquieu and the authors of the *Federalist Papers* observed—if the power to make laws is combined with the power to enforce them, liberty is endangered.[22] Not surprisingly, this issue was debated in several liberal democracies before the two World Wars, which saw the emergence of legislation empowering administrative institutions to make rules, including those concerning public safety, the supply of certain goods, and public order. In the past, those extensive powers were accepted under the pressure

[18] JB Auby, *Droit de la ville. Du fonctionnement juridique des villes au droit à la Ville* (2nd edn, LexisNexis 2018).

[19] Y Gaudemet, *Droit administratif* (21th edn, LGDJ 2015) 116.

[20] See P Craig, *Administrative Law* (5th edn, Sweet & Maxwell 2003) 398.

[21] See SA De Smith, 'Sub-Delegation and Circulars' (1949) 12 Modern L Rev 37, 43 (for the remark that 'many circulars do affect the rights of the public').

[22] See P Strauss, *Administrative Justice in the United States* (3rd edn, Carolina Academic Press 2016) 317 (discussing the impact of open government legislation) and Vedel and Delvolvé (n 4), 140.

of wartime. Today, administrative rules are accepted not only in civil emergencies, such as earthquakes or floods, but also in 'ordinary administration', such as market regulation. Administrative planning, similarly, falls under ordinary administration. The adoption of an ordinance, such as a city ordinance limiting municipal traffic or a zoning ordinance, is the most typical example of a power that affects the entire local population, although it may have a particular impact on specific individuals.

Thirdly, administrative rules raise issues from the perspective of control. There is often an unspoken assumption, perhaps more evident in older academic scholarship, that parliaments lack the expertise to adopt rules with technical content or may simply be unable to define all the rules necessary for complex societies. Whatever the intellectual soundness of this argument, the pertinent question is whether the current state of affairs is compatible with democratic principles.

D. The International and Supranational Dimensions

Lastly, it is important to acknowledge the impact or implications of international and supranational frameworks. 'Relevance' here refers to either the effects of existing rules and plans being determined by a supranational or international body, or the requirement to adopt such rules or plans in order to comply with the obligations arising from membership of such a body. Both EU law and World Trade Organization law exemplify the first scenario, while the second can be found in various areas of EU law. Additionally, the prospect of judicial review before supranational courts merits consideration.

The Treaty of Rome, establishing the European Economic Community (EEC), laid down a legal framework for the harmonisation of laws. The drafters of the Treaty were particularly concerned that divergent regulations could hinder the good functioning of the Common Market (later renamed 'single' market), for European business. To address this concern, Article 100 empowers the Council to issue directives for the 'approximation of such provisions laid down by law, regulation or administrative action in Member States as directly affect the establishment or functioning of the common market'. As Eric Stein, one of the first scholars to examine this power, notes, it was not intended to unify the legal systems of the Member States but to coordinate them.[23] Interestingly, it disregarded the traditional distinction between primary, secondary, and tertiary (or administrative) rules. Instead, the focus was on the nature and potential economic impact of national rules as regulations, emphasizing their potential effects on the mobility of economic factors and forces. The same rationale now underlies Article 114(1) of the Treaty on the Functioning of the European Union (TFEU), which grants EU institutions the authority to adopt 'the measures for the approximation of the provisions laid down by law, regulation or administrative action in member States' in relation to the establishment and functioning of the internal market.

More recently, Article X of the General Agreement on Tariffs and Trade (GATT) 1994 imposed three requirements on national authorities. The first is the requirement

[23] E Stein, 'Harmonization of European Company Laws' (1972) 37 Law & Cont Probl 318 at 323.

to publish their rules affecting trade 'promptly', so as to make them accessible to both other governments and traders.[24] Secondly, it required them to 'administer in a uniform, impartial and reasonable manner all its laws, regulations, decisions and rulings', in other words, to apply them in non-arbitrary ways. Thirdly, the Member States committed to maintain or institute 'judicial, arbitral or administrative tribunals or procedures for the purpose, inter alia, of the prompt review and correction of administrative action relating to customs matters' as soon as it would become practicable. Taken as a whole, these requirements confirm that what matters is not so much the status of legal rules but their capacity to govern the conduct of administrative agencies. Further evidence can be found in the ruling of the Appellate Body in a case concerning the European Commission, in which it stated that the obligation imposed on the contracting parties was to publish all rules 'of general application'.[25]

EU law also provides an interesting example of planning. The whole idea of the Common Agricultural Policy, which for many years was the largest in budgetary terms, was predicated on the premise that European administration would autonomously formulate plans regarding the quantities and prices of specific products, without interference from the courts. More recently, there has been a shift in the legal landscape concerning the autonomy of national administrations. Under the framework governing the EU recovery plan, there is now authority for administrative planning. The EU invested a huge amount of money in the Next Generation EU Recovery Plan to repair the social and economic damage caused by the coronavirus health emergency. As part of this initiative, all Member States are required to develop national recovery and resilience plans, which also include sector-specific plans, such as transport.

As European countries have sought to ensure better protection from administrative error and misuse or abuse of power, they have also agreed to allow their citizens and other individuals access to new judicial remedies beyond national boundaries. The European Court of Human Rights is the foremost jurisdiction of this type globally. Interestingly, the scope of its jurisdiction not only includes claims concerning individual administrative decisions but also rules and plans, particularly under Articles 6 and 8 of the European Convention on Human Rights.[26]

[24] Article X (1) GATT provides that: 'Laws, regulations, judicial decisions and administrative rulings of general application, made effective by any contracting party, pertaining to the classification or the valuation of products for customs purposes, or to rates of duty, taxes or other charges, or to requirements, restrictions or prohibitions on imports or exports or on the transfer of payments therefor, or affecting their sale, distribution, transportation, insurance, warehousing, inspection, exhibition, processing, mixing or other use, shall be published promptly in such a manner as to enable governments and traders to become acquainted with them.'

[25] WTO AB, WT/DS69/AB/R, 13 July 1998, *European Communities—Measures affecting the import of certain poultry products*, § 110. For further remarks, see P Ala'I, 'From the Periphery to the Center? The Evolving WTO Jurisprudence on Transparency and Good Governance' (2008) 11 J of Int Ec L 779 (for whom art X is fundamental as 'the embodiment of the principles of transparency and due process').

[26] See I Loveland, 'Injunctions, Planning Enforcement and Human Rights' (2002) 65 Modern L Rev 906.

III. Why Administrative Rulemaking and Planning Are Significant from the Comparative Perspective

After illustrating the increasing intrinsic importance of administrative rulemaking and planning, it may be appropriate to explain why the topic is also interesting from a comparative perspective. As observed earlier, this area is still scarcely studied and under-theorized.[27] Previous volumes in this series have dealt with various aspects of administrative adjudication, but it is now time to examine whether other forms of administrative action are subject to different constraints on power. In this regard, three questions will be briefly discussed: whether there are similar developments concerning the increase of rules and plans, whether there are comparable constraints on administrative decision-making, and, lastly and more specifically, whether any common standard of administrative conduct emerges with regard to procedural fairness and propriety.

A. A Parallel Development?

The first issue relevant to the comparative study of public law concerns the proliferation of administrative rules and plans. Is there, then, a 'parallel development', as Jean Rivero put it?[28] This aspect of the inquiry has two parts, one pertaining to the phenomenon itself and the other to the nature of rules and plans.

It is important to understand the role of executive regulation and planning in the discharge of administrative functions and powers and, more broadly, within society itself. Lawyers, adopting too narrow a focus, sometimes tend to emphasize the role of legislation as an instrument of policy. Not only does it place too much importance upon the 'rank' or binding force of legislation to guide society in a particular direction but it can also overlook instances where legislation can be modified by government regulations or decrees.

There are also some questions concerning not so much the plethora of labels given to executive rulemaking and planning (such as 'guidelines', 'instructions', 'codes of conduct', 'new frameworks', and similar terms), which is often confusing, but also concerning their inherent nature. Thus, for example, we should seek to understand whether there are acts with general content or effects that are formally distinct from regulations and, if so, whether they are subject to distinct norms regarding citizens' consultation or participation. Similarly, it is important to consider the various effects of plans, including how they affect existing decisions on land use and whether they provide mandatory or advisory guidance for the future.[29]

[27] F Morstein Marx, 'Administrative Regulation in Comparative Perspective' (1961) 26 Law & Cont Probl 307.

[28] J Rivero, *Cours de droit administratif comparé* (Les cours de droit 1957) 15 (noting the '*similitude des problèmes administratifs modernes, largement commandée par des facteurs techniques identiques de pays à pays*').

[29] A Dunham, 'A Legal and Economic Basis for Planning' (1958) 58 Columbia L Rev 650.

B. Fairness and Propriety in Non-Adjudicative Procedures

From another standpoint, rulemaking and planning also raise procedural issues. What matters is not only whether public authorities are doing the wrong thing but also whether they are acting in the wrong manner, such as not following prescribed procedures, omitting proper hearings for affected parties or neglecting to consider some relevant facts. Central to this issue are concerns about procedural fairness and propriety. Whether deviation from established principles and rules will invalidate the policy, rule, or plan is another question, which must be assessed in the light of judicial doctrines regarding the consequences that flow from procedural invalidity.

It is important to recognize that the traditional requirements of fairness and propriety, such as the right to be heard, have 'developed against the background of adversarial adjudication'.[30] The rationale of adjudication so ably grasped by Lon Fuller is the fact that 'it confers on the affected party a peculiar form of participation in the decision' potentially affecting its interests.[31] The question that arises, however, is whether this rationale has broader implications and significance. This may be the case, for example, when a public authority intends to expropriate someone of his or her property rights. Adjudication may also constitute the paradigm for the reduction of welfare benefits. However, despite its importance, adjudication is just one form or species of administrative action. What this suggests is that we should be ready to discuss whether alternative procedures may be more appropriate in certain circumstances. This does not necessarily imply that procedural fairness and propriety cannot be applied to non-adjudicative procedures. Rather, it suggests that legal scholars and judges should refrain from claiming that procedural obligations that presuppose a specific type of administrative action—adjudication—should be imposed in circumstances where other forms of administrative decision-making, affecting entire classes or categories of individuals, are at play.

It is important from the outset to be aware of the options at our disposal when thinking about these rules. All legal systems must determine the conceptual and practical distinctions between these rules and forms of executive rulemaking, including delegated legislation and regulations. However, these distinctions may vary considerably. Some legal systems may recognize a general norm—either enshrined in the formal constitution, as in Spain, or established through customary practice—providing for compulsory consultation. There may, or may not, be general legislation on administrative procedure that expressly governs the way administrative rules can be adopted, including consultation. Specifically, given the common assertion that rulemaking 'allows broader participation' in the making of agency policy,[32] it would be appropriate to ascertain whether this is indeed the case.

There is also an issue of the accessibility of any rule or plan adopted by a public authority. The question that arises is whether the failure to publish a rule would affect

[30] Craig (n 20) 453.

[31] L Fuller, 'The Form and Limits of Adjudication' (1978) 92 Harv L Rev 353, 364. See also MH Bernstein, 'The Regulatory Process: A Framework for Analysis' (1961) 26 Law & Cont Probl 329 (observing the persistence of an obsolete and inadequate conception of the regulatory process).

[32] See eg RA Merrill, 'Administrative Rule-Making' (1975) 30 Food, Drug & Cosm J 478, 479.

its validity or at least its effects, since the public would not otherwise have the opportunity to familiarize themselves with the new rules to be applied to them. There is some support, from a philosophical perspective, for the proposition that the norms of conduct applicable to everyone must be made public.[33] Legally there is also some support for the proposition that individuals who will be affected in some way by administrative rules or plans must know the contents of their rights and duties.[34] However, different legal systems may, and often do, regulate this matter in different ways.

C. Judicial and Non-Judicial Mechanisms of Control

Last but not least, there are various forms of control over rulemaking, including judicial doctrines that determine the possibility of challenging the acts that establish rules. For example, these acts may only be subject to collateral or indirect challenge, such as through recourse against an individual decision implementing a rule or a policy statement. Another variation may involve the judicial body with jurisdiction over rules, such as administrative or constitutional courts. There may also be different approaches regarding the liability in tort of public authorities, as noted in a case concerning a ban on importing agricultural products, which was discussed in the first book of this series.[35]

Moreover, as observed earlier, there remains the question of whether the exercise of the power to adopt policies or rules is accountable. For example, would greater parliamentary oversight be desirable? Similarly, within local government, is the role of elected bodies limited by bureaucrats, who influence planning in more than various ways?

IV. Common Core Research: Issues in Methodology

Our aim in this book is to examine administrative rulemaking and planning from the comparative perspective outlined in the previous volumes, again adopting a common core research approach, for which a brief explanation is warranted. This section proceeds on three different levels. First, I will summarize two views that have had a significant impact on how we think about comparative studies, namely those that

[33] I Kant, *Beantwortung der Frage: Was ist Aufklärung (1784)*, Engl trans by T Humphrey, *An Answer to the Question: What is the Enlightenment?* (Hackett Publ 1992), <https://www.nypl.org/sites/default/files/kant_whatisenlightenment.pdf> accessed 20 November 2024 (pointing out the importance of the 'public use of reason') (emphasis in the original).

[34] See Montesquieu, *L'esprit des lois* (1756; Flammarion 1979) book XI, chapter VI, 294 and J Madison, A Hamilton, and J Jay, *The Federalist Papers* (1788; Penguin 1987) XLVIII, at 310 (where Publius, that is Madison, argued that 'the concentrating in the same hands is precisely the definition of despotic government'). For a reappraisal of Montesquieu's theory, see C Eisenmann, 'L'Esprit des lois et la *séparation des pouvoirs*' in *Mélanges Carré de Malberg* (Librairie Duchemin 1977) 174. On the meaning of separation of powers in contemporary US law, see P Strauss, *Administrative Justice in the United States* (3rd edn, Carolina Academic Press 2016) 28 (discussing the regulation that executive agencies are authorized to adopt).

[35] See G della Cananea and R Caranta (eds), *Tort Liability of Public Authorities in European Laws* (OUP 2020) 201.

emphasize either commonality or diversity. I will also explain why both these views are lacking. Secondly, I will articulate the main methodological points that characterize the type of comparative research we have conducted, particularly the nature of our 'factual analysis'. In doing so, I hope to demonstrate the distinctiveness of our approach. A limitation arises from a choice that every comparative enquiry must face: the selection of legal systems for comparison. As will be discussed later, we have included a number of European legal systems (just over a fifth of the countries making up the Council of Europe) from different traditions. We have also included a couple of non-European legal systems, which may help provide a better understanding of what is common to Europe and what differentiates it from other legal traditions. All these choices will be explained more fully in the next sections.

A. Commonality *and* Diversity

We start from the premise that for several decades, many comparative studies have tended to emphasise either commonality or diversity.

In as far as we can claim a tradition of Western legal thought, it was founded on the idea that there was a common substrate driven by the re-elaboration of Roman law as taught in European universities. Thus, as Gino Gorla observed in his study of the *lex alius loci*, during the long period of *ius commune* (until approximately the eighteenth century), jurists and judges often cited legal sources and decisions from other jurisdictions,[36] thus emphasizing commonality. The dichotomy between civil law and English common law emerged gradually during the seventeenth and eighteenth centuries. At the end of the nineteenth century, this divergence was emphasized by Albert Venn Dicey, the Victorian constitutionalist. He argued that if there was a tradition of public law in England, it was grounded in the idea that there was, in fact, no such thing as a system of public law, still less of administrative law.[37] Dicey was certainly aware that 'a comparison between the administrative law of France and our English rule of law, if taken from the right point of view, suggests some interesting points of likeness, no less than of unlikeness'. However, he adopted a contrastive approach, asserting that *droit administratif* had no equivalent in the common law world. For him, it was 'in its content utterly unlike any branch of modern English law'.[38]

Quite the contrary, in the same years, Otto Mayer, the scholar considered to be the founder of German administrative law, pointed out the strong influence of French administrative law, either indirectly, when it was adapted to the realities of the host state,

[36] G Gorla, 'Il ricorso alla legge di un "luogo vicino" nell'ambito del diritto comune europeo' (1973) 96 Foro italiano 89; G Gorla, 'Civilian Judicial Decisions—An Historical Account of Italian Style' (1969–1970) 44 Tulane Law Review 740. For a retrospective of Gorla's scholarship, see L Moccia, 'Book Review, Gorla, Il diritto comparato in Italia e nel mondo occidentale e una introduzione al dialogo Civil Law – Common Law' (1985) 33 AJCL 533.

[37] AV Dicey, *Introduction to the Study of the Law of the Constitution* (10th edn, Macmillan 1954) 369. The treatise is now available at <http://files.libertyfund.org/files/1714/0125_Bk.pdf> accessed 20 November 2024.

[38] ibid 373.

or directly, when it was simply copied ('*simplement copié*').[39] More recently, there has been much talk about the 'convergence' of national administrative laws in the framework of European integration. Both Sabino Cassese and Jurgen Schwarze contributed to this body of literature. Cassese observed that there is a convergence of dualist and monist systems of judicial review.[40] Schwarze was among the first to explore the implications for the legal framework applicable to the European administration.[41]

Essentially, two approaches have emerged that emphasize commonality and diversity respectively, and may thus be termed 'integrative and contractive' or 'contrastive'.[42] As explained earlier, our intention in this comparative inquiry is not to claim that any of these approaches is inherently right or wrong. Rather, we argue that any approach that solely highlights analogies or differences is questionable from both the descriptive and normative perspectives. Descriptively, there is a significant risk that only the legal realities that align with the chosen perspective are examined.[43] In normative terms, the validity of any approach that emphasizes only commonality or diversity is equally flawed. Unlike many other global regulatory frameworks, regional legal orders are selective, since membership is reserved to the nations that share at least some broad public law values, such as democracy and respect for the rule of law and fundamental rights. This shared patrimony or substrate lies at the heart of two legal concepts formulated by the Court of Justice of the European Union. The first is the concept of 'general principles of law common to the legal orders of the member states', which was, so to speak, codified by the Treaty of Rome (1957) with regard to the liability in tort of European Community institutions and officials. The second is the concept of 'common constitutional traditions', referred to in Article 6 TEU.[44] The European Court of Human Rights, too, has often referred to the existence of a common legal

[39] See Mayer (n 14) 12. See also the review of Mayer's treatise by E Freund, (1906) 1 Am Pol Sc Rev 136 (observing that it was 'primarily an attempt to construct a scientific system', rather than a description of the law) and, on Mayer's role, E Forsthoff, *Lehrbuch des Verwaltungsrecht* (Beck 1966), French translation by M Fromont, *Traité de droit administratif allemand* (Bruylant 1969) 91 (distinguishing between two phases: before and after Mayer).

[40] S Cassese, 'Le problème de la convergence des droits administratifs: vers un modèle administratif européen' in *L'État de droit—Mélanges en l'honneur de Guy Braibant* (Dalloz 1996) 47. See also T Heukels and J Tib, 'Towards Homogeneity in the Field of Legal Remedies: Convergence and Divergence' in P Beaumont, C Lyons, and N Walker (eds), *Convergence and Divergence in European Public Law* (Hart 2002) 111 (same remark).

[41] J Schwarze, 'The Convergence of the Administrative Laws of the EU Member States' in FG Snyder (ed), *The Europeanization of Law: the Legal Effects of European Integration* (Hart 2000) 164.

[42] For this terminology, see RB Schlesinger, 'The Past and Future of Comparative Law' (1995) 43 AJCL 477.

[43] For similar remarks, see M Adams and J Griffiths, 'Against 'comparative method': explaining similarities and differences' in M Adams and J Bomhoff (eds), *Practice and Theory in Comparative Law* (CUP 2012) 279.

[44] Art 6 (3) TEU provides that 'Fundamental rights, as guaranteed by the European Convention for the Protection of Human Rights and Fundamental Freedoms and as they result from the constitutional traditions common to the Member States, shall constitute general principles of the Union's law'. For further analysis, see S Cassese, 'The "Constitutional Traditions Common to the Member States" of the European Union' (2017) 66 Riv trim dir pubb 943. The Court's elaboration of this phrase is illustrated by M Graziadei and R De Caria, 'The "Constitutional Traditions Common to the Member States of the European Union" in the Case-Law of the European Court of Justice: Judicial Dialogue at its Finest' (2017) 66 Riv trim dir pubb 949.

patrimony. Accordingly, a comparative analysis must consider both commonality and diversity[45] and seek to explain their respective importance.

B. Factual Analysis

After explaining that both commonality and diversity are relevant from a comparative perspective, it is time to clarify the purposes and nature of our comparative enquiry.

Our aim in this series is to examine some of the questions raised by comparative inquiry in the field of public law. I do not doubt that others will hold different views, among other things, on the nature of the questions that need to be addressed and their purposes. Comparative legal analysis may be, and has been, used for various purposes, including the search for 'the nature of things' (Montesquieu) and recourse to 'legal transplants' for improving domestic law and practice (Watson).[46] I myself, some years ago, used the comparative method in order to identify the standards of administrative conduct that could be codified for the EU administration.[47]

Our primary purpose in this research is different. It aims to advance knowledge on a range of issues that I believe are central to the study of public law but which, for various reasons, seem to be constantly neglected. These issues concern not so much how administrative action can be viewed through the lens of judicial review but how it must be considered in its own right.[48] It is precisely for this reason that the previous books in this series have focused on an important aspect of administrative adjudication—namely, decisions that impinge on private property[49]—as well as on the emergence of administrative procedure legislation in Europe.[50]

The methodology employed in this volume is consistent with that used in the previous books. There will be no attempt, therefore, to proceed from general moral propositions, *à la* Fuller.[51] Nor will there be a mere juxtaposition of national reports describing how a certain standard or set of standards of administrative conduct is shaped by legislation.

Although legal positivism is no longer the primary theory, it remains the largely dominant method, rooted in the view that law is a self-contained body of rules.

[45] For this general point, see P Craig, 'Comparative Administrative Law and Political Structure' (2017) 37 Oxford Journal of Legal Studies 947.

[46] Montesquieu (n 34) 115; A Watson, *Legal Transplants: An Approach to Comparative Law* (2nd edn, University of Georgia 1993).

[47] See P Craig, H Hofmann, and J-P Schneider (eds), *Reneual Model Rules on EU Administrative Procedure* (OUP 2017).

[48] For further remarks, see G della Cananea and M Andenas (eds), *Judicial Review of Administration in Europe. Procedural Fairness and Propriety* (OUP 2021).

[49] M Conticelli and T Perroud (eds), *Procedural Requirements for Administrative Limits to Property Rights* (OUP 2022).

[50] G della Cananea, A Ferrari Zumbini, and O Pfersmann (eds), *The Austrian Codification of Administrative Procedure: Diffusion and Oblivion* (OUP 2023).

[51] See LL Fuller, *The Morality of Law* (2nd edn, Yale UP 1969) 39 (discussing the various ways in which the law fails, in the sense that without the requirements discussed, the result is not simply that there is a 'bad system of law' but, rather, 'something that is not properly called a legal system at all'). See also J Boyle, 'Legal Realism and the Social Contract: Fuller's Public Jurisprudence of Form, Private Jurisprudence of Substance' (1993) 78 Cornell L R 371 (observing that, though Fuller owed much to legal realism, he examined 'a set of criteria that ..... *are deduced* from the very meaning of law') (emphasis in the original).

Consequently, many people tend to assume that solutions may be found deductively. However, this assumption is fraught with difficulties. First, the increasing volume of new legislation often results in a proliferation of rules within the field, making implementation more problematic. Secondly, and perhaps more importantly, while legislation may provide public administrators and judges with solutions in the majority of cases, in some instances it is unclear, obsolete, or simply absent. The solutions, therefore, will have to be found in the light of general principles, such as equality, due process of law, and proportionality.[52]

For these reasons, drawing inspiration from the methodology developed and used by Rudolf Schlesinger in the 1960s, our comparative inquiry takes the form of a 'factual analysis'. Its primary characteristic lies in its approach: rather than merely seeking to describe the specific legal institutions of a group of nations, the focus is on understanding how a particular set of problems would be addressed within the selected legal systems. Thus, the problems have to 'be stated in factual terms'.[53] The validity of this methodology was later confirmed in the context of the Trento project on the common core of European law.[54]

Our analysis is therefore of an experimental nature. Only experience can show, for example, whether all legal systems establish a general requirement to give reasons or exclude any general cloak of immunity for actions causing harm to individuals and corporations. In essence, what follows is an attempt to examine legal realities through experimental methods. Practically, as a first step, we formulated hypothetical cases and submitted them to national experts to ascertain whether they would be comprehensible and relevant to all of them.[55] It was only after the questionnaire had been approved, with some changes, that the second stage of our analysis got underway, namely hypothesizing on how these cases would probably be resolved in the legal systems selected for comparison. We are interested not only in the solutions provided by each legal system based on its operational rules but also in the varying importance of the legal formants,[56] including legislation, judicial decisions, governmental practices, and, last but not last, underlying theories of public law. In the third step, the solutions proposed by the national experts and the underlying rationales were compared in what can truly be called a legal comparison.

[52] G della Cananea and JB Auby (eds), *General Principles and Sector Specific Rules in European Administrative Laws* (OUP 2024).

[53] RB Schlesinger, 'Introduction' in RB Schlesinger (ed), *Formation of Contracts. A Study of the Common Core of Legal Systems* (Stevens & Son 1969). For further remarks, see O Kahn-Freund, 'Review of Schlesinger, Formation of Contracts. A Study of the Common Core of Legal Systems' (1970) 18 AJCL 429 (remarking that 'the hypothesis itself hardly needs verification, but the extent to which it applies, the extent it can be used as a working tool does so very much') and M Rheinstein, 'Review of R. Schlesinger, Formation of Contracts: A Study of the Common Core of Legal Systems' (1969) 36 Univ Chicago L Rev 448, 449.

[54] See M Bussani and U Mattei, 'The Common Core Approach to European Private Law' (1997–1998) 3 Colum J Eur L 339.

[55] A two-day workshop was held in Milan in October 2021, but the pandemic delayed completion of the research.

[56] On this concept, see R Sacco, 'Legal Formants: A Dynamic Approach to Comparative Law (I)' (1991) 39 AJCL 1.

C. The Questionnaire and Levels of Analysis

The questionnaire on which our comparative inquiry is based is divided into two parts. The first seeks to gather basic information about each legal system, including the presence of constitutional or legislative provisions laying down general principles concerning rulemaking and planning. The second comprises the hypothetical cases.

Collectively, these hypothetical cases concern three categories of procedural requirements beyond adjudication. There are, first of all, two cases concerning parliamentary oversight of administration, focusing particularly on asylum seekers and the admissibility of administrative rules limiting the exercise of discretion. Secondly, there are five cases concerning various requirements relating to administrative rulemaking, such as the duty to consult stakeholders and users, the giving reasons requirement, and the duty to publish regulations. Thirdly, there are three cases concerning the requirements applicable to planning, including the duty of consideration, the necessity of a cost-benefit analysis and, as a variant, an environmental impact assessment.

We are aware that this type of study is not without difficulties. First, finding clear answers to the hypothetical cases will not always be easy. Secondly, even when a solution can be identified, it may not be applicable across different contexts. As Stanley De Smith, an English public lawyer, put it, 'to prophesy the view that a court will take of the powers or duties of an administrative authority in a particular case must inevitably remain a hazardous undertaking'.[57] The practical utility of these solutions is, therefore, limited. On the other hand, as mentioned earlier, our goal is primarily to advance knowledge surrounding an important aspect of administrative and public law: administrative procedure. It is for this purpose that we are interested in exploring what is common and distinctive among countries like Austria, Italy, and Norway, but also whether these commonalities extend to some other legal systems worldwide, but not to others.

D. The Choice of Legal Systems

What has just been said also prompts a detailed explanation of a choice concerning the legal systems selected for comparison. As mentioned at the beginning of our comparative enquiry,[58] we had to steer a course between two contrasting options: either limiting the comparison to the usual three or four legal systems, based on the questionable assumption that they are the most important ones, or trying to cover a broader range of legal systems. In seeking a reasonable balance between these options, we chose to examine a dozen selected legal systems. We explain the reason for this choice in the next paragraph.

A word or two may be helpful to clarify why we did not follow the more or less outdated view that emphasized the divide between the two legal families in Europe: the

[57] S De Smith, 'Wrongs and Remedies in Administrative Law' (1952) 15 Modern L Rev 189, 190. See also PH Schuck and ED Elliot, 'Studying Administrative Law: a Methodology for, and Report on, Empirical Research' (1990) 42 Admin L Rev 519.

[58] See della Cananea and Bussani (n 1) 251.

civil and common law systems. First, despite its intellectual soundness in the field of private law, in the public law milieu, this view is intrinsically flawed as it conflates legal systems with several significant differences. As early as the nineteenth century, while the United States had a written constitution and judicial review of legislation, there was nothing similar in the United Kingdom. By the end of the century, while France and Italy had endowed their Councils of State with both judicial and advisory functions, neither the Austrian nor the German Empires followed suit. In the twentieth century, after Austria codified administrative procedure in 1925, the United States adopted a similar choice in 1946, and many European nations did the same, especially after 1989, including those re-establishing liberal democracy. Secondly, the term 'legal families' is conceptually inadequate, as it tends to emphasize what is common to a certain group of legal systems through inheritance, overlooking potential differences. Thirdly, from the legal perspective, the treaties emphasize a different concept: tradition. And, interestingly, they recognize the existence of both 'common constitutional traditions' (Article 6 of the Treaty on European Union (TEU)) and 'national traditions' (Article 67 TFEU).[59]

The French administrative scholar Michel Fromont has examined national administrative traditions and categorized them into four groups, focusing on both administrative organization and judicial review of administration.[60] The first includes France, Belgium, Italy, the Netherlands, and Greece, all of which have dualist judicial systems with both civil and administrative courts, and with bodies—the prototype of which is the French *Conseil d'État*—that also have advisory functions. The second group includes Austria, Germany, Switzerland, and Poland, where administrative courts have solely judicial functions and, unlike France, the liability of government officers is regulated by civil codes. The third group, which shares some features of the first two, includes Finland, Portugal, Spain, and Sweden. Lastly, the fourth group comprises the United Kingdom and the Republic of Ireland, as well as Denmark and Norway, all of which have a monist system of judicial review.

Fromont's treatise has the merits of putting traditions, rather than legal families, on centre stage, and adopts a more refined approach than the old one. However, it is debatable whether 'traditions', in this sense, constitute identifiable wholes. It is equally debatable whether these groups of administrative systems can be constructed on the basis of the presence of certain features or indicators rather than others, such as the constitutional bases of administrative power and the underlying theories of public law. Thus, for example, if the theory of 'illiberal democracy' were to be considered a foundational element of a particular legal system, it would inevitably set it apart from the rest of Europe.

However, I do not believe that these critical remarks should be taken to an extreme, going so far as to suggest that since reality is infinitely various, it cannot be classified and conceptualized. In truth, classifications can serve multiple purposes, including teaching. They are also useful for research, especially when choices must be made.

[59] Art 67 (1) provides that: 'The Union shall constitute an area of freedom, security and justice with respect for fundamental rights and the different legal systems and traditions of the Member States.'

[60] M Fromont, *Droit administratif des Etats européens* (PUF 2006) 13.

In this respect, however, Fromont's classification contains an evident limitation in that it is confined—with the exception of Poland—to what used to be called 'Western Europe'. It therefore leaves out several nations and neglects some legal systems that are particularly interesting from the perspective of administrative law. For example, the former Yugoslavia followed the Austrian legal systems in more than one respect, including administrative procedure legislation, thus providing an interesting example of diffusion,[61] and, after its dissolution it is equally interesting to consider the choices made by the new states.

In our comparative enquiry, we have attempted to include, first of all, legal systems that belong to all the traditions outlined by Fromont, as well as nations from Central and Eastern Europe (the Czech Republic and Hungary). Secondly, we included some of the traditionally 'major' European legal systems, such as Britain and Germany,[62] along with others that are of interest for comparative purposes, having largely drawn on others, as the Czech Republic and Hungary did with regard to the Austrian codification of administrative procedure. Thirdly, we included Norway, which is not a member of the EU but is part of the European Economic Area. Lastly, we included the EU itself for a number of reasons. One is that it shows how the same problems can be solved by a non-state entity. Another is that there has been discussion as to whether the EU should lay down precise rules governing its rulemaking activities.[63] It is interesting, therefore, to see how certain problems would be solved starting from existing rules. Lastly, we attempted to compare the Europe solutions with those found in two other regions of the world: China and the United States. The latter is often considered a model for rulemaking, while the former is particularly interesting due to the broad discretion enjoyed by the executive.

V. The Structure of this Book

The structure of this book essentially mirrors that of the previous volume in this series and is, therefore, divided into four parts, with this chapter included in the first part.

The second part consists of reports on the legal systems chosen for our comparative analysis. This includes the answers from national experts to some general questions concerning the distinction—either at the legislative level or in judicial doctrines—between adjudication, rulemaking, and planning, as well as the general principles governing the last two forms of administrative action.

The third part includes the answers given by experts to the hypothetical cases, constituting the core of our factual analysis and serving as the basis for the actual comparative analysis. Like in the previous books of this series, the disaggregation of these responses is designed to facilitate the analytical process.

[61] See S Lilic and M Milenkovic, 'Administrative Procedure in Former Yugoslavia and the Austrian Administrative Procedure Act' in della Cananea, Ferrari Zumbini, and Pfersmann (n 50) 119.

[62] Unlike in all the previous books, it was unfortunately impossible to include a study of the French legal system.

[63] See Craig, Hofmann, and Schneider (n 47).

The final part compares the solutions identified by the experts from the national legal systems—and their reasoning. The section begins with a chapter discussing the importance and implications of general legislation on administrative procedures adopted in the majority, but not all, of the legal systems included in our comparison. Additionally, there are two chapters dedicated to comparing the approaches to rulemaking and planning, respectively.

PART II
THE LEGAL SYSTEMS SELECTED FOR COMPARISON
BACKGROUND AND PERSPECTIVES

The second part of this book consists of reports on the legal systems chosen for our comparative analysis. This includes the answers from national experts to some general questions concerning the distinction—either at the legislative level or in judicial doctrines—between adjudication, rulemaking, and planning, as well as the general principles governing the last two forms of administrative action.

2
Austria

Stefan Storr and Sophie Praniess

I. Constitutional and Legislative Provisions on Rulemaking and Planning

The Austrian Federal Constitution specifies the forms of action the administration may use. According to the concept of 'relative unity of the legal source system' (*relative Geschlossenheit des Rechtsquellensystems*), the legislator may not create general types of legal sources that are not provided for by federal constitutional law.[1] Exceptions to this rule are only recognized to the extent that the constitutional legislator was already 'aware' of the intended form of action when passing the Federal Constitutional Act.[2] The distinction between the types of legal acts provided for in the Federal Constitution is directly related to the system of legal protection, as a specific form of legal protection is provided for each legal act. For example, legal protection against an (unlawful) ordinance can only be obtained by addressing the Austrian Constitutional Court,[3] whereas protection against the (unlawful) 'exercise of immediate administrative command and coercive power' (*Ausübung unmittelbarer verwaltungsbehördlicher Befehls- und Zwangsgewalt*) is obtained by addressing the administrative courts.[4]

In its established case law, the Austrian Constitutional Court has laid down that an ordinance is a general legal act issued by an administrative authority when exercising public law, regardless of its denomination. In this regard, self-governing institutions that are not territorial bodies may also be considered administrative authorities. The addressees of an ordinance are determined by the characteristics of the genre.[5] The normative effect of an administrative act is determined exclusively by its content.

The principle of legality is laid down in Article 18 paragraph 1 B-VG ('The entire public administration shall be based on law'). The issuance of ordinances by public authorities is established in Article 18 paragraph 2 B-VG ('Every administrative authority can issue ordinances on the basis of law within its sphere of competence').

The Austrian constitution does not provide for 'plans' as independent legal acts. Rather, plans must be classified within the existing system of legal forms of action. Plans are regularly—but not necessarily—qualified as ordinances. They can also be qualified as non-normative acts (eg plans and programmes for emission control).[6]

[1] VfSlg 17394/2004.
[2] *Bundes-Verfassungsgesetz* (B-VG) Orig Vers: BGBl 1/1930.
[3] Art 139 B-VG.
[4] Art 130 para 1 No B-VG.
[5] VfSlg 17203/2003.
[6] S 9 Federal Law for the Protection against Emissions caused by Air Pollutants (Emission Protection Law—Air, IG-L)—*Bundesgesetz zum Schutz vor Immissionen durch Luftschadstoffe* (*Immissionsschutzgesetz—Luft*, IG-L) Orig Vers: BGBl. I No 115/1997.

Stefan Storr and Sophie Praniess, *Austria* In: *Administrative Rulemaking and Planning in European Laws*. Edited by: Giacinto della Cananea and Angela Ferrari Zumbini, Oxford University Press.
DOI: 10.1093/oso/9780198867616.003.0002

The Austrian APA[7] does not regulate the issuance of ordinances. There is no other general law regulating 'planning' by the government or other authorities. According to the prevailing opinion in literature, in general, no procedural regulation is required for the issuance of an ordinance. Only ordinances issued by collegial bodies are exempt from this rule, as procedural provisions (ie decision-making by majority) are mandatory for such ordinances.[8] Another exception is the following: if a law is to be made executable by an ordinance, this law must provide all the essential details of the intended ordinance.

Nonetheless, there are specific laws comprising planning regulations, in particular spatial planning laws of the provinces or specific planning regulations, for example on the Integrated Network Infrastructure Plan (*Integrierter Netzinfrastrukturplan*, s 94 Renewable Expansion Act),[9] which must be developed in accordance with certain regulated principles.

Administrative acts directed at one or more identifiable individuals are generally not qualified as ordinances. The prohibition and termination of an assembly, for example, is executed as a 'decision'[10] or the 'exercise of immediate administrative command and coercive power' by an administrative authority[11] because the participants of the assembly are individually identifiable. However, there are exceptions to this rule. The order of a ban on squatting or the termination of illegal house squatting is carried out as an ordinance specifically provided for by law.[12]

II. Legal Effects of Administrative Rules and Plans

Three types of administrative ordinances are recognized under Austrian law.[13] The first type are implementing ordinances (*Durchführungsverordnungen*). Administrative authorities have the power to issue ordinances based on laws within their scope of action, as stated in Article 18 paragraph 2 B-VG. While explicit statutory authorization is not necessary, it is often present. Because ordinances may only be issued 'on the basis of the laws', those based on Article 18 paragraph 2 B-VG can only elaborate on the regulation of a law.[14] The purpose of these ordinances is to relieve the legislature and indirectly influence parliamentary law-making.

On the other hand, independent ordinances (*selbständige/verfassungsunmittelbare Verordnungen*), the second type of ordinance mentioned, are issued directly based on an authorization in the constitution. Like implementing ordinances, independent

[7] Federal General Administrative Procedure Act (*Bundesgesetz vom 21 Juli 1925 über das allgemeine Verwaltungsverfahren—Allgemeines Verwaltungsverfahrensgesetz*—AVG) Orig Vers BGBl 274/1925.

[8] HP Rill, 'Article 18' in B Kneihs and G Lienbacher (eds), *Rill-Schaeffer-Kommentar zum B-VG* (1st edn, Verlag Österreich 2001) rec 87.

[9] *Bundesgesetz über den Ausbau von Energie aus erneuerbaren Quellen* (Erneuerbaren-Ausbau-Gesetz—EAG) Orig Vers: BGBl. I No 150/2021.

[10] Supreme Administrative Court (Verwaltungsgerichtshof (VwGH)) 15 October 2009, 2007/09/0307.

[11] VfSlg 11132/1986.

[12] Ss 36 and 27 Police Act (*Bundesgesetz über die Organisation der Sicherheitsverwaltung und die Ausübung der Sicherheitspolizei* (*Sicherheitspolizeigesetz*—SPG)) Orig Vers: BGBl. No 566/1991.

[13] T Öhlinger and H Eberhard, *Verfassungsrecht* (13th edn, Facultas 2022) 269, 497.

[14] W Berka, *Verfassungsrecht* (8th edn, Verlag Österreich 2021) 666.

ordinances are considered legal ordinances (*Rechtsverordnungen*) and are legally binding. They can be issued in a form that supplements, represents, or amends the law and therefore have the same status as statutory law. The most notable examples of independent ordinances are 'emergency ordinances' (*Notverordnungen*) issued by the Federal President (*Bundespräsident*) (Art 18 para 3 and para 4 B-VG) and 'local police ordinances' (*ortpolizeiliche Verordnungen*) issued by municipal authorities (Art 118 para 6 B-VG).

Unlike the ordinances mentioned above, decrees (*Erlässe*) are classified as administrative ordinances (*Verwaltungsverordnungen*). They are issued by a superior authority addressed to a subordinate authority/authorities or staff member(s), defining the latter's organization and actions in greater detail. The subordinate authority is bound by the provisions of a decree, provided they are not incompatible with the law.

Nevertheless, a decree may be qualified as an implementing ordinance if it is phrased in an 'imperative' manner. If a decree is addressed to subordinate authorities but intends to have legal effects vis-à-vis private individuals, the Austrian Constitutional Court treats it as an implementing ordinance. Conversely, a decree is not an implementing ordinance if the superior authority only communicates its legal opinion without regulating the rights and duties of those subject to the law.

III. Procedural Requirements Concerning Rulemaking and Planning

In principle, there are no general laws regulating the procedure for issuing ordinances. In particular, there is no general right to be heard as a party, nor is there a general rule of procedural fairness. However, this may be different in relation to the scope of specific laws, such as the provincial spatial planning law.

Nevertheless, four points must be made in this regard.

First, the publication of ordinances is legally regulated. Ordinances issued by the federal government or federal ministers must always be published in the Federal Law Gazette (*Bundesgesetzblatt*), otherwise they are not lawfully enacted and must be annulled by the Austrian Constitutional Court. The same rule applies to ordinances issued by the regional government or a state governor (*Landeshauptmann*).[15] However, this requirement does not apply to ordinances issued by other authorities, such as the police force. Either there are specific requirements in a statute (eg publication on a municipal notice board) or other forms of notification are permitted (eg a public notice at the site of the authority, posting on the municipal notice board, publishing in a newspaper, announcement by loudspeaker, or a radio announcement).[16] It is important to ensure that the chosen form of publication corresponds to the ability and possibility of the relevant recipients to become aware of the ordinance. The Austrian Constitutional Court has derived the requirement of publicity from the principle of legal certainty.[17]

[15] For example, Styrian Public Notification Act (*Gesetz vom 15 Dezember 1998 über die Kundmachung (Steiermärkisches Kundmachungsgesetz)*) Orig Vers: LGBl. No 25/1999.

[16] Rill (n 8) rec 100.

[17] Rill (n 8) rec 87.

Second, an administrative authority must determine the factual, and therefore, legal requirements for issuing an ordinance, as well as the circumstances under which the issuance of an ordinance is admissible. This investigation must be carried out 'carefully and in detail'[18] and must be recorded in order to ensure the possibility of review by the Austrian Constitutional Court. This obligation has been derived from Article 18 B-VG and the principle of the rule of law.

Thirdly, if an ordinance significantly interferes with fundamental rights, greater specificity is required. The information relevant to the decision on the ordinance must be made clear during the issuing process, including all the circumstantial details required by law.[19]

Fourth, the principle of objectivity and the prohibition of arbitrariness apply. The Austrian Constitutional Court derives this requirement from the principle of objectivity. The principle of objectivity has hardly been defined so far, but it is an important 'catch-all' principle for reviewing state action. The prohibition of arbitrariness is particularly important regarding review by the Austrian Constitutional Court, as the court may only review certain actions by public authorities in terms of their compatibility with constitutional law. Both the principle of objectivity and the prohibition of arbitrariness have bearing on such proceedings.

Special requirements exist in Article 118 paragraph 7 B-VG, for example. A provincial government may transfer issues concerning a municipality to a state authority by ordinance, but only at the request of the municipality. According to section 94f of the Road Traffic Act,[20] the municipality must be heard before an ordinance by the provincial government is issued. According to section 14 paragraph 1 of the Waste Management Act,[21] the Federal Minister for Climate Action, Environment, Energy, Mobility, Innovation and Technology may determine waste management issues by ordinance, but only 'in agreement' with the Federal Minister of Labour and Economy. Other regulations impose the obligation to notify an ordinance to a higher authority (eg municipalities must notify ordinances to the provincial government as a supervisory authority)[22] or to obtain approval from the supervisory authority.[23]

In this context, not all procedural violations in proceedings before the Austrian Constitutional Court are significant. The Austrian Constitutional Court considers the violation of essential procedural rules for issuing ordinances 'significant', which results in ordinances being unlawful in the event of a violation of procedural rules, such as a curtailing of the parties' right to be heard.[24]

[18] VfSlg 11972/1989.

[19] Concerning COVID-19: VfSlg 20456/2021, referring to VfSlg. 20.398/2020, 20.399/2020.

[20] Road Traffic Act (*Bundesgesetz vom 6 Juli 1960, mit dem Vorschriften über die Straßenpolizei erlassen werden (Straßenverkehrsordnung 1960—StVO.* 1960)) Orig Vers: BGBl. No 159/1960.

[21] Waste Management Act (*Bundesgesetz über eine nachhaltige Abfallwirtschaft* (*Abfallwirtschaftsgesetz* 2002—AWG 2002)) Orig Vers: BGBl. I No 102/2002.

[22] Art 119a para 6 B-VG.

[23] Art 119a para 8 B-VG.

[24] VfSlg 16242/2001.

3
China

Xiaowei Sun

I. Introduction

This chapter concerns administrative rulemaking and planning in the Chinese legal system. There will be, first, a brief analysis of the constitutional framework. This will be followed by the answers to the questionnaire's general questions regarding the effects of administrative rules and plans and the principles governing them.

II. Constitutional and Legislative Provisions on Administrative Rules and Plans

The Chinese Constitution uses different terms to refer to the actions of administrative bodies. Thus, Article 89 of the Constitution provides that the State Council can 'adopt administrative measures, enact administrative regulations, and issue decisions and orders'.[1] Article 90 gives the ministries and commissions under the State Council the power to 'issue orders, directives and regulations'.[2] As for the local authorities, local people's congresses can adopt resolutions, plans,[3] and local regulations,[4] whereas local governments 'conduct administrative work' and 'issue decisions and orders'.[5]

Although there are theoretically two types of actions, namely regulations, resolutions, directives, and plans on the one hand, and decisions and orders on the other, no legal text clearly establishes such a distinction. Additionally, some administrative actions such as administrative measures, actions of conducting administrative work, and even some administrative decisions and orders cannot be classified so clearly.

[1] 规定行政措施，制定行政法规，发布决定和命令. Chinese-only footnotes are translations of the English in the main text.

[2] 发布命令、指示和规章.

[3] Art 99 of the Constitution: 'Within the limits of their authority as prescribed by law, they adopt and issue resolutions and examine and decide on plans for local economic and cultural development and for the development of public services' (依照法律规定的权限，通过和发布决议，审查和决定地方的经济建设、文化建设和公共事业建设的计划).

[4] Art 100 of the Constitution: 'The people's congresses of provinces, and municipalities directly under the Central Government, and their standing committees may adopt local regulations' (省、直辖市的人民代表大会和它们的常务委员会，在不同宪法、法律、行政法规相抵触的前提下，可以制定地方性法规).

[5] Art 107 of the Constitution: 'Local people's governments at or above the county level, within the limits of their authority as prescribed by law, conduct administrative work ... in their respective administrative areas; issue decisions and orders' (县级以上地方各级人民政府依照法律规定的权限，管理本行政区域内的 ... 行政工作，发布决定和命令).

Xiaowei Sun, *China* In: *Administrative Rulemaking and Planning in European Laws*. Edited by: Giacinto della Cananea and Angela Ferrari Zumbini, Oxford University Press.
DOI: 10.1093/oso/9780198867616.003.0003

Nevertheless, Administrative Litigation Law[6] indirectly distinguishes between 'administrative regulations, rules, and decisions with general binding [force]'[7] and other administrative actions. According to Article 13 of this law, the first cannot be challenged before the courts. An exception is made for decisions with general binding force. For example, Article 53 of the same law allows the plaintiff to file a request for review of a 'regulatory document'[8] when bringing a complaint against an administrative action based on this regulatory document.[9] In any case, the plaintiff cannot challenge a regulatory document directly. So the admissibility of the claim according to the Administrative Litigation Law can be seen as a criterion that allows a distinction to be made between administrative rulemaking and individual administrative decisions.

Otherwise, the Legislation Law (or Law on Legislation)[10] provides the procedures for making administrative regulations and rules detailed by the Regulations on Procedures for making administrative regulations[11] and the Regulations on Procedures for making administrative rules.[12] A circular of 31 May 2018, issued by the State Council, governs the production of administrative regulatory documents.[13] On 20 April 20, 2019, the State Council issued the Provisional Regulations on Major Administrative Decision-making Procedures.[14] These texts impose specific procedures on administrative rulemaking, whereas most individual administrative acts are regulated by texts according to their field of intervention, such as administrative licences, administrative penalties, or tax.

The combination of the texts referenced above shows that in China, administrative rulemaking is distinct from adjudication on procedural grounds and in relation to the admissibility of the complaint before the courts, even though there is no legal relevance for such a distinction. Otherwise, legal scholars tend to classify administrative actions into two groups: 'concrete administrative actions'[15] and 'abstract

6 行政诉讼法.

7 行政法规、规章或者行政机关制定、发布的具有普遍约束力的决定、命令.

8 规范性文件. Also called 'normative document'.

9 See W Cui, J Cheng, and D Wiesner, 'Judicial Review of Government Actions in China' (2019)1 China Perspectives 35–44; J Wang, 'Judicial Review of Regulatory Documents in Administrative Litigation in China' (2021)16 Asian Law Review 328–73.

10 立法法. The literal translation 'Legislation Law' or 'Law on Legislation' cannot express the exact meaning of this Chinese law, which is not limited to regulating legislative procedure. Indeed, this law provides the procedures for making administrative regulations and rules, as well as local regulations issued by local congresses. So the exact translation of this law should be 'Rulemaking Law' or 'Law on Rulemaking'. Nevertheless, we will use the literal translation, not only to refer to the official translation but also to foster familiarity with the Chinese notion of law, which includes all general normative documents issued by competent authorities, whether legislative or administrative.

11 行政法规制定程序条例.

12 规章制定程序条例.

13 关于加强行政规范性文件制定和监督管理工作的通知. According to this circular, regulatory documents are 'official documents, other than State Council regulations, decisions and orders, and departmental and local government rules that are formulated by a government authority according to statutory powers and procedures, publicly issued, involve the rights and obligations of the public, and have a general binding force and repeated applicability within a certain period' (除国务院的行政法规、决定、命令以及部门规章和地方政府规章外，由行政机关或者经法律、法规授权的具有管理公共事务职能的组织（以下统称行政机关）依照法定权限、程序制定并公开发布，涉及公民、法人和其他组织权利义务，具有普遍约束力，在一定期限内反复适用的公文).

14 重大行政决策程序暂行条例.

15 具体行政行为. Also called 'specific administrative action', see Wang (n 9).

administrative actions'.[16] This doctrinal distinction should be analysed in terms of three periods: before the adoption of the Administrative Litigation Law on 1989, from the adoption of this law to its amendment in 2014, and since the amendment.

Before the adoption of the Administrative Litigation Law in 1989, the distinction between concrete and abstract administrative actions was purely academic theory. It first appeared in an administrative law manual published on 1983,[17] According to the author, the criteria for distinguishing between concrete administrative action and abstract administrative action should be the object of the action: concrete administrative actions deal with specific cases or specific events, while abstract administrative actions do not.[18] This definition was accepted by most authors during this period.[19]

The legislation of 1989 on administrative litigation made 'concrete administrative action' a legal term. Article 2 of this text limited the scope of judicial review to 'concrete administrative actions' alone. A judicial opinion concerning the application of Administrative Litigation Law issued by the Supreme People's Court on 29 May 1991 (repealed)[20] clarified the definition of concrete administrative action as 'unilateral acts aimed at specific citizens, legal persons, or other organisations and susceptible to affect their rights and obligations'.[21] This judicial interpretation was once considered an official definition of concrete administrative action and was taken as a criterion for distinguishing concrete and abstract administrative actions.[22] However, no text mentioned the term 'abstract administrative action'. Some authors tried to classify the distinction between concrete and abstract administrative actions,[23] but no agreement has been reached on the meaning of 'specific'. The Supreme People's Court used this term to define concrete administrative action, without specifying its meaning. In practice,

16 抽象行政行为.

17 M Wang (王珉灿), *Administrative Law Outline* (行政法概要) (Law Press China (法律出版社) 1983).

18 ibid 98.

19 See C Pi (皮纯协), *China Administrative Law Manual* (中国行政法教程) (China University of Political Science and Law Press (中国政法大学出版社) 1988) 71; H Zhang (张焕光) and J Hu (胡建淼), *Principles of Administrative Law* (行政法学原理), China Labor and Personnel Publishing House (劳动人事出版社) (China Labor and Social Security Publishing House since 2013 (中国劳动社会保障出版社) 1989) 222; B Jiang (江必新), *Research on Administrative Litigation Issues* (行政诉讼问题研究) (China Police University Publishing House (中国人民公安大学出版社) 1989) 64.

20 关于贯彻执行〈中华人民共和国行政诉讼法〉若干问题的意见（试行）.

21 针对特定的公民、法人或者其他组织，就特定的具体事项，作出的有关该公民、法人或者其他组织权利义务的单方行为.

22 See Z Yu (喻志耀) and G Shi (石光柏), *Administrative Law and Administrative Litigation Law* (行政法与行政诉讼法) (Police Officer Educational Publishing House (警官教育出版社) 1994); S Fang (方世荣), *On Concrete Administrative Actions* (论具体行政行为) (Wuhan University Publishing House (武汉大学出版社) 1996); S Ying (应松年), *New Theory of Administrative Law* (行政法学新论) (China Fangzheng Press (中国方正出版社) 2004); B Ye (叶必丰), *Administrative Law and Administrative Litigation Law* (行政法与行政诉讼法) (China Renmin University Press (中国人民大学出版社), 2011); M Jiang (姜明安), *Administrative Law and Administrative Litigation Law* (行政法与行政诉讼法) (Peking University Press (北京大学出版社) 2011).

23 See S Zhang (张树义), 'On the Criteria for the Division of Abstract Administrative Actions and Concrete Administrative Actions' (论抽象行政行为与具体行政行为的划分标准) (1993) 1 China Legal Science (中国法学) 60–65; W Luo (罗文燕) and H Shi (石红卫), 'A New Statement on the Difference Between Concrete Administrative Actions and Abstract Administrative Actions' (具体行政行为和抽象行政行为区别标准新表述) (2004) 4 Journal of Zhejiang Industrial and Commercial University (浙江工商大学学报) 12–18; B Ye (叶必丰), 'Classification of Administrative Action: Notion Reconstruction or Thoroughly Overhauling' (行政行为的分类: 概念重构抑或正本清源) (2005) 23(5) Journal of China University of Political Science and Law (中国政法大学学报) 36–46.

different jurisdictions could consider the same administrative action concrete or abstract.[24] As the defining scope of administrative remedies was not fully decided by the classification of administrative action, there was no need, according to some scholars, to insist on a distinction between concrete and abstract administrative actions,[25] and it was even desirable to replace 'concrete administrative action' with 'administrative action' in the Administrative Litigation Law.[26] Their suggestions were heard.

III. Procedural Requirements for Rules and Plans and Their Effects

The 2014 amendment of the Administrative Litigation Law replaced the term 'concrete administrative action' with 'administrative action', although this change in the wording did not substantially modify the scope of judicial review of administrative actions.[27] Administrative regulations, rules, and most decisions with general binding force are still excluded from the scope of judicial review. Judicial review of a regulatory document is permissible only during a lawsuit against an administrative action based on this regulatory document.[28] The distinction between concrete and abstract administrative actions may still be useful to determine the question of *locus*

[24] For example, a local decision on modifying School districts that was considered to be an abstract administrative action by a subordinate court because it had general binding force could be used repeatedly, not being addressed to a particular individual ([2014] 甬海行初字第23 号裁定书). But the local Intermediate People's Court quashed the judgment of the subordinate court and considered the decision to be a concrete administrative action because it was addressed to a specific group of individuals and affected their rights and obligations ([2017] 浙03 行终226 号裁定书).

[25] H Luo (罗豪才), *Research on Administrative Judgment* (行政审判问题研究) (Peking University Press (北京大学出版社) 1990) 270; J Yang (杨解君), 'Questions on the Distinction Between Abstract Administrative Actions and Concrete Administrative Actions' (抽象行政行为与具体行政行为的划分质疑) (1995) 1 Journal of Central Leadership Institute of politics and Law (中央政法管理干部学院学报) 56–59; Ye (叶必丰) (n 23) 45–46; J Hu (胡建淼), *Administration and the Rule of Law* (行政与法治) (National Academy of Administration Press (国家行政学院出版社) 2014) 34.

[26] See Z Zhang (章志远), 'A Scientific Definition of the Concept of Administrative Action' (行政行为概念的科学界定) (2002) 16(4) Journal of Jiangsu Public Security College (江苏公安专科学校学报) 76–84; Z Hong (弘章) and R Zhou (周瑞军), 'Suggestions on Abolishing the Division of Concrete Administrative Actions and Abstract Administrative Actions In Legislation' (建议立法上取消具体行政行为与抽象行政行为的划分) (2006) 6 Journal of Liaoning Administration College (辽宁行政学院学报) 39–40.

[27] The 2014 version of the Administrative Litigation Law retains a provision from the 1989 version that excludes four groups of administrative actions from lawsuits, including 'administrative regulations, rules, decisions and orders with general binding force' (art 13). The Supreme People's Court set out other exclusions from judicial review in its Interpretation in Application of the Administrative Litigation Law (关于适用《中华人民共和国行政诉讼法》的解释), as adopted on 13 November 2017, including administrative guidance (行政指导行为), administrative actions without external effect (行政机关作出的不产生外部法律效力的行为), preparatory and deliberative acts (行政机关为作出行政行为而实施的准备、论证、研究、层报、咨询等过程性行为), internal supervisory acts (上级行政机关基于内部层级监督关系对下级行政机关作出的听取报告、执法检查、督促履责等行为), and administrative acts that have no actual effect on individuals and legal persons (对公民、法人或者其他组织权利义务不产生实际影响的行为).

[28] Art 53 of the Administrative Litigation Law.

standi before courts in the opinions of some specialists,[29] but it seems obsolete to others.[30]

One of the reasons for the rejection of the term 'concrete administrative action' is that many regulatory documents have concrete effects insofar as they can have legal effects on an individual's rights and obligations. Indeed, regulatory documents are used as references for issuing licences, assessing administrative penalties, or granting compensation or subsidies. This is also why the 2014 amendment formally provides for the judicial review of this documents. If this kind of judicial review is exceptional and partial in the framework of the Administrative Litigation Law, as mentioned above, some procedural requirements are imposed by the State Council in the Circular of 31 May 2018 with regard to administrative regulatory documents. These include the assessment and appraisal of their necessity, feasibility, and reasonableness; soliciting opinions from the public; legality review; collegiality in the adoption of decisions; and informing the public in due time.[31] Similar procedural requirements can be found in the Regulations on Procedures for making administrative regulations, the Regulations on Procedures for making administrative rules, and the Provisional Regulations on Major Administrative Decision-making Procedures. More formally, these texts envisage a public hearing for drafting regulations or rules which significantly affect a public interest or for which a major disagreement remains and which have an important impact on the individual's rights and obligations.[32]

Furthermore, Article 5 of the decision of 22 March 2004 of the State Council on the programme for the general implementation of the principle of legality in the administrations specifies six fundamental principles imposed on administrative authorities, as follows: (i) 'Be lawful', (ii) 'Be fair', (iii) 'Due process', (iv) 'Be efficient', (v) 'Be honest and trustworthy', (vi) 'Be responsible'. These requirements should be considered applicable to all administrative actions, rules, or adjudications.

However, there is a significant difference between individual administrative actions eligible for remedies before the courts and other administrative actions. The 2014 amendment of the Administrative Litigation Law introduced the notion of 'manifestly inappropriate' administrative actions in administrative litigation.[33] Article 70 of this law gives the courts the power to annul all or part of a 'manifestly inappropriate' administrative action and, if necessary, to order the administration to change its decision. Further, in Article 77, this law offers courts the possibility of reviewing a 'manifestly inappropriate administrative penalty'. Courts cannot decide on the appropriateness of individual administrative actions, but only on the legality of regulatory documents.

[29] H Zhou (周慧蕾) and C Ma (马程宏), 'On the Actionability of School District Division Decision' (论学区划分行为的可诉性) (2020) 6 Journal of Social Science of Harbin Normal University (哈尔滨师范大学社会科学学报) 56–59.

[30] M Liu (刘孟) and W Sha (沙卫鹏), 'Between the Abstract and the Concrete: Reflections on the Dichotomy of Administrative Action' (抽象与具体之间: 行政行为二分法之反思) (2021) 3 The South China Sea Law Journal (南海法学) 1–10.

[31] Arts 3, 4, 5, 6, 7, and 8 of the Circular on 31 May 2018.

[32] Art 22 of the Regulations on Procedures for Making Administrative Regulations; art 16 of the Regulations on Procedures for Making Administrative Rules; art 16 of the Provisional Regulations on Major Administrative Decision-making Procedures.

[33] Before the 2014 amendment of the Administrative Litigation Law, the court would discuss the proportionality of the penalty handed down when it was 'manifestly unjust', but only on matters pertaining to the administrative police (显失公正).

4
Czech Republic

Jiří Rajchl, Daniel Burda, and Gabriela Blahoudková

I. Constitutional and Legislative Provisions on Rulemaking and Planning

In the legal system of the Czech Republic, the basis for distinguishing between administrative rulemaking and individual decision-making can be found in the constitutional system. The differences between the two are not expressly defined, however they can be inferred from the way the two areas are regulated by law.

Concerning administrative rulemaking, the Constitution sets out an enumerated list of conditions under which implementing subordinate legislation can be adopted. Such subordinate legislation is referred to as executive regulations in this chapter. Ministries and other administrative authorities—as well as bodies of territorial self-governing units, when exercising state powers delegated to them by the state to be exercised in the name of the state (so-called delegated powers of territorial self-governing units)[1]—can only adopt regulations if they have been expressly authorized to do so by a statute.[2] The government, as the supreme executive body controlling the state administration, can adopt governmental regulations to implement laws within the limits of those laws without the need for express authorization.[3] However, given the stringent conditions and the risk of exceeding statutory limits, the legislature prefers to also seek express statutory authorization for the government. In this respect, it is necessary to reiterate that governmental regulations are of an implementing nature and cannot impose a duty in themselves without having sufficiently specific grounds set out in a statute.[4] Government regulations are thus not autonomous in the Czech legal system.

The situation is different in the case of the administrative rulemaking of territorial self-governing units within their autonomous powers (self-governance of municipalities and regions). In this case, the Constitution includes general authorization for such administrative rulemaking by municipalities and regions, which can impose duties on persons with no reference to a statute.[5] This type of rulemaking can thus be termed original. With some simplification, it can be said that territorial self-governing units can legislate if the administrative rulemaking is for municipal or regional purposes,

[1] Delegated powers are distinct from so called autonomous powers, ie independent powers of municipalities and regions.

[2] See art 79(3) of the Constitution.

[3] See art 78 of the Constitution.

[4] This is a so-called reservation of statutory regulation, enshrined, at the constitutional level, in art 4(1) and (2) of the Charter of Fundamental Rights and Freedoms (the Charter).

[5] See art 104(3) of the Constitution.

Jiří Rajchl, Daniel Burda, and Gabriela Blahoudková, *Czech Republic* In: *Administrative Rulemaking and Planning in European Laws*. Edited by: Giacinto della Cananea and Angela Ferrari Zumbini, Oxford University Press.
 DOI: 10.1093/oso/9780198867616.003.0004

provided it is not against the law and does not encroach upon expressly determined competences of the state administration.[6]

As for administrative decision-making, the powers are addressed at the constitutional level only within the framework of the fundamental principle that state power can be exerted only in the cases, within the limits, and in the manner prescribed by law (principle of legality),[7] and that duties may be imposed only on the basis of a statute and within its limits.[8] While more detailed regulation of individual administrative decision-making is left to the law, the adoption of administrative regulations is specifically addressed in the Constitution.

The differences can also be seen in the field of judicial review of the legality (and, as the case may be, constitutionality) of administrative regulations and individual administrative decisions. The Constitution guarantees individuals extensive judicial review of administrative decisions that affect their rights and duties[9] and this is conducted by the administrative judiciary. On the other hand, a judicial review of administrative regulations can only be initiated by public institutions and public officials as determined by law.[10] It is the Constitutional Court that decides in cases within the framework of an abstract review.[11] This is the so-called centralized model of judicial review. In contrast, individuals can only challenge the legality of an administrative regulation in court by challenging a specific act of the regulation's application. This act is usually a decision on the dismissal of an application for the grant of a right or a decision regarding an administrative contravention. Alternatively, individuals can challenge an actual intervention by an administrative body that is not grounded by a formalized decision, as long as the intervention is of an administrative law nature. General courts (which also include courts acting as administrative courts) have jurisdiction to review the legality and constitutionality of administrative regulations which they should apply in a particular case. If they find that an administrative regulation, or a part of it, breaks the law, then they do not apply it; however, they do not have the jurisdiction to cancel it.[12] This type of judicial review is referred to as a diffused model of judicial review and, at the same time, as a case-related judicial review (being associated with a particular case).

Details of the procedure for the preparation and adoption of administrative regulations are not regulated by law. By contrast, administrative processes and procedures concerning individuals are regulated in detail by the Code of Administrative Procedure,[13] which takes the form of a statute. The differing nature of abstract and concrete acts is not explicitly regulated. At the statutory level, only a decision is positively defined as an act by which the rights and obligations of persons determined by names are established, modified, cancelled, and/or bindingly determined.[14] This

[6] Executive regulations and regulations adopted by municipalities and regions within their autonomous powers are collectively referred to as 'administrative regulations' here.

[7] See art 2(3) of the Constitution and art 2(2) of the Charter.

[8] See art 4(1) of the Charter.

[9] See art 36(2) of the Charter.

[10] See s 64(2) of Act No 182/1993 Sb, on the Constitutional Court of the Czech Republic.

[11] See art 87(1)(b) of the Constitution.

[12] See art 95(1) of the Constitution.

[13] Act No 500/2004 Sb, the Code of Administrative Procedure.

[14] See s 67(1) of the Code of Administrative Procedure and, in particular, s 65(1) of the Code of Administrative Procedure.

definition complies with the administrative law doctrine which specifies two criteria to distinguish between abstract acts and concrete acts, namely the degree of generality from the point of view of the subject of the regulation (abstract/concrete), and the degree of personalization (non-personalized—addressed to an indefinitely determined circle of persons, or, on the other hand, personalized—addressed to a particular person or persons whose name is specified). Administrative regulations are abstract and non-personalized, whereas decisions are concrete and personalized. These distinguishing criteria are also applied by courts.

The Code of Administrative Procedure also regulates the issuance of measures of a general nature, which are considered a middle way between administrative regulations and administrative decisions.[15] The provision determining measures of a general nature is also the only statutory provision to expressly mention the link to other forms of administrative acts, albeit only negatively, as it includes the following wording: 'a measure of a general nature which is neither a legal regulation nor a decision'. The typical features and legal effects are also not positively defined here. The doctrine, however, defines this type of act as concrete (in terms of the subject of the regulation) but non-personalized. A measure of a general nature is not regulated in any specific way at the constitutional level. What they have in common with decisions is the opportunity for the persons concerned to comment on the factual solution, as well as the existence of the reasoning for the adopted solution and the possibility of judicial review. A feature they share with administrative regulations is, in particular, the non-personalized mode of publication.

II. Legal Effects of Administrative Rules and Plans

Administrative regulations bind their addressees in the same way as statutes. We only distinguish legal force in terms of hierarchy, so the rules contained in administrative regulations must comply with the Constitution and constitutional laws, statutes, and international treaties that are part of the legal system. Subordinate legislation puts the rules set out in laws into concrete terms, for example by setting out specific parameters for things and activities. Failure to satisfy requirements expressed in a prescribed manner can make it impossible to obtain permission to carry out certain qualified activities. This often applies to business activities, as well as building permits. Such activities require an administrative decision or permission, and failure to satisfy the requirements prescribed in administrative regulations can make obtaining permission impossible. Only rarely does a failure to adhere to administrative regulations represent a direct obstacle to carrying out activities that do not require a prior administrative decision. This occurs, for example, in the importing of foreign goods to the domestic market. What is more likely to constitute an obstacle to usual activities is the regulation contained in municipal bylaws, particularly the regulation governing conduct in public spaces.

[15] See Part VI of the Code of Administrative Procedure.

As a matter of principle, any violation of a duty should result in an adverse legal consequence as prescribed by law. Where the satisfaction of requirements prescribed in administrative regulations is merely a requisite for granting a permit to carry out an activity in the future, the adverse consequence is usually only the denial of the requested permit without any administrative sanctions. An administrative offence only occurs if the law specifies it (*nullum crimen sine lege*) and is more likely to happen when conducting qualified, especially business activities, and most frequently when carrying out an activity that requires an administrative permit. The permits issued also frequently establish requirements for carrying out such activities. Sanctions for violating duties outlined in permits are more common than sanctions for breaching duties stipulated in administrative regulations. The situation is different in the case of regulating public order by municipalities; the law establishes a general contravention consisting in the violation of a duty imposed by municipal bylaws.

III. Procedural Requirements Concerning Rulemaking and Planning

No requirements follow from the Constitution or laws for the process of adopting administrative regulations, which thus commonly takes place *in camera*. This contrasts with the public nature of the legislative process, which is regulated in detail by the Constitution and Codes of Procedure of both chambers of Parliament which take the form of statute. An exception to this practice is administrative rulemaking by municipalities and regions within the framework of their self-government; the regulations they adopt are considered at public sessions of municipal/regional councils, at which the citizens can present their standpoints.[16] The Act on the Collection of Laws thus regulates only the issues of the publication of some subordinate legislation and includes some rules regarding the drafting of it, however its scope is significantly limited.[17] Since 2022, there has existed an official centralized register of regulations adopted by regions, municipalities, and some state administrative bodies.[18] Detailed regulations are contained only in the internal directive of the government and also affect the creation of executive regulations by central administrative authorities.[19] The rules only allow comments to be made by certain public institutions and some umbrella private law organizations. A wide range of people have no legal right to influence the preparation and the content of executive regulations but can (passively) observe the comment procedure on the government information portal.

A different approach applies to general measures, which are regulated by the Code of Administrative Procedure. Parties involved can comment on the measures, and the owners of the properties concerned can raise objections. An administrative body

[16] See Act No 128/2000 Sb, on the establishment of municipalities, and Act No 129/2000 Sb, on the establishment of regions.

[17] Act No 222/2016 Sb, which has come into effect in 2024.

[18] Act No 35/2021 Sb.

[19] Government Legislative Rules, approved by the Government Resolution No 188 of 19 March 1998, as amended.

is required to decide on any objections raised, while it can address comments made through argumentation when giving reasons.

Regarding plans, it is necessary to distinguish between those that are legally binding and those that are not. Binding plans are drafted and approved in the form of a general measure; therefore, they are not considered to be rulemaking acts but rather a hybrid that straddles rulemaking and decision-making, and the regulation referred to above applies to them. However, special statutory regulation applies to the best known type of plan—that is, the local development plan—which is much more detailed and complex than the procedural regime for general measures set out in the Code of Administrative Procedure.

In conclusion, it can be said that the procedural requirements for the consideration of administrative regulations, administrative decisions, and measures of a general nature are substantially different. Furthermore, the principles of due process, fairness, and transparency are not ensured and applied in a comparable manner.

5
European Union

Edoardo Chiti

I. Constitutional and Legislative Provisions on Rulemaking and Planning

In the EU legal system, the legal relevance of administrative rulemaking, understood here as a concise formula referring to a variety of generally applicable measures, including plans, and distinct from adjudication, is acknowledged in the Treaty framework.

First, the categorization of legal acts in the Lisbon Treaty distinguishes between general and individual measures. Individual measures may take the form of a decision, defined as an act binding in its entirety that can be directed to individual addressees (see Article 288 of the Treaty on the Functioning of the European Union (TFEU), which follows the definition previously given by Article 14 of the European Coal and Steel Community (ECSC) Treaty). Rulemaking measures, which differ from individual decisions and are separate from legislative acts, can be adopted as delegated (Article 290 TFEU) and general implementing acts (Article 291 TFEU). The distinction between legislative measures, rulemaking subordinate to legislation, and individual decisions is also prominent in the case law of the European Court of Justice (ECJ), which has traditionally relied on the substantial criterion of the actual features of the measure in drawing such a distinction.

Secondly, several Treaty provisions by sector operate as legal bases for the adoption of rulemaking measures by EU institutions. For example, Article 108(4) TFEU empowers the Commission to adopt regulations relating to specific categories of state aid. Provisions in the fields of the internal market (Article 26(3) TFEU), economic policy (Article 121 TFEU), and labour policy (Articles 146–148 TFEU) refer to the use of non-binding guidelines by the Council.

Lastly, the system of judicial remedies distinguishes between general and individual measures, particularly through the rules on standing, to contest the legality of EU measures. In fact, Article 263(4) TFEU stipulates that non-privileged applicants' access to courts is subject to different requirements depending on the individual or regulatory nature of the challenged measure. The new regime introduced by the Lisbon Treaty is designed to overcome some of the difficulties traditionally encountered by non-privileged applicants in challenging the legality of EU norms. The real extent of the liberalizing effect of the reform, however, is still a matter of debate. In this context, the ECJ has interpreted the phrase 'regulatory act', which does not fit with the Treaty classification of legal acts, as referring to 'all acts of abstract general application apart from legislative acts'.[1]

[1] See eg Case C-583/11 P, *Inuit v European Parliament and Council*, ECLI:EU:C:2013:625.

Edoardo Chiti, *European Union* In: *Administrative Rulemaking and Planning in European Laws*. Edited by: Giacinto della Cananea and Angela Ferrari Zumbini, Oxford University Press.
DOI: 10.1093/oso/9780198867616.003.0005

EU legislation confirms the legal importance of administrative rulemaking as distinct from adjudication. Although no code of administrative procedure acknowledges the overall importance of rulemaking, several legislative provisions by sector establish a legal basis for the adoption of rulemaking measures by EU administrations. For example, some European agencies, such as the European Aviation Safety Agency (EASA), are called to participate, as technical actors, in procedures leading to the adoption of binding implementing rules, either assisting the Commission or directly adopting technical rules.

II. Legal Effects of Administrative Rules and Plans

It follows from the above that EU institutions and administrations may adopt a variety of binding rulemaking measures. These include (i) non-legislative measures adopted by the Commission or the Council under Articles 290 and 291 TFEU, and (ii) legally binding non-legislative measures adopted by EU institutions, bodies, offices, and agencies on the basis of sector-specific Treaty provisions or legislative acts (the example of EASA, mentioned above, is a case in point).

However, it is appropriate to stress the importance of non-binding rulemaking. Indeed, the EU order offers a diverse landscape of binding and non-binding rulemaking measures adopted by EU administrations. The latter are often informal and include guidance, application guides, communications and other soft-law instruments. For example, European agencies are often formally or *de facto* granted the power to issue soft-law acts, either to regulatees or other administrative bodies participating in the sectoral network they coordinate. Such measures make a substantial contribution to the smooth functioning of the policy sectors in question. The European Medicines Agency (EMA) is an excellent example of an organization that provides technical, scientific, and procedural guidance on the implementation of the EU pharmaceutical legislative framework, despite not being expressly granted rulemaking powers by the establishing Regulation. The guidance does not have the legal status of soft-law measures, which inherently present a tension between the form of non-binding provisions and the substance of rules that de facto affect and influence private parties' behaviour.

III. Procedural Requirements Concerning Rulemaking and Planning

The EU legal order has no general code of good administration or administrative procedure. While the European Ombudsman has advocated adopting such a code, the Commission has traditionally questioned the need for general legislation and pointed to the existing codification by sector, namely regulations establishing rules of good administration in specific fields, such as competition and state aid.

A proposal for 'innovative codification', combining the consolidation of existing laws with the introduction of new principles and rules, was advanced in European legal scholarship, with the Research Network on EU Administrative Law (ReNEUAL) in 2014. The 'Model Rules on EU Administrative Procedure', drawn up in the context of the project proposed a formal distinction between general and individual measures, put forward a normative argument for providing autonomous legal relevance to administrative rulemaking as distinct from adjudication, and established two distinct procedural disciplines.[2] A subsequent legislative proposal by the Legal Affairs Committee of the European Parliament (2016) rejected this approach, limiting itself to individual procedures and decisions. However, the ReNEUAL Model Rules are still a source of inspiration for ambitious and comprehensive future EU legislation on administrative procedure.

Despite the lack of a general code of administrative behaviour, there are several sources that impose general (not sector-specific) procedural obligations on public bodies when they adopt administrative rules. These comprise Treaty articles (such as Article 296(2) TFEU, prescribing a duty to give reasons), articles of the Charter of Fundamental Rights of the European Union (such as Article 41 establishing the right to good administration), ECJ case law (which has provided the requisites of due process and the rule of law), the European Ombudsman (see eg the Code of Good Administrative Behaviour approved by the European Parliament in 2001, intended to explain in more detail what the right to good administration envisaged by Article 41 of the Charter of Fundamental Rights should mean in practice), and the Commission (see eg the Code of Good Administrative Behaviour, adopted by the Commission on 13 September 2000, setting out the principles underpinning the administrative conduct of the Commission services, as well as a complaint procedure). Overall, the procedural requirements that emerge from this diverse set of sources do not differentiate between general and individual decisions. However, the same procedural requirements are implemented in partly different ways depending on the nature (either general or individual) of the measure to be adopted. While due process drives the functional rationale behind individual decision-making requirements, interest representation, exemplified by recourse to consultation, shapes and orients rulemaking procedures.

[2] The 'Model Rules on EU Administrative Procedure', <http://www.reneual.eu/projects-and-publications/reneual-1-0> accessed 22 November 2024.

6
Germany

Lilly Weidemann

I. Constitutional and Legislative Provisions on Rulemaking and Planning

Section 35 sentence 1 of the German Administrative Procedure Act[1] (hereafter referred to as the APA) defines an administrative act as 'any order, decision or other sovereign measure taken by an authority to regulate an individual case in the sphere of public law and intended to have a direct, external legal effect'. Legal norms, on the other hand, are abstract general regulations[2] that establish a generally applicable rule and are addressed to an indeterminate number of persons who are not known at the time of issuance of the norm. An administrative act therefore regulates a specific situation and has an individual addressee, which is why it is typically a 'specific individual' regulation. The essence of a legal norm, on the other hand, is that it regulates several issues and addresses several addressees; it is an 'abstract general' regulation.

Delimitation issues can arise in particular with regard to the general orders (*Allgemeinverfügungen*) provided for in section 35 sentence 2 APA. These are defined as administrative acts 'directed at a group of people defined or definable on the basis of general characteristics or relating to the public law aspect of a matter or its use by the public at large'. The general order concerns a specific situation but is general with regard to its addressees; it is a 'specific general' regulation. It is distinguished from a norm in that it concerns specific facts, as opposed to a legal norm that contains abstract general regulations.[3]

The distinction between 'abstract general' and 'specific general' regulations is only *apparently* clear-cut, as the situational relevance of a regulation cannot always be clearly identified, for example with regard to determining the navigability of a certain bay with watercraft or the definition of school districts.[4] According to case law, the form of action actually chosen is of key importance in such overlapping cases: if the measure takes the form of a legal norm, then it is not a general order.[5]

[1] Administrative Procedure Act of 25 May 1976 in the wording last promulgated on 23 January 2003 (Federal Law Gazette I, p 102), amended by art 4, para 8 of the Act to Modernise the Law on Costs of 5 May 2004 (Federal Law Gazette I, p 718).

[2] Federal Administrative Court, Order of 2 April 1993—7 B 38/93–, para 2, juris.

[3] Federal Administrative Court, Judgment of 9 June 1967—VII C 18.66–, BVerwGE 27, 181–89, para 10.

[4] M Knauff, '§ 35 VwVfG' in F Schoch and J-P Schneider, *Verwaltungsrecht* (4th edn, CH Beck 2023), para 199.

[5] Federal Administrative Court, Judgment of 17 June 2013—3 C 21/12–, BVerwGE 147, 100–18, para 11.

Lilly Weidemann, *Germany* In: *Administrative Rulemaking and Planning in European Laws*. Edited by: Giacinto della Cananea and Angela Ferrari Zumbini, Oxford University Press.
DOI: 10.1093/oso/9780198867616.003.0006

II. Legal Effects of Administrative Rules and Plans

The binding effect of administrative rules depends on the nature of the administrative instrument itself.

Administrative rulemaking can be categorised into three main types: statutory instruments or ordinances (*Rechtsverordnungen*), administrative regulations or directions (*Verwaltungsvorschriften*), and bylaws (*Satzungen*).

Statutory instruments (*Rechtsverordnungen*) are traditionally understood in substantive terms as subordinate and generally binding legal provisions issued by the executive (the so-called substantive concept of a statutory instrument). In recent literature, a formal definition of the term 'statutory instrument' has increasingly prevailed; it is based on the legislative body as well as the form and procedure by which the statutory instrument is issued, in particular its designation as a statutory instrument and the promulgation and citation of the authorizing law (the so-called formalized concept of a statutory instrument).[6]

The German constitution, the Basic Law,[7] establishes express limits concerning the form and procedure of delegation of legislative authority to the executive branch in the form of statutory instruments.[8] On the one hand, these relate to the authorisation to issue statutory instruments and are therefore addressed to the (delegating) legislator. On the other, the Basic Law also sets out requirements for authorization by the legislator; it establishes requirements for issuing statutory instruments aimed at the respective executive addressee of the authorisation.[9] The power to set statute-derived standards endows a statutory instrument with legally binding effect, in particular a binding effect vis-à-vis the courts.[10]

Bylaws (*Satzungen*) are legal provisions issued by a legal entity under public law within the scope of the autonomy granted to it by law and are effective for the persons belonging to and subject to it.[11] They derive from the constitutional principle of decentralization.[12] Issued by local government authorities or recognized autonomous bodies, such as universities or professional bodies, they regulate their own affairs independently, without specific statutory authorization.[13] Similar to statutory

[6] A Uhle, 'GG Article 80' in V Epping and C Hillgruber, *BeckOK Grundgesetz* (57th edn, CH Beck 2024) para 2 with further references regarding both views. Some stress the character of statutory instruments as forms of administrative action as opposed to its character as a source of law, see M Sachs, 'Normsetzung (Rechtsverordnung, Satzung)' in PF Bultmann and others (eds), *Festschrift Battis, Allgemeines Verwaltungsrecht: Institute, Kontexte, System* (1st edn, CH Beck 2014) 161; M Trips, *Das Verfahren der exekutiven Rechtsetzung* (Nomos 2006) 62.

[7] Basic Law for the Federal Republic of Germany in the revised version published in the Federal Law Gazette Part III, classification number 100-1, as last amended by the Act of 19 December 2022 (Federal Law Gazette I, p 2478).

[8] Art 80 Basic Law, see in detail Germany, Case 1 in Chapter 15.II.E.

[9] Uhle (n 6) para 5.

[10] B Remmert, 'GG Art. 80' in G Dürig, R Herzog, and R Scholz (eds), *Grundgesetz Kommentar* (CH Beck 2023) para 212.

[11] Federal Constitutional Court, Order of 9 May 1972—1 BvR 518/62–, BVerfGE 33, 125–71, para 103.

[12] See M Martini, 'Normsetzung und andere Formen exekutivischer Selbstprogrammierung' in A Voßkuhle, M Eifert, and C Möllers, *Grundlagen des Verwaltungsrechts*, Band II (3rd edn, CH Beck 2022) 417–512, 441.

[13] V Mehde, 'GG Art. 28' in Dürig, Herzog, and Scholz (eds) (n 10) para 207.

instruments, bylaws are generally abstract and apply within a specific locality or to organs and individuals associated with the relevant autonomous bodies.[14]

Administrative regulations (*Verwaltungsvorschriften*) are regulations that 'make binding statements for an abstract variety of administrative matters without being aimed at a direct external legal effect'.[15] They are addressed by a superior authority to subordinate authorities or by a superior to his or her subordinate administrative staff.[16] By setting out a standardized and generalized clarification of laws in writing, they serve the interest of the legal interest of a uniform administrative practice.[17] Administrative regulations only have a de facto external effect if, and insofar as, the authorities act in accordance with them.[18] They can be divided into different types. Norm-interpreting regulations contain instructions on the interpretation and application of statutes, in particular in the case of undefined legal terms without scope for judgement, especially with regard to limit value determinations in the safety and technology sector. Administrative regulations specifying standards relate to 'open' prerequisites of a statute with undefined legal terms in which the authorities have room for discretion, particularly in the area of safety and technology. Discretionary administrative regulations are not based on the facts of the case but refer to the legal consequences that result from them. They presuppose the fulfilment of the statutory requirements and are intended to ensure the uniform exercise of discretion as far as the legal consequences are concerned, and specifically to ensure the equal or uniform distribution of public funds to which there is no legal entitlement.[19]

III. Procedural Requirements Concerning Rulemaking and Planning

Apart from some notable sector-specific exceptions (eg urban land-use planning), administrative rulemaking in Germany is characterized by a considerable lack of procedural regulations. The concept of procedure is only weakly developed in this area of public law. This applies to the procedure for issuing statutory instruments, bylaws, and administrative regulations. Legal scholarship is also insufficient in this regard.[20] Generally speaking, a procedural doctrine of administrative rulemaking does not exist, although some scholars advocate for its creation.[21]

[14] Remmert (n 10) para 210.

[15] Federal Constitutional Court, Order of March 2nd, 1999—2 BvF 1/94–, BVerfGE 100, 249–63, para 38.

[16] Suerbaum, 'GG Art. 84' in Epping and Hillgruber (eds) (n 6) para 49.

[17] Geis, 'VwVfG § 40' in Schoch and Schneider (eds) (n 4) para 171.

[18] H Schmitz, 'VwVfG § 1' in P Stelkens, H J Bonk, and M Sachs (eds), *Verwaltungsverfahrensgesetz* (10th edn, CH Beck 2022). See Germany, Case 3 on Chapter 15.IV.E for more details.

[19] Schmitz (n 18) para 213 ff.

[20] Notable exceptions are eg C Gößwein, *Allgemeines Verwaltungs(verfahrens)recht der administrativen Normsetzung?* (Duncker & Humblot 2000); Trips (n 6).

[21] E Schmidt-Aßmann and W Schenk, 'VwVfG Einleitung' in Schoch and Schnerider (eds) (n 4) para 26; Trips (n 6) 61.

The APA does not regulate administrative rulemaking.[22] Its scope of application is limited to administrative proceedings aimed at issuing an administrative act or concluding a public law contract in accordance with section 9 APA.[23] The historic law-maker intentionally excluded administrative rulemaking from the scope of application.[24] However, it is argued that—notwithstanding sections 9 and 35 APA—procedures of administrative rulemaking are, according to their primary dogmatic classification, administrative procedures and therefore subject to the general principles of administrative procedures according to the APA.[25]

Notably, specific provisions come into play concerning the 'legally-binding planning procedure' (*Planfeststellungsverfahren*—paragraphs 72 et seq APA). This special administrative procedure leads to a planning decision, in other words an administrative act,[26] and thus falls under section 9 APA. It pertains to the proposed plan of a project developer for a stationary project that has spatial connections and impinges at either the local or supra-local level, such as highways, railway or power lines, airports, or waste disposal sites.[27] The planning decision determines the lawfulness of a project with regard to all public interests affected by it (section 75 paragraph 1 APA). In most cases, the authority disposes of a scope for planning within which it has to balance the public and private interests affected by the project.[28]

[22] The APAs of the *Länder* do not apply to administrative rulemaking, either. A notable exception is the General Administrative Law for the State of Schleswig-Holstein of 2 June 1992, GVOBl. 1992, 243, 534, see ss 53 et seq.

[23] According to s 9 APA, for the purposes of the APA, administrative procedure shall be the activity of authorities having an external effect and directed to the examination of basic requirements, the preparation and adoption of an administrative act, or to the conclusion of an administrative agreement under public law; it shall include the adoption of the administrative act or the conclusion of the agreement under public law.

[24] In drafting the APA, the legislator was of the opinion that the regulation of administrative acts was of greater urgence and that the regulation of administrative rulemaking would supersede the limits of an Administrative Procedures Act; see Trips (n 6) 103 with further references, 185.

[25] U Stelkens, 'Rechtsetzungen der europäischen und nationalen Verwaltungen' (2012) 71 Veröffentlichungen der Vereinigung der Deutschen Staatsrechtslehrer 369, 388; differing opinion: Gößwein (n 20) 92 ff.

[26] Federal Administrative Court, Judgment of 14 February 1975—IV C 21.74–, BVerwGE 48, 56–70, para 28.

[27] W Neumann and C Külpmann, 'VwVfG § 72' in Stelkens, Bonk, and Sachs (eds) (n 18) para 3.

[28] N Kämper, 'VwVfG § 72' in J Bader and M Ronellenfitsch, *BeckOK VwVfG* (61st edn, CH Beck 2023) para 6.

7
Hungary

Lilla Berkes and Balázs Szabolcs Gerencsér

I. Constitutional and Legislative Provisions on Rulemaking and Planning

As a starting point, it should be noted that Hungarian substantive law traditionally did not follow the classical *actus* jurisprudence, that is, it did not distinguish between acts of public administration on the basis of whether they were individual or normative, while administrative jurisprudence dealt in detail with the dogmatics of acts, following the German model.[1]

The basis of this understanding is that only what has been duly enacted and promulgated by the bodies empowered to legislate is considered law, and this law cannot be changed by the subjects and practitioners of the law.[2] The types of legal norms and the authorized bodies are defined in the Fundamental Law[3] and the Act on law-making;[4] in other words whoever or whatever does not fall within this scope is not a law-maker, and the result of their activity is not a law. In this sense, the task of the public administration, insofar as we are not talking about administrative bodies also empowered to legislate, is to implement the law and not to create it.[5]

Along these lines, Article T)[6] of the Fundamental Law lays down the basis for legislation, and Article T is implemented by the Act on law-making, which distinguishes between laws and public law regulatory instruments.[7] The latter are internal acts of law which only have effect within the state organization. Regarding this system, there is no fundamental difference between the old Constitution and the old Legislative

[1] A Patyi, *A közigazgatási működés jogi alapjai* (Dialóg Campus Kiadó 2017) 107–13.

[2] A Tamás, 'A jogalkotási dilemmák modern demokráciában' in L Ficzere, M Molnár, and A Tamás, *Tanulmányok a közigazgatási szervezeti és jogi intézményei köréből* (Unió 1995) 127–37, 132–33.

[3] <https://njt.hu/jogszabaly/en/2011-4301-02-00≥ accessed 22 November 2024.

[4] Act CXXX of 2010 on law-making <https://njt.hu/jogszabaly/en/2010-130-00-00≥ accessed 22 November 2024.

[5] A Tamás, *A közigazgatási jog elmélete* (Szent István Társulat 2005) 68–69.

[6] Article T): '(1) Generally binding rules of conduct may be laid down in the Fundamental Law and in laws adopted by an organ having legislative competence specified in the Fundamental Law and promulgated in the official gazette. A cardinal Act may lay down different rules for the promulgation of local government decrees and of laws adopted after the initiation by the Government of the declaration of state of war or state of emergency, or under a special legal order. (2) Laws shall be Acts, government decrees, prime ministerial decrees, ministerial decrees, decrees of the Governor of the Hungarian National Bank, decrees of the heads of independent regulatory organs and local government decrees. (3) No law shall conflict with the Fundamental Law. (4) Cardinal Acts shall be Acts, the adoption and amendment of which requires the votes of two thirds of the Members of the National Assembly present.'

[7] S 1(1) The scope of this Act shall cover a) laws, and b) normative decisions and normative instructions (hereinafter jointly 'public law regulatory instruments').

Lilla Berkes and Balázs Szabolcs Gerencsér, *Hungary* In: *Administrative Rulemaking and Planning in European Laws.*
Edited by: Giacinto della Cananea and Angela Ferrari Zumbini, Oxford University Press.
 DOI: 10.1093/oso/9780198867616.003.0007

Act, although the latter used the term 'instrument of organization of public law' for internal acts.

It is clear, however, that the system of norms cannot be described in such a closed way. There have always been examples of law-enforcement (adjudicative) bodies acting as regulators, due to the diversity of social relations and in order to make their operation and application of law more predictable. Such rules have been made possible, at best, by sectoral legislation but, on the whole, this issue has not been addressed in the administrative law literature, so the scope of these instruments is not clear.

The Constitutional Court (CC) sought to curb this tendency as early as 1992, when it ruled in CC Decision 60/1992 (XI. 17.) that

> the publication and practice of issuing and guiding by means of legal guidance documents, circulars, guidelines, directives, opinions and other informal interpretations of law from ministries and other central state bodies, without regard to the guarantee rules of Act XI of 1987 on Legislation,

was unconstitutional. The core of the constitutional problem was the proliferation of these instruments, which had no binding force but which, in practice, behaved as if they were legal acts, often with de facto legislative content. The result was a 'law without form' which, by taking precedence over the promulgated legislation of the bodies vested with legislative powers by the Constitution, often undermined its effectiveness. Although the law of the time allowed for the issuing of so-called legal guidelines, they were not binding and were intended to assist the law enforcement (adjudicative) bodies in their work and ensure uniform implementation of the law. In contrast, the instruments challenged by the Constitutional Court were, in its view, creating legal uncertainty and making the behaviour of legal entities and law enforcement bodies unpredictable. Although the interpretation of the law and the legal application aspects they contained had no legal force or binding content, having been issued by the central bodies of the state administration, they were and could actually be capable of misleading the addressees and being followed by them as binding rules.

In 2009, the Constitutional Court finally annulled the entire legislative act. In its reasoning, the Court stated that over the years, the Act had come into conflict with the modern constitutional doctrines of legislation.[8] The ruling stated that other legal instruments of state governance cannot take over the function of legislation, but it failed to take into account the growing importance of administrative legislation and the Court's failure to require constitutional rules for its creation.[9] The new (and current) Act on law-making adopted after the CC decision therefore only recognizes the instruments of the normative decision and the normative instruction, but it has also recognized and, in effect, 'legalized' other legal regulatory instruments which could be issued by another act but whose integration into the legal system had not been

[8] L Csink, 'Sources of Law' in A Zs Varga, A Patyi, and B Schanda (eds), *The Basic (Fundamental) Law of Hungary. A Commentary of the New Hungarian Constitution* (Clarus Press 2015) 63–77, 66.

[9] J Tóth, '121/2009. (XII. 17.) AB határozat—jogalkotás szabályozása' in F Gárdos-Orosz, and K Zakariás (eds), *Az alkotmánybírósági gyakorlat. Az Alkotmánybíróság 100 elvi jelentőségű határozata 1990–2020* (Társadalomtudományi Kutatóközpont, HVG-ORAC Lap- és Könyvkiadó 2021) 777–96, 784, 789.

generally clarified.[10] Thus the concept of 'other legal instrument' was introduced, which is defined as an instrument that can be issued on the basis of an act.[11] This includes, for example, the power to issue a recommendation granted by the Media Act.[12]

A further regulatory development is worth highlighting. The new Code of Administrative Court Procedure[13] has introduced the 'administrative acts of general scope to be applied in a specific case, and not falling under the scope of the Act on law-making' into the application of the law.[14] According to the explanatory memorandum to the Act, this concept has been applied by the Court of Justice of the European Union in a number of decisions, and it is therefore necessary to include this type of act as an administrative act. This includes, for example, regulations of public bodies. The concept specifically refers to the fact that these are general provisions applicable to a specific (individual) case, since they typically give rise to specific decisions and, in that context, to the unlawful nature of the general provision. The Commentary on the Act points out that the Act has opened up the possibility of a direct judicial challenge to soft law. The public administration 'regulates' by means of new types of acts which cannot be classified as traditional mandatory administrative acts, but by which, in adopting them, the public authority nevertheless determines the management of the administrative matters falling within its competence and, through them, the conduct of individual cases. These administrative acts do not have a specific addressee (they are therefore normative) but they do influence the conduct, the legal action, or the legal consequences of the legal entities. In this way, the Act has followed the trends in the development of European law.[15] However, the judicial practice related to this concept is not yet visible.[16] The Code of General Administrative Procedure[17] (APA) does not address the issue at all.

[10] B Varsányi 'A régi és az új jogalkotási törvény összehasonlítása' MTA Law Working Papers 2014/55, 3 <http://real.mtak.hu/121278/1/2014_55_Varsanyi.pdf≥ accessed 22 November 2024.

[11] S 24(3): 'No other legal instruments that may be issued on the basis of an Act to regulate the activities and operation of state organs or statutory professional bodies shall conflict with any law or public law regulatory instrument.'

[12] For example s 9(8): 'The Media Council shall make recommendations concerning the fundamental aspects of judicial principles relating to the detailed guidelines governing the ratings referred to in Subsections (2)–(7), the signs to be used prior to and in the course of broadcasting the various programs and the method of communicating the rating if justified by public interest related to the protection of minors or by the uniform approach to the protection of minors.' Act CLXXXV of 2010 on Media Services and on the Mass Media <https://njt.hu/jogszabaly/2010-185-00-00≥ accessed 22 November 2024 (no official English translation available)

[13] Act I of 2017 on the Code of Administrative Court Procedure <https://njt.hu/jogszabaly/en/2017-1-00-00≥ accessed 22 November 2024.

[14] S 4(3)c)(3): 'Administrative acts shall include administrative acts of general scope to be applied in a specific case, and not falling under the scope of the Act on law-making.'

[15] G Barabás, KF Rozsnyai, and AG Kovács (eds), *Nagykommentár a közigazgatási perrendtartásról szóló 2017. évi I. törvényhez* (Wolters Kluwer Hungary 2018)

[16] Only three cases are available. In one case, reference is made to the epidemiological procedural rules of the national medical officer, but since the applicant was (wrongly) of the opinion that these rules could not be challenged, they were not examined on the merits (Curia of Hungary Kfv. 37.174/2023/4.). In one case, the air quality plan was not classified as a normative act (Curia of Hungary Kfv. 37.700/2020/5), and in one case the traffic sign was classified by the Curia as an administrative act of general scope (Curia of Hungary Kfv. 37.393/2020/5).

[17] Act CL of 2016 on the Code of General Administrative Procedure <https://njt.hu/jogszabaly/en/2016-150-00-00≥ accessed 22 November 2024.

In terms of planning, showing a comprehensive picture of the issue is not really possible. The previous APA included provisions for an audit plan in the context of an administrative audit.[18] However, this solution is no longer followed in the current legislation, on the grounds that, for the authority, the rules were entirely of an internal administrative or organizational nature rather than general procedural provisions. However, the sectoral legislation may continue to include requirements in this respect as additional rules. This can be considered a type of planning.

The various forms of social consultation can also be seen as a form—or rather a part—of planning. On the one hand, public participation in the preparation of legislation is regulated by an act,[19] but this only covers acts, government decrees, and ministerial decrees. It does not cover local government decrees, nor is there any obligation to do so in the Local Government Act.[20] They may, however, hold public hearings, which is provided for in their rules of organization and operation.[21] There may also hold other forms of consultations too.[22] Local governments may, or may not, consult the public and interested bodies on any matter. Typically, this takes place before major construction projects but there are also many good practices in other areas of local government legislation.[23] In line with this, local governments have the possibility to consult with the population, interest groups, civil and business organizations, and religious communities on the draft of the town plan, the government decree on the

[18] Act CXL of 2004 on the General Rules of Administrative Proceedings and Services s 91: '(1) The authority shall draw up an audit plan containing inter alia the subject matter of scheduled inspections, the period inspected, the timetable and means of the inspections, the criteria for inspections and other particulars defined by the head of the authority. The audit plan is not required to indicate permanent control functions. (2) The authority shall prepare an audit report concerning the implementation of the functions set out in the audit plan, covering also the regulatory inspections conducted during the inspected period, which are not specified in the audit plan, and the findings of the inspection before the closure of the next inspection period, containing also the amount of inspections conducted and their results, the types of infringements revealed, and other statistical data specified by the head of the authority. (3) The authority shall publish the audit plan and the audit report on its website and shall post them in the customer area of its offices. The audit plan shall be made public in a manner and to the extent so as not to jeopardize the outcome of the inspections.'

[19] Act CXXXI of 2010 on public participation in the preparation of legislation <https://njt.hu/jogszabaly/2010-131-00-00≥ accessed 22 November 2024 (no official English translation available)

[20] Act CLXXXIX of 2011 on Local Governments in Hungary <https://njt.hu/jogszabaly/2011-189-00-00> accessed 22 November 2024 (no official English translation available)

[21] S 53(1): 'The representative body shall determine the detailed rules of its operation in its decree on the rules of organization and operation. The representative body shall provide for the following in the decree on the rules of organization and operation: i) public hearings; Section 54 The representative body shall hold a public hearing at least once a year which is announced in advance where the population and the representatives of locally interested organizations may ask questions and make proposals in issues related to local public affairs. Responses to the proposals and questions raised at the public hearing shall be given within fifteen days at the latest.'

[22] S 53(3): 'In the rules of organization and operation, the representative body shall specify the self-organizing communities that shall have the right of consultation at the meetings of the representative body and its committees as well as the rules of forums (village policy forums, urban policy forums, city quarter meetings, village meetings etc.) serving direct information and involvement of the population and associations in the preparation of important decisions. The representative body shall be informed on their standpoint and on minority opinions arisen in these forums.'

[23] L Kiss, *Önkormányzati jogalkotás, szabályozás és dereguláció. Empirikus kutatások eredményeinek felhasználásával* (Dialóg Campus Budapest 2020) 102–03.

visual environmental of the town, and the manual of the visual environmental of the town (so-called partnership consultation).[24]

It should also be noted that in the planning process, the weight given to consultation depends on the weight given to it by the legislation (it does not require it but merely requires consultation, with no legal consequence; however, it attaches a legal consequence to the failure to consult, eg nullity). There is more likely to be a legal consequence in the event of failure to consult other public bodies than the failure to consult civil society.

II. Legal Effects of Administrative Rules and Plans

Since there is no comprehensive regulation of the issue, and it is a constitutional requirement that these administrative rules cannot behave as normative acts, there is no explicit provision for their binding effect. The name of these rules also indicates that they are not formally binding, for example recommendations, methodological guidelines. But as previously mentioned, they may have such effects indirectly and are therefore now subject to judicial control.

As for the audit plan, the explanatory memorandum of the previous APA stated that the prior planning and publicity of the audit provides a basis for carrying out an effective audit in line with those of the audit, protecting the rights of clients, allowing them to prepare and preventing possible breaches of the law. In general, the audit plan binds the authority as to the conduct, procedure, and subject matter of the audit. However, irrespective of the audit plan, the authority may, depending on the legal regulation, launch an official control at any time, either on the basis of a request, a notification, or on the basis of its own knowledge. Sector-specific regulation currently follows this practice.

In general, public participation in the various planning phases is not an obligation but an opportunity, and there are no direct legal consequences if it is not taken. Even if the law (an act or the local government decree) requires some type of participation for the drafting of a law, since participation (in general) is not a constitutional requirement, the failure to have it does not necessarily invalidate the drafted law.

III. Procedural Requirements Concerning Rulemaking and Planning

Regulatory activity of the public administration is a rather exceptional phenomenon in the Hungarian legal system, so only the Legislation Act contains a general rule. The 2010 Act on Legislation contains principles and milestones that must, or may, be taken into account in any regulatory task, but this depends on the type and form of the regulatory act. The also-mentioned 'other legal instrument' introduced by section 24(3) of the Act on Legislation connects to the criteria of the general legislation, which

[24] § 12(4) of the Act LXXIV of 2016 on the protection of the visual environmental of the town <https://njt.hu/jogszabaly/2016-74-00-00> accessed 22 November 2024 (no official English translation available).

is an obligatory code for the regulative measures that fall under the scope of the Act. This law does have measures on due process, fairness, and transparency.

For any other regulatory or planning act, outside the Act on Legislation, the general rule is a guideline but not a mandatory condition of validity.

Lex specialis rules may appear as the rules of organization and operation of specific sectors, which may contain prescriptions on the procedure for regulation. However, these processes are closer in nature to the legislation than to individual decision-making.

8
Italy

Leonardo Parona

I. Constitutional and Legislative Provisions on Rulemaking and Planning

In the Italian legal system, administrative rulemaking—broadly understood here as administrative action leading to the adoption of administrative rules and acts of general applicability—and planning are distinct from adjudication from both the theoretical and practical points of view, with significant consequences in terms of the applicable legal regime. The importance of rulemaking as an autonomous concept, however, varies depending on the various legal formants and according to the perspective taken for analysis.

More precisely, although the Italian Constitution (which came into force in 1948) envisions neither an express nor implicit distinction between administrative rulemaking and planning on the one hand, and adjudication on the other[1] (with only few general provisions on administrative action), this distinction emerges, instead, from statutory law. This is true with regard both to the general law on administrative procedure, enacted in 1990 and to special legislation, which, at least since the first half of the twentieth century, has implicitly recognized the legal significance of such a distinction.

As far as the first one is concerned, with significant systematic consequences for Italian administrative law, the general law on administrative procedure explicitly excludes rulemaking and the procedures leading to the adoption of general administrative acts from the scope of application of most of its guarantees and provisions, starting with those on participation and the duty to give reasons.[2] As a consequence,

[1] For instance, when establishing the right to judicial protection of legitimate interests and rights towards public authorities, art 113 Const only refers to 'administrative acts' which include both general administrative acts (such as those issued through rulemaking and planning) and individual acts (stemming from adjudicatory procedures). It will be nonetheless clarified later that, notwithstanding the existence of a constitutionally protected right to judicial review (see also art 24 Const), the distinction between these two types of acts bears important consequences for the actual exercise of the right to judicial protection, especially in terms of standing. It is worth noting that art 117(6) Const, on the normative powers of the state and the regions, refers at to 'regulatory powers'. The provision, however, does not address the distinction between administrative procedures of rulemaking and adjudication at issue here but concerns instead the relationship between primary legislation and secondary normative acts, ie regulations, as well as the allocation of competences between the state and the regions. Concerning administrative acts of a general, but neither abstract nor innovative nature, not sharing the feature of normative acts, see AM Sandulli, 'Sugli atti amministrativi generali a contenuto non normativo' (1954) IV Foro it 217 ff. More broadly on this topic, see G della Cananea, *Atti amministrativi generali* (Cedam 2000); MC Romano, 'Atti amministrativi generali' (ad vocem) in S Cassese (ed), *Dizionario di diritto pubblico* (Giuffrè 2006) 491.

[2] More precisely, art 13, para 1 of Law No 241/1990 establishes that '[t]he provisions of this Chapter shall not apply to the activities of the public administration for the issuance of regulatory, general, administrative,

Leonardo Parona, *Italy* In: *Administrative Rulemaking and Planning in European Laws*. Edited by: Giacinto della Cananea and Angela Ferrari Zumbini, Oxford University Press.
DOI: 10.1093/oso/9780198867616.003.0008

rulemaking and planning procedures only follow the general principles of administrative procedure codified in the first articles of the 1990 law.[3] Rather, they are regulated in greater detail by special laws, which grant them autonomous relevance and establish specific and heterogeneous legal regimes. This does not mean, however, that participation is necessarily and automatically excluded in these kinds of procedures.

Some examples may serve to clarify this observation. First of all, since 1942, when Law No 1150 was approved, urban planning and land use procedures were given a general statutory framework. The law—now operating as a framework regulation, further implemented by regional legislators, due to their shared legislative competence in this matter—allows every citizen to access planning projects and submit written observations, providing even stronger participation (in the form of objections) for parties specifically affected by certain provisions of the planning act (mainly the urban municipal plan). Secondly, it should be noted that even earlier, when Italy was confronted with the consequences of the Great Depression, and then again after the Second World War, numerous ministerial rules, as well as general acts of local and central administrative bodies, established prices, tariffs, and technical requirements in very different economic sectors.[4] Thirdly, with the establishment of independent administrative authorities in the 1990s, these bodies were granted wide regulatory powers across a variety of economic sectors. The organic laws governing such authorities establish—with certain differences—the procedures that they must comply with when issuing regulations. These procedures notably include requirements for public consultations, similar to the US notice and comment model.[5] This requirement makes a significant contribution to indirectly reinforcing the accountability of the exercise of regulatory powers by authorities lacking direct democratic legitimacy, as they operate independently from political authorities. Fourthly, the legislators pay particular attention to planning procedures and the adoption of certain general acts in the fields of public works for the construction of strategic infrastructures, public procurement, and environmental protection when transposing EU harmonization directives. In these fields, in fact, participatory guarantees such as public debate and public consultation through strategic environmental assessments have been finally introduced

planning and programming acts for which the specific rules governing the formation of training remain'. Art 3, para 2 of the same law also provides that the duty to give reasons, which in Italy has a broad scope of application (both in case of favourable and unfavourable acts), does not apply to normative and general administrative acts. With specific regard to the requirement to give reasons in relation to general administrative acts, see M Cocconi, 'L'obbligo di motivazione degli atti amministrativi generali' (2009) 3 Rivista trimestrale di diritto pubblico 707 ff.

[3] The Constitutional Court has in fact long stated (see Judgment No 355/2002) that the general principles referred to in Law No 241/1990—and, in particular, those contemplated by art 2(2), which requires the public administration to conclude the procedure within the deadline defined by law—must also be applied to general administrative planning and programming acts

[4] See G della Cananea, 'The Growth of the Italian Executive' in P Craig and A Tomkins (eds), *The Executive and Public Law* (OUP 2005) 243.

[5] On this topic, see E Chiti, 'La disciplina procedurale della regolazione' (2004) 3 Rivista trimestrale di diritto pubblico 679. The Constitutional Court has insisted on the concept of 'procedural legality' and the importance of granting participation by stating that 'the difficulty of rigorously predetermining by law the prerequisites of the administrative functions attributed to the authorities would lead to an inevitable prejudice to the needs underlying the legal reserve, if at least forms of participation of sector operators in the process of drawing up the documents were not foreseen' (see Judgment No 69/2017)

in Italy.[6] Other examples from sector-specific legislation might, of course, be added to this brief overview.

Moving on from statutory law to judicial construction and legal doctrine, it must be acknowledged that it is thanks to the latter that the distinction between general administrative acts, adopted at the conclusion of rulemaking or planning procedures, and individual acts, issued following adjudicatory processes, has been theorized in Italy. In fact, despite the initial difficulties found by public law scholarship in relation to the possibility of reconciling the idea that an administrative act could lay down rules or produce general effects with the separation of powers,[7] this distinction now represents a tenet of Italian administrative law. The distinction is built upon the differing nature, function, and effects of general administrative acts compared with individual ones, and carries significant implications for the procedures that must be followed for their adoption (as already mentioned), and for the judicial protection available against them, both in terms of standing, and of the available remedies.

II. Legal Effects of Administrative Rules and Plans

Among the heterogeneous acts considered so far, it is possible to distinguish between those with binding effects and those that do not have such effects. This distinction, however, is not clear cut, given the uncertainties in classifying certain general administrative acts and how they differ from normative ones. Both formal and substantial criteria have therefore been adopted in order to distinguish among the various types of administrative acts producing general effects. Looking at the substance of the act, rather than at its formal categorization, a distinction can be made between acts whose scope of application—especially the subjective one—is indeterminate both *ex ante* and *ex post*, thus sharing the abstract nature of normative acts and qualifying as such; and acts issued to be applied to a group of individuals, which can be determined *ex post*. These acts are considered in terms of general administrative acts,[8] whereas the former mainly take the form of regulations, that is, secondary sources of law which can be mainly issued by the Executive, regions, local bodies, and independent administrative authorities. As far as the Executive's regulatory power is concerned, Article 17 of Law No 400/1988 (which concerns the discipline of the government's activity and the organization of the Presidency of the Council of Ministers)[9] provides their general

[6] See G della Cananea, 'Exit or Voice? *Debat Public* Goes to Italy' (2019) 2 European Public Law 157 ff.

[7] See on this point G della Cananea, 'Administrative Rulemaking in Italy: Theories and Practice' in J-B. Auby (ed), *Droit compare de la procedure administrative. Comparative Law of Administrative Procedure* (Bruylant 2016) 247 ff, 248. On this point, also BG Mattarella, 'Participation in Rulemaking in Italy' (2010) 2 Italian Journal of Public Law 339 recognizes that 'the principle of division of powers is not fully operational in the Italian legal system'.

[8] As clarified by the Council of State, Plenary Meeting No 9/2012. See on, this topic, M Ramajoli and B Tonoletti, 'Qualificazione e regime giuridico degli atti amministrativi generali' (2013) 1 Diritto amministrativo 60 ff; C Cudia, 'L'efficacia 'dimensionale' dell'atto amministrativo: il caso dei destinatari degli atti amministrativi generali' (2016) 4 Diritto amministrativo 719 ff.

[9] Law No 400/1988 also regulates the power of the government to adopt acts bearing the force of primary law (as envisioned by arts 76 and 77 Const), such as legislative decrees and law decrees (arts 14–16 of the Law).

legal regime, establishing the procedure that must be followed for their adoption and distinguishing among various types of regulations.[10]

When addressing the issue of their binding or non-binding nature, it is first necessary to point out that certain plans (eg regional or provincial territorial plans) as well as most general administrative acts, such as interpretative and informative circulars, directives, and guidelines, are directed at other public bodies and administrations, with the consequence that they produce no direct binding effect on private individuals.[11] Instead, rules directed at citizens and businesses (such as regulatory acts issued by ministers or independent authorities) and other general acts governing their activities (such as urban plans and building rules adopted by local bodies) possess binding authority when the law so provides. In such cases, a violation of these regulations by an individual constitutes a breach of the law in the broad sense, leading to potential administrative sanctions. For instance, if a public utility company disregards the billing rules or tariffs established by the competent independent regulatory authority, it may be fined by the body, which can also issue injunctions to ensure compensation for consumers. Similarly, a private individual building or renovating a house in violation of the urban municipal plan constitutes building abuse, which, depending on its gravity, can be sanctioned by the municipality even with a demolition order.

III. Procedural Requirements Concerning Rulemaking and Planning

As mentioned earlier, although Italy enacted a general law on administrative procedure in 1990, most of its provisions do not apply to rulemaking and planning. Consequently, only sector-specific legislation regulates these areas. Nonetheless, some regulatory and soft-law acts of general applicability address specific aspects rather than the entire procedure of rulemaking. For example, guidelines on public

[10] The provision establishes that by decree of the President of the Republic, following a resolution of the Council of Ministers, after hearing the opinion of the Council of State, which must be issued within 90 days upon receiving the request, regulations may be issued to regulate: (i) the execution of laws and legislative decrees, as well as EU regulations; (ii) the implementation and integration of laws and legislative decrees containing rules of principle, excluding those relating to matters reserved to regional competence; (iii) matters in which there is a lack of regulation by laws or acts having the force of law, provided that these are not matters reserved to the law; (iv) the organization and functioning of public administrations according to the provisions dictated by law.

[11] Nonetheless, a violation of these types of acts by administrations themselves might have consequences in terms of the lawfulness of their action, which may constitute either a violation of the law or an abuse of power. More precisely, when a decision is challenged in court because it is incompatible with a provision (a circumstance that can be relatively easily proven), it can be quashed as unlawful. Conversely, if it conflicts with general administrative acts, this aspect can be taken into consideration within the more complicated proof of the presence of abuse of power. Regardless of this distinction, if the violation is proven and judicially ascertained, the act conflicting with either a normative act or a general administrative act will anyway be annulled by an administrative court. It should also be added that the principle *iura novit curia*, whereby in the event of controversy, the judge refers to and applies a provision without the need for the party to submit it, only applies in case of normative acts and not with regard to general administrative acts. Hence, in the event of a violation of the latter, the party must explicitly argue on the point and prove the breach.

consultation were adopted in 2017.[12] However, they only introduced a series of general principles aimed at ensuring that 'public consultation processes are capable of leading to informed and quality decisions and are as inclusive, transparent and effective as possible'. They do not constitute, therefore, an operational manual with practical indications on which consultation techniques to use and how to actually carry out a public consultation. Additionally, state administrations (with the exception of independent administrative authorities) must comply with the requirements concerning the regulatory impact assessment.[13]

[12] On 9 March 2017, the Department of Public Functions of the Presidency of the Council of Ministers published the 'Guidelines on public consultation in Italy', subsequently adopted by Ministerial Directive (Directive No 2/2017 published in the Official Gazette of 14 July 2017, No 163).

[13] See Decreto del Presidente del Consiglio dei Ministri (Council of Ministry President's Decree) (dPCM) 15 September 2017, No 169 (which substituted the previous dPCM No 170/2008).

9
Netherlands

Jacobine van den Brink, Louise Verboeket, and Veerle van Waarde

I. Constitutional and Legislative Provisions on Rulemaking and Planning

The Dutch General Administrative Law Act (GALA, *Algemene wet bestuursrecht*) is centred around the notion of the decision (*besluit*), which is defined in Article 1:3(1) GALA as a written decision by an administrative authority (*bestuursorgaan*) containing a legal act under public law. This definition is quite broad: it encompasses both single-case decisions (*beschikkingen*)[1] and decisions of general scope (*besluiten van algemene strekking*).[2] Administrative rulemaking and planning lead to decisions of general scope as they are addressed to an undefined number of people in an undefined number of cases. Decisions of general scope, and thus administrative rulemaking and planning, can be subdivided into general binding regulations (*algemeen verbindende voorschriften*), policy rules (*beleidsregels*), and other decisions of general scope (*overige besluiten van algemene strekking*), including concretising decisions of general scope (*concretiserende besluiten van algemene strekking*). Policy rules are defined by law, namely Article 1:3(4) GALA. The definition of a general binding regulation and making a decision of general scope concrete can be derived from case law.[3] There is no overarching legal definition of a plan, but some plans constitute decisions as defined by Article 1:3(1) GALA since they are intended to have legal consequences. A common example of a plan constituting a decision, more specifically a general binding regulation, is a zoning plan (*omgevingsplan*).[4]

This rather tricky distinction between different types of decisions matters because it determines whether or not an administrative action can be reviewed by an administrative court (*bestuursrechter*). According to Article 8:1, in conjunction with Article 8:3 GALA, access to administrative courts (*beroep*) is only possible if a claimant seeks to challenge a decision that concerns a single-case decision or a concretising decision of general scope. Vice versa, access to administrative courts is not possible if a claimant seeks to challenge a general binding regulation or a policy rule. Depending on their specific status as a decision of general scope, plans may be subject to judicial review by

[1] Art 1:3(2) GALA.

[2] It should be noted that decisions of general scope do not include Acts of Parliament, as these are issued by the First and Second Chamber of the States General (*Eerste en Tweede Kamer der Staten-Generaal*), which are not deemed to be administrative authorities under art 1:1(2) GALA.

[3] See eg ABRvS 15 April 2020, ECLI:NL:RVS:2020:1067 for the definition of the general binding regulation and CRvB 26 August 2022, ECLI:NL:CRVB:2022:1859 for the definition of the concretising decision of general scope.

[4] See art 2.4 Environment and Planning Act (*Omgevingswet*).

Jacobine van den Brink, Louise Verboeket, and Veerle van Waarde, *Netherlands* In: *Administrative Rulemaking and Planning in European Laws*. Edited by: Giacinto della Cananea and Angela Ferrari Zumbini, Oxford University Press.
 DOI: 10.1093/oso/9780198867616.003.0009

administrative courts. For some plans, the law establishes the possibility of judicial review by administrative courts.[5] The jurisdiction of Dutch administrative courts is thus limited. However, they are able to rule indirectly on the legality of a general binding regulation or a policy rule through a single-case decision or a concretisingdecision of general scope which is based on the said general binding regulation or a policy rule.[6] This type of judicial review is called incidental review (*exceptieve toetsing*). Recourse must be made to civil courts (*civiele rechter*) to challenge a general binding regulation or a policy rule directly. However, when it comes to a general binding regulation that creates enforceable rights or obligations through an implementing decision, a so-called indirectly effective regulation (*indirect werkende regeling*),[7] the Supreme Court (*Hoge Raad*) declares a direct action against general binding regulations brought by individual citizens or their interest groups inadmissible.[8] After all, in such a case, a party concerned (*belanghebbende*) can appeal against the implementing decision to the administrative court, which can then rule indirectly on the legality of a general binding regulation or a policy rule. Examples of indirectly effective regulations that can have an indirect effect include subsidy (*subsidieregelingen*) and taxation schemes (*belastingregelingen*). As a result of this case law, administrative courts are the primary route to assess whether indirectly effective regulations conflict with higher law through incidental review. The rationale behind this is, first, the specialization argument.[9] As the administrative court has jurisdiction to rule on appeals against decisions based on the general binding regulation, this court is also the most appropriate body to determine any possible conflict between the regulation and higher law. Secondly, the Supreme Court's jurisprudence prevents conflicting rulings between administrative and civil courts, which could occur if the civil court route were open. General binding regulations that have direct effect, meaning regulations that apply immediately without the need for an appealable decision, can be appealed to the civil court.[10] In this case, citizens cannot be expected to ignore the prohibition or order and appeal to the administrative courts against a subsequent enforcement decision in order to question the legality of the underlying general binding regulation.[11]

Unlike administrative rulemaking and planning, adjudication does not constitute a decision. This is because judges cannot issue decisions as they are not deemed to be administrative authorities according to Article 1:1(2)(c) GALA. The GALA thus recognizes the legal relevance of administrative rulemaking and planning as distinct from adjudication. Decisions of general scope have general legal consequences for

[5] Regarding zoning plans, see art 2 Appendix 2 to the GALA.

[6] See eg ABRvS 4 March 2015, ECLI:NL:RVS:2015:622, which formally resulted in the annulment of the single-case decision in question but de facto entailed a declaration of the illegality of the underlying general binding regulation through incidental review. The current standard of incidental review is set out in CRvB 1 July 2019, ECLI:NL:CRVB:2019:2016-2019.

[7] See RBJ Schutgens, 'Rechtsbescherming tegen algemene regels: tijd om de Awb te voltooien' in WJM Voermans, RJB Schutgens, and ACM Meuwese (eds), *Algemene regels in het bestuursrecht*, VAR-reeks No 158 (Boom juridisch 2017) 95–145.

[8] See Supreme Court 9 July 2010, ECLI:NL:HR:2010:BM2314 (*Staat/Vreemdelingenorganisaties*), Supreme Court 22 May 2015, ECLI:NL:HR:2015:1296 (*Privacy First/Staat*), and Supreme Court 3 June 2016, ECLI:NL:HR:2016:1049 (*SCAU/Universiteiten*).

[9] Schutgens (n 7) 103.

[10] Schutgens (n 7) 105 ff.

[11] Supreme Court 3 June 2016, ECLI:NL:HR:2016:1049, para 4.2.2.

the public at large, while administrative court rulings only affect the legality of the decision(s) in question.[12] Some judgments, however, are intended to have an effect on the underlying law or future rulings. These usually regard the interpretation or application of a legal definition or a general principle of good administration (*algemeen beginsel van behoorlijk bestuur*) and may be preceded by a non-binding opinion (*conclusie*) handed down by an advocate-general.[13]

II. Legal Effects of Administrative Rules and Plans

Under Dutch law, administrative rules and plans usually have legally binding effects. As for administrative rules, these qualify as decisions under Article 1:3(1) of the GALA. Furthermore, to be a decision, an administrative action requires legal effect. More specifically, administrative rules constitute decisions of general scope and can, as such, be subdivided into general binding regulations (*algemeen verbindende voorschriften*), policy rules (*beleidsregels*), and other decisions of general scope (*overige besluiten van algemene strekking*), including concretising decisions of general scope (*concretiserende besluiten van algemene strekking*). First, general binding regulations by definition constitute rules that must be followed.[14] Whether the infringement of a general binding regulation can constitute an impediment to the exercise of an individual's rights or give rise to a sanction depends on the content of the general binding regulation and the legal basis for such consequences in the underlying Act of Parliament (*wet in formele zin*).[15] Secondly, according to Article 4:84 GALA, an administrative authority must act in accordance with its policy rules, unless doing so would disproportionately affect one or more interested parties in relation to the objectives of the policy rule. Such a policy rule by itself is not a sufficient legal basis for an impediment to the exercise of an individual's rights or the imposition of a sanction; these consequences must be grounded in law, meaning a general binding regulation and an underlying Act of Parliament. Thirdly, concretising decisions of general scope have legally binding effects, but these decisions derive this effect from the underlying general binding regulation, as such decisions make concrete the applicability of a general binding regulation in terms of time, place, and object. A concretising decision of general scope can be relevant with regard to the infringement of a general binding regulation and thus an impediment to the exercise of an individual's right or the imposition of a sanction, but, like policy rules, they do not constitute a sufficient legal basis for these consequences.

[12] Art 8:70 and 8:72 GALA.

[13] Art 8:12a GALA. See eg ABRvS 2 February 2022, ECLI:NL:RVS:2022:285 (*Harderwijk*), which introduced a revised standard of review with regard to the proportionality of discretionary decisions.

[14] See eg ABRvS 2 August 2017, ECLI:NL:RVS:2017:2105, and ABRvS 15 April 2020, ECLI:NL:RVS:2020:1067.

[15] The Dutch Constitution differentiates between rights that may be restricted by an Act of Parliament (*bij de wet*) and rights that may be restricted by, or pursuant to, an Act of Parliament (*bij of krachtens de wet*). In the first case, a general binding regulation may not restrict the right; only an Act of Parliament can do that. In the latter case, a general binding regulation may restrict the right, but only in so far as the general binding regulation has an Act of Parliament as its basis.

As for administrative plans, some constitute decisions as defined by Article 1:3(1) GALA and thus have legal consequences. Infringement of a plan may not, in and of itself, lead to an impediment to the exercise of an individual's rights or the imposition of a sanction. Again, these consequences require a general binding regulation and an underlying Act of Parliament.[16]

III. Procedural Requirements Concerning Rulemaking and Planning

A focal point of Dutch administrative law are the so-called general principles of good administration (*algemene beginselen van behoorlijk bestuur*). Some of these principles are codified in the GALA, such as the principle of impartiality in Article 2:4 GALA, the principle of due care (*zorgvuldigheidsbeginsel*) in Article 3:2 GALA, the principle of *détournement de pouvoir* (*verbod van détournement de pouvoir*) in Article 3:3 GALA, the proportionality principle (*evenredigheidsbeginsel*) in Article 3:4 GALA, and the duty to give reasons (*motiveringsbeginsel*) in Articles 3:46 and 3:47 GALA. However, some principles are not (yet) codified and are thus based on case law, such as the principle of legal certainty (*rechtszekerheidsbeginsel*), the principle of legitimate expectations (*vertrouwensbeginsel*),[17] and the principle of equality (*gelijkheidsbegin sel*).[18]

The principles codified in chapter 2 of the GALA apply to all decisions, including administrative rules and plans. The principles codified in chapter 3 apply unconditionally to all decisions, apart from general binding regulations. According to Article 3:1(1)(a) GALA, the principles of due care, *détournement de pouvoir*, and proportionality only apply to general binding regulations in so far as these principles are not incompatible with the nature of the general binding regulation in question. According to Article 3:1(1)(b) GALA, the duty to give reasons does not apply to general binding regulations. Some procedural requirements only apply to single-case decisions but not to administrative rules and plans, such as the requirements in Title 4.1 GALA. Other procedural requirements, such as the public preparatory procedure in Division 3.4 GALA, are optional and can be applied depending on the (delegated) legislation.

[16] See eg art 1a(1) Economic Offenses Act (*Wet op de economische delicten*) in conjunction with art 5.1(1)(a) Environment and Planning Act (*Omgevingswet*).

[17] The current standard of review for the principle of legitimate expectations is set out in ABRvS 29 May 2019, ECLI:NL:RVS:2019:1694 (*Amsterdams dakterras*). Regarding the recipients of long-term subsidies, the principle of legitimate expectations is codified in art 4:51 GALA.

[18] See eg ABRvS 2 November 2016, ECLI:NL:RVS:2016:2927 (*Speelautomatenhal Vlaardingen*). Compare with art 1 Dutch Constitution (*Grondwet*).

10
Norway

Eivind Smith

I. Constitutional and Legislative Provisions on Rulemaking and Planning

The Administrative Procedure Act (APA) (statute of 10 February 1967) explicitly recognizes and builds on the distinction between administrative acts of an individual or general character. The distinction appears in section 2 (Definitions) as follows:[1]

> For the purposes of this Act, the following terms shall have the following meanings:
> a. administrative decision, a decision made in the exercise of public authority which generally or specifically determines the rights or duties of private persons (individual persons or other private legal persons);
> b. individual decision, an administrative decision relating to the rights or duties of one or more specified persons;
> c. regulation, an administrative decision relating to the rights or duties of an indefinite number or an indeterminate group of persons.

As far as the criterion 'generally or specifically determines the rights or duties of private persons' (letter a) is concerned, the last paragraph of section 2 explicitly provides that the provisions of the APA apply even to acts determining the rights or duties of 'administrative agencies that, in relation to the specific regulation, have the same interest or status as a private party'. A municipality that deals with a case where a branch of the central government apparatus seeks a permit to construct an office building provides an example.

Letter b deals with what could be called 'rulemaking' or even 'delegated legislation'. In addition to some general provisions relevant for all kind of administrative activity (disqualification/conflict of interest, secrecy, and so on), those addressing rulemaking in particular may be found in chapter VII, which is much shorter and less constraining than those regarding individual acts (chapters IV–VI). Chapter VII contains namely:

- Section 37 on the administration's obligation to investigate the case, submit a motivated draft regulation to 'public and private institutions and organisations for enterprises, professions [etc.] or interest groups which the regulations will concern, or whose interests are particularly affected' and to receive and consider the statements received after the time limit of the hearing,

[1] Unofficial translation of the Norwegian version of the Act provided by the Ministry of Justice and Public Security for information purposes only. Legal authenticity remains with the Norwegian version as published in Norsk Lovtidend.

Eivind Smith, *Norway* In: *Administrative Rulemaking and Planning in European Laws*. Edited by: Giacinto della Cananea and Angela Ferrari Zumbini, Oxford University Press. © Eivind Smith 2025. DOI: 10.1093/oso/9780198867616.003.0010

- Section 38 on the publication of the regulation,
- Section 39 on the legal effect of failure to publish, and
- Section 40 on the binding effect of regulations (unless properly amended) even for the administration itself.

Unlike chapters IV–VI on individual acts, APA chapter VII does not contain provisions on, *inter alia*, the right to have access to relevant documents for the 'parties', the obligation to provide a written justification for the act, or the right to appeal.

II. Legal Effects of Administrative Rules and Plans

By virtue of the definition itself, regulations constitute an important form of the 'exercise of public authority, which generally or specifically determines the rights or duties of private persons (individual persons or other private legal persons)'. In short, they are 'legally binding'. This implies that they may, according to the character of each provision, constitute an impediment to the exercise of the individual's rights or give rise to a sanction.

The distinction between legally binding and other general formal statements by no means excludes the present day proliferation of general statements ('comments', 'guidance', etc) from the relevant ministries, statements that are not legally binding for private legal subjects (including publicly owned companies and administrative agencies that, in relation to the specific regulation, have the same interest or status as a private party). In practice, such instruments may easily, notwithstanding their formal status, cause 'binding' effects similar to those supposed to flow from proper regulations.

Even if hierarchical 'instructions' or 'orders' are legally binding for the relevant subordinate agents or agencies, they fall outside the scope of APA chapters IV–VII because they are not binding for 'private persons' etc, as defined by section 2.

III. Procedural Requirements Concerning Rulemaking and Planning

Insofar as they are legally binding, they count as regulations under the 1967 act. At the same time, they may even constitute a number of individual acts when directly binding for particular actors concerned (for instance, owners of property submitted to the provisions of the relevant plan on land use).

Moreover, statutory norms regarding various kinds of plans contain specific, more rigorous provisions concerning public hearings and other proceedings during the preparation process compared with those established by the 1967 act.

In general, norms regarding due process, fairness, and transparency apply to public authorities even when they adopt administrative rules or make plans. In principle, these requirements broadly apply to individual and regulatory acts, but they may produce a different impact due to the specific contexts of the different kinds of enactments; for instance, general provisions regarding conflicts of interest will normally be far less consequential when applied to rulemaking than to individual enactments

11
Portugal

Rui Guerra da Fonseca

I. Constitutional and Legislative Provisions on Rulemaking and Planning

The Portuguese legal system recognizes the legal relevance of administrative rulemaking and planning as distinct from adjudication. However, both administrative forms of action, although closely intertwined, must be addressed separately.

The Portuguese Constitution (CRP)[1] reflects a system of norms under which administrative rules coexist normally with legislative rules, and administrative rulemaking is a normal way of pursuing administrative action. In a similar vein, the Code of Administrative Procedure (CPA)[2] thoroughly regulates the procedure for the adoption of administrative rules (Articles 97 ff) and its concept, need for legal basis, relationships between administrative rules, effects, validity, and administrative guarantees (Articles 135 ff).

The CRP addresses administrative rules scattered throughout different sets of constitutional norms. These norms cover normative acts in general, the powers of distinct administrative bodies, guarantees, and substantive public policies and fundamental rights. We will focus on the most important norms of each group.

Regarding normative acts in general, the CRP clearly states that administrative regulations must expressly mention the legislative acts they are intended to regulate or that establish the powers for their approval (Article 112/7 CRP). In principle, government regulations[3] should take a specific form (*decreto regulamentar*) when this is established by law and in the case of independent regulations (Article 112/6 CRP),[4] in which case they must be promulgated by the President of the Republic (as happens in the case of acts of a legislative nature: Article 134/*b)* CRP). However, the government

[1] The Portuguese Constitution of 1976 has undergone several amendments, the last one in 2005.

[2] The CPA (Decree-Law No 4/2015, 07/01, significantly amending the first CPA of 1991, is the Portuguese APA.

[3] These are approved by the government in the context of its administrative function. This clarification is important because in Portugal, the government also holds a legislative function, allowing to issue decree-laws of a legislative nature. When exactly the government must make use of one or the other function or type of act is something that cannot be explained here. Nevertheless, it is worth noting that the CRP does not systematically or universally establish a clear-cut distinction, so the answer depends on many variables, including the substance and context of the act).

[4] Independent regulations are a type of administrative regulation marked by their innovative nature in comparison with the law. Typically, the law merely grants authority to issue them without specifying particular legal provisions that the regulation would then detail (see M Aroso de Almeida, *Teoria Geral do Direito Administrativo* (7th edn, Almedina 2021) 233 ff). About regulations directly grounded on the CRP, see P Otero, *Direito do Procedimento Administrativo*, I (Almedina 2016) 300–301.

Rui Guerra da Fonseca, *Portugal* In: *Administrative Rulemaking and Planning in European Laws*. Edited by: Giacinto della Cananea and Angela Ferrari Zumbini, Oxford University Press.
DOI: 10.1093/oso/9780198867616.003.0011

typically has broad discretion when it comes to choosing from other forms for its regulations that do not require presidential intervention.

As for administrative bodies distinct from the Government, the CRP also assigns powers to issue administrative regulations to the governments of the Azores and Madeira, which are autonomous regions (Articles 227 and 233/4 CRP), as well as to municipalities (Article 241 CRP). In any case, it is generally understood that administrative bodies have the power to issue administrative regulations when their functions require it, even if the law is not always clear on the matter.

Concerning guarantees, the CRP also expressly lays down a fundamental right to challenge administrative norms with external effects[5] that harm a person's rights or legally protected interests in a court of law (Article 268/5 CRP).

When it comes to substantive public policies and fundamental rights, planning is actually a public task regarding which the CRP addresses administrative rules or regulations. The CRP deals with various types of planning, namely socio-economic, urban, and environmental. We can discern constitutional influence in the administrative rules that relate to all of them, but the most explicit reference is to urban planning. In fact, Article 65(4) requires the state, autonomous regions, and municipalities to establish rules for the occupation, use, and transformation of urban land. These rules should be determined through normative planning instruments. Since municipalities do not have legislative powers, this is an implicit call for administrative rulemaking.

II. Legal Effects of Administrative Rules and Plans

In general, the answer is positive. In the Portuguese legal system, administrative rules and plans have legally binding effects. Some administrative rules and plans may consist of, or contain, mere recommendations,[6] but they are normally considered to have binding effects (both on persons and the public bodies that issue them). In any case, a distinction should be made between administrative rules in general and those regarding plans, as will be seen in what follows.

As the question implies, the violation of administrative rules can have negative consequences on the exercise of individual rights. For example, Article 10 of the Regulation on Academic Fraud in Masters and PhD Courses at the Faculty of Law of the University of Lisbon[7] states that if fraud in student work is discovered, the thesis submitted or its evaluation discussion will be considered invalid. This is in addition to any disciplinary action or sanctions that may be taken according to other regulations clearly stating that fraud determines the ineffectiveness of the thesis submitted or its

[5] This is also a complex concept, but these regulations generally contrast with regulations that have mere internal effects generally of an organizational kind and regulating the internal organization or structure of a specific administrative body or agency.

[6] Otero (n 4) 302, with reference to art 136/4 CPA.

[7] The University of Lisbon is a public university, and the Faculty of Law is one of its autonomous departments. On the authority of public universities to issue administrative rules in Portugal, see L Pereira Coutinho, *As Faculdades Normativas Universitárias no Quadro do Direito Fundamental à Autonomia Universitária* (Almedina 2004).

discussion for the purposes of evaluation (without prejudice to disciplinary action and sanctions according to other regulations).

It is also common for the infringement of an administrative rule to result in sanctions, in accordance with the law. Decree-Law 433/82, dated 27 October,[8] establishes the general legal framework for administrative penalties that administrative authorities may impose. These penalties are of two types: those with minimum and maximum amounts determined by law and which differ depending on whether the offender is an individual or a legal entity. The other type of penalty is the ancillary sanction, such as the loss of assets belonging to the offender or a ban on carrying out a profession or activity that requires public authorization.[9] Administrative rules may then specify which, according to specific situations, establishing what specific conduct may result in these sanctions. There are thousands of examples from municipalities, other public bodies, and the government. One of the latter is the 'Decreto Regulamentar 22-A/98, 1 Outubro' on traffic signs, imposing fines of 250 to 1250 euros on those who tamper with traffic signs, specifically by cluttering them with posters or other items that may interfere with their purpose.

The effects of plans, especially urban and spatial plans, are binding and specifically regulated. The Law 31/2014, dated 30 May, establishes the foundation of a system that includes various plans and programmes for land, urban, and spatial planning, based on the general principles of public policy. Programmes tend to have a broader territorial scope (such as national, regional, or multi-municipal) or a special substantive scope. Plans, on the other hand, tend to have a more specific, namely municipal scope, but they can also be multi-municipal. The former are binding only on public authorities, while the latter are also directly binding on private individuals (Article 46/1 and 2).[10] The national policy programme on territorial spatial planning is approved by parliamentary law, but all other programmes and plans are administrative rules approved by the government (usually in the form of a resolution of the Council of Ministers) or other public authorities, namely municipalities, and are ratified by the government.[11]

A last note concerns maritime spatial planning. According to Law 17/2014, dated 10 April (on the general basis of public policy on spatial planning and management of the national maritime spaces),[12] the system of maritime spatial planning consists of two types of instruments: situation plans and allocation plans (Article 7). Both take the form and have the nature of administrative rules, and both are binding on public authorities, as well as private individuals (Article 4(3) of Decree-Law 80/2015).

[8] Last amended by Law 109/2001, 24 December.

[9] Art 21.

[10] Also, art 2 of Decree-Law 80/2015, 14 May (last amended by Decree-Law 45/2022, 8 July), on the legal regime of territorial spatial planning.

[11] This is, of course, a very broad picture based on several norms of Law 31/2014 and Decree-Law 80/2015. According to the latter, however, special or sectoral programmes may be approved by a decree-law (of a legislative nature) if this is required by a specific law (art 51).

[12] Amended by Law 1/2021, 11 January.

III. Procedural Requirements Concerning Rulemaking and Planning

The CRP has an entire title dedicated to public administration, and its first article, Article 266, expressly states that public administrations aim to promote the public interest, while always respecting the rights and legally protected interests of citizens (section 1). Therefore, public bodies and administrative agents are always subject to the Constitution and the law, and they must act according to the principles of equality, proportionality, justice, impartiality, and good faith (section 2). Article 268 covers citizens' guarantees *vis-s-vis* public administration. Some of these are procedural, namely notification and giving reasons for administrative acts (section 3), the establishment by law of a deadline for administrative response when citizens request certain information (6), and—particularly important here—the right to challenge administrative rules that harm their rights in a court of law (5).

According to Article 65/5 (housing and urban planning), the Constitution guarantees the participation of those with interests in the elaboration of urban planning rules or other instruments relating to planning the physical occupation of land.

Also, as mentioned above[13] the CPA thoroughly regulates the procedure for adopting administrative rules (Articles 97 ff), as well as the concept, need for a legal basis, relationships between administrative rules, effects, validity, and administrative guarantees (Articles 135 ff). But the CPA also contains a large cast of general principles and rules applicable to all administrative activity (including the approval of administrative rules) which specify the said constitutional provisions and deal precisely with due process, fairness and transparency (Articles 3–19). Transparency and impartiality are also the main concerns of Articles 69 to 76, which deal precisely with situations impeding the participation of administrative agents in decisions that could benefit themselves or persons close to them, and other situations in which they should ask to step aside for similar reasons.

The government is also bound by a Code of Conduct aiming to guarantee transparency, impartiality, and other general principles.[14] Namely, government members and their staff must refrain from conduct that could, directly or indirectly, be objectively interpreted as an attempt to benefit improperly a specific person or entity. Breaking these and any other rules of conduct outlined in the Code only results in the accountability of other members of the government (or individuals working within their offices or under their supervision) to the Prime Minister.[15]

[13] See answer to R Guerra da Fonseca, 'Portugal—Case 1', Chapter 15.II.J in this book.

[14] The latest version of this Code of Conduct was approved by Resolution of the Council of Ministers 42/2022, 9 May. Formally, it qualifies as an administrative rule because it adheres to one of the formats that governmental regulations are legally required to have (art 138 CPA).

[15] Although there is also a reference to these CPA rules (see arts 5 and 6).

12

Sweden

Patricia Jonason and Björn Forssén

I. Constitutional and Legislative Provisions on Rulemaking and Planning

Criteria[1] for distinguishing general decisions (*normbeslut*) and individual decisions stem from the *travaux préparatoires*[2] and administrative case law. A comprehensive description of these criteria can be found in Supreme Administrative Court decision 2016 ref 59.[3] According to the Court:

> Standard decisions are characterised by the fact that they are in principle binding on authorities and individuals and that they do not refer only to a concrete case but have general applicability. The latter requirement may be considered fulfilled if a regulation refers, for example, to situations of a certain kind or certain types of actions, or if it is directed to or otherwise affecting a generally defined group of persons, such as all companies that carry on a certain type of activity.

Beyond this criterion, of a rather *ratione personae* character, the Court also mentions temporal criteria:

> Prescriptions that concern only a short period of time would sometimes be seen as decisions in an individual case and therefore fall outside the scope of what can be considered a normative decision for which the prescription applies.

Additionally, courts use a criterion concerning the territorial scope of application. The judgment reads: 'Even the question of whether the decision has a larger or smaller geographical area of application is significant in the assessment of whether it constitutes a normative decision.'

[1] It should be mentioned that a constitutional reform in 2010 meant a clearer distinction in the Swedish legal order between judicial adjudication (*rättskipning*) and administration/administrative adjudication (*förvaltning*). A division was introduced in the Constitution (the Instrument of Government) between the two. Judicial adjudication and administrative adjudication now have their own chapter. Chapter 11 only contains rules on judicial adjudication, whereas the rules on administration are to be found in chapter 12. This was due to a series of reforms largely resulting from decisions from the European Court of Human Rights concerning the right to court trials, which, *inter alia*, made it necessary to clarify the courts' unique position in the constitutional system. E Holmberg and others, *Grundlagarna Regeringsformen Successionsordningen Riksdagsordningen* (3rd edn, Norstedts Juridik 2012).

[2] See prop. 1973:90 p 203 f, prop. 1975/76:112 p 62 ff.

[3] This decision makes reference to the *travaux préparatoires* mentioned in the previous footnote but also to another administrative judgment, RÅ 1986 ref 108.

Patricia Jonason and Björn Forssén, *Sweden* In: *Administrative Rulemaking and Planning in European Laws*. Edited by: Giacinto della Cananea and Angela Ferrari Zumbini, Oxford University Press.
DOI: 10.1093/oso/9780198867616.003.0012

II. Legal Effects of Administrative Rules and Plans

The Swedish legal system clearly distinguishes between binding and non-binding administrative rules. The first category consists of the government's normative decisions, as well as public authorities' and municipalities' legally binding general norms (*föreskrifter*). The second category encompasses so-called official advices (*allmänna råd*), which consist of a determined legal category of statutes of a non-binding nature and supplementing a statute (Act of Law or ordinances). Among the non-binding administrative rules there are also rule that are not related to a specific statute, such as recommendations (*rekommendationer*).[4]

The violation of rules that belong to the second category of administrative rules cannot lead to the imposition of sanctions, while the violation of rules that belong to the first category may do so.

According to case law, some rules that seem non-binding at first sight have nevertheless been considered to have factual effects on individuals.[5]

III. Procedural Requirements Concerning Rulemaking and Planning

General duties applicable to the adoption of administrative rules are to be found at the constitutional, legislative, and regulatory levels.

The Constitution (Instrument of Government) lays down in its section 2, chapter 7, the obligation of the government to consult stakeholders when 'preparing Government business', which includes the elaboration of administrative rules. Thus, in these cases, the constitutional provision requires that:

> the necessary information and opinions be obtained from the relevant public authorities. Information and opinions shall be obtained from local authorities as necessary. Organisations and individuals shall also be given the opportunity to express their opinion as needed.

In addition to the aforementioned provision, which only applies to the government and pertains to the duty to consult and grant stakeholders the opportunity to express their opinions, the Constitution also establishes a general obligation of objectivity that applies to all public authorities and affects the adoption of administrative rules. Indeed, section 1, chapter 9 of the Constitution establishes the obligation for 'Courts of law, administrative authorities and others performing public administration functions' to 'pay regard in their work to the equality of all before the law' and to 'observe objectivity and impartiality'. According to Wenander, this provision implies, among

[4] For more details about the categories of statutes mentioned, see H Wenander, 'Sweden: Non-binding Rules Against the Pandemic—Formalism, Pragmatism and Some Legal Realism' (2021) 12 European Journal of Risk Regulation 127–42.

[5] The Supreme Administrative Court case, RÅ 2004 ref 8, the so-called Olive Oil Case, which, according to Wenander, 'establishes a possible route for challenging non-binding decisions'; Wenander, 'Sweden' (n 4) 137.

other things, the requirement for public authorities to have a 'sufficient factual basis' (*tillräckligt faktaunderlag*) in order to take decisions.[6] According to the same author:

> The authorities' regulations, general advices and other recommendations ...must meet basic requirements of reasonableness in relation to established knowledge, something that is to some extent connected with the interest in predictability.[7]

At the legislative level, some of the provisions of the Administrative Procedure Act (2017:900) (APA), apply to the adoption of administrative rules, such as those concerning the principles of legality, objectivity, and proportionality (section 5, APA),[8] as well as the provision on disqualification in cases of conflict of interest (section 16, APA).[9] However, while all provisions of the APA apply to the adoption of individual decisions, not all of them apply to the adoption of administrative rules. For instance, the provision on communication (*kommunikationsskyldigheten*) (section 25, APA)[10] (a prerequisite for the right of the party to express its views before the authority takes a decision) and the one on the duty to state the reasons for the decisions (section 32, APA)[11] do not apply to the adoption of administrative rules.

It is interesting to note that the government is not technically required to comply with the APA, as it does not apply to it. However, it typically follows the Act in practice.[12]

At the regulatory level, the ordinance (2007:1244) on Impact Assessment in Legislation (*förordningen (2007:1244) om konsekvensutredning vid regelgivning*) imposes some requirements on administrative authorities under the government (*förvaltningsmyndigheter under regeringen*), deciding on regulations or general advice. According to section 4, first paragraph No 2, the mentioned authorities have the obligation to:

> investigate the cost of the rules and other consequences in necessary scope as well as giving Government authorities, municipalities, regions, organisations, the business community, and others who are affected in terms of costs or in any other significant way the opportunity to comment on the matter and the impact investigation.

[6] H Wenander, 'Rättssäkerhet i förhållande till myndigheters föreskrifter och allmänna råd' in R Sannerholm and K Djurberg Malm (eds), *Rättsstaten i den svenska förvaltningen—en forskningsantologi* (OOS 45, Statskontoret 2022) 36 refers to T Bull, 'Objektivitetsprincipen' in L Marcusson (ed), *Offentligrättsliga principer* (4th edn, Iustus 2020) 113.

[7] (Our translation): H Wenander, 'Rättssäkerhet i förhållande till myndigheters föreskrifter och allmänna råd' in Sannerholm and Djurberg Malm (eds) (n 6) 36.

[8] ibid 35. Refers to his article from 2021, p 136.

[9] ibid 38.

[10] ibid.

[11] Wenander, 'Rättssäkerhet i förhållande till myndigheters föreskrifter och allmänna råd' (n 7) 39.

[12] See eg HFD 2011:10.

13
United Kingdom

John Morison and David Mark

I. Constitutional and Legislative Provisions on Rulemaking and Planning

It is well known that the United Kingdom does not have a formal written constitution as such and, consequently, there is no formal constitutional provision that establishes or protects process rights in the context of administrative rulemaking in general, or in the planning context in particular. Of course, irrespective of the impact of Brexit, the national constitutional framework remains conditioned by international legal instruments. Some of these, such as the UN Declaration of Human Rights stating that 'everyone has the right to take part in the government of his country',[1] do seem suggestive of participation rights, although primarily concerned with establishing first generation basic political rights. In a similar way the International Covenant on Civil and Political Rights, enshrines a right of self- determination to all peoples, so that 'they freely determine their political status'.[2] Other commitments also exist, such as the International Labour Organisation Convention 169 on the rights of Indigenous and tribal peoples in independent states, which asserts a similar, very general level right to prior consultation for such peoples regarding development plans that may affect their 'lives, beliefs, institutions and spiritual well-being and the lands they occupy or otherwise use'.[3] The Aarhus Convention of 1998 too requires public consultation in environmental decision making.

II. Legal Effects of Administrative Rules and Plans

Outside these international arrangements, at the national level there are a number of ways in which rulemaking and decision-making by administrative actors are regulated and controlled. First there is parliamentary control. The formal position is that Acts of the UK Parliament that delegate rulemaking functions generally provide for some sort of parliamentary control over how those functions are exercised. In terms of parliamentary restrictions on administrative rulemaking, and in contrast to the United States or some European jurisdictions, there are few formal impediments on the

[1] Universal Declaration of Human Rights, arts 21(1), 21(3).

[2] International Covenant on Civil and Political Rights, art 1(1). This article works in tandem with art 25 (b), which guarantees all citizens the ability 'to vote and to be elected at genuine periodic elections'.

[3] The International Labour Organization Convention 169 on the Rights of Indigenous and Tribal Peoples in Independent States, 1989, art 7(1). Only 20 countries have ratified this to date.

John Morison and David Mark, *United Kingdom* In: *Administrative Rulemaking and Planning in European Laws*. Edited by: Giacinto della Cananea and Angela Ferrari Zumbini, Oxford University Press.
DOI: 10.1093/oso/9780198867616.003.0013

degree to which the legislature may control the executive and administrative agencies. As a result of the dominance of ideas about sovereignty of Parliament, control by the legislature can never be said to be unconstitutional, leaving only practical and conventional limits on Parliament's control.[4] Acts delegating rulemaking powers will generally (although not invariably) contain a provision that rules be laid for approval before one or both Houses of Parliament and subject to various procedures, affirmative or negative or simply for note, before coming into effect. There is no formal rationale or criteria for the procedure to be adopted, although those rules that substantially affect primary legislation or taxation or create new criminal offences are generally subject to more scrutiny. There may also be statutory requirements for consultation, although again the rationale for when these are deployed is not clear. Changes to regulation concerning social security, for example, require consultation as do some elements of local governance. The type and level of consultation varies in both its format and its effectiveness.[5]

The devolved legislative bodies too have requirements about consultation. Northern Ireland perhaps led the way here initially with requirements that public authorities promote equality of opportunity and consult widely about the effect of their policies on persons of different sex, religious belief, political opinion, racial group, age, marital status, or sexual orientation, and those with a disability or with dependents.[6] A section in the Government of Wales Act 2006, titled '"Inclusive" approach to exercise of functions', details how consultation should take place in relation to a whole range of schemes from local government to business, and from regulatory impact to sustainable development. There are also particular areas where enhanced consultation is required.[7] Further, the Scottish Ministerial Code commits the Scottish government to developing consultation procedures to make possible a participative approach to legislation and decision-making.[8] There are also a number of best practice guides, such as the UK Cabinet Office's *Consultation Principles* (2018)[9] and equivalents from the devolved governments, although their status is merely to indicate best practice in a rather general way.

4 J Beatson, 'Legislative Control of Administrative Rulemaking: Lessons from the British Experience' (1979) 12 Cornell International Law Journal 200–20.

5 See E Page, *Governing by Numbers* (Hart Publishing 2001) and S Pywell and T West, *Delegated Legislation: What Types Are There, and How Are They Made: A Procedural Explainer* (Hansard Society 2023) <https://assets.ctfassets.net/n4ncz0i02v4l/3nxOz49ep4E9nUbucqhyE/6dc755b3f966a5ea30046c251a16dc35/Delegated_Legislation_Explainer_Dec_2023_FINAL.pdf?utm_source=HansardSociety> accessed 23 November 2024.

6 See The Northern Ireland Act 1998, s 75.

7 For example, the Planning (Wales) Act 2015 requires ministers to make a statement about their proposals for public participation and a full report on its success.

8 See *Scottish Ministerial Code: 2023 Edition* para 3c <https://www.gov.scot/publications/scottish-ministerial-code-2023-edition/pages/15/> accessed 23 November 2024; the *Key Principles Shaping Scotland's Parliament* <https://webarchive.nrscotland.gov.uk/https:/www.parliament.scot/visitandlearn/Education/18651.aspx> accessed 23 November 2024; and the website listing active consultations <https://consult.gov.scot> accessed 23 November 2024.

9 <https://assets.publishing.service.gov.uk/media/5aafa4f2e5274a7fbe4fbacb/Consultation_Principles__1_.pdf> accessed 23 November 2024.

III. Procedural Requirements Concerning Rulemaking and Planning

In the absence of general provisions much of the policing of administrative decision-making has fallen to the courts within common law parameters. The courts have taken a general view that while a duty to consult does not arise in all circumstances, there are four main instances where consultation is required. First, where there is a statutory duty to consult as above. Second, where there has been a promise to consult. Third, where there has been an established practice of consultation. Fourth, where, in exceptional cases, a failure to consult would lead to conspicuous unfairness. Without these elements there is no obligation to consult. Beyond this there is no general common law duty to consult persons who may be affected by a decision but where there is a legitimate expectation of such a consultation a common law duty may arise.[10] There is, in addition, the general common law duty on a public body 'to act fairly', which is perhaps a rather different idea to a democratic right to participation, and relates more closely to ideas of good administration and procedural fairness. As Lord Steyn has remarked, 'context is everything',[11] and where decisions affect an individual's fundamental rights the courts have been willing to infer more enhanced process rights, particularly to ensure decision-making that enhances ideas of participation in terms of justice and democracy.[12]

The courts have also developed views on what makes an adequate (if not a good) consultation. Essentially, the position is that unless there are statutorily prescribed procedures, and subject to the overall requirements of fairness, the decision-maker will usually have a broad discretion as to how a consultation exercise should be carried out. There are however fundamental ground rules to be followed. The most commonly known formulation of these rules are known as the Gunning Principles or Sedley Principles, from the arguments offered by Stephen Sedley QC, accepted by the court in *R v Brent London Borough Council, ex parte Gunning*, and subsequently approved by the Court of Appeal.[13] The Gunning Principles require that (i) consultation must take place when the proposal is still at a formative stage, (ii) sufficient reasons must be put forward for the proposal to allow for intelligent consideration and response, (iii) adequate time must be given for consideration and response, and (iv) the product of consultation must be conscientiously taken into account.

In contrast to the United States where the general position is that administrative discretion should in all possible cases be exercised within rules ascertainable in advance, and that policy should be standardized as far as possible, the UK approach holds that within its legal limits discretion should be free, and administrators allowed to produced the best solution in the given context.[14] This idea, that within administrative

[10] See *R (ota Moseley) v London Borough of Haringey* [2014] UKSC 56.

[11] *R (Daly) v Home Secretary* [2001] UKHL 26, [2001] 2 AC 532, 548.

[12] See further judicial discussion of this in *Re Reilly's Application* [2013] UKSC 61, [2014] AC 1115; and *R (Moseley) v Haringey LBC* [2014] UKSC 56, [2014] 1 WLR 3947.

[13] (1985) 84 LGR 168, 169. See also Simon Brown LJ in *R v Devon County Council, ex parte Baker* [1995] 1 All ER 73 and *R v North and East Devon Health Authority, ex parte Coughlan* [2001] QB 213, [108].

[14] See further B Schwartz and W Wade, *Legal Control of Government: Administrative Law in Britain and the United States* (Clarendon Press 1972) and R Baldwin, 'Governing with Rules: The Developing

rulemaking discretion must be retained, has been expressed judicially as the 'no fettering rule'.[15] The impact of this rule within the context of developments of judicial review in more recent times has come under question. One commentator concludes that its role has 'changed from being a doctrine which preserves administrative discretion to one which regulates the development and application of administrative rules'.[16]

Agenda' in G Richardson and H Genn (eds), *Administrative Law and Government Action* (Clarendon Press 1994) 168.

[15] See the landmark cases in this area, *R v Port of London Authority ex p Kynoch* [1919] 1 KB 176; and *British Oxygen Co Ltd v Minister of technology* [1971] AC 610.
[16] A McHarg 'Administrative discretion, administrative rule-making, and judicial review' (2017) 70 Current Legal Problems 267, 271.

14

United States of America

Jeffrey Lubbers and Giacinto della Cananea

I. Constitutional and Legislative Provisions on Rulemaking and Planning

In the US legal system there are both constitutional and legislative provisions regulating administrative procedure. First and foremost, there is the Due Process Clause, which is enshrined into the federal Constitution. The Fifth and Fourteenth Amendments require that federal and state governmental authorities abide by certain procedures, in order to protect the essential interests of all; that is, life, liberty, and property. This is one of the Bill of Rights protections that serve to ensure liberty in the face of contrary governmental action. The Due Process Clause has both a procedural limb and a substantive one. The substantive limb concerns the limits to collective action contrary to individual rights, for example, the right to privacy, right to have children or to have your child learn a foreign language, or the rights guaranteed in the Bill of Rights. The procedural limb, which is of greater interest here, does not require simply a fair trial before the courts. It has been widely interpreted, to encompass the requirement of a neutral decision-maker, the right to receive notice and to have a fair hearing before an adverse decision is taken, and a requirement to give reasons.[1]

Considered as a whole, these requirements grant not only that fundamental fairness is respected in administrative adjudication, but also that decisions are taken in a sound manner.[2] However, the precise amount of procedural protection may, and does, vary depending on the nature of both the protected interest of the individual and the collective interest that requires governmental action.[3]

It was not until the New Deal manifested its impact on individual freedoms that a legislative framework was adopted at federal level. The federal Administrative Procedure Act (1946)[4] is important, in this respect, for three reasons: it provided

[1] See KC Davis, 'The Requirement of Opportunity to be Heard in the Administrative Process' (1942) 51 Yale Law Journal 1093. See also PL Strauss, *Administrative Justice in the United States* (3rd ed, Carolina Academic Press 2016) 257 (examining the various sources of protections for federal administrative procedure).

[2] See Davis (n 1) 1093, arguing the 'purpose of a hearing in the administrative process is to assure enlightened administrative action', and J Mashaw, *Due Process in the Administrative State* (Yale UP 1986), for whom there are three rationales of due process; that is, accuracy, competence, and dignity.

[3] See US Supreme Court, *Mathews v Eldridge*, 424 US 319 (1976) and, for further comments, J Mashaw, 'The Supreme Court's Due Process Calculus for Administrative Adjudication in Mathews v. Eldridge: Three Factors in Search of a Theory of Value' (1976) 48 Unit Chicago L Rev 28 and, more recently, J Lubbers and P Verkuil, 'Alternative Approaches to Judicial Review of Social Security Disability Cases Report to the Social Security Advisory Board' (March 2002) (reprinted in (2003) 55 Admin L Rev 731).

[4] Originally enacted June 11, 1946 by Pub L No 404, 60 Stat. 237, Ch 324, §§1–12. Codified at 5 USC §§ 551–59, 701–06, 1305, 3105, 3344, 5372, 7521.

Jeffrey Lubbers and Giacinto della Cananea, *United States of America* In: *Administrative Rulemaking and Planning in European Laws*. Edited by: Giacinto della Cananea and Angela Ferrari Zumbini, Oxford University Press.
 DOI: 10.1093/oso/9780198867616.003.0014

standardized legal boundaries on federal agency procedures,, it developed the distinction between rulemaking and adjudication and, finally, it had a significant influence on state administrative procedure. Although the APA is formally a statute like many others, it has a fundamental importance because it protects the individual's rights against governmental interference. Several commentators, therefore, include it within the statutes that have a constitutional relevance and significance.[5] The APA, moreover, clearly distinguishes between rulemaking and adjudication. Under Section 2(c), (now 5 U.S.C. section 551(4)) a 'rule' means:

> the whole or any part of agency statement of general or particular applicability and future effect designed to implement, interpret, or prescribe law or policy or to describe the organization, procedure, or practice requirements of any agency and includes the approval or prescription for the future of rates.

By contrast, an 'order' includes 'the part of the final disposition ... of any agency in any matter other than rule making but including licensing' and is the result of administrative adjudication.

The APA, which applies to all agencies in the Executive Branch of the federal government, sets out the general procedures for various types of rulemaking. It defines the seldom-used procedures for 'formal' rulemaking (the requirements they impose for oral hearings are cumbersome and are said to 'ossify' agency action).[6] The APA's procedures for so-called informal rulemaking, under which the agency need only publish a 'notice of proposed rulemaking' and provide an opportunity for anyone to file written comments, are used for most rules that are intended to be binding on the public. Some issuances that are within the broad definition of 'rule', including many that are intended only to provide guidance to the public, may be issued without any pre-publication procedure. There are also certain subject-matter exceptions from notice and comment.

It should be added that the APA has exerted an indirect influence on state rules governing administrative procedure. Soon after its entry into force a Model State APA was adopted, and subsequently revised. Nearly all the states have adopted an APA for their state agencies, always including a section on rulemaking.

Although planning has become important in administrative practice, especially at state and local level, it is not covered by the federal APA. Other statutes require specific planning procedures in a range of areas, including environmental protection, forest service, coastal zone management, fisheries, and other types of natural resources.

II. Legal Effects of Administrative Rules and Plans

Administrative rules can have the same force and effect as a statute, if they have been properly issued and have withstood any judicial review. Hence, they are often called

[5] See E Garrett, 'The Purposes of Framework Legislation' (2005) 14 J Contempt Legal Issues 717; B Ackermann, 'The Living Constitution' (2007) 120 Yale L J 1737.

[6] For further analysis, see PR Verkuil, 'Rulemaking Ossification—A Modest Proposal' (1995) 47 Admin L Rev 453 and JS Lubbers, 'Achieving Policymaking Consensus: The (Unfortunate) Waning of Negotiated Rulemaking' (2008) 49 S Tex L Rev 987.

'legislative rules', and they can be binding and enforceable against regulated parties, including both individuals and firms.[7] By the same token, agencies must respect the constitutional limitations imposed on federal authority. Thus, in the 1970s, two cases decided by the Supreme Court,[8] involved challenges to rules issued by the (former) Interstate Commerce Commission (ICC). In both cases, the regulated firms argued that promulgation of the rules violated the Interstate Commerce Act, the APA, and the Due Process Clause because they were issued using the informal procedures of section 553, while the formal procedures of APA should have been used. The Supreme Court rejected those claims, first holding that due process did not apply to prospective rules that treated regulated parties similarly, and second, that the formal rulemaking provisions of the APA did not apply unless the agency statute contained particular phrases requiring a hearing 'on the record'.

III. Procedural Requirements Concerning Rulemaking and Planning

A. Judicial Doctrines

As observed earlier in Part I, in the US, due process requirements (deriving from the 5th and 14th Amendments of the Constitution) apply to individualized determinations that involve questions of adjudicative fact, not general determinations that involve questions of legislative fact or policy.[9] For these latter questions, under section 553 of the APA, it suffices that the agency assures receipt and consideration of public comments before regulations are adopted. Thus, the APA-prescribed rulemaking procedures of notice and comment (allowing written comments on the proposed rule) but not requiring trial-type (or even oral) hearings, are deemed to be fair procedure. In some situations, Congress may prescribe more formal hearing procedures for rulemaking. Further requirements were imposed on agencies by the courts, beginning in the 1970s. The consequence was a shift from the initial model of rulemaking (called the 'transmission belt') to another, which was called 'the interest-representation model' with a view to pointing out the increasing range of protected interests, not dissimilar from political representation.[10]

Another change occurred when the Supreme Court admonished lower courts not to require procedures beyond those required in the APA (or other statutes). Its ruling in *Vermont Yankee*[11] is of crucial importance in this respect, because it implied a restraint on judicially imposed requirements. In previous years, federal courts had

[7] For a distinction between non legislative interpretative rules and statements of policy, see W Funk, 'A Primer on Non-legislative Rules' (2001) 53 Admin L Rev 1321.

[8] *United States v Allegheny-Ludlum Steel Corp.*, 406 US 742 (1972) and *United States v Florida East Coast Railway*, 410 US 224 (1973).

[9] *Compare Londoner v Denver*, 210 US 373 (1908) *with Bi-Metallic Investment Co. v State Board of Equalization*, 239 US 441 (1915).

[10] RB Stewart, 'The Reformation of American Administrative Law' (1975) 88 Harvard L Rev 1667, at 1767.

[11] *Vermont Yankee Nuclear Power Corp. v Natural Resources Defense Council*, 435 US 519 (1978).

broadly interpreted new statutes, such as the Clean Air Act, expanding the scope of judicial review of agency procedure. The Supreme Court took the opposite view. It held that courts cannot impose procedural requirements on agencies beyond those established by statutes. According to then-Professor Antonin Scalia, *Vermont Yankee*

> produced what, in an era of judicial activism, is a remarkably self-denying opinion, abjuring judicial responsibility for the development of federal administrative procedure except in the relatively narrow area where requirements are imposed by the Due Process Clause.[12]

A leading expert of administrative law later observed that the Court could not have made plainer its view that the D.C. Circuit had overstepped its proper role and illegitimately used its judicial review function to advance its judges' own policy preferences.[13]

B. Presidential and Congressional Review

While *Vermont Yankee* did constrain judicial review of agency rulemaking procedures to some extent, Presidents and Congress showed increasing interest in reviewing agency rules before they could be finalised.[14] Starting with incipient review of some environmental rules in the Nixon administration, presidential review expanded into a clearance system in the Reagan administration, whereby proposed or final rules could not be issued before a review by the Office of Management and Budget (OMB) in the White House. Although this was controversial at first, once President Clinton issued his own Executive Order 12,866[15] creating a somewhat more selective and transparent version of the Reagan clearance system, the review process became accepted on a bi-partisan basis and has now become entrenched to the point where Executive Order 12,866 has been retained by every subsequent President. It requires executive branch agencies to submit all significant rules to OMB for approval before they can be issued. Moreover, any rule with an economic impact of over $100 million must be accompanied by a cost-benefit analysis.

Congress, for its part, enacted some additional statutes that added requirements to those in the APA for rulemaking (such as one that requires special analyses for rules that affect small businesses).[16] It also began attaching legislative veto provisions to numerous rulemaking statutes, which allowed Congress (or sometimes one house of Congress) to veto a rule issued by an agency before it could go into effect. The Supreme

[12] A Scalia, 'Vermont Yankee: The APA, the D.C. Circuit, and the Supreme Court' [1978] Supreme Court Review 345.

[13] Gillian Metzger, 'The Story of the Vermont Yankee. A Cautionary Tale of Judicial Review and Nuclear Waste' (2005) Columbia Law School, Public Law Research Paper no 92, 26.

[14] For a history of White House and congressional review, see J S Lubbers, *A Guide to Federal Agency Rulemaking* (6th edn, Am Bar Ass'n 2018) 12–39.

[15] Exec. Order 12,866, Regulatory Planning and Review, issued Sept. 30,1993, 58 Fed. Reg. 51,735 (Oct. 4 1993), available at https://www.archives.gov/files/federal-register/executive-orders/pdf/12866.pdf.

[16] The Regulatory Flexibility Act, Pub. L No 96-354, 94 Stat. 1164–70 (1980).

Court put an end to this practice in 1983 by holding that this was unconstitutional legislative action because the process lacked both bicameralism and presentment of the bill to the President.[17] In response, in 1996, Congress enacted the Congressional Review Act,[18] which provided a constitutional process for congressional veto (with presidential concurrence) of agency rules. While it has only been used sporadically, it has taken on more importance as a technique for newly elected Presidents from the same party as the new Congress to overturn rules of a previous administration from a different party.

Overall, this increased presidential and congressional review of rules, combined with a more intense, Supreme Court-mandated, review of agencies' *substantive* rulemaking authority, has made agency rulemaking a far more complicated process than that required by the APA.

[17] *Immigration and Naturalization Service v Chadha*, 462 US 919 (1983).
[18] Pub L No 104–221 § 251, 110 Stat. 847, 868–74.

PART III
CASES

The third part includes the answers given by experts to the hypothetical cases, constituting the core of our factual analysis and serving as the basis for the actual comparative analysis. Like in the previous books of this series, the disaggregation of these responses is designed to facilitate the analytical process.

15
Cases

Several Authors

I. Questionnaire

Giacinto della Cananea and Angela Ferrari Zumbini

Case 1—Parliament and administrative procedures concerning asylum seekers (parliamentary control)
Case 2—Toys World and standardless adjudication (limiting and structuring discretion)
Case 3—The rules of the game: Allocating few licences (duty to consult stakeholders; protection of expectations)
Case 4—The newcomer who was not consulted (duty to consult all stakeholders equally)
Case 5— 'Parents for school preservation' and closing down a school (duty to consult users; duty to give reasons)
Case 6—Ms Rand and the legal effects of partially unpublished administrative rules (duty of publication)
Case 7—Bellevue and hastily reviewed taxi licence standards (protection of procedural expectations)
Case 8—Sun City: Urban planning, private property, and procedural fairness (duty of consideration)
Case 9—Old Park and the new tram route (cost-benefit analysis)
Case 10—A gold mine plan with no environmental impact assessment (environmental impact assessment)

A. Case 1—Parliament and Administrative Procedures Concerning Asylum Seekers (Parliamentary Control)

Primary legislation regarding immigration grants the Minister of Internal Affairs the authority to issue an order that defines in detail the administrative procedures for the treatment of asylum seekers. However, the legislation requires the Minister to present the order to Parliament, which has 30 days to comment or request changes before the order comes into force. The order is laid before Parliament, but before the 30-day deadline expires, the Minister decides to give force to the order and publishes it on the Ministry's website, stating that it is vital that the order come into force immediately.

Would Parliament consider this to be a disregarding of its legislation and therefore invalid? Could the order be challenged before the courts on grounds of invalidity?

Several Authors, *Cases* In: *Administrative Rulemaking and Planning in European Laws*. Edited by: Giacinto della Cananea and Angela Ferrari Zumbini, Oxford University Press. © Several Authors 2025.
DOI: 10.1093/oso/9780198867616.003.0015

B. Case 2—Toys World and Standardless Adjudication (Limiting and Structuring Discretion)

Parliamentary legislation has provided for public money to be granted to toy manufacturers that promote greater environmental awareness among children under the age of 10. According to this legislation, the Department of the Environment (DE) can award grants for the 'new games'. The DE establishes some rules of practice, including one whereby it would not award grants for any game costing more than €50 (or the equivalent in another currency). Toys World (TW) applies for a grant for a new game but its application is rejected on the grounds that the price of the game for the public would be €55, thus exceeding the €50 limit.

TW thus brings a claim before the competent court, asserting that, before defining its rules of practice or standards, the DE should have consulted stakeholders instead of acting unilaterally. The DE objects that no legislative provision requires it to consult stakeholders before adopting any rule or policy.

Setting aside the substantive issues (eg whether there is conflict with EU norms on state aid or equivalent legislation outside of the EU), would the competent court give any weight to a claim based on the lack of consultation of stakeholders? If so, would it strike down the disputed rejection of TW's application? Or would it require the DE to reopen the consultation phase?

C. Case 3—The Rules of the Game: Allocating Few Licences (Duty to Consult Stakeholders; Protection of Expectations)

The primary legislation regarding slot machine arcade licences gives regional authorities the power to establish rules for granting them, including the ability to set the maximum number of licences available. After a recent election and a subsequent shift in policy, one of these regional authorities decides to change its policy regarding slot machine arcades. Instead of the former maximum of just one licence, the authority will now allow up to five licences within the region. Due to the experimental nature of the new policy, the licences will be granted for a period of two years. The authority publishes its new policy in its official journal and on its website. Those who want to apply for a slot machine arcade licence, including the current licence holder, have one month to submit their application. After that, the authority will assess and rank the applications based on the criteria listed in the policy. During the application period, the authority publishes an amendment to its policy to the effect that the applications will also be scored in relation to a 'prevention plan' that should contain the measures the participants will include to prevent gambling addiction.

Although local market players are content with the greater number of available slot machine arcade licences, they challenge the new policy before the competent court, arguing that the authority should have consulted them before setting the validity period at two years. This does not offer enough time to recover the costs to prepare the application for a licence, let alone the investments needed to purchase and maintain slot machines. According to the authority, however, there is no legislative provision requiring it to consult stakeholders before establishing the licence validity period. The local market players also argue that the authority should not have added the prevention plan to the selection criteria after the application period had already begun. The authority responds that applicants have enough time to add a prevention plan to their application for a licence. Furthermore, the prevention plan is just one of the selection criteria and is thus not strictly necessary to obtain a licence.

Based on national (non-EU) law, including general principles, would the court uphold the authority's arguments, or would it endorse the local market players' claim? In the latter case, how would it act?

D. Case 4—The Newcomer Who Was Not Consulted (Duty to Consult All Stakeholders Equally)

A new railway company, Bullet Trains (BT), has entered the market, which has been dominated by just two incumbents for several years. Before establishing new tariffs, the Department of Transport (DoT) decides to consult with all stakeholders, although it is under no obligation to do so. However, the DoT consults only the two incumbents without engaging with the newcomer, BT.

BT then challenges the new tariffs before the competent court, arguing that it should have been consulted on the grounds that (i) the conduct of the DoT infringes the principles of procedural fairness, and (ii) its conduct prevented the regulator from obtaining information from all the relevant sources. It thus argues that the new tariffs are unlawful or, at least, not binding on it. The DoT responds that, according to the sector-specific rules governing railway transport, there was no obligation to consult all the stakeholders.

Would the court uphold the DoT's argument, or would it endorse the claim brought by BT, the newcomer? In the latter case, would it strike down the contested tariffs, or would it affirm that they are not binding on BT? Otherwise, would it accord BT some form of financial compensation?

E. Case 5—'Parents for School Preservation' and Closing Down a School (Duty to Consult Users; Duty to Give Reasons)

A local authority decides to close down a school on the assumption that the number of students requiring education is steadily decreasing. It thus publishes its decision on its website and allows interested parties 10 days to submit comments and supporting documents. Several documents are sent to the local authority by students and parents' associations, requesting it to review its decision to close the school. However, only 10 days after the three-day term expires, the authority gives notice of the end of the public consultation and publishes its decision, which is unchanged.

A parents' association, 'Parents for School Preservation' (PSP), challenges the decision to close the school before the competent court, arguing that (i) no evidence has been provided for the falling numbers requiring education within the local community, and (ii) the duty to consult has not been taken seriously as consultations were not held when the decision-making process was still in the formative stage, and the local body did not allow sufficient time for adequate consideration and response. The authorities reply that (i) the number of births is falling across the country, with inevitable consequences on schooling, and (ii) national legislation does not require local authorities to carry out consultation for a specified number of days.

Would the court accept the argument of the responding authority, or would it support PSP's argument that the decision to close the school was unjustified and not preceded by adequate consultation? Would the decision be quashed in the latter case?

F. Case 6—Ms Rand and the Legal Effects of Partially Unpublished Administrative Rules (Duty of Publication)

During a pandemic, the Minister of Health issues an order setting the prices for various types of face masks. This order also establishes fines for those who do not apply them. The Minister announces that the order will be published in the official journal, as required by existing legislation. But it is published only in part, without specifying the prices for the various types of face mask. Moreover, it is published on the Health Department's website rather than in the official journal.

When Ms Rand, a pharmacist, is fined by the local authority for selling the masks at a different price, she challenges the fine before the competent court. Ms Rand argues that the order must be published in full for it to be considered valid and to have any legal effect. She believes that her freedom to trade cannot be limited outside of the cases and forms provided for by legislation. The Health Department responds that the order is valid, despite not having been published in the official journal. It argues that in today's world, a government website has the potential to reach more people than the official journal can.

Would the court uphold Ms Rand's arguments based on the failure to publish in the official journal? If so, what would it do?

G. Case 7—Bellevue and Hastily Reviewed Taxi Licence Standards (Protection of Procedural Expectations)

The Municipality of Bellevue, a coastal town, has issued several taxi licences over the years. The city council provided assurance that it would give notice or embark upon consultation before changing its policy concerning taxi licensing. However, in view of an international sailing yacht competition which was to take place six months later, the Municipality of Bellevue made two changes to its policy: (i) white was the most common colour for Bellevue taxis, but some were blue, yellow, green, or other colours; nevertheless, the City Board ruled that all taxis had to be white in order to be easily recognized; (ii) it also ruled that, instead of the traditional working-hour limits, no taxi driver may drive for more than eight hours per day.

Taxi Drivers, a local association challenges the new policy on both economic and legal grounds. Economically, it argues, the new policy implies higher and unforeseen costs. Legally, it continues, since the Bellevue administrators gave a straightforward assurance, they should be held to it. In particular, those administrators should not be allowed to make the proposed changes without providing notice or consulting with others. The legal action brought by Taxi Drivers against the new policy presents both arguments.

Would the court be willing to accept Taxi Drivers' arguments, and, if so, how would it act?

H. Case 8—Sun City: Urban Planning, Private Property, and Procedural Fairness (Duty of Consideration)

When the administrators of the municipality of Sun City elaborated the draft local plan, they specified that the new proposed policy was not to permit the construction of new buildings but only the restructuring of existing ones. However, although the administrators received several representations from consultees who contested the new policy, they did not refer to these representations in their final statement, nor did they explicitly state the reasons why they did not follow these representations.

Residents in the Suburbia neighbourhood, the one most affected by this municipal policy, challenge the procedural failings. Sun City responds that there is no express statutory requirement to engage in debate with consultees. The Suburbia residents then bring a case before the competent court, arguing that (i) decision-makers must, as a general principle, adopt a fair procedure before reaching a decision that may adversely affect a group of people; and (ii) the report produced by the Sun City officials does not satisfy the requirement to consider all representations made by consultees (the duty of consideration) as it says nothing about opposing views.

Would the court endorse Sun City's argument? Or would it side with Suburbia, relying on the judicial doctrines of fair administrative procedure?

I. Case 9—Old Park and the New Tram Route (Cost-Benefit Analysis)

The municipality of Moderna has decided to construct a new tramway line to help alleviate transport issues in a central area of the city. The area in question is home to a public park called Old Park, which is often crowded with local residents. According to current national and local regulations, any new transportation project must satisfy the two criteria of being both 'feasible and prudent'. Moderna believes that the cost of building the tramway line through parks is lower than in any other area.

Citizens to Preserve Old Park, an association of residents and other individuals, challenges Moderna's project on the grounds that it does not meet the above requirements. The association believes that Moderna has not weighed the costs and benefits to determine whether alternatives exist that could avoid the destruction of Old Park. It decides to sue the municipality.

Would the court be satisfied with Moderna's position, or would it require that an adequate cost-benefit analysis be carried out before deciding?

J. Case 10—A Gold Mine Plan with No Environmental Impact Assessment (Environmental Impact Assessment)

Terranova, a regional authority, has decided to promote the exploration of new gold mines as part of its plan for developing economic activities within its territory. No environmental impact assessment (EIA) was carried out before adopting the plan.

During the exploration process, before mining actually commences, some groups of residents and other persons concerned about the likely impact of mining bring a case before the competent court. They argue that (i) Terranova erred insofar as it adopted the plan without making any attempt to integrate environmental consideration into its policy; (ii) the plan is unlawful because it provides no EIA whatsoever before licences for mining are issued, although scientific studies warn about the pollution of both water and the atmosphere, as well as the destruction of the ecosystem, with potentially lethal consequences for human beings.

Would the court simply verify whether there is a specific obligation to conduct an EIA in this sector, and, if there is no such obligation, would it dismiss the case? Or would it draw on constitutional values and principles, such as the need to protect human health and the environment, as well as referring to international treaties? If so, would it nullify the challenged plan, or would it require Terranova to conduct an adequate EIA before issuing licences?

II. Case 1—Parliament and Administrative Procedures Concerning Asylum Seekers (Parliamentary Control)

A. Austria

Stefan Storr and Sophie Praniess

First, it must be determined whether the order is a decree, with only internal effect (as stated earlier), or an implementing ordinance, with external effect. Under Austrian administrative law, both implementing ordinances and decrees are referred to as administrative ordinances (but, as mentioned before, this terminology may lead to confusion).

If the order concerns the rights and obligations of asylum seekers, which is assumed for the purposes of this analysis, it must be classified as an implementing ordinance with external effect. In this case, two aspects are important.

First, the Parliament must be consulted if provided for by statute. Failure to comply with the statutory obligation of prior consultation constitutes a significant procedural violation. Therefore, if the ordinance is violated, it is considered unlawful and will be annulled in accordance with the Austrian Constitutional Court's established case law.

Second, in this case the implementing ordinance was published incorrectly. Implementing ordinances issued by federal ministers must be published in the Federal Law Gazette.[1] The report was not published as required by law but was instead released on the Ministry's homepage. If the publication of the implementing ordinance is unlawful, the Austrian Constitutional Court will annul it.[2]

The approach of the Austrian Constitutional Court is unusual in that it determines an administrative ordinance issued by an administrative authority to be an ordinance regardless of its label if it regulates the rights and obligations of those subject to the law. Whether the issuing authority designates the regulation as such (or otherwise) is irrelevant. The interpretation in question is not necessarily covered by Article 139 B-VG, which has resulted in criticism from legal scholarship.[3]

Applied to the case at hand, the Austrian Constitutional Court's approach results in the Minister's order being interpreted as an implementing ordinance with external effect. Following classification, the ordinance will be repealed—without substantive review by the court—due to its unlawfulness resulting from non-compliance with statutory publication requirements.

If the Minister's regulation is considered an administrative ordinance without external effect, it would be deemed to be a decree. Its unlawfulness would result from the lack of prior parliamentary consultation as provided for by statute. However, such a decree cannot be annulled by the Austrian Constitutional Court, regardless of its

[1] S 4 Federal Act on the Federal Law Gazette (*Bundesgesetz über das Bundesgesetzblatt 2004* (*Bundesgesetzblattgesetz—BGBlG*)) Orig Vers: BGBl I No 100/2003.

[2] Art 89 B-VG.

[3] W Antoniolli and F Koja, *Allgemeines Verwaltungsrecht* (3rd edn, Manz 1996) 165.

unlawfulness. Austrian constitutional law does not provide a remedy to annul ordinances with only internal effect, only providing remedies against unlawful ordinances with external effect.

B. China

Xiaowei Sun

Parliament will inform the minister of the procedural breach but will approve the order if there is no substantial violation of its legislation. The order cannot be challenged directly in court, but it can be contested by way of exception when an individual act based on this order is challenged.

Regarding the case before Parliament, the Legislation Law endows Parliament with the power to change or annul an administrative rule in the following five situations (Article 96):

1. If it exceeds the scope of its authority.
2. Where it is contrary to provisions of a higher ranking rule. This rule applies when there are conflicting provisions in different rules and, if a ruling is made by the relevant body, one of the provisions should be changed or removed.
3. Where the provisions of a rule are considered inappropriate and should therefore be altered or annulled.
4. Breach of legal procedure.[4]

In formal terms, the minister did not follow the procedure as outlined in the primary legislation. This action could be considered a procedural violation by Parliament. In practice, a minor procedural breach like this will not cause Parliament to invalidate an order from the ministry since Parliament is concerned with the effectiveness of public action. If there is no material breach of the primary legislation, Parliament will simply notify the ministry.

The minister's order can only be reviewed by the court in the context of a trial concerning an individual action.

According to Article 53 of the Administrative Litigation Law:

> Citizens, legal persons or other organisations who believe that a regulatory act formulated by the State Council or local people's government on which the administrative act is based is illegal may request the review of the regulatory act when a lawsuit is filed against the administrative act.[5]

According to Article 64 of the same law:

[4] （一）超越权限的；（二）下位法违反上位法规定的；（三）规章之间对同一事项的规定不一致，经裁决应当改变或者撤销一方的规定的；（四）规章的规定被认为不适当，应当予以改变或者撤销的；（五）违背法定程序的。

[5] 公民、法人或者其他组织认为行政行为所依据的国务院部门和地方人民政府及其部门制定的规范性文件不合法，在对行政行为提起诉讼时，可以一并请求对该规范性文件进行审查。

> During the administrative suit, if the court determines that the regulatory act is not lawful as provided for in Article 53 of this Law, this regulatory act will not be considered as the legal basis for the contested administrative act, and a regularisation recommendation will be issued to the administrative authority.[6]

More specifically, the Supreme People's Court issued a Judicial Interpretation of 13 November 2017 regarding the application of the Administrative Litigation Law[7] (Article 148). In it, the court determined that, when reviewing a regulatory act, it may consider whether the administrative organ has exceeded its competence or violated articles of legal procedure.[8] The Supreme Court specifies four unlawful situations as follows:

1. The administrative authority exceeds its statutory competence or the scope delimited by law and regulations
2. The regulatory act is not in compliance with the law or superior regulations
3. The regulatory act has no legal basis, and illegally increases obligations or restricts rights of citizens, legal persons or other organisations
4. The administrative authority failed to comply with legal approval procedures and publication procedure, or committed a serious procedural breach.[9]

The question is whether the court can review the procedural compliance of the regulatory act by way of exception, as it does for individual acts. Until now, there has been no precedent for ascertaining the existence of such a review. In this regard, scholars are divided into two opposing groups: one supporting the need for such a review, while the other remains hesitant.

The first perspective suggests that procedural compliance is a necessary element of the validity of any administrative act, whether it is individual or regulatory. In order for a regulation to be considered valid, it must adhere to consultative processes. Such obligations are specified in legal texts.[10]

The second perspective does not concern a complete rejection of reviewing the procedural compliance of regulations in exceptional cases. It regards, instead, the practical implications. First, there would be an inconsistency between the consequences of a procedural breach of an individual act and that of a regulatory act. The former is annulled by the court, while the latter is struck down but continues to exist and apply. It is possible that the courts will not adopt the same solution until the Supreme People's Court decides on the regulation.

[6] 人民法院在审理行政案件中，经审查认为本法第五十三条规定的规范性文件不合法的，不作为认定行政行为合法的依据，并向制定机关提出处理建议。

[7] 关于适用《中华人民共和国行政诉讼法》的解释.

[8] 人民法院对规范性文件进行一并审查时，可以从规范性文件制定机关是否超越权限或者违反法定程序、作出行政行为所依据的条款以及相关条款等方面进行。

[9] （一）超越制定机关的法定职权或者超越法律、法规、规章的授权范围的；（二）与法律、法规、规章等上位法的规定相抵触的；（三）没有法律、法规、规章依据，违法增加公民、法人和其他组织义务或者减损公民、法人和其他组织合法权益的；（四）未履行法定批准程序、公开发布程序，严重违反制定程序的.

[10] Beyond the Regulations on Procedures for the Formulation of Administrative Regulations of 16 November 2001 (行政法规制定程序条例), in certain specific areas, the requirement for consultation in the drafting of regulations is provided by legislation.

Lastly, the two sides agree that review is limited to the part of the regulation relevant to the individual act in question. This is in no way a general review of the entire text, which is distinct from the trial.

C. Czech Republic

Gabriela Blahoudková

Under the Czech Constitution, ministries, other bodies of state administration, and bodies of local self-governance can adopt their own administrative regulations if they are authorized to do so by statute. The statutory authorization must be specific, unequivocal, and clear.[11] The ministries can adopt administrative regulations on the basis and within the limits of a statute, and the legislation resulting from their activities is referred to as 'ministerial regulations'. In doing so, the administrative authorities participate, in a way, in the creation of complex legal regulations. But state power can only be exerted in manners prescribed by statute. Therefore, conditions regulating the status of asylum seekers can be laid down by a ministerial regulation, but procedural rules must be stipulated by a statute. The scenario indicated is thus inappropriate for the Czech legal system.

At the same time, the adoption of ministerial regulations is the manifestation of state power, where the procedural rules for their adoption are contained in the Government Legislative Rules. The Rules are adopted in the form of a government resolution and are thus binding only internally. The Rules unify the procedures for the preparation of regulations at ministries and other central bodies of public administration, and, under the Rules, the bodies which draft (ministerial) regulations submit the drafts through the electronic library. A group of persons, determined by the Rules, can subsequently provide feedback[12] to the submitting body. Although Parliament is not included among these persons, the fundamental principles of consideration can be illustrated by the functioning of working committees that consider and recommend regulations. The regulations cannot be published in the Collection of Laws until a draft regulation has been considered by the working committees and amended in compliance with the committees' standpoints prior to signing. However, the Legislative Rules do not include express regulation of procedures in cases where a ministerial regulation has not been considered by the committees and a declaration regarding the amendment of the regulation in compliance with the committees' standpoints has not been attached. Such an absence (ie the absence of an express regulation of procedures when a regulation has not been considered by the committees) is understandable, given that such a situation should never occur. Since Legislative Rules are internally binding, their breach should not lead to the unlawfulness of the regulation; therefore, if the regulation were published, it would become a valid part of the legal system.[13]

[11] Judgment of the Constitutional Court of 21 June 2000, File Ref No ÚS 3/2000.

[12] Art 16 (1) and art 15 of the Government Legislative Rules.

[13] Moreover, the Government Legislative Rules are a mere internal regulation and do not establish a legal right to a particular mode of consideration (Judgment of the Constitutional Court, File Ref No Pl ÚS 7/03).

The intermediate step of obtaining approval from another body or by considering it is not used when adopting legislation (including regulations). Such a condition can occasionally be seen in the case of other forms of abstract acts, particularly those adopted by professional self-government for the purposes of self-regulation. This includes, for example, special competences of the Ministry of Justice with respect to the regulations of selected professional chambers. These special competences are necessary because the professional regulations can also affect persons who are not members of the respective chamber. For example, the Act on Notaries and their Activities requires certain regulations adopted by the Notarial Chamber of the Czech Republic to be approved by the Ministry of Justice in order to be valid. If the Notarial Chamber applied a regulation that did not meet the requirements, an interested party would be allowed to seek protection before the court. The Ministry of Justice approves the examination code, disciplinary code, and rules of practice of the Chamber of Licensed Enforcement Agents. The Czech Bar Association is required to submit all professional rules and regulations adopted by its bodies to the Ministry of Justice within 30 days. If the Minister of Justice determines that a professional regulation of the Association violates the law, he or she has the right to request that the court reviews it. The court can only determine whether the professional regulation conflicts with the law and annul the regulation or part of it in the context of a subsequent judicial review. In such cases, the Ministry of Justice acts as the supervisory authority.

In other cases, a special statute prescribes mandatory consultations for particular types of subordinate legislation. This is the case, for example, of certain regulations that are submitted for consultation to the European Central Bank pursuant to a Council Decision of 29 June 1998 on the consultation of the European Central Bank by national authorities regarding draft legislative provisions (98/415/EC). What can also be mentioned is the duty of notification for technical regulations set out in Directive (EU) 2015/1535 of the European Parliament and of the Council of 9 September 2015, which sets out a procedure for the provision of information in the field of technical regulations.

However, the Czech legal system does not have a general rule that invalidates abstract acts when a formal requirement is not satisfied. Only authorized bodies can determine the validity and effects of legal regulations. Parliament could logically object that a statutory procedure has not been observed when adopting a regulation, but it has no right to repeal it. A regulation can be directly amended or repealed by the ministry that adopted it. The Parliament could abolish a ministerial regulation by passing a statute through the legislative process, but the statute would need to be an amendment or revocation of authorization and the enactment of new legal regulation in the form of primary legislation.[14] Once a regulation has been published in the manner required by law, it becomes a valid part of the legal system.

Furthermore, in the Czech legal system, a distinction must be made between unlawfulness and non-existence. If any form of administrative activity is non-existent, it has never existed and thus cannot have legal consequences. In contrast, the issue of unlawfulness must be raised before the court. If we assume that the Czech legal system

[14] Judgment of the Constitutional Court of 20 October 2004, File Ref No Pl ÚS 52/03.

allows for the determination of a procedure through a regulation which must be presented in Parliament prior to its publication, and this was not complied with, then the non-compliance would not, under the applicable rules, render the regulation null and void. This is because the regulation was still adopted by a competent body, despite the fact that (only) certain procedural rules were not adhered to. This procedural deficiency may, however, cause the regulation to be unlawful.

The Constitutional Court has never addressed the issue of providing Parliament with sufficient time to express its opinion on a regulation. However, a violation of the procedure to the extent indicated would likely be grounds for abolishing a regulation based on it, as it would be considered unlawful. The Constitutional Court is the only court that can abolish regulations. It has the power to do so when a motion is put forward by at least 25 deputies, 10 senators, the ombudsman, the Government, or other qualifying applicants. Only individuals or legal entities who bring a constitutional complaint, and if the circumstance which is the subject of the constitutional challenge occurred as a consequence of the application of such a regulation, may make a proposal for its abolishment.[15] In addition to the review by the Constitutional Court within the general system of courts, there is also a so-called diffused review process. This process allows general courts to assess the compliance of administrative regulations with statutes. If there are discrepancies between the regulations and the statutes, the courts have the right not to apply the regulation. This procedure does not, however, lead to the abolition of the unlawful regulation.

D. European Union

Edoardo Chiti

Adapted to the specific features of the EU order, this hypothetical case envisages a situation in which the EU legislator grants the Commission administrative rulemaking responsibilities. As the exercise of rulemaking powers is authorized by EU primary legislation, one can reasonably assume that the situation is one of 'delegated' rulemaking under Article 290(1) pf the Treaty on the Functioning of the European Union (TFEU), which states that 'a legislative act may delegate to the Commission the power to adopt non-legislative acts of general application to supplement or amend certain non-essential elements of the legislative act'. In this hypothetical case, more specifically, the delegating legislation has subjected the exercise of administrative rulemaking to a specific procedural requirement involving the European Parliament. This is one of the two possible sets of (non-mutually exclusive) conditions to which delegation is subject under Article 290 TFEU. In fact, the Council or the European Parliament may subject the delegation to a condition which empowers either of these institutions to revoke the delegation. Otherwise, the delegated act may enter into force only if no objection has been expressed by the European Parliament or the Council within a period set by the legislative act. The hypothetical case refers to this second option,

[15] S 74 of Act No 182/1993 Sb on the Constitutional Court.

but it should be noted that the primary legislation would only allow the European Parliament to object to the draft but without comment, unless we consider the conditions listed in Article 290 TFEU to be non-exhaustive.

The publication of the rulemaking order by the Commission before the expire of the deadline on the basis of an emergency claim would be regarded by the Parliament as a breach of its legislation and might be challenged before EU courts. Indeed, delegated acts are subject to judicial review by the EU courts, which ensure their conformity with the delegation provided for in the basic act. Judicial control extends to ensuring that the procedures laid down in the delegating act are followed. The EU courts would most likely uphold the European Parliament's claim. Admittedly, there is no recent case law to refer to, as the European Parliament has challenged a delegated act only once since the entry into force of the Lisbon Treaty and the introduction of the new classification of EU acts.[16] But the criteria for the review developed over the previous decades by the European Court of Justice (ECJ) under Articles 202 and 211 of the European Community Treaty (ECT), including compliance with the procedures defined in the delegating act, remain applicable under the new Lisbon model. One should also consider that the new taxonomy of acts introduced by the Lisbon Treaty conveys a specific understanding of institutional balance, one which aims to ensure the prominence of the legislature and its ability to control executive rulemaking by the Commission. The procedural conditions envisaged by Article 290(2) are, in this perspective, important instruments of political oversight of subordinate rulemaking.

It is within this framework—the ECJ's consolidated case law on executive rulemaking, on the one hand, and the new rationale introduced by Lisbon, emphasizing democratic control over executive rulemaking, on the other—that the Commission's emergency claim must be assessed. The argument that 'it is vital that the order comes into force immediately' would not be regarded, as such, as an appropriate justification for the adoption of the rulemaking measure before giving the European Parliament the opportunity to object. Given its rather nuanced case law on the relationship between basic and implementing acts, it is possible that the ECJ might accept an exception to the procedural requirement laid down by primary legislation. However, such an exception would certainly be interpreted narrowly and subjected to a more stringent obligation to give reasons.

E. Germany

Lilly Weidemann

In Germany, an 'order' would constitute a statutory instrument (*Rechtsverordnung*), which would be invalid due to the absence of consent by Parliament. This invalidity can be invoked before a court.

[16] Case C-286/14, *European Parliament v European Commission*, ECLI:EU:C:2016:183, concerning a Commission delegated regulation on the Connecting Europe Facility and revolving around the distinction drawn between 'amending' and 'supplementing' the basic act.

Article 80 section 1 of the Basic Law states that the Federal Government, a Federal Minister, or the *Land* governments may be authorized by a law to issue statutory instruments. The content, purpose and scope of the authority conferred must be specified in the law. According to section 2 of the same provision, in specified cases the consent of the *Bundesrat* (the Federal Parliament that represents the 16 *Länder*, ie 'federated states', of Germany) is required for statutory instruments issued by the Federal Government or a Federal Minister.

The constitutionality of these participative rights of Parliament has been controversial.[17] In a decision of 1959, the Federal Constitutional Court affirmed the admissibility of such control reservations in favour of the parliamentary plenum. It explained that, in principle, the Basic Law reserves law-making to the legislature. However, in the event of a breach of this principle, it also recognizes the authorization of the executive to legislate. However, authorizations to issue statutory instruments requiring the consent of Parliament do not contribute to the clear demarcation of the responsibilities of the executive and legislative branches; they do, however, contain a minus compared to the full delegation of law-making to the executive. In any case, they are compatible with the Basic Law for those areas where the legislature has a legitimate interest in delegating law-making to the executive, but—due to the importance of the regulations to be made—also in reserving decisive influence on the enactment and content of the regulations to itself.[18]

Overall, Article 80 can be understood as an elementary formulation that makes concrete the principle of the separation of powers and the rule of law. The provision separates the powers of the legislature and the executive in the area of law-making and also ensures that executive law-making is bound by the requirements of the legislature. The exclusion of the executive's independent right to issue statutory instruments thus represents both a limitation of its power to legislate and a link between this executive-derived power to legislate and the requirements of the legislature. Being derived sources of law, statutory instruments are always subordinate to parliamentary acts, which they are therefore—at least in principle—unable to amend or even override; statutory instruments can neither break through nor outweigh laws. Lastly, a concrete manifestation of the principle of democracy emerges in the derived right to issue statutory instruments, as executive legislation can only operate within the framework established by the legislature and thus within the framework established by the principle of popular sovereignty. Ultimately, the provision also ensures the primacy of parliamentary decision-making in the sphere of executive legislation. Thus, Article 80 can be understood, at its most marginal, as a manifestation and an article that partially makes concrete of the principle of the federal state, namely in the context of the power of authorization in favour of state governments and the participation of the *Bundesrat* as well as its right of initiative with regard to statutory instruments requiring approval.[19]

If a statutory instrument requires the approval of the *Bundesrat* in accordance with Article 80 paragraph 2 Basic Law, this is a prerequisite for the statutory instrument to

[17] A Uhle, 'Verordnungsgeberische Entscheidungsmacht und parlamentarischer Kontrollvorbehalt zur verfassungsrechtlichen Zulässigkeit verordnungsspezifischer Kontrollbefugnisse des Parlaments unter besonderer Berücksichtigung der Rechtsprechung des BVerfG' [2002] Neue Zeitschrift für Verwaltungsrecht 15–21, 16.

[18] Federal Constitutional Court, Order of 12 November 1958, BVerfGE 8, 274–332, para 184.

[19] M Brenner, 'GG Art. 80' in H v Mangoldt, F Klein, and C Starck (eds), *Grundgesetz Kommentar* (7th edn, CH Beck 2018) para 15.

take effect.[20] If approval is refused, the procedure for issuing the statutory instrument is terminated.[21] Since, in the case given, consent was not given before the publication of the order, the order would not take effect.

The invalidity of a statutory instrument can be invoked in court in various ways. An individual can request an indirect review of the statutory instrument within an action for annulment—if the statutory instrument serves as a basis for an administrative act affecting him or her—or commence a(n) (atypical) declaratory action[22] under Article 43 paragraph 1 Code of Administrative Court Procedure[23] before the administrative court. An abstract judicial review by the Federal Constitutional Court is also available under Article 93 paragraph 1 no 2 of the Basic Law, which can be brought by the Federal Government, a *Land* government, or by one-quarter of the Members of the *Bundestag*. The *Bundesrat* itself is not entitled to bring such an action before the Federal Constitutional Court, but the *Länder* governments constituting the *Bundesrat* may do so.

F. Hungary

Lilla Berkes and Balázs Szabolcs Gerencsér

First, to answer the second question: in relation to legislation, administrative courts only have jurisdiction over local government decrees and normative decisions and instructions (the Curia can annul them or, in the event of failure to adopt a decree, grant the county government office[24] the right to adopt them).[25] Therefore, only the Constitutional Court can decide on the invalidity of a ministerial decree. However, the court may initiate proceedings before the Constitutional Court if it finds that it should apply a rule of law that is unconstitutional in an individual case.[26]

[20] B Remmert, 'GG Art. 80' in G Dürig, R Herzog, and R Scholz (eds), *Grundgesetz Kommentar* (CH Beck 2023)para 178.

[21] ibid.

[22] Higher Administrative Court of Berlin-Brandenburg, Order of 16 April 2021—OVG 1 S 43/21–, para 4, juris.

[23] Code of Administrative Court Procedure in the version of 19 March 1991 (Federal Law Gazette I page 686), most recently amended by art 5, subs 24 of the Act of 21 June 2019 (Federal Law Gazette I p 846)

[24] Fundamental Law of Hungary, art 17(3) The capital or county government offices shall be the territorial state administration organs of the government with general competence.

[25] Fundamental Law of Hungary, art 25(1) Courts shall administer justice. The supreme judicial organ shall be the Curia. (2) Courts shall decide on criminal matters, civil disputes, the lawfulness of administrative decisions, the conflict of local government decrees with any other law and their annulment, the establishment of omission by a local government of its obligation based on an Act to legislate, and on other matters specified in an Act.

[26] Act CLI of 2011 on the Constitutional Court, s 25

(1) If a judge, in determining a specific case in progress is bound to apply a legislation that he or she perceives to be contrary to the Fundamental Law, or which has already been declared contrary to the Fundamental Law by the Constitutional Court, the judge shall stay the judicial proceedings and, in accordance with Article 24(2)(b) of the Fundamental Law, submit a petition to the Constitutional Court for declaring that the legislation in question or any provision thereof is contrary to the Fundamental Law, and/or the exclusion of the application of the legislation that is contrary to the Fundamental Law.

(2) Based on the petition, the President shall take measures to put the case on the agenda at a time considered appropriate for reasons of compliance with the time limit prescribed under Article 24(2)(b) of the Fundamental Law. <https://hunconcourt.hu/act-on-the-cc/> accessed 23 November 2024

Hungarian law does not provide for a parliamentary procedure for delivering an opinion on the adoption of a ministerial decree.

If such were the case, the question of whether this kind of opinion-giving intervention of the Parliament is of constitutional significance would be relevant for determining the invalidity of the ministerial decree. The Constitutional Court's 30 years of practice on invalidity can be summarized roughly as follows: not all breaches of the rules of legislative procedure entail invalidity but only those of constitutional significance, and what is of such significance is decided on a case-by-case basis. It is also true that this practice has so far been confined to acts, while no such question has arisen in the case of decrees.

In the present case, it should be borne in mind that the Parliament is the supreme representative of popular sovereignty, which certainly distinguishes it from the other actors involved in other types of consultative processes. It should also be noted that it was the will of Parliament that the procedure described in the example should be adopted, which is why it was regulated by an act. These are both very strong arguments in favour of declaring it invalid. On the other hand, the legislation was laid before the Parliament, which had the opportunity to comment on it (so, they could have discussed it). What is more, if the legislation only requires the Minister to submit the decree to Parliament, then the Minister has formally done so, so it is questionable how much significance the subsequent procedure bears. (In public authority proceedings, for example, according to judicial practice, if only consultation is required, but not consideration of its content, the obligation is fulfilled by seeking the opinion of the person concerned. A similar logic can be assumed from the Constitutional Court's practice.) This argues against invalidity because it reduces the assessment of the gravity of the infringement. A third factor is why it is important for the order to come into force immediately and whether it is of pressing importance. Taking this into account, it is conceivable that invalidity would not be declared. It should be noted that the Parliament may, where appropriate, debate the legislation and require changes afterwards, but it also has the means to overrule the legislation in an act (although this is not so viable).

G. Italy

Leonardo Parona

In the Italian legal system, the act in question would constitute a ministerial regulation: an act qualifying as formally administrative but with a substantially normative nature (ie having general and abstract effects). Ministerial regulations are secondary sources of law that are (i) subordinated to statutory law; (ii) can be adopted—in conformity with the principle of legality—only when envisioned by a specific legislative provision (as in the case at issue);[27] (iii) are issued in the form of ministerial decrees;

[27] According to the Plenary Meeting of the Council of State, 4 May 2012, No 9, 'in principle, it must be excluded that the regulatory power of the Ministers and, more generally, of the Government can be exercised through "atypical" acts, of a non-regulatory nature, especially where the legislative provision that attributes the power does not provide anything'. See also Council of State, Sec VI, 30 November 2016, No 5036.

(iv) are adopted following a procedure that requires, in brief, a prior opinion of the Council of State, a notice to the President of the Council of Ministers, and subsequent verification by the Court of Auditors (as established by Law No 400/1988).[28]

The law conferring regulatory powers upon the Minister can eventually establish further procedural requirements, such as the duty to submit the proposed regulation to Parliament in order to receive comments, as in the case at issue here. If the regulation finally adopted is incompatible with the law—either for procedural grounds, as in the current case, or for substantial violations—the act is unlawful and can, in principle, be challenged in court as any administrative act would be. Nonetheless, the normative nature of the regulation bears several consequences on the regime of judicial contestations, starting from those concerning standing requirements. As a matter of fact, direct judicial review of the regulation before an administrative court, which is theoretically available,[29] might turn out to be inaccessible in practice.

Before elaborating on this remark, which lies at the heart of the issue addressed by the present question, two clarifications seem necessary for completeness' sake. First, ministerial regulations, despite being sources of law, cannot be directly challenged before the Constitutional Court, since they do not constitute statutory law (ie acts with the force of primary law).[30] Secondly, a ministerial regulation cannot be directly challenged before an ordinary judge, although the latter could disapply it, if relevant for the decision of a given case, under Article 5 of Law No 2248/1865, Annex E.

As already mentioned, what matters most from our standpoint is judicial review and its limitations, as provided by the administrative court when a regulatory act is challenged. As far as direct challenges to obtain the annulment of the act are concerned, the remedy is available in theory—given the formally administrative nature of ministerial regulations—but excluded in practice[31] due to lack of standing, which is a direct consequence of the normative nature of regulations.

Even in the case discussed here, in fact, the regulation does not directly or individually affect any specific physical or legal person, making any action against it inadmissible.[32] Only when a ministerial regulation is enforced through an individual

[28] In order to evade the controls and the procedure established by Law No 400/1988, Ministers have often resorted to the so-called escape from the regulation, meaning that they issued decrees not formally acknowledged as regulatory. Nonetheless, this circumstance does not change the substance of the question addressed here. On this topic, see B Tonoletti, 'Fuga dal regolamento e confini della normatività nel diritto amministrativo' (2015) 2–3 Diritto amministrativo 388 ff.

[29] In fact, according to art 113(1) and (2) Const: 'The judicial protection of rights and legitimate interests against acts of the public administration ... is always permitted' and '[s]uch judicial protection may not be excluded or limited ... for particular categories of acts.'

[30] A ministerial regulation, as in the case at issue, could nonetheless become relevant in a judgment on the conflict of powers brought to the Court by another power of the state, such as Parliament (art 39, 87/1953).

[31] This is true apart from when an act formally classified as a regulation actually produces the effects of an individual decision (lacking, therefore, the typical features of a normative act). In these cases, the act can be challenged by the affected party in an administrative court within 60 days from its publication, which is not, however, the case of the hypothetical discussed here.

[32] Under art 35(1) of the Code of Administrative Process, enacted with Legislative Decree No 104/2010 (CAP). As a partial and—at least historically—controversial exception, a regulation like the one at issue in the current case could theoretically be challenged in court by an association or by a private or public organization active for the protection of interests ensured by the violated legislative provision. That would be the case, for instance, of a non-governmental organization (NGO) concerned with the protection of asylum seekers' rights. This option, however, would reasonably be successful—and the action would not be

measure (for instance, the denial of an asylum application), can the former then be—collaterally—challenged in court. Enforcement measures affecting individuals and adopted according to the procedure established by the ministerial regulation can, in fact, be challenged in the lower courts. It is within the latter that the conflict between the regulation and the law can be addressed, since it is only with the enforcement measure that the unlawfulness of the regulation produces a prejudicial effect on asylum applicants or other affected individuals. A double claim, against both the ministerial regulation and the enforcement measure, is therefore necessary in these cases.

Two further clarifications are necessary. On the one hand, when an annulment action is successful, and the administrative court consequently quashes the regulation (as well as the enforcement measure), broader effects then stem from the judgment. In fact, the annulled regulation ceases to produce effects also in relation to other cases, being declared *tamquam non esset*. On the other hand, even in the absence of a specific action by an affected party (the aforementioned double challenge), if the ministerial regulation applies to a case to be adjudicated by an administrative court, the latter can disapply it—as established by the Council of State after a long debate in legal scholarship.[33] Disapplication, however, only affects the given case, unlike the annulment of the regulation.

Ultimately, the solution to the case would not be very different, even in the case in which the act in question would be qualified as a ministerial circular rather than a regulation—a solution, albeit improbable, that is nonetheless worth mentioning, given the uncertainties that characterize the categorization of these types of acts. Circulars, in fact, do not truly qualify as normative acts, only bearing internal effects and amounting to binding instructions that the Minister directs to ministerial offices, concerning the way in which the law is to be interpreted (*circolari interpretative*) or applied (*circolari normative*). Even in this case, an act applying a circular that is incompatible with the law could be challenged in court and deemed unlawful, leading to its annulment. The unlawfulness would stem from the fact that the circular, upon which the challenged act is based, is in itself unlawful, and individual acts issued in violation of a circular are generally annulled due to abuse of power.[34]

declared inadmissible for lack of standing—only if the violation regarded a provision protecting the rights or collective interests represented by the body. In our case, instead, the regulation was adopted in breach of a legislative provision requiring the Minister to respect a specific deadline in order to allow Parliament to express its view. No individual or collective right, therefore, was directly affected by said violation.

[33] Both in so-called exclusive jurisdiction (where the administrative court also decides on subjective rights), as established by the Council of State, Sec V, 26 February 1992, No 154, and, more generally, in the general jurisdiction of legitimacy, according to Council of State, Sec V, 26 September 2013, No 4778 (although that solution is not always fully accepted, as in Council of State, Sec VI, 21 March 2017, No 1265, and Sec V, 3 October 2015, No 515).

[34] If properly motivated, nonetheless, individual measures can exceptionally depart from circulars (since they are not normative acts).

H. Netherlands

Jacobine van den Brink, Louise Verboeket, and Veerle van Waarde

The order of the Minister of Internal Affairs that sets out in detail the administrative procedures concerning the treatment of asylum seekers qualifies as a ministerial regulation (*ministeriële regeling*) under Dutch law according to the definition in Instruction 3.18 of the Legislative Drafting Instructions (*Aanwijzingen voor de regelgeving*). The procedure for the drafting stage of a ministerial regulation is quite simple, as described in Instructions 207–218 of the Plan of Legislative Drafting (*Draaiboek voor de regelgeving*). First of all, drafts of ministerial regulations do not need to be submitted to the Council of State (*Raad van State*) for advice. In addition, the Council of Ministers (*ministerraad*) and Parliament (*Eerste en Tweede Kamer*) need not be involved in the preparation of a ministerial regulation. This means that the only formal elements during the drafting stage of a ministerial regulation are (i) the enactment by the minister, and (ii) the publication of the ministerial regulation. However, according to Instruction 2.35 of the Legislative Drafting Instructions, a preliminary scrutiny procedure (*voorhangprocedure*) can be carried out in some cases in order to allow Parliament to be involved in the drafting process of a ministerial regulation. There are four forms of parliamentary involvement, established in Instructions 2.36–2.40 of the Legislative Drafting Instructions: (i) controlled delegation (*gecontroleerde delegatie*), (ii) conditional delegation (*voorwaardelijke delegatie*), (iii) temporary delegation (*tijdelijke delegatie*), and (iv) delegation subject to approval by law (*delegatie onder het vereiste van goedkeuring bij wet*). In this case, the draft of the ministerial regulation must be presented to Parliament, which will have 30 days to review it, express its observations, and exchange ideas with the Minister of Internal Affairs. Therefore, controlled delegation, in accordance with Instruction 2.36, seems to be applicable in this case. Before the draft of the ministerial regulation is sent to Parliament, the draft must be discussed in the Council of Ministers (*ministerraad*).

According to Article 89(3) of the Dutch Constitution (*Grondwet*), in conjunction with Articles 5(a) and 8 of the Publication Act (*Bekendmakingswet*), a ministerial regulation must be published in the Government Gazette (*Staatscourant*) in order to take effect. The fact that the Minister of Internal Affairs decides to give force to the order and publish it on the Ministry's website would have no legal effect under Dutch law, as the ministerial regulation is not published in the Government Gazette. Hence, the ministerial regulation would be regarded as invalid in the Dutch legal system. The order cannot be challenged directly before the administrative courts, however, as a ministerial regulation qualifies as a general binding regulation (*algemeen verbindend voorschrift*) under Dutch law.[35] A claim for judicial review (*beroep*) cannot be lodged against a decision containing a general binding regulation, as set out in Article 8(3)(a) of the General Administrative Law Act (GALA, *Algemene wet bestuursrecht*). Therefore, an action against the ministerial regulation should be brought before the

[35] Compare with ABRvS 3 January 2007, ECLI:NL:RVS:2007:AZ5491, in which a subsidy cap (*subsidieplafond*) was declared invalid, because it was published on the Ministry's website instead of in the Government Gazette.

civil courts. However, the Supreme Court (*Hoge Raad*) declares inadmissible any direct action against general binding regulations that create enforceable rights or obligations through an implementing decision brought by an individual citizen or their interest groups.[36] General binding regulations that have direct effect, meaning regulations that apply immediately without the intermediary of an appealable decision, can be appealed directly to the civil court.[37] Given the facts of the case, it is unclear whether the order that defines the administrative procedures concerning the treatment of asylum seekers qualifies as a general binding regulation with direct or indirect effect. This depends on the content of the regulation, which is unknown. If the ministerial regulation qualifies as a general binding regulation with direct effect, the ministerial regulation can be appealed directly to the civil court. The civil court will most likely issue a declaratory decision (*verklaring voor recht*) to the effect that the ministerial regulation is non-binding, as the regulation is not published in the Government Gazette and, therefore, has no legal effect.[38] If the ministerial regulation only has indirect effect, citizens must ignore the prohibition or order an appeal to the administrative court against a subsequent enforcement decision in order to challenge the legality of the underlying general binding regulation.[39]

I. Norway

Eivind Smith

With an extraordinary exception at the very beginning of the COVID-19 pandemic, the example has no practical bearing in Norway, neither in general nor when it comes to the procedure regarding the treatment of asylum seekers.

Keeping this caveat in mind, it would certainly be regarded as a case of disregard of Parliament, with the political consequences (criticism, distrust) that the Norwegian 'negative' parliamentary system might command.

The legal validity of the order, however, is quite another matter. First, the question could not be submitted to the judiciary *in abstracto*. Secondly, the disorderly manner in which the order was issued may be invoked as an argument in favour of the invalidity of individual administrative acts, supposedly refusals to grant asylum. In this case, I regard it as most likely that the fault would be considered a procedural rather than a material fault. If so, the argument would be decisive if the court finds a reason to believe that the outcome of the individual case would have been different (ie beneficial

[36] See Supreme Court 9 July 2010, ECLI:NL:HR:2010:BM2314 (*Staat/Vreemdelingenorganisaties*); Supreme Court 22 May 2015, ECLI:NL:HR:2015:1296 (*Privacy First/Staat*); and Supreme Court 3 June 2016, ECLI:NL:HR:2016:1049 (*SCAU/Universiteiten*).

[37] RBJ Schutgens, 'Rechtsbescherming tegen algemene regels: tijd om de Awb te voltooien' in WJM Voermans, RJB Schutgens, and ACM Meuwese (eds), *Algemene regels in het bestuursrecht*, VAR-reeks No 158, (Boom juridisch 2017) 105 ff.

[38] Compare with Rb 's-Gravenhage 31 December 2008, ECLI:NL:RBSGR:2008:BG8465. However, this judgment was overruled by the Supreme Court (*Hoge Raad*), because the NEN norms (*NEN-normen*) did not qualify as general binding regulations (*algemeen verbindende voorschriften*), so publication under the Publication Act was not necessary. See HR 22 June 2012, ECLI:NL:HR:2012:BW0393.

[39] Supreme Court 3 June 2016, ECLI:NL:HR:2016:1049, para 4.2.2.

to the asylum seeker) had the order not been issued before the expiration of the time limit. Provided that most parts of the procedural order would have been unaffected by the minister's disregard, however, the latter would not entail the invalidity of the refusal to grant asylum. However, different hypotheses may, of course, be envisaged.

J. Portugal

Rui Guerra da Fonseca

In the Portuguese system, 'primary legislation' can mean a parliamentary law, or a decree-law issued by the government as both the Parliament and the executive have legislative powers.[40] In this case, the former appears to be the most logical possibility.

Parliament could have legislated on the matter itself but instead it chose to confer that competence on the Minister, whose powers are administrative in nature. By doing so, Parliament refrains from using its legislative powers and instead opts for administrative rulemaking. The law (Code of Administrative Procedure, CPA) does not grant Parliament any powers of intervention in this process. Of course, this could be seen as a possibility granted only, and specifically, by this 'primary legislation' for this case, but it would be a problem from the point of view of the separation of powers. In fact, Parliament has no administrative function (the Portuguese Constitution (CRP) reserves that to the government as the superior body of the public administration).[41] Therefore, it cannot participate in the creation of administrative rules or issue them itself.[42] If Parliament wishes to act on this, it should legislate according to the proper procedure, from beginning to end, ultimately annulling the Minister's order. In this sense, according to jurisprudence of the courts and doctrine, the 'primary legislation' breaches the principle of separation of powers (Article 111 CRP) as does the intervention of Parliament in an administrative procedure.[43]

But leaving that aside and treating this intervention ('make comments or require changes') as any other legally required phase of an administrative procedure ('before the order comes into force'), could the Minister dismiss this phase or step on the grounds of urgency?[44] In the CPA, urgency can justify overlooking some procedural steps. For example, if a person's rights or interests are affected by an administrative decision, they have the right to be heard before that decision is made. This applies to both administrative acts (Articles 121 ff) and regulations (Article 100). If the decision

[40] See CRP, arts 112, 161, and 198. In the autonomous regions of Madeira and the Azores the respective parliamentary assemblies also have legislative powers but only within their territory.

[41] See art 182.

[42] Leaving aside administrative rules concerning its own managerial affairs, such as personnel or the use of installations.

[43] On the existence of administrative functions reserved to the government and other administrative bodies except Parliament, see P Otero, *Legalidade e Administração Pública—O Sentido da Vinculação Administrativa à Juridicidade* (Almedina 2003) 749 ff. Also Ac Central Administrative Court-South, Proc Np 572/10.1BELSB, 01-10-2020.

[44] The Minister does not assert the unconstitutionality of the 'primary legislation' as a justification to overlook the phase or step.

is urgent, the hearing can be dispensed with (Articles 100/3 al. *a)* and 124/1 al. *a)*), but reasons for doing so must be given, and an objective justification must be presented.

Theoretically, it would be possible to bypass this and other procedural requirements if a state of administrative emergency were declared. This would enable the Minister to not comply with all of the CPA's procedural requirements if the desired results could not be achieved otherwise (Article 2/2). But this is truly a situation of 'exceptional legality'[45] and an extremely unusual occurrence. The former, though still an exception, is a normal one specifically contemplated by law.

However, the regulation cannot come into effect by simply being published on the Ministry's website. It must also be published in the Official Journal of the Republic (*Diário da República*).[46]

Of course, Parliament could consider the Minister's action as a disregard for its legislation (notwithstanding its probable unconstitutionality). But it would not have standing to question the Minister's order (regulation) in an administrative court of law. The Portuguese Code of Process in the Administrative Courts of Law (CPTA) grants administrative courts the power to nullify an administrative rule on grounds of illegality, with general effect, or for a specific case (Articles 72 ff). However, according to the rules of standing, the initiative to challenge the regulation would rest on those who claim they have been damaged by its application, or the Public Prosecutor's Office, or any others (natural or legal) who protect objective values safeguarded by the CRP.[47] It is important to remember that Parliament can use its legislative powers to act on the Minister's regulations.

K. Sweden

Patricia Jonason and Björn Forssén

In principle, the Swedish government would not require parliamentary authorization to adopt a legal framework defining in detail the administrative procedures concerning the treatment of asylum seekers. This would fall under the so-called residual power (*restkompetens*) of the government in accordance with section 7, chapter 8 of the Instrument of Government.[48]

[45] Otero, *Legalidade e Administração Pública* (n 43) 996 ff.

[46] See art 139 CPA and art 119/1 al. *h)* CRP.

[47] Such as public health, the environment, urban and territorial planning, quality of life, the protection of cultural heritage, and public property (arts 73/1 and 9/2 CPTA).

[48] S 7, chapter 8 states 'The Government may adopt: 1. provisions relating to the implementation of laws; and 2. provisions which do not require adoption by the Riksdag under fundamental law.' Regarding residual power, see prop 1973:90, p 139; E Holmberg and others, *Grundlagarna Regeringsformen Successionsordningen Riksdagsordningen* (3rd edn, Norstedts Juridik 2012) 357, 358, 385, 390, and 396; and A Eka and others, *Regeringsformen—med kommentarer* (Karnov Group 2018) 386 second para No 2. The term 'implementing of laws' (Swedish, *verkställighet av lag*) is not fully clear. See Holmberg and others (n 48) 390 and 392. However, it is evident that in the form of 'implementing of laws' nothing may be decided that can be deemed a previously non-existing encroachment in the individual's personal or economical circumstances according to s 2, para 2 of chapter 8 (Instruments adopted by the *Riksdag*).

However, an authorization from Parliament, the *Riksdag*, would be required if the regulation, which concerns relations between individuals and public institutions, entails 'obligations of individuals, or which otherwise encroach on their personal or economic circumstances' (section 2, 2 st, chapter 8 Instrument of Government).

If we assume that the actual regulation generates these kinds of consequences for individuals, then the rules fall under the scope of what is called parliamentary primary legislation.

Having normally been examined by the *Riksdag*, the provisions as understood here may be adopted by the government upon authorization by the *Riksdag* (section 3, chapter 8, Instrument of Government).[49] When assessing its authorization, the *Riksdag* may decide that provisions adopted by virtue of its authorization will be submitted to it for examination (section 6, chapter 8, Instrument of Government).[50]

Here follow two examples of the submission mechanism in action. The first involves temporary delegation of power to the government by the *Riksdag* (in the form of amendments of the Contagious Disease Act (2004:168)),[51] which enabled the government to promptly take measures to fight the spread of COVID-19.[52] The amendments included a mechanism for submitting each decision made by the government to the *Riksdag* for examination. This submission had to be made immediately after the decision was taken, meaning either the same day or the day after.

The second example concerns the Act (1988:97) on the procedures to be followed by municipalities, administrative authorities, and courts during times of war or threat of war, which empowers the government to decide—by decree—about the application of the provisions of the Act, under certain circumstances. According to this Act, regulations adopted by the government 'must be submitted to the Riksdag within one month of its issuance'.

The *Riksdag* also decides on the consequences after the submission. In the abovementioned case of a delegation during the COVID-19 pandemic, the amendment to the Contagious Disease Act prescribed that if the *Riksdag* agreed with the government's assessment, the ordinance would remain in effect until the validity period ended. If the *Riksdag* disagreed with the government's decision on the need for measures, it had the power to withdraw the delegation of regulatory power by passing a law. Alternatively, the ordinance could be withdrawn or replaced by law. According to Act (1988:97) concerning the procedure of municipalities, administrative authorities, and courts during times of war or threat of war, the ordinance will cease to apply if it is not submitted to the *Riksdag* in time or if the *Riksdag* does not approve it within two months of submission.[53]

[49] See also Holmberg and others (n 48) 377.

[50] See prop 1973:90, p 139. See also Holmberg and others (n 48) 388; Eka and others (n 48) 381.

[51] See P Jonason and Th Larue 'The Covid-19 Pandemic and the Swedish Parliament: How to Make Use of a Flexible Constitutional Framework' in E Cartier, B Ridard, and G Toulemonde (eds), *The Parliament in the Time of Coronavirus* (Robert Schuman Foundation 2020) 5.

[52] See SFS 2020:242, lag om ändring i smittskyddslagen (2004:168); prop 2019/20:155.

[53] See also Eka and others (n 48) 381–83.

This submission mechanism is intended to allow the *Riksdag* to exercise *a posteriori* control (*eftergranskning*);[54] that is, after the provisions have already been adopted.

Thus, the questions 'Would the *Riksdag* consider this a disregard of its legislation and, thus, as being invalid?' and 'Could the order be contested before the courts on grounds of invalidity?' are not pertinent to the Swedish legal order. The submission mechanism to Parliament is not meant as a consultation mechanism but as a monitoring mechanism in the hands of the *Riksdag* on regulations already adopted and entered into force. Moreover, in Swedish Constitutional law, the *Riksdag* can always take decisions on any matters it chooses and change any rules enacted by the government (decrees) by passing an Act (section 8, chapter 8, Instrument of Government).[55]

L. United Kingdom

John Morison and David Mark

Within this scenario Parliament has specified that there should be a formal process. This scenario can therefore be addressed rather succinctly, as failure to follow this process to make law in the prescribed way would not be overlooked by Parliament. When making rules or procedures relating to the treatment of asylum seekers the Minister is operating under powers given by Parliament. If powers are being exercised outside the scope of the power granted it is *ultra vires* and the courts will strike down the rules as being invalid.

M. United States of America

Jeffrey Lubbers and Giacinto della Cananea

In the United States the Congress could not require the immigration agency (or any other agency) to subject its orders to congressional veto or congressionally mandated changes. As a result, the order could be contested before the courts.

The *Immigration and Naturalization Service v Chadha* case (1983) is of salient importance in this respect.[56] The case concerned a legislative veto provision established by the Immigration and Nationality Act that permitted one house of Congress to invalidate suspension-of-deportation rulings. Jagdish Rai Chadha, born in Kenya, was a graduate student in a US university when his student visa expired. As Kenya had gained independence from Britain by the time his student visa expired, he should have been deported to Kenya, where, however, he would not have been accepted as a citizen. Following a hearing,

[54] (Our translation): 'Ultimately, the review of such regulations that are subject to submission is part of the Parliament's overarching control over how governmental power is exercised', in Eka and others (n 48) 381.

[55] 'The powers conferred on the government to adopt provisions in a particular matter do not preclude the Riksdag from adopting provisions in the same matter in an act of law'. See also Holmberg and others (n 48) 396 and 397; Eka and others (n 48) 389.

[56] 462 US 919 (1983).

an immigration judge suspended Chadha's deportation. But the House of Representatives voted to deport Chadha. He then sued the Immigration and Naturalization Service (INS) and both houses of Congress. The Supreme Court, by a 7–2 majority, overturned legislative vetoes on the ground that such a legislative shortcut without bicameralism and presentment to the President for signature or veto is unconstitutional.

Before the Supreme Court's decision, a commentator observed that the 'use of the veto in that case to override an agency adjudication presented a particularly onerous deprivation of Chadha's due process right to fair treatment by the INS'.[57] After the judgment, another commentator read the whole case in light of the constitutional guarantees, observing that, on the one hand, 'the *Chadha* opinion, in characterizing the legislative veto as an exercise of legislative power, adopted a definition of legislative action which presumes absolute non-delegation' to a subunit of itself.[58] Separation of powers and due process thus constitute barriers against the excesses of the legislative branch. The *Chadha* decision was soon after applied to invalidate over 200 statues that had attached legislative veto provisions to agency rulemaking statutes.

However, this does not prevent legislation to mandate a period for Congress to comment on it before it goes into effect (and presumably mandate that the agency respond to such comments). If that were the requirement and the agency flouted the requirement, the agency would have violated the procedural law and the action would be overturned by the courts and remanded back to the agency to conform to the statute. Moreover, Congress in 1996 enacted a statute, the Congressional Review Act, which allowed it to disapprove agency rules through an expedited procedure, but one that required both bicameralism and presentment.

[57] KE Johnson, 'Limiting the Legislative Veto: Chadha v. Immigration & Naturalization Service' (1981) 81 Columbia L Rev 1721.

[58] ES McMahon, 'Chadha and the Nondelegation Doctrine: Defining a Restricted Legislative Veto' (1985) 94 Yale L J 1493 and 1497.

III. Case 2—Toys World and Standardless Adjudication (Limiting and Structuring Discretion)

A. Austria

Stefan Storr and Sophie Praniess

According to Austrian law, the distinction between state aid granted under public law and state aid granted under private law is essential. Most aid is granted under private law, as the rules and regulations that apply are less stringent.[59]

Procedural rules can be issued without consulting potential applicants beforehand. Judicial legal protection is provided by civil courts. The competent civil court will review whether the limitation of aid to manufacturers of games priced no more than €50 is in compliance with the law. Article 17 B-VG states that the competency provisions of Articles 10–15 B-VG, which divide legislative and executive powers, may not affect the position of the Federation and the states as the holders of civil rights in any way. The prevailing doctrine in Austria concludes that private sector administration (*Privatwirtschaftsverwaltung*) should be approached in a fundamentally different way from state administration (*hoheitliche Verwaltung*). Specifically, the principle of legality of Article 18 paragraphs 1 and 2 B-VG does not apply to private sector administration,[60] so state aid granted under private law does not require a dedicated foundation in the law. This type of aid is often given in the form of a contract.

Even though state aid can be granted under public law, there is no requirement that potential applicants must be heard in advance. If the provision granting state aid is issued in the form of an implementing ordinance, the Austrian Constitutional Court does not have jurisdiction. Only administrative courts provide legal protection against the decision of an authority that rejects an application. This decision is issued in an administrative procedure in which parties are able to claim their rights and legal interests.[61] If the administrative court questions the validity of an administrative ordinance, it is legally required to refer the matter to the Austrian Constitutional Court. However, the Austrian Constitutional Court will not annul an administrative ordinance on the grounds that an applicant was not heard with regard to their rights and interests in advance of issuing an ordinance, as there is no legal obligation to do so.

B. China

Xiaowei Sun

The court will probably not endorse the local market players' claim, which is based on the lack of consultation.

[59] See S Storr, 'Allgemeiner Teil' in B Raschauer, D Ennöckl, and N Raschauer, *Wirtschaftsrecht* (4th edn, Manz 2021) 7.
[60] See Storr (n 59) 59.
[61] S 37 AVG.

As regulatory acts, the rules defined by the DE can be reviewed by the court in the light of Articles 53 and 64 of the Administrative Litigation Law[62] by way of exception. Two situations of illegality could arise under the Judicial Interpretation of the Supreme People's Court of 13 November 2017 relating to the application of the Administrative Litigation Law:[63]

- The regulatory act has no legal basis, and illegally increases obligations or restricts rights of citizens, legal persons, or other organizations
- The administrative authority failed to comply with legal approval procedures and publication procedure or committed serious procedural breach

We will focus on the second issue, which concerns the lack of consultation. Before discussing the powers of the court, it is important to note that there are rules in China that require consultation during draft rulemaking.[64] Leaving these rules aside, we can consider a scenario in which there is no legislative provision requiring consultation with stakeholders before adopting any rule or policy. The question is whether the court will deem the lack of consultation a 'serious procedural breach' according to the Judicial Interpretation of the Supreme Court.

In the event of a lack of a legal specification regarding the consultation procedure, in practice, the courts often rely on the concept of 'due process'. As to the content of this concept, the Supreme People's Court explained in its Judicial Interpretation of 2017 that it refers to 'fundamental procedural rights, such as the right to be heard, the right to make observations, and the right to defend oneself'.[65]

Since the year 2000, many administrative decisions have been overturned because the interested party was not given a sufficient opportunity to be heard by the administration and to present all of their arguments before the decision was made. As a result, an intermediate court declared that when a decision is likely to affect the rights and duties of an interested party, their participation in the proceedings is a fundamental element in ensuring the fairness of the administrative procedure. Being heard is an essential condition for the participation of interested parties.[66]

Under the supervision of the Supreme People's Court, the Intermediate People's Court of Beijing developed the concept of 'due process' in a case concerning an administrative sanction.[67] Two principles emerge from its judgment.

First, the substance of the 'due process' principle resides in the requirement to hear the arguments of the interested party before a decision that could undermine his or her rights is taken. 'Due process' is a minimum requirement for procedural fairness.

[62] Regulations on Procedures for the Formulation of Administrative Regulations of 16 November 2001 (行政法规制定程序条例).

[63] ibid.

[64] Art 67 of the Legislation Law, arts 16 and 46 of the Regulations on Procedures for the Formulation of Administrative Regulations.

[65] Supreme People's Court, Judicial Interpretation of 13 November 2017 relating to the application of the Administrative Litigation Law, art 96.

[66] Intermediate People's Court of Nantong, Jiangsu (江苏省南通市中级人民法院), 2015, No 00169 (通中行终字第00169号).

[67] Intermediate People's Court No 2 of Beijing (北京市第二中级人民法院), 2017, No 01-277 (京01行终277号).

Although there may not be a legally defined procedure, the activities of the administration are still subject to procedural limitations. The administration must take appropriate measures in accordance with the principle of 'due process' and is not free to exercise its discretion.

Secondly, the participation of the interested party in the administrative procedure is necessary to ensure the principle of 'due process' is upheld and that the procedure and its result are fair. In order to participate in the procedure, it is important that the interested person has a complete and fair understanding of the facts and interests involved. They should be able to make observations and present their arguments. Participation should not be reduced to a mere formality.

However, these principles were established in a case involving litigation over an individual action. As stated in Case 1, there is no precedent for the court to review a regulatory act, such as an individual act, on procedural grounds.

Indeed, courts are very hesitant to review a regulatory document on procedural grounds, as they know that a procedural breach may cause the document to be invalidated in its entirety. There are no rules allowing the courts to validate an act that is vitiated by a procedural breach, in such a way as for the review of individual acts.[68]

In practice, courts allow authorities to correct procedural breaches after the fact. For example, a local traffic authority imposed a speed limit without consulting the public. The court validated the act, stating that the procedural breach did not impinge on the effects of the act since the authority had published its decision in the local press.[69]

C. Czech Republic

Gabriela Blahoudková

First of all, it should be noted that in the Czech Republic there is generally no legal right to be awarded grants from public budgets.[70] Providers of grants thus have wide discretion to determine the rules for awarding them. Setting up a number of grant calls can also be highly variable. It is therefore difficult to challenge the grant call in court as it is primarily up to grant providers to decide which types of projects they want to support and under what conditions.

In the Czech Republic, grant rules are not usually published in any standardized form of administrative activity, such as an administrative regulation or a measure of

[68] Art 74 of the Administrative Litigation Law specifies two cases in which a court can declare the unlawfulness of an individual act vitiated by a procedural breach, but not annul it:

(1) The annulment of the unlawful act can be seriously prejudicial to the State's interests or those of the public;

(2) The procedural breach is slight and does not have a real impact on the plaintiff's rights.

[69] Intermediate People's Court of Qiannan Buyi and the Miao Autonomous Prefecture, Guizhou Province (贵州省黔南布依族苗族自治州中级人民法院), 2017, case No 27-6（黔27 行终6 号）.

[70] See s 14(1) of Act No 218/2000 Sb, on budgetary rules (the act regulating the financial management of the state, that is, also the provision of grants from the state budget), and s 10a (2) of Act No 250/2000 Sb, on budgetary rules of territorial units (the act which regulates the financial management of municipalities and regions, that is, also the provision of grants from their budgets).

general nature. Instead, they are typically published without being bound by any procedures, as a call for applications for a grant. This call describes the grant conditions in detail, including the types of projects or activities that will be supported based on the relevant call, the persons or entities for which the grant is intended, and other relevant information.[71] At the same time, the conditions for awarding the grant are specified in detail. These parameters are then included in the administrative decision on awarding the grant, or the decision makes reference to them, at least to the appropriate extent. Alternatively, the parameters may be included in a public contract that replaces this decision.[72] In this respect, the law does not contain any procedural rules that would make it necessary to consult the stakeholders. From the point of view of Czech law, the DE's statement that 'there is no legislative provision requiring it to consult stakeholders before adopting any rule or policy' is correct. In the case of a dispute before the court, the fact that the conditions of the grant were not consulted with the stakeholders in advance would be irrelevant.

As explained above, the rules for awarding grants cannot be challenged directly in court. For one thing, they are not published in a standardized form of administrative activity, so there is no specific procedural tool (type of action) with which to challenge them. Additionally, the rules do not represent an immediate intervention in individual public rights, so protection through a subsidiary action in administrative justice, a so-called action against an illegal administrative intervention, cannot be sought either. What is important is that such an intervention in the rights of an applicant would potentially be represented by an administrative decision (i.e., an individual act) that rejects a specific application. In this respect, the Act on budgetary rules provides for two possible outcomes: one, there is a procedural decision—including discontinuance of the grant application procedure if the application was filed by a person who does not fall within the pool of eligible applicants or if the application is incompatible with the subject of the call;[73] and second, it is a decision on the merits—dismissal of the application[74]. Both types of decision can be challenged before an administrative court. It would then also be possible, within the action brought, to dispute the setting of the grant conditions in the call. Regarding the specific objections that could be made to the grant conditions, it must be reiterated that it would not be possible to object successfully that the conditions had not been discussed with stakeholders (prospective applicants) in advance; the duty to consult does not follow from the law. In general, the court would only have limited room for a review of the conditions; in fact, according to present case law, administrative courts can only sanction conditions that are 'unreasonable and clearly unacceptable in a democratic state respecting the rule of law'.[75] Discriminatory conditions are an example of such conditions.

It can be concluded that TW's direct action contesting the grant conditions would not be admissible; the action against a decision regarding TW's application for a

[71] See s 14j of the Act on budgetary rules, and s 10c of the Act on budgetary rules of territorial units.

[72] A decision is made in cases where the grant is provided from the state budget; a public contract is awarded where the grant is provided from the budgets of territorial self-governing units. We will consider only the situations where the grants draw on the state budget, as in this scenario.

[73] See s 14j(4)(b) and (d) of the Act on budgetary rules.

[74] See s 14m(1) of the Act on budgetary rules.

[75] See the judgment of the Supreme Administrative Court of 23.5.2018, File Ref No 6 Afs 8/2018-37.

grant—grounded merely in the arguments presented (the absence of preliminary consultations)—would be dismissed.

D. European Union

Edoardo Chiti

In the specific context of the EU legal order, this hypothetical case may be understood to refer to a situation in which an EU primary legislation adopted by the European Parliament and the Council requires implementation by the Commission. Unlike the typical cases of subordinate rulemaking envisaged by Articles 290 and 291 TFEU, however, such primary legislation does not explicitly delegate or authorize the Commission to exercise implementing regulatory powers. The 'rules of practice' mentioned in the summary of the case seem to be administrative rules unilaterally adopted by the Commission. They predefine the criteria to which the award of grants by the Commission itself is made subject, including a requirement that games should not cost more than €50. In this way, the rules of practice cannot be considered purely internal administrative regulations. Instead, they provide guidance to applicants on how the Commission will apply the relevant primary legislation.

The nature of the 'rules of practice' deserves some attention. As unilateral administrative rules with external effect, they differ from the various soft-law measures widely used by the Commission and other EU administrations, such as European agencies, to guide applicants' behaviour. The overall function of soft-law measures used by EU administrations to guide private actors' behaviour is to provide advice to applicants, marketing authorization holders, and other interested parties on the most appropriate way to fulfil their obligations under primary EU legislation. Given their function, their legal status is that of measures inherently in tension between the form of non-binding provisions and the substance of rules de facto affecting and conditioning private parties' behaviour. The rules of practice adopted by the Commission in this hypothetical case, instead, do not simply clarify the appropriate way of fulfilling obligations laid down in primary EU legislation with a view to ensuring the smooth implementation of existing rules. Rather, they establish the rules through which the Commission will exercise the power stemming from the basic act to award grants for new games. In other words, the rules of practice structure how the Commission performs the executive tasks granted to it by primary legislation. Given their function, they should be classified as binding both on the Commission, as self-assumed obligations designed to regulate the exercise of implementing power, and on applicants, whose applications will be assessed on the basis of the criteria established by the rules of practice.

The legal dispute before EU courts would revolve around two main interconnected issues. One concerns the validity of the rules of practice adopted by the Commission, particularly their compliance with the relevant primary legislation, while the other concerns the failure to consult with stakeholders.

Regarding the first issue, one may assume that the ECJ would dismiss the argument that the disputed measure is invalid. One of the principles developed in the case law on executive rulemaking since the early 1970s and consolidated over the years is that the

Commission has wide powers of discretion and action. Once the basic regulation has laid down the essential rules governing a certain matter in particular, the Commission may be conferred with a general implementing power without having to specify the essential components of the delegated powers.[76] The Commission may therefore add new elements, such as general criteria that must be adhered to in implementing tasks.

The second issue would be addressed by the ECJ in a rather formalistic manner, referring to the existing sources of EU administrative law. The ECJ would refer to the circumstance that the requirement to consult in rulemaking procedures is not a general obligation under EU law, as it is not established by any EU general legislation, such as a code of administrative procedure, nor does it stem from the principle of the rule of law or other general principles of EU law as currently developed by the EU courts. While EU political institutions and administrations must respect the overarching principle of the rule of law, which includes a number of constitutional guarantees, such as the principle of effective procedural and judicial protection, these constitutional protections mainly relate to due process and defensive procedural guarantees. Interest representation mechanisms, that is to say, procedural guarantees concerning the exercise of rulemaking powers, have so far not been addressed in ECJ case law. Despite many attempts by applicants seeking to extend the right to be heard to general measures, the ECJ has consistently held that the right to be heard only applies to acts of direct and individual concern to the applicant. The only obligations to consult incumbent on EU authorities are those specified in the article upon which the rulemaking measure is based.[77] Accordingly, in a situation like the hypothetical case here, the ECJ would uphold the Commission's decision to adopt a number of implementing criteria without consulting the stakeholders because no formal rule imposes mandatory consultation in this case.

E. Germany

Lilly Weidemann

The court would probably not find a breach of a duty of consultation in this case.

According to prevailing opinion, the participation and consultation of affected parties in administrative rulemaking procedures are not required unless expressly prescribed by law.[78]

[76] Case C-240/90, *Germany v Commission*, ECLI:EU:C:1992:408.

[77] See, for example, Case C-104/97, *Atlanta AG and others v Commission of the European Communities and Council of the European Union*, ECLI:EU:C:1999:498, § 39.

[78] Federal Court of Justice, Judgment of 2 October 1986—III ZR 99/85–, juris para 14; Higher Administrative Court of Rhineland-Palatinate, Judgment of December 2nd, 1985—10 C 26/85, NVwZ 1987, 243–46, 243 et seq; D Kallerhoff and T Mayen, 'VwVfG § 28' in P Stelkens, HJ Bonk, and M Sachs (eds), *Verwaltungsverfahrensgesetz* (10th edn, CH Beck 2022) para 28; opposing view: F Hufen and T Siegel, *Fehler im Verwaltungsverfahren* (Nomos 2021) para 743; H Pünder, 'Democratic Legitimation of Delegated Legislation–A Comparative View on the American, British and German Law' (2009) 58(2) The International and Comparative Law Quarterly 353–78, 374 ff.

A duty to consult does not arise from section 28 APA, since this provision only requires the affected party to be heard before an administrative act is issued.[79] Prevailing opinion also denies the requirements for analogous application.[80] The justification is seen in the orientation of section 28 APA towards individual legal affection, as clearly expressed in paragraphs 1 and 2 no 4[81] of the provision. In addition, specific legislation, insofar as it contains consultation rules, has very different forms, ranging from the informal consultation of individual professional associations to broad public participation as in construction planning law as a specific form of democratic participation. In view of the generally strict nullity resulting from failure to adhere to special statutory consultation obligations when setting standards, subject to the provisions of specific legislation on irrelevance, these heterogeneous standards do not provide a sufficient basis for drawing analogies.[82]

The Basic Law does not prescribe consultation with affected individuals before issuing administrative rules either. Article 103 paragraph 1 of the Basic Law[83] only establishes the right to be heard in court. Also, the general principle of the rule of law arising from Article 20 paragraph 3 of the Basic Law[84] does not require the participation of the affected parties in the standard-setting procedure itself. Rather, their rights are sufficiently guaranteed by the fact that they have the opportunity to seek judicial protection against measures taken against them by the authority on the basis of the statutory instrument.[85]

The opposing view objects that subordinate acts frequently interfere directly with the rights of individuals.[86] The principle of 'protection of basic rights by means of procedures' (*Grundrechtsschutz durch Verfahren*) would require at the very least that those directly affected by the subordinate act be consulted.[87]

However, even according to the latter opinion, the obligation to consult would probably not apply in the present case. According to section 28 paragraph 1 APA, before an administrative act affecting the rights of a participant may be executed, the latter must be given the opportunity to comment on the facts relevant to the decision. However, the rights of the participant are not infringed if approval of the requested grant establishes a right of the participant for the first time, as this does not interfere

79 As seen in L Weidemann, 'Germany' in chapter 6 para. III in this book, the scope of application of the APA is limited to administrative proceedings aimed at issuing an administrative act or concluding a public law contract in accordance with its s 9. In addition, s 28 para 1 APA provides that before an *administrative act* affecting the rights of a participant may be executed, the latter must be given the opportunity of commenting on the facts relevant to the decision (emphasis added).

80 J-P Schneider, 'VwVfG § 28' in F Schoch and J-P Schneider (eds), *Verwaltungsrecht* (CH Beck August 2022) para 34 with further references.

81 According to s 28 para 2 no 4 APA, a hearing may be omitted when not required by the circumstances of an individual case and in particular when the authority wishes to issue a general order or similar administrative acts in considerable numbers or administrative acts using automatic equipment.

82 Schoch and Schneider (eds) (n 80) para 34.

83 Art 103 para 1 states: 'In the courts every person shall be entitled to a hearing in accordance with the law.'

84 Art 20 para 3 Basic Law: 'The legislature shall be bound by the constitutional order, the executive and the judiciary by law and justice.'

85 Higher Administrative Court of Rhineland-Palatinate, Judgment of 2 December 1985—10 C 26/85—10 C 26/85, NVwZ 1987, 243–46, 243 et seq.

86 Hufen and Siegel (n 78) para 743 ff.

87 M Trips, *Das Verfahren der exekutiven Rechtsetzung* (Nomos 2006) 173 ff.

with the previous legal position of the party involved. Such an encroachment is to be recognized if the administrative act changes the previous legal position of the party involved to his disadvantage, or imposes a legal obligation on them, especially if it requires them to do or refrain from doing something. On the other hand, it is not enough if the issuance of an administrative act that is intended to grant a legal position is rejected.[88]

It should be noted that if the consent of other bodies is legally required for the adoption of a statutory instrument, one that has been adopted without the required consent is invalid; according to prevailing opinion, this also applies to other forms of participation.[89] This is because the applicable constitutional provisions which stipulate that statutory instruments may only be issued by the authorized bodies of the executive with special statutory authorization and only within the framework defined by the legislature,[90] which must determine the content, purpose, and scope of the authorization it grants to issue statutory instruments in the law (cf. Article 80 paragraph 1, sentence 2, Basic Law). In addition, it may also regulate the procedure to be followed by the legislator in enacting the law. For example, it may—within the limits of the Constitution—provide for the consent of other constitutional bodies or even weaker forms of participation (participation, consultation, agreement) by other bodies, organizations, or experts. Such statutory provisions are also part of the authorization to which the legislator is bound. Its power to legislate derives exclusively from the legislator and is limited from the outset in accordance with the statutory provisions.[91] However, this reasoning does not apply where the legislator decided not to prescribe any form of participation in the rulemaking process.

F. Hungary

Lilla Berkes and Balázs Szabolcs Gerencsér

The rules of practice referred to in the example are precisely the kind of rules that may be subject to the jurisdiction of administrative courts to review 'administrative acts of general scope to be applied in a specific case and not falling under the scope of the Act on law-making'. As this provision does not yet have a case law, we can only speculate. One important question is whether the DE has been given the power to adopt such rules. If it makes rules behaving like legislation without such authorization, this may raise the question of unconstitutionality and may even be annulled by the court. In the case of legal consequences, the court can also decide on its scope (*ex tunc, ex nunc, pro*

[88] Federal Administrative Court, Judgment of 14 October 1982—3 C 46.81—BVerwGE 66, 184; see K Ritgen, 'Section 28' in H-J Knack and H-G Henneke (eds), *Verwaltungsverfahrensgesetz: VwVfG* (9th edn, Wolters Kluwer 2010) para 8; R Engel and M Pfau, 'Section 28' in T Mann, C Sennekamp, and M Uechtritz (eds), *Verwaltungsverfahrensgesetz* (2014 Nomos) para 32, in each case with further references concerning the state of the dispute.

[89] Federal Administrative Court, Order of 25 October 1979—2 N 1/78, NJW 1980, 1763–65, 1763.

[90] Federal Constitutional Court, Order of 2 June 1964 - 2 BvL 23/62 –, BVerfGE 18, 52-65, at 59.

[91] Federal Administrative CourtOrder of 25 October 1979— – 2 N 1/78 –, BVerwGE 59, 48-56, at 48.

futuro).[92] The court can also say that these rules are not considered to constitute a law (if there is no mandate to adopt them as a law); additionally, the court examines the legality of the decision taken and the criterion (the €50 limit) in the decision does not follow from the law and therefore annuls the decision. But since the claim expressly relies on the failure to consult, the relevant question here would be whether consultation is compulsory (whether there is a legal obligation to consult, there is a legal provision creating such an obligation), and what importance the legislation itself, which provides for it, attaches to consultation. If there is no legal consequence for failure to consult, or if consultation is not provided for in the legislation in the first place, the courts would not assess the failure to consult, either in relation to the decision or the rules.

G. Italy

Leonardo Parona

In the Italian legal system, after the enactment of the general law on administrative procedure in 1990, procedures for distributing economic benefits of any kind (such as the grants awarded for new games by the DE in the given case) are regulated, in general terms, by Article 12 of the aforementioned Law No 241/1990.[93]

More precisely, according to Article 12(1), the granting of subsidies, financial aid, and the award of economic benefits of any kind to public and private individuals and entities is subject to the prior determination of the criteria and procedures for awarding grants. These are established by the public administration awarding grants in accordance with the relevant laws. The second paragraph adds that effective compliance with the established criteria and procedures must be evident from the reasons provided by the administration for each individual grant award decision.

Sector specific legislation establishing economic benefits (such as parliamentary legislation allowing the DE to award grants to toy manufacturers for greater environmental awareness in the given case) can, of course, further specify the procedures for establishing the criteria and the procedures for awarding grants.

[92] Act I of 2017 on the Code of Administrative Court Procedure, s 92(1): 'The court shall annul the administrative act with retroactive effect as of the date of its communication, if a) the administrative act is null and void or invalid on grounds specified by law, or has an essential deficiency as to form for which it is to be considered not to exist, b) the infringement caused by the violation of substantial rules of the preceding administrative procedure cannot be remedied in the action, c) the administrative organ based its act solely on legal provisions not applicable in the case, or d) amending the administrative act is not allowed. (2) If justified by the protection of public interest, legal certainty or an especially important interest of the persons affected by the judgment, the court shall set aside the administrative act, indicating the exact date when it becomes ineffective. The annulment referred to in the Act must be understood to refer also to setting aside.'

[93] For a detailed analysis on this topic see A Police, 'Prevedibilità delle scelte e certezza dell'azione amministrativa' (1996) 2 Diritto amministrativo 697 ff, who argues that art 12 cannot be considered to have 'general application' since it is limited to disbursements for which the administration does not receive any direct economic advantage (ie a price), and only to those in which disbursement criteria have not been directly determined by the legislator, but rather by the public administration itself. In broader terms, see A Police, *La predeterminazione delle decisioni amministrative. Gradualità e trasparenza del potere discrezionale* (Edizioni Scientifiche Italiane 1997).

The acts through which public administrations establish criteria and procedures for awarding grants, such as the rules of practice adopted by the DE in this case, qualify as general administrative acts. Procedures leading to the adoption of these types of acts, however, are excluded from the scope of application of the rules on participation established by Law No 241/1990, as specified in Article 13(1).

Moreover, Article 12 of the law does not require public administrations to consult the public before establishing criteria and procedures for awarding grants. The only requirement is that the procedures and criteria conform to the organic law and other special laws applicable to the proceeding authority. It is therefore within the boundaries prescribed by the latter normative framework that public administrations can exercise their discretion when adopting this type of general administrative acts. The underlying idea is that, by exercising discretion at an early stage (through the adoption of a general administrative act), the administration is subsequently bound when deciding on the awarding of grants to specific individuals. This ensures that the adoption of individual measures is substantially bound and non-discriminatory.

As a consequence, a public administration is obliged to consult the public or allow participation before adopting a general administrative act only if mandated by a specific primary or secondary law provision—a requirement which, however, is quite infrequent with regard to this type of acts.

In our case, for instance, when Parliament decided to grant public money to toy manufacturers that promote greater environmental awareness in children under the age of 10, it could well have required the DE to consult stakeholders before establishing any rules of practice or deciding how to award the grants. Parliament could have even allowed the consultation to include submissions of written observations by the general public, not just the most representative stakeholders. Moreover, the DE itself could have chosen to conduct consultations voluntarily, as sometimes occurs at the ministerial level in Italy.[94]

We ought nonetheless to stress that the rules of practice could not be challenged in court by stakeholders, nor by TW, for the mere lack of consultation in the absence of a specific rule mandating such consultation.

It may be useful to add that the rules of practice, as well as any equivalent general administrative act, could be challenged if they appear patently unreasonable or if they establish criteria and procedures for awarding grants that are manifestly disproportionate, illogical, or discriminatory.[95] However, successfully proving such grounds for unlawfulness, especially in cases involving acts of general application and with wide discretion—as in the given case—is a difficult task for a claimant seeking judicial review. Moreover, Italian administrative courts tend to be quite deferential in this regard. As a consequence, TW could surely try to argue that the rules of practice (and the rejection of its application) are unlawful, since it might be considered unreasonable—and therefore an abuse of power under Article 21-*octies* of Law No

[94] For a list of public consultations conducted by the Ministry of economics and finance (both on normative acts and on general administrative acts), see <https://www.mef.gov.it/comunica-con-noi/consultazione/index.html#> accessed 23 November 2024.

[95] On the direct judicial review of general administrative acts (in particular notice of tenders or of public competitions) see Council of State, Plenary Meeting, 29 January 2003, No 1.

241/1990—not to consult any stakeholders before establishing the criteria and procedures for awarding grants. Nonetheless, it is indeed improbable that a court would consider this argument sufficient to declare the rules of practice patently unreasonable and, consequently, to quash them or issue an injunction ordering the DE to reopen the consultation phase.

H. Netherlands

Jacobine van den Brink, Louise Verboeket, and Veerle van Waarde

In the case at hand, the DE establishes rules of practice, including one whereby it would not award grants for any game costing more than €50 (or the equivalent in another currency). Under Dutch law, these rules of practice could either qualify as a general binding regulation (*algemeen verbindend voorschrift*) or as a policy rule (*beleidsregel*). A request for judicial review (*beroep*) cannot be directly lodged against a decision containing a general binding regulation or a policy rule as laid down in Article 8(3)(a) of the GALA. However, since the grant application of TW is rejected, we have a single-case decision (*decision*) under Dutch law.[96] A claim for judicial review can, in fact, be lodged against a single-case decision. In an action against the single-case decision before the administrative courts, TW could argue that (the establishment of) the formulation of a general binding regulation or policy rule is incompatible with the law or a general principle of law. This procedure is called incidental review (*exceptieve toetsing*) and allows general binding regulation and policy rules to be reviewed indirectly. Because of this, it is not possible to bring an action against a breach of the rules of practice in a civil court.[97]

Under Dutch law, there is, in principle, no obligation for public authorities to consult the parties concerned (*belanghebbenden*) prior to the establishment of general binding regulations and policy rules.[98] There is, however, a practice whereby the parties concerned are consulted before establishing regulations. Consultations can take different forms. Sometimes, ministries will approach people directly, while on other occasions they will have recourse to online consultations. These two forms are generally used when an Act of Parliament (*wet in formele zin*) is adopted. It is also possible to submit general binding regulations and policy rules for consultation, but this is not a legal obligation. In the procedure against the rejection of the single-case decision, TW could argue that the rules of practice are in breach of the principle of due care (*zorgvuldigheidsbeginsel*)[99] because the parties concerned have not been consulted. We

[96] Art 1:3(2) GALA: 'The meaning of a single-case decision is: a decision which is not of a general scope, including the rejection of a request of such a decision.'

[97] Supreme Court 9 July 2010, ECLI:NL:HR:2010:BM2314 (*Staat/Vreemdelingenorganisaties*); Supreme Court 22 May 2015, ECLI:NL:HR:2015:1296 (*Privacy First/Staat*); and Supreme Court 3 June 2016, ECLI:NL:HR:2016:1049 (*SCAU/Universiteiten*).

[98] Commissie Europeanisering algemeen bestuursrecht VAR, *Europa en het algemeen bestuursrecht. Burger en bestuur in de gemeenschappelijke rechtsorde* (Boom juridisch 2021) 98.

[99] This principle is laid down in art 3:2 GALA: 'When preparing an order an administrative authority shall gather the necessary information concerning the relevant facts and the interests to be weighed.'

are not aware of any precedent where such an argument has led to a general binding regulation or policy rule being declared non-binding or set aside by a Dutch administrative court.

There is an exception to the rule that public authorities are not required to consult the parties concerned prior to the establishment of general binding regulations and policy rules. This exception applies when the DE decides that the uniform public preparatory procedure (*uniforme openbare voorbereidingsprocedure*) is applicable. This procedure is described in Division 3.4 GALA. The Explanatory Memorandum of the GALA states that the uniform public preparatory procedure is used in the preparation of a decision that will affect a large number of parties or other persons, unknown to the administrative authority (*bestuursorgaan*).[100] This procedure is usually applicable in the drafting of single-case decisions, but it can also be used in the formulation of general binding regulations[101] or policy rules. In this case, the administrative authority must deposit the application of the general binding regulation or the policy rules as laid down in Article 3:11(1) GALA. Thus, the application or draft must be published in a government-issued gazette, stating who will have the opportunity to present their opinion (*zienswijze*) and how they may do so.[102] Article 3:15(1) GALA states that the uniform public preparatory procedure is, in principle, to be used for the parties concerned. However, Article 3:15(2) GALA allows statutory regulation or administrative authority to provide other persons with the opportunity to state their opinions. In principle, the time limit for stating a view is six weeks.[103] This shows that a claim based on the lack of consultation of stakeholders will only be likely to succeed if the uniform public preparatory procedure is provided for in a statutory regulation or an order of the DE. As far as we are aware, the uniform public preparatory procedure is never applicable in the preparation of grant schemes in the Netherlands.

I. Norway

Eivind Smith

The question leaves some doubt about the formal character of the relevant 'rules of practice'. If they fall under the definition in APA section 2 letter c, cf letter a, they should clearly have been submitted for public (written) hearing according to the provisions of APA section 37. In that case, the absence of a hearing constitutes a clear violation of the APA. If, on the other hand, the ministry only decided how to handle the budgetary grant in a situation, the 'rules' fall outside the scope of APA chapter VII. This would normally be the case even if those 'rules' were issued in the form of an internal instruction legally binding on the relevant agent or agency.

100 *Kamerstukken II* 1999/2000, 27023, 5, p 6.
101 See eg art 43(1)(a)(b) Fertiliser Act (*Meststoffenwet*) and art 4 Water Authority Act (*Waterschapswet*).
102 Art 3:12 GALA in conjunction with art 12 Publication Act (*Bekendmakingswet*).
103 Art 3:16(1) GALA.

In both cases, the 'rules' may have been issued, for instance,

- because the ME presupposes the need to handle a number of applications substantively greater than the money available,
- by reference to the need to simplify the internal procedures during an initial 'test period',
- in order to favour less expensive toys; or
- because the environmental impact of the measure would be greater if attached to toys available to a broad group of consumers than to more exclusive toys.

Provided we are faced with a formal 'regulation', TW might succeed insofar as the lack of public hearing may have had a bearing on the outcome of the individual case. As the 'rules' may have a solid basis in the government's policy as informed by the budgetary grant, however, this need not at all necessarily be the case.

If the 'rules' are regarded solely as internal orders, the outcome of the case would not depend on the absence of a public hearing at all, but rather on the rationale for the individual outcome, considering the underlying intentions of Parliament in allocating funds for the respective goal.

J. Portugal

Rui Guerra da Fonseca

The Portuguese CPA establishes forms of participation for stakeholders in the procedure leading up to the approval of administrative rules as a normative implication of the principles of democracy and respect for individuals' rights and legitimate interests in administrative procedure (Articles 98 ff). Before examining specifics, however, it is important to clarify the legal meaning of the facts of the case.

The parliamentary legislation in question does not seem to expressly mandate administrative rules for its implementation. Nevertheless, (i) it grants the DE the instrumental power to award grants to achieve legislative goals ('to promote greater environmental awareness in children under the age of 10'); (ii) and without further specifications, which are, of course, needed to render such legislation operative. This qualifies as a legislative call and authorization (albeit with implicit aspects) for administrative rules of execution. So, the 'rules of practice' or 'standards' established by the DE, which are normative and applicable to those falling within their scope of application, qualify as a set of administrative rules or regulations for procedural purposes (Article 135 CPA).

Hence, public notice of the beginning of the procedure must be publicly announced on the DE's website so that any stakeholder can come forward and be recognized as an interested party. This recognition grants them the right to make suggestions (Article 98 CPA). Furthermore, the regulation appears to directly and immediately affect the rights and legitimate interests of individuals, so its preliminary version must undergo a prior hearing (*audiência prévia*) lasting no less than 30 working days. All individuals qualified as an interested party may participate in these proceedings, which can be in written or oral (Article 100/1 and 2 CPA).

In cases where the number of interested parties is excessive, the prior hearing may be replaced with a public consultation. The preliminary version of the regulation will be published in the Official Gazette (*Diário da República*) and on the DE website, inviting suggestions and observations for a duration of 30 working days (Articles 100/3 al. *c)* and 101.º/1 and 2 CPA).

If these procedural steps are not adhered to, the regulation will be deemed invalid (Article 143/1 CPA).

Therefore, TW has a legitimate grievance and may file a claim before an administrative court of law. TW is directly and immediately affected by the administrative rules in question because establishing the price of the eligible games alone excludes the company away from any public grant. Consequently, TW can seek a declaration of illegality regarding the rules in question with general effects (Articles 72/1 and 73/1 al. *a)* CPTA). Moreover, TW seems to have already applied for the grant anyway, and can concurrently challenge the decision denying the grant (an administrative act) along with the aforementioned claim of illegality.[104]

The regulation in question has no deadline for claims. While other procedural shortcomings before approval only allow for a challenge to the legality of administrative rules within a six-month deadline, the omission of public consultation is deemed too significant to be bound to such a strict time limit by law (Articles 144 CPA and 74 CPTA).

The court could strike down the administrative regulation in question on these grounds, and, since it is an administrative set of rules mandated by law, the court could also (theoretically) order the procedure to be repeated, this time with public consultation, to ensure that the final regulation complies with the law (Articles 137 CPA, and Articles 77, 95/4, and 5 CPTA). However, the court cannot dictate the specific provisions of the regulation, which is discretionary, so separation of powers draws the line there, but it can establish the essential criteria that must be met. Furthermore, TW can also request an interim measure to suspend the administrative rules in question due to the likelihood of their being unlawful while this main lawsuit is pending (otherwise, the funds for these grants could be depleted before the main dispute is resolved).[105]

K. Sweden

Patricia Jonason and Björn Forssén

The government has, in principle, an obligation to consult stakeholders, public authorities (national and local), and other actors, according to section 2, chapter 7, Instrument of Government, for the preparation of its business (*beredningskravet*).[106] This obligation

104 See art 4/2 *b)* CPTA.
105 See art 130 CPTA.
106 See also Holmberg and others (n 48) 326; Eka and others (n 48) 326–28.

applies to the government's participation in the legislative process, including the creation of a bill, and to its own internal business, such as adopting regulations or decisions. In this second case, the obligation to consult stakeholders is less stringent. Moreover, the Constitution distinguishes between the stakeholders who should be consulted. The consultation of public authorities is mandatory, while for other actors, it occurs 'as necessary'. The government has a certain margin of manoeuvre to decide how the consultation should be carried out. The forms for the preparation demand are not thoroughly described, but the obtaining of opinions must generally be made in writing and, in the end, it is the government itself which, under constitutional responsibility, decides the scope of the preparation activity in each case.[107]

TW may have the right to bring a claim to the Supreme Administrative Court (*Högsta förvaltningsdomstolen*) against the rules enacted by the government on the basis of the Act (2006:304) on Judicial Review of Certain Government Decisions (ie on *rättsprövning*). The appeal is open when the government's decisions entail determining the individual's civil rights and obligations in the meaning of Article 6(1) of the European Convention of Human Rights.[108]

For the purposes of this exercise, we will assume (although it is not certain in reality) that the issue at hand falls within the scope of this provision.[109]

According to the above-mentioned judicial procedure, the Court examines the lawfulness (*laglighet*) of the decision but is not competent to control its appropriateness (*lämplighet*), as it is the case otherwise for ordinary appeals.

This means that the competent court, the Supreme Administrative Court, may only overturn a decision when the decision is unlawful (*strider mot en rättsregel*). However, a decision is not invalidated if the error is clearly insignificant to the decision. The question that needs to be addressed in this case is whether the violation of this procedural rule could have affected the outcome.

In the case at hand, if by chance the court considers that the decision was unlawful and that the error was significant enough to affect for the outcome of the decision,[110] which is unlikely, the court could simply overturn the decision or revoke it and send the case back to the government.

[107] See Eka and others (n 48) 327.

[108] See also Holmberg and others (n 48) 220.

[109] In order to assess whether art 6 ECHR is applicable, it must be discerned whether the dispute may be considered real and serious, relates to a right under national law, and whether the right is a civil one: Wiweka Warnling-Nerep *Rättsmedel Om- & överprövning av förvaltningsbeslut* (Jure 2015) 203. See HFD 2011 ref 10; HFD 2011 ref 22; HFD 2016 ref 49; HFD 2018 ref 46; and HFD 2019 ref 10.

[110] In some cases of judicial review, the Supreme Administrative Court has concluded that the obligation to communicate under s 2, chapter 7 of the Instrument of Government was not fulfilled, and that it was not obvious that this procedural error had no bearing on the decision. The government's decisions were therefore revoked by the court and the question remanded to the government for new treatment, See Holmberg and others (n 48) 328, where the following cases by the Supreme administrative court are mentioned: RÅ 1992 not 161; RÅ 1996 ref 28; RÅ 2008 not 110; and RÅ 2008 not 111.

L. United Kingdom

John Morison and David Mark

There is no statutory requirement for consultation in this instance. In the absence of such a requirement, or any procedural legitimate expectation of consultation in the light of past practice,[111] it is not clear that the courts would infer such a requirement. The application by TW relates to a product selling for slightly more than the sum specified in the DE's rule of practice. The parliamentary statute is presumably silent on the specifics of the scheme, leaving a degree of discretion to the DE as to values and such like. As mentioned above, it is a basic rule of administrative law that an authority entrusted with discretion under statute must retain of itself the option of exercising that discretion on a case-by-case basis (the 'no fettering' rule). In instances where, for example, there may be a limited number of licences to grant or places on a scheme to offer, or as here, resources to offer, the courts will be unwilling to fetter the discretion of the administrator. Of course, before an issue of fettering is raised, it must be clear that the policy itself is lawful, and that it is not so rigid as to amount to an unacceptably high threshold for individual applications to cross. This may encourage TW to argue that that the scheme is ultra vires the empowering statute and that TW should have been given an opportunity for a fair hearing, and that the absence of this amounts to procedural impropriety. Decision-makers should not 'shut their ears'[112] to individual applications solely on the grounds that an authority has a particular policy in place. TW's challenge would depend on the reasonableness of the authority's decision, and related arguments over whether DE had failed to take into account TW's representations, as well the proportionality of the decision.

M. United States of America

Jeffrey Lubbers and Giacinto della Cananea

In the United States, since the DE's action would be a 'rule', in the sense in which this term is intended by the APA, it would normally have to follow the APA's notice-and-comment procedures before establishing a binding requirement such as this one. However, the APA also contains some exemptions from notice and comment. One is for 'rules of agency organization, procedure, or practice'. However, since this rule contains a substantive requirement (no grants for toys above €50), a court would be likely to determine that the procedural rule exemption would not apply. But there is also an exemption for rules relating to 'public property, loans, grants, benefits or contracts'. This so-called proprietary exemption would apply here. It is a very broad exemption that may have made sense in 1946 when the APA was enacted, but today would allow many important rules of great public interest to be issued without public comment.

[111] See further *Council of Civil Service Unions v Minister for the Civil Service* [1985] AC 374.
[112] *R (A) v Home Secretary* [2021] UKSC 37, [2021] 1 WLR 3931.

So, even though Congress has not heeded calls to eliminate it, many agencies have voluntarily agreed not to invoke it, and in other statutes (relating to government contracts, benefits, and property (eg national parks)), Congress has explicitly required notice and comment in those statutes. But, based on the question's facts, there is no mention of that, so the exemption from notice and comment would apply, and the rule could go forward.

IV. Case 3—The Rules of the Game: Allocating Few Licences (Duty to Consult Stakeholders; Protection of Expectations)

A. Austria

Stefan Storr and Sophie Praniess

As explained above, the authority is not legally obliged to consult with arcade operators before determining the licence validity period. The legality of the authority changing the award criteria after the application period has started must be analysed critically under Austrian law. Amendments to concession documents are not legally prohibited. However, the Federal Concessions Award Act (BVergG Konz)[113] defines a set of rules that must be observed in the event of subsequent amendments to the concession documents. Section 23 para 4 BVergG Konz stipulates[114] that the authority must inform all bidders of any amendments to concession documents. The information should be provided in such a ways as to grant the bidders sufficient time to adjust their bids, if necessary. Under no circumstances is it permitted to subsequently modify the subject matter of the concession, the award criteria, or the minimum requirements.

In addition to the Federal Act on the Award of Concession Contracts, general legal principles may also apply. These include the principle of legitimate expectations and the principle of fair competition. In a society organized according to the rule of law (*Rechtsstaat*) the protection of legitimate trust and expectations of those subject to the law is indispensable. Dispositions made in justified reliance on abstract provisions of the law cannot be subject to change due to subsequent amendments. Therefore, all bidders can trust that the rules under which they submitted their tender will not be changed after submission. The authority can only lawfully change the rules and conditions of an ongoing tender if all potential bidders are informed individually and given sufficient time to modify their submission accordingly. Otherwise, the change is deemed 'unfair' and therefore unlawful.

In this case, the authority published an amendment to the award criteria during the application period. As not all potential bidders were informed in due manner and time, it must be concluded that the competent court would consider the changes made by the authority unlawful. Whether further violations of the applicable regulations have occurred is of secondary importance in the event of a violation of the fundamental principles, since for this reason alone the action is not lawful.

[113] Federal Act on the Award of Concession Contracts (Federal Concessions Award Act 2018—*BVergGKonz* 2018), Federal Law Gazette I No 65/2018—*Bundesgesetz über die Vergabe von Konzessionsverträgen* (*Bundesvergabegesetz Konzessionen 2018—BVergGKonz 2018*), Orig Vers: BGBl I No 65/2018—implementing Directive 2014/23/EU of the European Parliament and the Council of 26 February 2014 on the award of concession contracts, OJL 94 28.3.2014, p 1.

[114] In case of negotiations.

B. China

Xiaowei Sun

The court would probably not endorse the local market players' claim about consultation, but it may endorse the one based on the challenge to the addition of the prevention plan, declaring this act unlawful and recommending the authority remedy the irregularity.

As a regulatory act, the new regional policy can be reviewed by the court in the light of Articles 53 and 64 of the Administrative Litigation Law[115] by way of exception. Two situations of illegality could arise under the Judicial Interpretation of the Supreme People's Court of 13 November 2017 relating to the application of the Administrative Litigation Law:[116]

- The regulatory act has no legal basis, and illegally increases obligations or restricts rights of citizens, legal persons, or other organizations;
- The administrative authority failed to comply with legal approval procedures and publication procedure or committed a serious procedural breach.

With respect to the first issue, the addition of the prevention plan can be considered to increase obligations as defined by the Judicial Interpretation. In 2018, the Supreme People's Court published a guiding case[117] concerning a rejection of medical payment by Social Insurance.[118] In this case, the local Social Insurance Office made a rule regarding the reimbursement of medical care. According to this rule, local citizens must choose public hospitals when seeking medical care outside their city if they are to receive reimbursement. The court considers this rule to be a restriction of citizens' rights and believes it is not in compliance with the superior regulation. The regulatory act made by the local Social Insurance Office would be declared unlawful, and the authority would have to make a new decision on the plaintiff's claim.

Regarding the second issue, as stated in Case 2, courts are very hesitant to review a regulatory document on procedural grounds. If there is no legal obligation to consult, the court will not consider the lack of consultation when determining the validity period of the licence.

[115] Intermediate People's Court of Qiannan Buyi and the Miao Autonomous Prefecture, Guizhou Province (贵州省黔南布依族苗族自治州中级人民法院), 2017, case No 27-6（黔27 行终6 号）.

[116] ibid.

[117] Supreme People's Court, October 30, 2018, Guiding Case No 1. 'Guiding cases' refer to cases with judgments that have taken legal effect and which have gained wide public attention, deal with basic principles of law, and are representative, complicated or novel, or any other cases that have a guiding function. Guiding cases play a significant role in unifying the application of legal standards, providing guidance in the judicial work of lower courts. The jurisprudence of the Supreme People's Court does not constitute Guiding cases, which are chosen by the Court for instructional purposes. Judgments are public documents published by the courts. They can be viewed on the website of the Supreme People's court: https://wenshu.court.gov.cn accessed 23 November 2024. But only Guiding cases, commented on by the Supreme Court, with special juridical value attributed to them by the Organic Law of the People's Courts (art 18).

[118] Intermediate People's Court of Rizhao, Shandong Province (日照市中级人民法院), 2016, case No 2016-11-9, (鲁11行终9号).

C. Czech Republic

Jiří Rajchl

By way of introduction, a few remarks should be made on the general framework of the case description itself from the point of view of national circumstances. The delegation of licensing powers to regional authorities would need to be regulated in more detail by a law that would define how, and through which type of process, applicants are to be selected and licences granted. In the Czech Republic, the power to set procedural rules independently cannot be delegated to territorial self-governing units. It is desirable that territorial self-governing units be able to influence or exclusively determine whether or to what extent, if any, they consider it appropriate to allow slot machine arcades in their territory. Local derogations may relate only to an interest in the material resolution of the issue at hand, but the procedural aspect of the decision-making must remain uniform throughout the state and is reserved to the law.[119] A law would apply to the decision-making, namely the Code of Administrative Procedure, which contains special procedural rules for the selection of applications.[120] However, these special rules can only be applied in situations where another law allows it. To this end, a law delegating the competence to determine the number of slot machine arcades to regions, as well as the rules for their location, would be necessary. The law should also allow the application selection process. The problem is that laws do not typically use the aforementioned special procedural regulation to distribute property that is limited in quantity. Applications are not decided collectively but rather on an individual basis, with time and capacity being key factors. This approach cannot be regarded as optimal. To resolve the case, we must assume that the best administrative procedure for selecting the best applications will be followed. This procedure is conducted according to the Code of Administrative Procedure, but the regions have autonomous powers. In reality, the number and location of slot machine arcades are determined by municipalities through a municipal bylaw adopted within their autonomous powers. A decision to grant a licence to operate a slot machine arcade is issued in administrative proceedings within delegated powers, but this is not a competition.[121]

In the legal system of the Czech Republic, it is currently not possible to challenge a future selection policy in court. Applicants for licences, whether they are still considering submitting an application or have already submitted one along with all the necessary supporting documents, do not have the right to sue in the administrative justice system for any reason. An action against a decision cannot be taken before a decision is made; similarly, an action for failure to act is not available since non-activity is not pleaded. The third type of action, against an intervention by an administrative authority, cannot currently be used in the early stages of proceedings in which an

[119] Art 2(3) of the Constitution stipulates, *inter alia*, that state authority may be asserted only in the manner provided for by law. The concept of state authority is to be interpreted as including public authority in a broad sense.

[120] See s 146 of Act No 500/2004 Sb, the Code of Administrative Procedure.

[121] Act No 186/2016 Sb, to regulate gambling.

administrative decision is to be made afterwards. This type of action is more universally applicable in terms of forms of administrative activities, but it is of a subsidiary nature. In administrative justice, defence through these kinds of claims is admissible only against alleged encroachment upon rights already taking place. It cannot be used as a precaution aimed at merely preventing encroachment upon the rights themselves.[122] The law regulating administrative justice provides for the institution of a motion for an interim measure, but it can only be used in the context of an action that has already been filed. Therefore, it does not extend the possibility of defending one's rights in administrative justice on its own. All applicants will be subject to the procedural limits described above, regardless of their factual objections. Furthermore, when deciding on the conditions for the licence parameters, it is important to consider whether the selection criteria and other requirements should be published as part of a call for licence applications or if they should be previously regulated in a municipal bylaw. The inclusion of normative provisions in legal statutes would further limit the scope of judicial review in regard to basic criteria.

A further consideration, which goes directly to the root of the question, can thus only be made on the assumption that judicial review takes place already based on decisions on the dismissal of applications, that is, where a licence has not been granted, and after ordinary remedies have been exhausted. However, such a construction essentially makes it impossible for successful applicants who have obtained the licence to challenge the limitation of the validity of the licence to a period of two years, because they had been informed of the limited validity in advance, and they entered the competition in full awareness. By submitting their applications, all applicants express their understanding of the conditions and confirm that they have assessed whether or not it may be profitable for them to use the licence from the economic point of view. Actions brought by unsuccessful applicants must therefore have had to do with other parameters. The licence validity period is a parameter that cannot be influenced by the applicants in their projects. Quite the opposite, it is an attribute which is unilaterally set by an administrative authority in its decision. If some applicants are not successful, it must be as a result of other circumstances. In this respect, an objection to the limited licence validity period can hardly become a relevant ground for a review of the lawfulness of the decision. One can only imagine that, given a short period of operation, an applicant cannot achieve positive numbers within the framework of other criteria, such as investment in the slot machine arcades themselves and their surroundings, or commitment to voluntary contributions to the municipal budget. As the two-year limitation applies equally to everyone, no applicants are being given an advantage, and despite the causal link outlined, this could not, therefore, be considered a relevant factor.

If we imagine that there was some form of legal defence against the terms of the competition, a material objection to the limited licence validity period of two years would still not succeed. The administrative authority is not required to consult with potential actors or interested parties when setting parameters. The administrative authority is presumed to have knowledge of the factual background and the needs of the

[122] Act No 150/2002 Sb, the Code of Administrative Justice.

regulated sector. If the entity does not have sufficient knowledge, it has to decide how and to what extent it will acquire or refine the necessary knowledge. If the administrative authority deems it necessary, it may conduct a survey or formal discussion to gather input and arguments. However, it is under no obligation to do so, and the addressees have no legal right to demand it. If a survey or discussion is conducted, it is important that it is not unreasonably selective and allows all potential interested parties, or those with certain characteristics required for participation in the competition, to participate. Therefore, the only potential issue is unfair selection, not whether or not consultations are held.

For many years, licences in the Czech Republic were granted to operate individual slot machines for only 12 months.[123] However, at that time there was a legal right to be awarded the licence. Currently, slot machine arcade licences are granted for a maximum of three years, which suggests that the two-year licence validity period in the scenario presented here would not be entirely inappropriate. Limiting the validity period is in the public interest because it allows people to assess the consequences of conducting such businesses and respond accordingly. Given the potential impact on public order, crime, and the financial behaviour of certain citizens, it is reasonable to maintain the possibility of reassessment and response. Operators do not have to purchase the slot machines; they can simply lease them for a fixed period of time. It should be noted that municipalities have the right to ban the operation of slot machine arcades in their territory through a municipal bylaw.

Slot machines are permitted for negative reasons, offering a legal alternative to illegal use. There may also be positive financial reasons, but these must never outweigh the protection of other public interests. A strict approach to this type of business activity is supported by both the public and the judiciary, which conducts reviews. Since the case at hand concerns this type of business, and the point is not to suppress the existing operation but to potentially expand it, complaints from potential applicants would not attract much attention or sympathy. Nor would the courts be motivated to look for new legal constructions that would allow review.

A relevant ground for objection is the change of criteria during the application period. Conditions have changed after some applications may have already been submitted, while others may still be in progress. Applicants may have already spent time and money preparing their application and supporting documents, or they may have already started negotiating with other parties. While the content of the prevention plan may not be the only factor in the decision, its absence could still be significant, and taking another parameter into account will be important for the ultimate outcome. Preparation of the prevention plan may be cross-referenced to other measures in the application, so it is not just an isolated elaboration of an additional document. It is completely unacceptable to change the conditions during the application period, regardless of any social or rational justification for the new parameter. This unacceptability cannot be justified in any way. Furthermore, the argument that there is no legal right to be granted a licence and that the administrative authority is not obliged to grant all five licences, or any at all, does not help the case.

123 Compare s 18 of Act No 202/1990 Sb, to regulate lotteries and other similar games, which was in effect until the end of 2016.

However, the fundamental issue is again a procedural one. A change in the criteria during the application period can only be challenged after a decision has been made on the rejection of an application or a decision not to grant a licence after all ordinary remedial measures have been exhausted. It is therefore necessary to wait until the procedure has been completed, unless the administrative authority terminates it earlier. If conditions change during the application period, the results of the selection procedure will be annulled in court. However, there is no legal way to challenge the licence awarding process during the administrative procedure; that is, for example, immediately after a new criterion has been set. There is no preventive defence available. The administrative authority's course of action would, in any case, be wrong. If the other conditions are met, it is possible to claim compensation for any damage caused by maladministration.[124]

D. European Union

Edoardo Chiti

In the EU context, this hypothetical scenario could be reformulated as one in which EU legislation, whether a regulation or a directive, is implemented by the administrations of Member States rather than those of the EU. National authorities are responsible for granting slot machine arcade licences and for creating the rules that govern the procedures for issuing them. The approach to implementation followed by the EU legislator is therefore one of 'indirect execution', a method established since the early years of the European Community (EC), assigning primary responsibility to the administrations of Member States while leaving room for them to interact with the Commission and allowing the EC institutions to set the rules of the administrative framework to be applied at the national level. Seen in this perspective, this method of implementation substantially promotes an EU-driven indirect administration rather than purely decentralized execution, as suggested by studies which clearly distinguish between exclusively direct and exclusively indirect modes of policy delivery. In this specific case, the EU legislator has adopted legislation by sector that directly affects the powers of national administrations when implementing this specific EU policy, but it has left Member States, and in particular their competent national authorities, with the power to regulate the procedures for carrying out their tasks.

Since the hypothetical case involves indirect execution, the validity of the measures adopted by the national authority would be challenged before the competent national court. The ECJ, however, might intervene in the litigation if asked to provide a preliminary ruling on interpretation, with a view to assessing the compliance of the national measures with EU law. The preliminary reference, for example, might be used to ask two questions concerning interpretation: whether the EU legislative provisions granting national authorities the power to regulate the licensing procedure should be interpreted as

[124] Under Act No 82/1998 Sb, regulating liability for damage caused by a decision or maladministration when exercising public powers.

requiring those authorities to consult with stakeholders, and whether they exclude the possibility of national authorities adding new elements such as a prevention plan once the procedure and application period have started.

Regarding the first question, we suggest that the ECJ would not consider the lack of consultation a violation of EU law. As we observed in relation to the previous hypothetical case, the duty of consultation in rulemaking procedures is not considered by the EU courts as a general obligation under EU law because it is neither established by EU general legislation, nor can it be derived from the general principles of EU law as currently developed by the ECJ. The obligation to consult applies to all components of the EU administrative system, which includes EU, national, and mixed structures functionally oriented to implement EU laws and policies, although this obligation only applies when sector-specific provisions require it. Admittedly, there are many examples of EU regulations and directives granting rights to participate in rulemaking proceedings before national regulatory bodies. However, this is not the case in the specific circumstances of this hypothetical case, as it is clear that national authorities can put in place their own licensing procedures. It should be noted that a regulatory choice that allows national authorities to exercise their discretion would be fully consistent with the EU's commitment to respect the administrative autonomy of Member States. In the absence of any obligation to consult in EU positive law, the ECJ would most likely consider the decision by a national regulatory authority to allocate licences through a procedure that does not do so to be compliant with basic EU legislation.

The ECJ would also answer the second preliminary question, asking whether the national authority should not have added the prevention plan to the selection criteria after the opening of the procedure, in the negative. The EU principle of legitimate expectations, as developed by the ECJ in its well-established case law applicable to both EU and national authorities,[125] requires that economic players to be legally and factually informed ('prudent and discriminating').[126] This extends reasonably to situations where applicants are required to add new elements to their applications after the procedure has started, provided that the new requirement does not alter the equal treatment and competition between the applicants in the procedure. Moreover, if a legitimate expectation is found to exist, the ECJ might well give precedence to the overriding public interest of preventing gambling, which is the objective of the addiction prevention plan introduced by the national authority.

E. Germany

Lilly Weidemann

The court would probably reject the local market players' claim insofar as it concerns consultation before setting the licence validity period at two years. As seen in the previous case, according to prevailing opinion, it is not a requirement to consult

[125] Case C-230-231/09, *Hauptzollamt Koblenz v Kurt Etling, Thomas Etling* (C-230/09); *Hauptzollamt Oldenburg (C-231/09) v Theodor Aissen, Hermann Rohaan*, ECLI:EU:C:2011:271, § 74.

[126] See eg Case C-265/85, *Van den Bergh BV et Van Dijk Food Products (Lopik) BV* v *Commission of the European Communities*, ECLI:EU:C:1987:121, § 44.

affected parties in administrative rulemaking procedures unless expressly prescribed by law.[127]

The court would, however, most likely uphold the market players' claim regarding the addition of the prevention plan to the selection criteria after the start of the application period. The court would probably confirm a breach of the subjective right of the applicant to a transparent and non-discriminatory procedure. Amending the selection criteria after the start of the application period would probably be regarded as a breach of the principle of equality and the principle of a transparent and predictable procedure. By publishing the selection criteria, the authority was bound to these admission requirements for reasons of equal treatment and could not subsequently deviate from them.[128] If the authority publishes criteria for obtaining a specific licence, it is generally bound by the announced criteria when deciding on the consideration and evaluation of the applications received. This results in a self-imposed obligation (derived from the principle that the administration is bound by its own acts, *Selbstbindung der Verwaltung*) that makes any subsequent deviation not based on compelling reasons and only disadvantages, or favours some of the applicants, appear to breach the principle of equal treatment (Article 3 paragraph 1, Basic Law) and the requirement of a constitutional, that is a fair, procedure.[129] This self-imposed obligation does not only arise with regard to the first case of application but can already occur with the announcement of a planned procedure by administrative regulation (anticipated administrative practice, *antizipierte Verwaltungspraxis*).[130]

The general principle of equal treatment is enshrined in Article 3 paragraph 1 of the Basic Law, and the requirement of a transparent and predictable course of proceedings stems from the rule of law requirement for fair (administrative) procedures. The essential principles of a constitutional procedure include the right to a fair one.[131]

Since the authority has non-justiciable discretionary powers in the selection of applicants when determining evaluation criteria, procedural safeguards for the selection decision are of particular importance. Only strict compliance with the procedure can justify, with regard to Article 19 paragraph 4 Basic Law[132] and the principle of effective judicial protection which it enshrines, a lower level of control over the substantive decision, which can mean the exclusion of the applicant from the market due to the application of discretionary powers. Fundamental rights are essentially ensured here due to the way the procedure is organized. Only criteria known in advance can sufficiently limit the exercise of discretion and avoid discrimination through hidden decision-making criteria. This means, among other things, that an applicant only has to accept the selection of another applicant if this has occurred in a transparent and non-discriminatory procedure.

[127] See L Weidemann, 'Germany' in this book, Chapter 15, III. E., fn 78 for references.

[128] Administrative Court Hamburg, Order of 20 September 2012—11 W 1658/12, BeckRS 2013, 47973; Administrative Court Cologne, Judgment of 16 October 2008—1 K 4507/08–, para 31, juris.

[129] Higher Administrative Court of North Rhine-Westphalia, Order of 28 February 2013—4 A 500/10–, para 13, juris.

[130] Higher Administrative Court of Bavaria, Order of 4 December 2023—22 ZB 22.2621–, para 14, juris.

[131] Administrative Court Düsseldorf, Order of 18 May 2021—3 L 59/21–, paras 19–20, juris with further references.

[132] Art 19 para 1 sentence 1 Basic Law stipulates: 'Should any person's rights be violated by public authority, he may have recourse to the courts.'

The transparency requirement is intended to ensure, among other things, that all potential applicants are adequately informed about the selection criteria, that they can adapt to them, and that the selection of applicants is comprehensible on the basis of the published criteria and can be objectively justified.

The criteria for a successful application must already be established before the call for applications and must be specified in it. First, this is the only way to enable interested parties to make a well-founded decision as to whether they wish to participate in the concession procedure. Secondly, it is intended to counter the risk of criteria being tailored to individual applicants who are already known. This should be countered from the outset by disclosing all relevant criteria.[133]

The relevant criteria must be formulated clearly, precisely, and unambiguously, both for the fulfilment of the minimum requirements and for the selection decision, and must be known in advance so that every applicant can inform himself properly and understand and interpret their meaning. Every applicant must be able to assess the requirements in order to submit an adequate and the best possible bid under all circumstances.

Disclosure of criteria only at a later stage runs the risk that criteria will be tailored to individual applicants.[134]

F. Hungary

Lilla Berkes and Balázs Szabolcs Gerencsér

The most fundamental operating principle of the Hungarian public administration is that it is subordinate to the law: what the law authorizes it to do, it can and does do; what the law does not authorize, it does not do. There is also an interpretation of this that the public administration is not characterized by flexibility. In the present case, since there is no express provision in the act to consult, most authorities would not consult and, due to the lack of legislative provision, there can be no legal consequences. On the other hand, the fact that it does not consult when drafting procedural rules does not prevent it from asserting the principle of cooperation and that of exercising its powers according to their purpose in the procedure, which are already enshrined in the APA.[135] The conclusion that can be drawn from a combined interpretation of these principles is that the public authority must seek to promote the exercise of the rights of the party, which is fundamentally contradicted if it changes the 'rules of the game' and imposes additional obligations during the course of the

[133] Administrative Court Frankfurt, Order of 27 May 2015—2 L 3002/14.F–, paras 42–44, juris.

[134] Administrative Court Frankfurt, Order of 27 May 2015—2 L 3002/14.F–, paras 45–48, juris.

[135] S 2 (Principle of legality): 'The administrative authority (hereinafter 'authority') shall act on the basis of authorisation by law, exercising its powers within the framework of the law and according to their purpose. (2) When exercising its powers, the authority shall act a) in compliance with the requirements of professionalism, simplicity, cooperation with the party and the principle of good faith, b) complying with the requirements of equality before the law and equal treatment, without undue differentiation and partiality, c) within the time limit specified by law, within a reasonable time.' <https://njt.hu/jogszabaly/en/2016-150-00-00> accessed 23 November 2024.

procedure. The authority's defence is not reassuring in this respect either, as it basically implies an unpredictable application of the law, since it is not clear what the consequences are if someone does not comply with the additional condition. While rulemaking consultation would not be required by the court in the absence of a legal provision to that effect, a new tender procedure would.

G. Italy

Leonardo Parona

The case poses at least two important issues from the perspective of Italian administrative law principles applying to the allocation of scarce public resources. The first concerns the procedure followed by regional authorities for adopting policies such as the one for granting slot machine arcade licences and specifically regarding the issue of participation and the alleged duty to consult stakeholders. The second issue relates to the addition of further requirements (such as the one referring to the prevention plan) to the selection criteria originally established after the application period has already started. This issue can be framed in terms of administrative action departing—in the course of the proceeding—from a prior decision, where the administration had previously established criteria to which it had committed to adhere (namely a change to the 'rules of the game').

As far as the first aspect is concerned, it is necessary to start with the qualification of the act establishing the policy and the procedures for granting the licences in order to determine the legal framework that regulates its enactment. Acts such as the one in question, which are adopted to regulate specific types of situations and cases (and are therefore not abstract in nature), qualify as general administrative acts, even though they concern a potentially indeterminate and unknown number of individuals (at least *ex ante*). As already clarified in the answer to the general and introductory questions, the rules on participation established by the general law on administrative procedure (Articles 7 ff of Law No 241/1990) do not apply to general administrative acts unless sector-specific laws explicitly require it.

As a consequence, in the given case, unless the legislative provision conferring on regional authorities the power to adopt rules on the procedures for granting licences expressly mandates them to conduct public consultations, no obligation to ensure participation can be said to originate from statutory law.

Public administrations can, of course, voluntarily decide, at their discretion, to ensure participation (either establishing this requirement through secondary regulations or following such conduct as an administrative practice). In the given case, however, there is no indication that the regional authority decided to do so. Consequently, a court would therefore endorse the authority's position based on a plain and literal interpretation of the applicable primary and secondary law.

A partial derogation from the solution that has just been outlined comes from judicial construction. It should be noted that, under certain limited circumstances, a minority view in administrative case law has affirmed that public authorities, bound by the principle of due process, might be required to carry out public consultations when the formally general administrative act to be adopted actually affects only a limited number of identified individuals.[136] In this case, however, the duty to consult stakeholders does not apply because the act is a general one but because it substantially produces the same effects as an individual measure.

Coming to the second aspect, it should be noted that changing the rules of the game, both in general terms and in the specific circumstances of the given case, may conflict with several principles regulating administrative action in the broad sense (ie encompassing the adoption of both general and individual administrative acts). These principles have been developed over several decades in administrative case law and, to a significant extent, have been codified both in Article 97 Const, which establishes the principles of impartiality and good administration, and in Article 1(1) of Law No 241/1990, which, among others, includes the principles of publicity and transparency. In 2020, moreover, paragraph 2-*bis* was added to the latter provision, requiring relations between citizens and public administrations to comply with the principles of collaboration and good faith. This addition is particularly relevant to the case at hand, as it provides greater normative support for the protection of legitimate expectations. The new provision, as clarified by the Plenary Meeting of the Council of State, codifies 'a rule of general applicability of administrative action, which is founded in the constitutional principles of impartiality and good administration (Article 97(2) Const)'.[137]

As a consequence, when subsequent administrative action departs from criteria previously established through a general act that was made official through publication, allowing the public to know and rely on them, the administration's conduct might be found to exceed its power, especially if no adequate reasons are provided. If the criteria had been previously established by the enabling legislation itself, or by a normative act (such as a regulation), then the unlawfulness of departing from these criteria would be more easily ascertained by the court and automatically annulled as breaching the law (with no possibility of exemption for the administration unless explicitly provided for by the law).

In the case at issue, the court would therefore endorse the local market players' claim, stating however, that the latter should also challenge the enforcement measure, affirming its unlawfulness for applying a different criterion from the one originally established.

H. Netherlands

Jacobine van den Brink, Louise Verboeket, and Veerle van Waarde

According to Dutch law, holding a slot machine arcade licence (*speelautomatenhalvergunning*) is considered a limited right (*schaars recht*). Since there are only a limited number of licences available, there may not be enough available to satisfy all applicants. As established by the *Speelautomatenhal Vlaardingen* judgment, administrative authorities need to adhere to specific rules when

[136] See Tuscany Administrative Court, Florence, s I, No 214/2017.
[137] Council of State, Plenary Meeting No 21/2021.

allocating such limited rights.[138] These rules are based on the national[139] principle of equality, which in this context serves to create equal opportunities through a level playing field (*beginsel van gelijke kansen*). Put simply, the administrative authority (*bestuursorgaan*) must in some way create room for (potential) applicants to compete for the available limited right (*mededingingsnorm*). The administrative authority must therefore comply with a requirement of temporariness (*tijdelijkheidseis*) and an obligation of transparency (*transparantieverplichting*). As to the temporariness requirement, a limited right may not, in principle, be granted indefinitely, since this would de facto rule out equal opportunities to obtain the limited right. The current holder of the limited right would then have a disproportionate advantage over newcomers wanting to obtain the limited right.[140] As for the obligation of transparency, the authority must ensure an appropriate degree of transparency (*passende mate van openbaarheid*) with regard to the availability of the limited right, the allocation procedure, the application period, and the selection criteria. To this end, the authority must use a means that will allow (potential) applicants to be notified of the upcoming allocation procedure before it starts.[141] The obligation to make room for (potential) applicants to compete for the available limited right may be restricted by the underlying (delegated) legislation. However, it is important to note that such a restriction cannot be so strict as to eliminate all opportunities to compete for the limited right. Furthermore, the (delegated) legislation and/or its Explanatory Memorandum must show that the interest of equal opportunities has been weighed by the legislator and found insufficient to override other interests demanding less, or no, competition.

It is clear that adding the prevention plan to the selection criteria after the application period has already started is a breach of the principle of equality, and specifically the obligation of transparency. Indeed, the obligation of transparency requires the regional authority to publish the selection criteria *prior* to the start of the allocation procedure. The regional authority may clarify its selection criteria after the allocation procedure has started, but this clarification may not amount to the addition of a new selection criterion.[142]

With regard to consulting local market players before fixing a licence validity period of two years, it should be noted that there is no general legislative provision stating that the regional authority must do so. Based on the principle of due care set out in Article 3:2 GALA and the duty to give reasons in Article 3:46 GALA, however, the regional authority is obliged to investigate whether the licence validity period is reasonable, meaning

[138] ABRvS 2 November 2016, ECLI:NL:RVS:2016:2927 (*Speelautomatenhal Vlaardingen*), building on CBb 3 June 2009, ECLI:NL:CBB:2009:BI6466 (*Swiss Leisure Group*).

[139] This means that these rules also apply in strictly national cases. This interpretation of the national principle of equality is, however, inspired by the case law of the Court of Justice of the European Union on the obligation of transparency; see ABRvS 12 April 2017, ECLI:NL:RVS:2017:994. The *Speelautomatenhal Vlaardingen* judgment is thus an example of the voluntary 'Europeanization' of national law.

[140] Building on CBb 15 May 2012, ECLI:NL:CBB:2012:BW6630 (*Zondagavondwinkel Wassenaar*) and CBb 24 August 2012, ECLI:NL:CBB:2012:BX6540 (*Supermarkt Castricum*).

[141] Such as a website or local newspaper. See ABRvS 9 March 2016, ECLI:NL:RVS:2016:661.

[142] See eg CBb 19 December 2007, ECLI:NL:CBB:2007:BC2460; CBb 8 January 2010, ECLI:NL:CBB:2010:BL3125; CBb 21 December 2011, ECLI:NL:CBB:2011:BU9729; and Rb Noord-Holland 18 December 2018, ECLI:NL:RBNHO:2018:11609. See also Opinion of the State Councilor A-G Widdershoven 25 November 2016, ECLI:NL:RVS:2016:1421 (*Speelautomatenhal Vlaardingen*) paras 4.15 and 4.18.

whether it is sufficient for applicants to recover their investments.[143] This obligation requires some form of market research, which may entail a market consultation. Case law shows a high degree of judicial scrutiny on this matter, meaning that the regional authority would have to state sufficient reasons if it did not conduct market research or a market consultation before setting the licence validity period at two years.[144] No such reasons seem to be present in this case.

Now that we have established that both the amendment of the allocation procedure and the absence of a market consultation on the licence validity period are most likely unlawful under Dutch law, the question is how a Dutch court would handle the situation. This depends on the route that the local stakeholders decide to take. The first, most frequently used, route is to apply for a licence and wait for the decision by the regional authority. If it is granted, the applicant will probably only want to appeal the licence validity period. If the licence is not granted, the applicant will probably want to appeal both the amendment of the allocation procedure and the licence validity period, if the ruling leads to a new allocation procedure. In any case, the applicant can lodge a claim for judicial review (*beroep*) against the decision and argue that it was taken in breach of the principle of equality, the principle of due care, and the duty to give reasons. The administrative court will then annul the decision, which will most probably mean that the local authority will have to organize a new allocation procedure for the slot machine arcade licences. Additionally, it is advisable to request the administrative court grant interim relief (*voorlopige voorziening*) in the interlocutory proceedings (*voorzieningenrechter*), suspending the allocation procedure.[145] The second route is to bring an action against the allocation procedure before the civil court. The civil court will probably declare the underlying general binding regulation(s) and/or policy rule(s) illegal (*onverbindend*). It is advisable—and a more commonly used action before the civil court in such cases—to ask the civil court to grant interim relief (*kort geding*), so that the civil court can (temporarily) stop the regional authority going through with the allocation procedure, at least in its current form.[146]

I. Norway

Eivind Smith

Nothing indicates that the licences are issued against financial compensation. We therefore suppose that the example does not refer to a formal tender but simply a

[143] Opinion of the State Councillor A-G Widdershoven 25 November 2016, ECLI:NL:RVS:2016:1421 (*Speelautomatenhal Vlaardingen*) para 6.3.

[144] See eg Rb Den Haag 27 August 2019, ECLI:NL:RBDHA:2019:8907; ABRvS 21 July 2021, ECLI:NL:RVS:2021:1588; and CBb 20 December 2022, ECLI:NL:CBB:2022:821.

[145] Art 8:81(1) GALA. See eg CBb (vzr) 29 July 2010, ECLI:NL:CBB:2010:BN4119; Rb Oost-Brabant (vzr) 19 January 2018, ECLI:NL:RBOBR:2018:279; and Rb Limburg (vzr) 17 December 2020, ECLI:NL:RBLIM:2020:9985.

[146] See eg Rb Amsterdam (vzr) 17 March 2023, ECLI:NL:RBAMS:2023:1529.

process engaged in order to select the beneficiaries of a number of vacant public licences that do not fall under the strict legal regime of public procurements.

Being adopted by virtue of explicit legislative provisions, the 'rules on the procedures for granting such licences' qualify as regulations under Norwegian law by reference to APA section 2 letter c. This entails the obligation to submit a draft version of the rules to a public (written) hearing of interested actors or groups before the regulations are issued.

As presented in the example, however, the conflict does not seem to concern matters of procedure but of substance, namely regarding the licence validity period and the added prevention plan. The court is likely to uphold the authority's arguments regarding both contested measures.

J. Portugal

Rui Guerra da Fonseca

This case must be addressed as an 'as though' scenario since the Portuguese gambling laws[147] establish a clear division of powers between the government and local authorities. In brief, the use of slot machines is considered as a form of gambling only permitted in casinos[148] and the issuance of authorizations and licences falls within the purview of the government, also involving the General Inspectorate for Gambling. Since 2018, municipalities have gained some powers in this area, but only regarding certain activities deemed 'similar to gambling', which do not include slot machines.[149] Consequently, slot machines are not found in bars or restaurants, and the number of casinos is limited.[150] Bearing this in mind, let us proceed 'as though ...'.

The change in regional authority policy, with the resulting increase in the number of licences within the region, appears to be lawful; at least, there is no evidence to the contrary. The same can be said regarding the other aspects of the regulation adopted by the regional authority.

The local market players make two kinds of claims: the first is procedural and has to do with prior consultation; the second is substantive and dual in nature. It concerns the two-year validity of each licence and the addition of a prevention plan with measures to prevent gambling addiction as a criterion for selecting applications for licences after the application period had already commenced.

Regarding the procedural claim, let us bear in mind the discussion in response to Case 2. The administrative rules in the present case do not appear to directly and

[147] See Decree-Law 422/98, 2 December, last amended by Decree-Law 9/2021, 29 January.

[148] See art 4 of Decree-Law 422/98, 2 December. Possible exceptions under special governmental authorization include tourist events and hotels or similar places (art 7).

[149] The main characteristic of these 'similar modalities' is that the prizes are pre-established (like tombola or raffles or lottery): art 159.

[150] In 2018, Law 50/2018 of 16 August established a general framework for the transfer of powers to municipalities, including the issue of modalities akin to gambling. Following this, Decree-Law 98/2018 of 27 November addressed the specifics of the power transfer in this specific sector. The division of powers between central government and the autonomous regions of Madeira and the Azores is more complex and cannot be addressed here.

immediately affect the rights and legally protected interests of the market players: in fact, they need to apply for the licences, and adjudication (or its denial) will come in the form of an administrative act which will express a decision on the distribution of a 'scarce good' to which the market players have no a priori entitlement. Consequently, there is no legal obligation on the regional authority to conduct a prior hearing of potentially interested parties (Article 100/1 CPA). However, the nature of the subject matter of this administrative regulation seems to warrant public consultation (Article 101/1), given its intent to distribute a 'scarce good' with ramifications for community life and the economic opportunities and choices of market players. Thus, there should have been a public consultation,[151] which means that, regarding this procedural aspect, the market players have a valid grievance and could seek recourse before the administrative courts. Since the regulation has no direct and immediate impact on them, they should challenge the administrative acts that determine their individual circumstances (such as denying each licence or establishing conditions they consider unlawful) and concurrently contest the legality of the regulation, seeking to obtain its non-application (even if only in relation to those parts or rules that they deem illegal and detrimental).[152]

On the first substantive claim, regarding the two-year validity period for each licence, the market players could argue that the primary legislation is silent on the matter, so the regulation, being innovative, has exceeded its intended scope, making it illegal due to a lack of legal foundation. But the regional authority could, in turn, argue that this openness was exactly what the legislator intended and that this should be considered an independent regulation with a very broad margin of discretion. The market players would then only be able to challenge the regulation on the basis of unconstitutionality, claiming, for instance, that the two-year time limit disproportionally restricts their fundamental right to economic freedom (Article 61 CRP). This argument does not appear to be strong, however. The primary legislation empowers regional authorities to establish a maximum number of licences, which is in itself a way of granting particularly ample discretionary authority to manage a 'scarce good' in pursuit of, and protecting, public and social interests. And this broad discretion could be interpreted as being sufficient for creative decision-making to safeguard the possibility of other players entering the market or ensuring their periodic renewal, thereby promoting economic democracy (market opportunities). The market players do not seem to have a strong legal argument here. If they had been heard in public consultation on this matter, and the regional authority had maintained the two-year validity period, could they still claim the illegality or unconstitutionality of a material solution such as this? Probably not.

[151] See 'Portugal—Case 2', section III.J in this chapter.

[152] The CPTA establishes different means of challenging operative regulations directly and immediately (without the need for any act of adjudication) and those which are not; the first can be challenged alone. The courts can declare them illegal with general effects; while the latter can only be challenged incidentally along with the administrative act of application, and the courts may only determine their non-application in relation to a particular case. Only the Public Prosecutor can use the first type of challenge against the latter type of regulations (art 73 CPTA). On this, see JC Vieira de Andrade, *A Justiça Administrativa* (19th edn, Almedina 2021) 217 ff; M Aroso de Almeida, *Manual de Processo Administrativo* (2th edn, Almedina 2021) 114, 252–53.

Regarding the second substantive claim, the issue of retroactivity arises in relation to the introduction of the prevention plan as a scoring criterion for applications. Without a doubt, the regional authority's addition of this new criterion after the application submission deadline began constitutes a new criterion. It is, therefore, a retroactive change to the regulation since the deadline had already occurred.[153] Moreover, this new criterion imposes additional demands on applicants as it is a new item that they must include the applicants that have already submitted their applications will feel compelled to do it again now with a plan, and the ones that still have not drafted one will have to the take this criterion into consideration. All in all, the new criterion is retroactive and makes the situation for applicants more difficult.

The retroactivity of regulations is illegal when they impose duties, penalties, or burdens that adversely affect rights or legally protected interests, or change the conditions for their exercise (Article 141/1 CPA). This is precisely the case in hand. The objection raised by the regional authority, suggesting that applicants have enough time to add a prevention plan to their applications is irrelevant. All applicants must have had equal opportunity and sufficient time available since the opening of the procedure. And the argument that the prevention plan is only one of the selection criteria does not stand either: since it is one of the criteria, it is relevant. Introducing this criterion not only violates the prohibition of retroactivity (Article 141/1 CPA) but it is also in breach of several principles that bind administrative activity: the protection of the rights and interests of persons (Article 4 CPA), equality (Article 6 CPA), and possibly even impartiality (Article 9 CPA), and good faith (Article 10 CPA).

Faced with this situation, and considering the previously mentioned challenges regarding administrative rules, an administrative court could deem these changes inapplicable and order the administrative authority to make decisions concerning the licences without taking the prevention plans into consideration.

K. Sweden

Patricia Jonason and Björn Forssén

We suppose that the county administrative board (*länsstyrelsen*), which is a national regional public authority, has been given jurisdiction to decide on regional rules regarding slot machine arcade licences.

As an administrative authority under the government (*förvaltningsmyndighet under regeringen*), the county administrative board has an obligation to

> investigate the cost of the rules and other consequences in necessary scope as well as giving Government's authorities, municipalities, regions, organisations, the business community and others who are affected in terms of costs or in any other significant way, the opportunity to comment on the matter and the impact assessment,

[153] See art 12 of the Civil Code (considered a general rule on retroactivity regarding all areas of law).

before deciding on regulations or general advice (section 124, paragraph 1of regulation (2024:183) on Impact Assessments).[154]

For the purposes of this exercise, we suppose that the local market players have standing before the court.

The court would not endorse the arguments of the public authority that there is no legal requirement to consult stakeholders before setting the licence validity period, as the obligation to consult is laid down in the regulation (2024:183) on Impact Assessments.

However, the court would probably not consider the lack of consultation. Indeed, as H Wenander puts it: 'The obligation to hear individuals is … diffuse (*obestämd*) and seems to a large extent to be left to the authority's free discretion.'[155] Furthermore, the same author states that

> the requirement for impact assessments as outlined in the regulation is not focused on safeguarding individuals' legal security, but rather on financial management and general administrative policy issues with cost-related and other consequences.[156]

Wenander concludes that '[i]t is hard to imagine situations where a court could examine the application of the impact assessment requirements more closely in relation to an individual's interest in legal security'.[157]

So, the court would probably disregard the arguments brought by the appellants. Instead, the Parliamentary Ombudsman (officially *Riksdagens ombudsmän* or—in ordinary parlance—*Justitieombudsmannen*, JO) would be a possible forum for this kind of issue, albeit only for the purpose of lodging a complaint in principle.[158] The Ombudsman has the power to make critical observations but not to overturn a decision.[159]

L. United Kingdom

John Morison and David Mark

Schemes for awarding licences are familiar territory in discussions of how fairness requirements operate within their context. The leading authority, *McIness v Onslow*

[154] *Förordningen (2024:183) om konsekvensutredningar.*

[155] (Our translation) Henrik Wenander, 'Rättssäkerhet i förhållande till myndigheters föreskrifter och allmänna råd' in Richard Sannerholm and Karl Djurberg Malm (eds), *Rättsstaten i den svenska förvaltningen—en forskningsantologi*, OOS 45 (Statskontoret 2022) p 37.

[156] ibid.

[157] ibid.

[158] The JO examines, for example, setting out of guidelines by public authorities through the lens of the principle of objectivity (*saklighet* and *opartiskhet*). See eg JO 2021/22, p 115, where the JO investigated the National Board of Health and Welfare's (*Socialstyrelsens*) model for adopting national non-binding guidelines for the care of depression and anxiety from the requirements of objectivity.

[159] The JO's decisions, of course, in practice influence authorities and municipalities' work with the drawing up of recommendations, which the officials are supposed to abide by.

Fane,[160] relates to a boxing manager applying for a licence. Here Megarry VC sets out three categories of applications. First, there are licensees who may lose their existing licence, and here the common law will have maximum protections; secondly, there are those who are applying for the renewal of their licence, and here there are significant, although reduced, protections from the common law; and thirdly, those who are making an application for a licence for the first time, where the procedural protections are lesser.

In this instance there is a current licence holder who is being required to apply within what is effectively a new scheme. This does not amount to forfeiture as such, although the timing of the scheme and the new conditions involved suggests that the existing licence holder may have his licence effectively removed. This would seem to suggest that a relatively high degree of procedural protection is appropriate including, for example, advance notification of the proposed decision; an opportunity to make oral and written submissions before the decision is taken; and reasons for any subsequent decision. While there seems not to be any statutory requirement in the primary legislation that there should be a consultation process, it may be considered that there is procedural legitimate expectation of consultation as the new scheme has the potential to remove existing licences and so affect the livelihood of the existing stakeholder. The likelihood of this would be increased if there were a practice of consultation with stakeholders, and this were now being disregarded. The new condition, relating to the prevention plan introduced after the application period has begun, is something that may increase the chances of a successful challenge of the reasonableness of the authority's decision. There is limited notice of this change, and it might reasonably be thought to be something that stakeholders should have been consulted about and allowed sufficient time to make their case. The Authority's contention that this is only one of several selection criteria, and may not indeed be necessary, suggests a lack of transparency about the criteria for making the decision and perhaps indicates that 'good administration' is not served by a scheme where the grounds for challenge are not clearly articulated. If and when the Authority is required to give reasons for its decision (and although there is no universal requirement for this, it would seem likely the common law would require this in the interests of fairness)[161] it is difficult to see the Authority being able to provide reasons that are 'adequate and intelligible'.[162]

This scenario also suggests a potential overlap with the common law and human rights principles. The local market players are engaged in an economic activity and could well be construed as a property right in terms of Article 1 of Protocol 1 ECHR and, on foot of that, a 'civil right' within the meaning of Article 6 ECHR. Were the court to be persuaded of this not only would the common law procedural protections be available but so too would the protections under the Human Rights Act 1998.[163] Finally, the Authority may wish to offer the idea of 'public interest' in support of its prevention plan, and so suggest that common law rules of fairness might have reduced

[160] [1978] 1 WLR 1520.

[161] See further *R v Home Secretary, ex parte Doody* [1994] 1 AC 531.

[162] See Forbes J in *R v Mental Health Tribunal, ex p Pickering* [1986] 1 All ER 99, 102.

[163] S 6 of the Human Rights Act requires that public authorities act in a way that is compatible with the Convention rights that have effect under the Act.

application. While 'national security' may have some undoubted power to limit procedural entitlements, it less clear that this unarticulated claim of public interest would be persuasive.

M. United States of America

Jeffrey Lubbers and Giacinto della Cananea

In the United States, the federal government would presumably have the authority to regulate arcade games under the Interstate Commerce Clause, Article I, section 8 of the Constitution, which gives Congress the power 'to regulate commerce with foreign nations, among states, and with the Indian tribes'. In the US federalist system, it would be possible, though rare, for the federal legislation to authorize devolving regulatory authority to the states. The question speaks of regional authorities. This could mean regional offices of the federal agency or it could mean the states. Each state has its own administrative procedure act, though most of them are somewhat similar to the federal APA (as observed in the answer to the first introductory question). For this question, it is assumed that federal administrative law applies.

There are several questions here. The first is whether the agency should have allowed notice and comment on the change from one to five licences in the geographical area. This would be a rule, and there does not appear to be an applicable exemption from notice and comment, so the answer would be 'yes'. However, to challenge that procedural violation in court someone would have to have standing. Maybe citizens opposed to raising the number of licences would be able to show they were adversely affected, but the market players would hardly be able to show they were hurt by the expansion (unless they had argued for more than five). But, as to the temporary nature of the licence and the late additional requirement, they would have standing and would have a good claim for a procedural violation.

They could also argue that the policy changes were arbitrary and capricious. According to the ruling of the Supreme Court in *FCC v Prometheus Radio Project*, this standard of review, prescribed by the APA for review of rules and policy changes, requires

> that agency action be reasonable and reasonably explained. Judicial review under that standard is deferential, and a court may not substitute its own policy judgment for that of the agency. A court simply ensures that the agency has acted within a zone of reasonableness and, in particular, has reasonably considered the relevant issues and reasonably explained the decision.[164]

What the Court applied is a test of reasonableness that implies a somewhat deferential approach.

Nevertheless, the agency's rationale could be deemed to be unreasonable for failing to take into account the challengers' legitimate concerns, although the action might

[164] 592 US 414, 423 (2021).

not be substantively reviewable at all if the court found that the legislation provided the agencies with complete discretion as to the number of licences to allow. Even so, it might not provide discretion on the length of the licences or the selection criteria. The facts do not provide enough information to know what law applied to this decision, but it is probable that at least the procedural challenge should still be heard. The remedy would be a remand to allow an opportunity for notice and comment. After that, substantive challenges would still be available. If the challengers prevailed, the agency would have to start over.

V. Case 4—The Newcomer Who Was Not Consulted (Duty to Consult All Stakeholders Equally)

A. Austria

Stefan Storr and Sophie Praniess

As there is no legal requirement for a hearing, the authority exercises its discretionary powers to determine whether consulting with stakeholders is necessary for adequate decision-making. When discretionary powers are granted, the authority may choose from several equally permissible decisions. If, as in this case, the authority has the power to act but is not required to do so, the Austrian legal system refers to the 'discretion to act' (*Handlungesermessen*). However, discretionary power granted to the authority does not imply entirely unrestricted decision-making. The authority must exercise its discretion in accordance with the law in order for its actions to be lawful.

The need for consultation may arise for two reasons. First, the authority must conduct 'fundamental research' to determine the factual basis for regulation. The composition of cost parameters in regulated industries may be part of this research. If a hearing is necessary to obtain the required information, then all potentially interested parties must be given the opportunity to participate. If the DoT conducts research to determine the composition of cost parameters in applied tariffs, it is not only obliged to consult with the incumbents but with all the parties potentially involved. The DoT's argument that it is not obliged to hear the parties before making a decision loses its validity as soon as hearings are initiated with at least one party. The Austrian legal system—in this respect—has adopted an all-or-none approach.

The second reason why it may be necessary to consult all parties is to ensure equality. It is unfair to allow only two out of three stakeholder companies to comment, as this may lead to discrimination against the third. This limitation poses a potential violation of the principle of equality.

Both a lack of required fact-finding and a violation of the principle of equality may lead to the conclusion that the authority has taken an arbitrary approach to regulation. The Austrian Constitutional Court will declare an arbitrarily imposed tariff order null and void (annulment of the contested tariffs). The procedure to be followed depends on the specific details of the tariff order.

In addition to the annulment of the contested tariff order, the Federation is responsible for any damage caused by the unlawful action of persons acting as its organs while executing the laws.[165]

[165] Art 23 B-VG, s 1 para 1 Public Liability Act (*Bundesgesetz über die Haftung der Gebietskörperschaften und der sonstigen Körperschaften und Anstalten des öffentlichen Rechts für in Vollziehung der Gesetze zugefügte Schäden* (*Amtshaftungsgesetz*—AHG)), Orig Vers: BGBl No 20/1949.

If BT receives financial compensation, this could be considered a public liability. However, the principle of the priority of primary legal protection against state acts[166] requires that such action be taken before secondary liability applies. Compensation for damages is not due if the injured party could have avoided the damage by recourse to a legal remedy or by filing a complaint with an administrative court and appealing to the Supreme Administrative Court.[167] Therefore, in the case of *BT vs DoT*, a claim of liability against the state will not be successful until a primary remedy has been sought.

B. China

Xiaowei Sun

The court may rule in favour of BT, declare the DoT's actions unlawful, and strike down the contested tariffs.

In China, rail transport is not open to private providers. The service is provided by China Railway,[168] which is a state-owned company. There are still no rules relating to rail infrastructure charges. However, the government has very recently declared its intention to open up the rail transport market.[169] As for the telecommunications market, there will be rules in this area. We can cite the Regulation on Telecommunications[170] as an example.

Article 27 of this regulation states that the Information Industry Department, Financial Department, and Authority for Prices will decide the infrastructure charges, which will then be approved by the State Council. Such an act may constitute a 'major administrative decision' within the meaning of the Provisional Regulation of April 20, 2019, on Major Administrative Decision-Making Procedures.

According to Article 6 of this text:

> Major administrative decisions shall be made under the principle of democratic decision-making, opinions shall be fully solicited from all parties, and it shall be guaranteed that the people participate in decision-making through various channels and forms.[171]

[166] S Storr, 'Primärrechtsschutz und Sekunddärrechtsschutz in Europa' in A von Bogdandy, PM Huber, and L Marcusson (eds), *Handbuch Ius Publicum Europaeum IX* (CF Müller 2021) 178, 229.

[167] S 2 para 2 AHG.

[168] 中国国家铁路集团有限公司.

[169] State Council, Notice on Railway Construction Planning (关于进一步做好铁路规划建设工作的意见), 15 March 2021.

[170] 中华人民共和国电信条例.

[171] 作出重大行政决策应当遵循民主决策原则，充分听取各方面意见，保障人民群众通过多种途径和形式参与决策。

Article 12 of the same text states that,

> The decision-making authority shall prepare draft decisions with extensive and in-depth investigation and research, comprehensive and accurate information, and full consultation and coordination.[172]

According to the Judicial Interpretation of the Supreme People's Court relating to the application of the Administrative Litigation Law, courts can verify whether an administrative act complies with a superior regulatory administrative act.[173] Thus, the court can review the DoT's action in the light of these provisions. If the court finds that the opinions were not 'fully solicited from all parties' and that the DoT did not prepare its draft decision after 'full consultation and coordination', the decision on new tariffs may be judged unlawful.

C. Czech Republic

Jiří Rajchl

The essential question for any judicial review of the tariffs is the form of the regulation. If it is implemented as an administrative regulation, the legal system of the Czech Republic does not yet afford individuals a direct defence. A motion to repeal subordinate legislation may only be filed by entities or groups of persons defined by law. In this case, the government, a group of at least 25 deputies or at least 10 senators, the regional council, the ombudsman, and a person who has filed a constitutional complaint against the interference of a public authority in constitutionally guaranteed rights and freedoms.[174] BT would first have to wait and obtain an act of enforcement, for example by not following the tariff and applying different fares. This would result in a decision imposing a fine or disqualifying it from carrying out its activities. However, it is extremely risky to secure an act of enforcement in this way simply for the purposes of proceeding further, and entrepreneurs would probably only do so if they knew that they were only facing a fine and not the restriction of, or disqualification from, activities, or in a situation where adherence to the new tariff would be incompatible with their other activities.

If an administrative decision on the fine were actually obtained, it would be possible, after the exhaustion of ordinary remedies, to challenge the decision by taking administrative action. This would allow the decision to be challenged on the grounds that it was based on an unlawful executive regulation. Although the administrative court does not have the power to repeal the executive regulation, it may refuse to apply it on the grounds that it contravenes the law, with consequences only for the case in question.[175] However, the likelihood that a court would not apply an executive regulation containing the tariff is very low if the reason for not doing so is not the unlawful

172 决策承办单位应当在广泛深入开展调查研究、全面准确掌握有关信息、充分协商协调的基础上，拟订决策草案。

173 Art 148 of the Judicial Interpretation.

174 See s 64(2) of Act No 182/1993 Sb, on the Constitutional Court.

175 See A 95(1) of the Constitution.

content of the tariff itself but only the violation of the principle of equality in preceding consultations. Prior consultations with stakeholders are not a legal requirement, and they are thus a voluntary action by the administrative authorities responsible for the content of the executive regulation.[176] Inequality during the drafting of an executive regulation would not necessarily result in the denial of the application of the instrument before administrative courts or the annulment of the statutory instrument by the Constitutional Court. There would be some possibility if the specific requirements of the incumbents were clearly reflected in the content of the statutory instrument, and, at the same time, they made BT's position more difficult, or if BT's position was worsened by the fact that, unlike the requirements of other entities, its potential requirements were not incorporated in it.

If a tariff only sets out fares and does not lay down any other rules for rail transport, it should be considered a measure of a general nature. The law could explicitly determine the form of the tariff. However, even in the absence of such explicit determination, the suggested form should be preferred as the most appropriate for the nature of the administrative activity in question. According to standard procedures, issuing a general measure involves publishing a draft of the measure, and then allowing the opportunity for objections and comments.[177] If the DoT had only communicated with the two incumbents prior to the publication of the draft, but BT had been given the opportunity to present its standpoint in the process prior to the issuance of the final tariff, the preceding omission would be rectified. However, we infer that in this case BT had no opportunity to respond to the draft tariff at all. In the Czech legal system, such a situation could occur where a law relating to the relevant sector, such as the Railways Act, would exclude the application of general regulations contained in the Code of Administrative Procedure, stating that a draft is not published, but a general measure is issued in simplified proceedings without the possibility of raising objections. The addressees of the public body concerned have legal recourse against general measures without the need for an intermediary act for the application of a law.[178] The existence of a specific type of action, like the general regulation of proceedings, significantly expands the possibilities for procedural objections, including the objection of inequality in the right to be heard.

When an administrative authority unlawfully excludes the possibility of objections and comments, the court would endorse BT's argument and annul the measure of a general nature. In a case where objections and comments are excluded by law in simplified proceedings, the situation would be more complex. It is likely that the inequality created would be perceived more intensely than in the case of a legal regulation, although the rationale of this difference in approach is not entirely clear. The external view may be that while it is common for statutory instruments to be drafted without involving the recipients of the rules, an administrative authority must reflect the reality of the environment and may thus monitor and consult the situation in the

[176] Except as provided for under the Government Resolution on the General principles on regulatory impact assessment, see art 5.3 of Government Resolution No 922 of 14 December 2011, as amended on 1 July 2023.

[177] See ss 171 and 172 of Act No 500/2004 Sb, the Code of Administrative Procedure.

[178] See s 101a Act No 150/2002, the Code of Administrative Justice.

field. However, in the case of a general measure, the right of stakeholders to take part in procedures and to be treated equally by the administrative authority is expected as a matter of course. The chances of annulment would be increased by the fact that at least some of the requests or arguments of the two incumbents were heard or that BT's requests and arguments might have been considered in a similar way had BT been approached. On the other hand, if it were clear that none of the companies' requests could have been considered and that they were not reflected in the resulting tariff in any way, it would be unlikely that the measure would be annulled. If the court were to accept BT's argument that there may have been a link between the administrative course of action and the resulting tariff, the court would annul the general measure but not declare it ineffective against BT. A tariff that only partially binds would be inconsistent with the nature of a general measure and would create a different type of inequality. An administrative court does not have the authority to decide on compensation for BT. However, BT may seek compensation from the state in civil proceedings.

In conclusion, if the tariff were to be implemented as an administrative regulation, the unequal treatment by the DoT could become a matter of concern for the Office for the Protection of Competition, and the DoT itself could face a heavy fine for discrimination. When exercising its public powers, a public authority must not distort competition without justifiable reasons, particularly by favouring a particular competitor or group of competitors.[179] However, the Office for the Protection of Competition does not have the authority to supervise administrative authorities that perform activities under the Code of Administrative Procedure, including the issuance of general measures.

D. European Union

Edoardo Chiti

When adapting this hypothetical case to the EU institutional and legal system, one might consider the reality of the current allocation of tasks between EU and Member States' authorities and imagine a situation in which the relevant regulatory administration is a national agency implementing EU law. However, the point of the hypothetical case is not to discuss consultation in relation to composite administrative proceedings but to reflect on the standards that should inform de facto consultation and, in particular, the possibility of carrying out a selective consultation procedure. In this context, it is appropriate to refer to a situation in which EU primary legislation by sector confers on the Commission the task of setting railway and other transport tariffs. In effect, the EU legislation that applies to this case does not require the Commission to afford interested parties the opportunity to comment on the draft regulatory measure within a certain period. The Commission decided to consult all the stakeholders but only heard two of the three incumbents, namely those who had always been present in the sector, leaving out the newcomer.

[179] See s 19a of Act No 143/2001 Sb, on the protection of competition.

The EU courts would not endorse the newcomer's claim that the new tariffs are unlawful due to the fact that it should have been admitted to the consultation procedure.

The claim would be assessed in the light of a clear legal framework, which has been previously recalled in relation to hypothetical cases. As has already been stated, consultation is not a general obligation under EU law. According to the consolidated orientation of the EU courts, which is not likely to be modified in the near future, despite the strong arguments brought by applicants and scholars, participation rights in rulemaking procedures only exist when they are expressly provided for in positive law by sector, such as a Treaty article, a regulation, a directive, or a decision. This position is in stark contrast to the principle laid down in relation to individual decision-making proceedings. In such proceedings, the ECJ has held that there is a general rule that a person affected by a decision taken by a public authority must be given the opportunity to be heard and has considered such a general rule to form an integral part of the rights of defence, the observance of which constitutes a general principle of EU law.[180] In relation to rulemaking procedures, the only obligations to consult are those envisaged in the article on which the rulemaking measure is based.

In this hypothetical scenario, the Commission decided to consult despite the absence of any binding legal provision requiring consultation by sector. The consultation was carried out on a purely de facto basis. Admittedly, in its 2002 Communication on Consultation, the Commission established a consultative regime laying down a number of principles and minimum standards that the Commission itself should respect when it considers it appropriate to consult interested parties and the public at large. This approach takes seriously the functional rationale of consultation, and its fundamental principles and standards are consistent with this rationale. But the Commission remains entirely free to decide whether or not to consult, and the principles and standards are declaredly not legally binding. If the Commission decides to make a particular rulemaking measure subject to consultation, it may opt for what it considers the most appropriate way to carry out the consultation. In this context, namely in the absence of an obligation to consult stemming from a positive law provision (Treaty article, regulation, directive, or decision), there is no available mechanism to challenge the Commission's decision before the EU courts, including the decision to engage in selective consultation. It should be noted that if a newcomer is excluded from the consultation procedure, they would also find it difficult to demonstrate standing to challenge the measure, as Article 263(4) requires private parties to be directly concerned by the regulatory act.

E. Germany

Lilly Weidemann

The court would probably uphold BT's arguments concerning the failure to engage in consultation. While there is—according to prevailing opinion (see 'Germany—Case

[180] See eg Case C-560/14, *M v Minister for Justice and Equality, Ireland, Attorney General*, ECLI:EU:C:2017:101, § 25.

2' section III.E this chapter)—no general obligation exists to consult affected parties in administrative rulemaking procedures unless it is expressly prescribed by law. The obligation to consult BT would arise in this case based on the principles of procedural fairness and the authority's obligation to carry out appropriate fact-finding. First of all, if parties are given the opportunity to participate, the procedural principles of equal opportunities and plurality apply.[181] This means that the authority may not arbitrarily exclude newcomer BT from the consultation process.

Secondly, the authority is required to determine the facts accurately.[182] This includes consulting all the material information required to prepare the decision, assess its consequences, and weigh up the specific interests in each case.[183] Although the extent of this duty depends on the specific circumstances of each case, in a situation where there are only three incumbents, the obligation would arguably mean consulting all of them.

It is, however, debatable whether BT could invoke the violation of the obligation to consult in court. In Germany, the duty to consult before setting new tariffs concerning rail transport is regulated by the Passenger Transportation Act (*Personenbeförderu ngsgesetz*). In this regard, the Higher Administrative Court of Bavaria has held that the obligation to consult does not serve to safeguard the rights of individual entrepreneurs, but rather, in addition to determining the facts and collecting material for an appropriate decision, and to introduce relevant aspects that are important for the regional authorities affected by the 'requested' traffic. An individual entrepreneur could not then claim that a violation of the provision imposing the obligation to consult had occurred.[184]

The Higher Administrative Court of Saxony-Anhalt, by contrast, expressed *obiter dicta* that the individual entrepreneur could in fact invoke the breach of a duty to consult precisely because the consultation is intended to enable a full understanding of the facts and is therefore a prerequisite for an appropriate decision regarding the legislative act to be adopted.[185]

It follows from this that an action of judicial review of the tariffs according to section 47 paragraph 1 Code of Administrative Court Procedure might be inadmissible. Pursuant to section 47 paragraph 2 of that Code, applications may be made by any natural person or body corporate claiming to have been aggrieved by the legal provision or its application. It would depend on the view one adopts with regard to the nature of the provision on consultation (either serving public interests alone or intended to serve individual interests as well), whether the legitimate right to bring an action of judicial review before the court would be regarded as fulfilled or not. It should be noted that, if the action is admitted, judicial review would comprise an objective review of the tariffs and would not be limited to a review of the infringement to which the applicant refers.[186]

[181] Hufen and Siegel (n 78) Rn 787.
[182] ibid Rn 789.
[183] ibid Rn 733.
[184] Higher Administrative Court of Bavaria, Judgment of 18 December 2000—11 N 98.3199–, para 40 et seq.
[185] Higher Administrative Court of Saxony-Anhalt, Judgment of 16 June 2022—3 K 196/19–, para 85.
[186] Higher Administrative Court Bremen, Judgment of 20 December 2016—1 D 83/14–, para 38, juris.

F. Hungary

Lilla Berkes and Balázs Szabolcs Gerencsér

Price regulation under the law in Hungary is a legislative task, so, for example, the media authority or the energy authority can issue such regulation (both are independent regulatory organs that can adopt decrees and normative instructions). In this power, it is governed by general legislative rules which do not require mandatory consultation with stakeholders. Nor is it indicative of a requirement for consultation in the case of non-legislative regulation, so the authorities would be unlikely to carry out such consultation. If such consultation did take place, it would not in itself render the regulation unlawful. However, from a competition law perspective, it may be questionable whether such coordination could constitute unlawful intervention in the market.

By way of comparison, consultation may also be required by law, for example in the context of a consultation on an energy network development plan.[187] Failure to do so would constitute an unlawful procedure, which would justify a negative court decision.

G. Italy

Leonardo Parona

Acts whereby public administrations, such as the DoT in this case, establish tariffs, qualify as general administrative acts. As already mentioned there is no general statutory obligation for public administrations to consult the public before issuing this type of acts in the Italian legal system,[188] a circumstance which has been often reiterated in the case law regarding acts setting tariffs.[189] Obligations of this kind, rather, are sometimes established by sector-specific legislation and can, if necessary, be judicially imposed when a seemingly general act actually produces the effects of an individual decision, as it immediately and directly affects specific subjects.[190]

In the field of public services, such as that of railway transport at issue in the present case, Italian primary and secondary law require some forms of consultation before establishing tariffs. It should be noted that Article 2(23) of Law No 481/1995, which introduced rules to ensure competition and regulate public services, and, for the first time in Italy, established independent authorities to regulate these services, imposes

[187] Act LXXXVI on Electricity of 2007, s 25 para (4): 'The Agency shall hold a public consultation of network users on the network development plan in accordance with the procedures published by the Agency and publish a reminder of the outcome on its website.' <https://njt.hu/jogszabaly/2007-86-00-00> accessed 23 November 2024

[188] Art 13 Law No 241/1990.

[189] See eg Council of State, Sec VI, No 2309/2009; Tuscany Administrative Court, Florence, Sec I, No 350/2018; Lazio Administrative Court, Rome Sec II, No 3666/2015; Sec III, No 1700/2014.

[190] See 'Italy—Case 3', section IV.G in this chapter, and Tuscany Administrative Court, Florence, Sec I, No 214/2017.

on these authorities the obligation to establish, within their internal regulations, some forms of participation and, in particular, to carry out regular hearings with stakeholders.[191] Moreover, with specific regard to the railway sector, the Council of State has affirmed that railway companies have a legitimate expectation that changes to the tariff system will take into account their effects on enterprises, especially in terms of the burden of costs and economic and financial balance.[192]

Nonetheless, this case concerns a different scenario, where, regardless of any statutory obligation, the administration voluntarily decided to carry out some forms of consultation before establishing tariffs, but did so without involving the newcomer.

The issue therefore concerns the exercise of procedural discretion by the DoT, a discretion which has been exercised in an allegedly unlawful manner. Although public administrations are free to decide whether to ensure participation before adopting general administrative acts, once they decide to do so, they must act in conformity with the previously mentioned general principles of administrative law codified in Article 97 Const and Article 1 Law No 241/1990,[193] among other legal requirements.

Consulting only some stakeholders while ignoring others might appear to conflict with the principles of procedural fairness, equal treatment, impartiality, and the need to fully ascertain relevant facts and interests before adopting an administrative act, even when the latter is of a general nature. At the same time, however, requiring a public administration to consult every potentially affected party is certainly burdensome and might run contrary to the principles of efficiency. Public administrations are typically bound to the rule that they 'cannot aggravate the procedure except for extraordinary and justified needs imposed by the investigation phase'.[194]

Consequently, the court's solution would probably be complex: it would acknowledge that the DoT is right in arguing that it was under no statutory obligation to ensure participation or to carry out consultations. Nevertheless, since the DoT chose to consult with all the stakeholders, the court would partially uphold BT's claim by affirming that the DoT should have exercised its discretion in a lawful manner, and then assessed whether it actually did so in this case. To declare the new tariffs unlawful and order their annulment simply because one stakeholder (BT) was not consulted by the DoT would appear, however, to be an extreme measure.[195] Before an administrative

[191] For the sake completeness, it should however be noted that art 2(12)(h) of Law No 481/1995 envisages the participation of electricity service operators and user representatives in the preparation of the general acts of the supervisory authority. However, it does not include the obligation for an explicit evaluation of the written and oral deductions made by the participants.

[192] This consideration reinforces the need to take into account railway companies' interests also through various forms of consultation when setting or changing tariffs. See Council of State, s VI, No 4067/2021. This conclusion stems from the consideration that tariffs for services of general economic interest must ensure the economic-financial balance of the enterprise's investment and management, irrespective of the specific methodology actually used to establish tariffs (Council of State, Sec VI, No 6119/2019).

[193] In a similar case, a local body setting tariffs decided voluntarily—although it was not legally required to do so—to give reasons for establishing a specific tariff. The administrative court, therefore, affirmed that, although the administration was under no obligation to provide reasons, since it actually did so when it exercised its authority to set tariffs, it is then the court's duty to review the legitimacy of this authority, also with regard to the reasons given (Lazio Administrative Court, Rome, Sec II, No 3666/2015).

[194] Art 1(2), Law No 241/1990.

[195] In fact, as consistently affirmed in case law (also with regard to individual procedures, where participatory guarantees are even stronger), 'procedural guarantees are put in place to safeguard tangible interests

court, the DoT could in fact demonstrate that the investigation phase had nonetheless been complete, that it had gathered extensive information, and that it had fully and adequately ascertained the facts and balanced the various interests involved. Given the discretionary nature of the DoT's authority when setting tariffs, it is reasonable to assert that the court could only annul the act if the tariffs are clearly illogical or unsupported by facts. The situation would change, of course, if there were a statutory requirement to consult with newcomers too (although this interpretation might still be open to interpretation). Essentially, while theoretically possible, annulling the new tariffs appears to be an improbable solution in this case.

Moving on to the second issue, in the Italian context, the question of whether the new tariffs could be considered non-binding on BT amounts to asking whether the administrative court has the authority to disregard them in this particular case. The answer is negative: administrative courts—which adjudicate these types of disputes concerning legitimate interests—are not in fact empowered to disregard illegitimate administrative acts, except in certain extraordinary circumstances, which do not apply here. They can only annul unlawful administrative acts when the action is brought within 60 days of their publication, or, in the case of what has already been clarified in terms of the double claim, together with the action to annul the act of enforcement—such as, in our case, the one to apply the new tariff system to BT.[196]

Regarding the last issue raised in the question, that of financial compensation, it should be noted that this remedy is theoretically available under Article 30 of the Code of Administrative Procedure, though probably unviable in practical terms, in light of the circumstances of our case due to a number of related, but distinct, reasons.

First, compensation for damages arising from an administrative act can only be awarded if a court finds the act unlawful, and, as explained above, this outcome might not be easy for BT to achieve.

Secondly, even supposing that BT obtains the annulment of the unlawful tariffs, it would be difficult to argue—and prove—that it still suffered damage that must be compensated, since the prejudicial act has been eliminated. Moreover, to demonstrate the existence of such damage (which cannot simply be indemnified on the basis of presumptions) may prove complicated both in terms of actual loss and foregone profits. Merely establishing the unlawfulness of the act is not sufficient to warrant compensation.

and must not result in unnecessary procedural burdens'. Consequently, they cannot be reduced to a mere formalistic ritual, with the consequence, from the standpoint of effective administrative action, that private individuals must not only assert the breach of their own right to participate, but must also specifically identify or indicate the factual or evaluative elements that might have influenced the final outcome of the decision-making process if they had been taken into consideration (in these terms, see Council of State, Sec VI, No 8859/2022, but see also Council of State, No 1405/2019; Sec II, No 6687/2020; Sec IV, No 6824/2018).

[196] On the issue of standing to challenge acts that establish or modify tariffs, see Lazio Administrative Court, Rome, Sec II, No 3666/2015.

H. Netherlands

Jacobine van den Brink, Louise Verboeket, and Veerle van Waarde

First, it should be noted that Dutch Railways (*Nationale Spoorwegen* or *NS*) is the principal passenger railway operator in the Netherlands. As such, it holds the sole national transport concession.[197] Thus far, Dutch courts have deemed NS' de facto monopoly position legal.[198] Concessions for most regional or urban transport services are allocated via public tendering procedures. The case will therefore regard regional and urban transport.

Under Dutch law, there is no general legislative provision demanding that the concession provider consult all stakeholders before setting new tariffs.[199] The sector-specific rules governing railway transport only prescribe that the concession provider must consult consumer organizations before changing existing tariffs or setting new ones for the public transport concession.[200]

EU law does not require the concession provider to consult all stakeholders before setting out new tariffs. Some general procedural rules for awarding public transport concessions are set by EU Regulation 1370/2007, more commonly known as the Public Service Obligation (PSO) Regulation. The PSO Regulation imposes general principles similar to the general principles of public procurement law (meaning the principles of equal treatment, non-discrimination, proportionality, and transparency).[201] The PSO Regulation does not, however, require concession providers to consult with all stakeholders before setting out new tariffs in the Program of Requirements.

More specific procedural rules for awarding public transport concessions are set out by Dutch concession providers in their general Tender Procedure Regulations (*Aanbestedingsreglement*) and in a specific Program of Requirements (*Programma van Eisen, PvE*) for each concession. These rules usually refer to an open market consultation, and it is common practice in Dutch public transport concession procedures to consult all potential candidates through open market consultation, which is publicly announced.[202]

The case at hand seems to indicate that the underlying procedural rules do not require the concession provider to organize an open market consultation; it does so voluntarily. Under these circumstances and on the basis of the PSO Regulation, the principle of equal treatment obliges the concession provider to consult not only with the two incumbent railway companies but with newcomer BT as well. A relevant factor

197 Art 67(2) Passenger Transport Act 2000 (*Wet personenvervoer 2000*).

198 Most recently in Rb Den Haag (vzr) 13 December 2022, ECLI:NL:RBDHA:2022:13391.

199 Tariffs can also be regulated by delegated legislation. See arts 30 and 33 Passenger Transport Act 2000 in conjunction with the Passenger Transport Decree 2000 (*Besluit personenvervoer 2000*).

200 See arts 31(1), 44(3), and 66a(2) Passenger Transport Act 2000.

201 See eg art 4 PSO Regulation.

202 Market consultations for concession procedures are regularly announced on TenderNed, the Dutch government's online tendering system. See also the legislative proposal for a Transport Sector Tariffs Regulation (*Regeling tarieven transportsectoren*), which sets out all kinds of tariffs for the transport sector, including railway companies. A public consultation of this Regulation was announced on the general website for internet consultation (see <https://www.internetconsultatie.nl/regeling_tarieven_transportsectoren> accessed 23 November 2024).

in this application of the PSO Regulation is that there are only a few market players for such public transport concessions. These market players are usually known to the concession provider. If there are many market players eligible for a concession, this would justify consulting with only a few market players. The concession provider then has to share the results of the closed market consultation with the other contenders.[203] In conclusion, the concession provider, in this case, has either to consult with all stakeholders, including newcomer BT, or with none of them.

Legal recourse must be made to the High Administrative Court for Trade and Industry (*College van Beroep voor het bedrijfsleven, CBb*) as the court of first and only instance. The CBb is an administrative court, so newcomer BT would have to contest the decision to award the public transport concession (assuming that the concession was not awarded to BT). BT does not necessarily have to also contest the decision to not award the public transport concession to BT.[204] If the CBb endorses BT's claim, it will annul the awarding decision. The concession provider will thus have to organize a new concession procedure in compliance with the ruling. The CBb would not affirm that the tariffs are not binding on BT.

Additionally, BT can ask the administrative court in the interlocutory proceedings (*voorzieningenrechter*) of the CBb to grant interim relief (*voorlopige voorziening*), more specifically to suspend the concession procedure until the concession provider has consulted with BT on the new tariffs.[205] It would be wise for BT to do so. This is because, in order for BT's claim to be lodged successfully, BT would need to make a claim regarding not being consulted by the concession provider as soon as possible. Otherwise, the CBb may rule—by analogy with the *Grossmann* judgment[206] of the Court of Justice of the European Union—that the concession provider had the legitimate expectation that BT would accept the concession procedure that the concession provider wished to follow without being consulted about the new tariffs first. By not complaining and/or lodging an appeal for interim relief, BT risks forfeiture of its right to judicial review.[207]

As a side note, regardless of any prior market consultation, contenders in a concession procedure can challenge tariffs set in the Program of Requirements before the competent court by claiming that the tariffs are disproportionate or otherwise unlawful.[208]

I. Norway

Eivind Smith

The answers reasonably depend on the pre-established status in the relevant rail market and the current and/or likely upcoming space for BT within it. Supposing that

[203] See Rb Zeeland-West-Brabant (vzr) 29 July 2015, ECLI:NL:RBZWB:2015:5028, para 4.8.
[204] See CBb 5 April 2011, ECLI:NL:CBB:2011:BQ0455.
[205] Art 8:81(1) GALA.
[206] CJEU 12 February 2004, ECL:EU:C:2004:93 (*Grossmann*).
[207] See CBb 10 July 2014, ECLI:NL:CBB:2014:244.
[208] See eg Rb Den Haag (vzr) 5 October 2016, ECLI:NL:RBDHA:2016:11869 and, subsequently, at appeal, Gerechtshof Den Haag 14 February 2017, ECLI:NL:GHDHA:2017:260.

the tariffs fixed by the DoT apply to the two actors present in the relevant market, the decision must be regarded as an individual administrative act falling under the regime of individual consultations with each 'party to the case' according to APA chapter IV. This requirement is satisfied, whereas there is no obligation to consult an actor (BT) not already a part of the relevant market and not taking part in a public bid for a third licence (or similar).

J. Portugal

Rui Guerra da Fonseca

As the previous cases show, the Portuguese administrative law system is based on the opposite principle to the one asserted by the DoT. The Portuguese CPA stresses the principle of participation (Article 12), which requires administrative bodies to ensure that citizens are involved[209] in the formulation of administrative decisions that concern them by hearing them before those decisions become final. The most common use of this prior hearing (*audiência prévia*) is before the adoption of specific administrative acts.[210] However, as we have seen, this procedural step can also occur before administrative rules are adopted (Article 100 CPA).[211] As the CPA is a general rule of subsidiary application covering all administrative action in all sectors of administrative activity,[212] its requirement regarding prior hearings will only be set aside in a specific sector if another legal rule creates an exception (which is the argument of the DoT, even if the case presupposes that there is no general rule in the first place). However, making such an exception would be constitutionally questionable since the CRP states that administrative procedure is regulated by special law that must ensure citizens' participation in the formation of decisions or deliberations that concern them. In other words, the prior hearing can be considered a constitutional requirement, and once legislative provisions secure it, they can be seen as a materialization of a fundamental right. But let us proceed under the assumptions of the case, especially that there was no legal obligation for procedural consultation.

In this context, the DoT's decision to consult with existing stakeholders amounts to the use of discretionary powers to introduce a non-mandatory procedural step towards the approval of administrative rules establishing the new tariffs. Consequently, although it is initially discretionary, this new step is subject to certain legal demands, as it is not arbitrary but merely discretionary. In fact, even if the DoT was not required to take this step, once it does it must proceed according at least with constitutional and legal principles of administrative activity, as this step is a procedural moment and thus

209 Along with any associations dedicated to their interests.

210 Administrative acts consist of decisions concerning specific situations and normally regard specific persons (determined or determinable from the outset). The legal concept of administrative act (*ato administrativo*) is set out in art 148 CPA.

211 Portugal Case 3—IV.J in this chapter.

212 See art 2 CPA.

not a-juridical. Principles like equality and non-discrimination, impartiality, respect for citizens' rights, and good faith—to name but a few—apply. Again, this marks the difference between discretionary and arbitrary power.

Furthermore, once the DoT takes this step, it becomes self-bound to follow through. If the action was not legally required, but the public authority deemed it necessary, then it is reasonable for stakeholders to trust its importance, and for the DoT to see it through, all the while adhering to general principles. This does not mean that the DoT will do what they suggest. Ultimately, it is the DoT's decision. However, at least all of their suggestions will be taken into consideration.

We are not sure what is meant by the statement that BT had just 'entered the market', but we assume that this could not have happened without the knowledge of the DoT. Therefore, consulting only with the two incumbents, leaving out 'the newcomer', is an evident act of discrimination and breaches the principle of equality (Article 6 CPA; Article 266/2 CRP).

What is more, not giving BT the opportunity to be heard leads to a biased decision. Bias can be analysed from a subjective perspective, which means not favouring A to the detriment of B, or not harming A to favour B. Alternatively, bias can be analysed from an objective perspective by considering all the relevant facts and *only* the relevant facts. The case in question calls for the second perspective: failing to provide all stakeholders with equal opportunities to be heard may result in a non-objective decision by the public authority, as it may depart from analysing all relevant information (Article 9 CPA).

So, the arguments of the 'newcomer' seem solid, and the DoT's response does not seem to stand. The new tariffs are invalid because they violate general principles of administrative law as set out in Article 143 of the CPA. As the illegality is substantive rather than procedural or formal, it can be found unlawful at any time and declared such by competent public authorities or administrative courts (Article 144 CPA; Articles 72 and 74 CPTA).

It is not entirely clear how these administrative rules regarding the new tariffs would operate in practice. In any case, they appear to be immediately effective and directly prejudicial to the 'newcomer' as this is obligated to put them into practice and face consequences in its relationships with clients. BT thus seems to be entitled to bring a claim before an administrative court regarding legality with general mandatory force and not only the non-application of the regulation to its specific situation (ie 'not binding [only] on it') (Article 73/1 al. *a)* CPTA). However, applying different administrative rules to different railway companies would certainly disrupt the market, which would be questionable according to EU principles and rules. Therefore, although some form of economic compensation may be theoretically possible (considering the framework of civil liability of public authorities arising from unlawful acts), it is difficult to imagine it in this case.

K. Sweden

Patricia Jonason and Björn Forssén

Even if there are no obligation to consult in specific railway legislation, the government has, in principle, a duty to consult stakeholders, public authorities (both national and local), and other actors, in accordance with section 2, chapter 7 of the Instrument of Government, in the carrying out of its business.[213] This obligation applies both when the government participates in the legislative procedure (in the process of drafting a bill) and when it carries out its own affairs, such as adopting regulations or decisions. The obligation to consult is weaker in the second scenario. Furthermore, the Constitution distinguishes between the stakeholders who should be consulted. It is mandatory to consult with public authorities while only has to do so, 'as necessary', when it concerns the other stakeholders. The government therefore has a room for manoeuvre when deciding to what extent it is necessary to consult stakeholders other than public authorities.

If the decision is considered to be a general decision (*normbeslut*),[214] that is, concerning general instruments as opposed to an administrative decision in a specific case,[215] then it cannot be subject to legal review.[216] The only sanction would be a political one when the Constitutional committee (*konstitutionsutskottet*) reports on how the government has performed its activities.

If the decision is considered to be an individual decision, the remedy will be the so-called *rättsprövning* (judicial review),[217] where the court may only examine whether the decision is unlawful (*strider mot en rättsregel*) or not. The court would not endorse BT's claim as it would not consider the decision unlawful with regard to the margin of manoeuvre of the government in applying the rules for the preparation of its decisions.

L. United Kingdom

John Morison and David Mark

Without a specific statutory requirement or a legitimate expectation-based duty, there is no general legal obligation upon decision-makers to undertake a consultation within the United Kingdom. However, the law is clear that where consultations *are* undertaken for whatever reason, either voluntarily or otherwise, they 'must be conducted

[213] On the requirement to consult, see especially 'Sweden—Case 1', section II.K in this chapter. See also Holmberg and others (n 48) 326.

[214] The decision mentioned in Case 6 seems corresponds to the criteria which define general decisions (*normbeslut*). See *inter alia* Wiweka Warnling-Nerep *Förvaltningsbeslut—Överklagande, rättsprövning och annan domstolsprövning* Studentlitteratur 2010) 181 and SOU 2024:11, p 122.

[215] See Holmberg and others (n 48) 348 and SOU 2024:11, p 122.

[216] See *inter alia* SOU 2024:11, 107. For case law, see eg a government decision concerning the temporary prohibition of driving scooters (in this case the government acted as an appellate body and restricted the ability to grant exemptions from the prohibition). This decision to change municipal rules (*kommunala föreskrifter)* constituted a general decision (*normbeslut)* and could not be subject to judicial review (*rättsprövning* (HFD mål 3291-20) 14 December, 2020. See 'Sweden—Case 2', section III.K in this chapter, regarding the so-called *rättsprövning*.

[217] See weden—Case 2', section III.K in this chapter.

properly to satisfy the requirements of procedural fairness'.[218] The criteria for which is outlined by the Gunning Principles, established in *R v Brent London Borough Council, ex parte Gunning*[219] and reaffirmed in *R (Moseley) v London Borough of Haringey*.[220]

Consultations play a vital role in providing decision-makers with diverse perspectives and facilitating stakeholder engagement[221] and in this scenario, BT contends that it is their exclusion from any consultation that is itself inherently unfair. Therefore, a critical issue in this scenario is determining whether the DoT's actions have, despite no formal obligation, engendered a legitimate expectation to consult BT, which makes their exclusion a breach of procedural fairness. See the GCHQ[222] case which makes clear that in certain circumstances an unmet expectation of consultation can potentially constitute a breach of procedural fairness.

In considering this issue, given the tariffs' impact upon BT, there are several cases that support an expectation of consultation. Take *R (Greenpeace Ltd) v Secretary of State for Trade and Industry*[223] which emphasized the judiciary's aversion to inadequate engagement, (albeit from a statutory standpoint), similarly consider the *R (Article 39) v Secretary of State for Education*[224] matter, in which the court criticized selective consultation, particularly when excluding those most impacted. Further, in *Bank Mellat v HM Treasury (No 2)*[225] the courts held the common law requirements of fairness can require consultation of a party affected by a decision.

The above case law indicates a judicial preference for thorough stakeholder engagement in consultations, particularly of parties that could be affected by a decision. Echoing these principles, the UK government has previously articulated that it is committed to effective consultation targeted at, and easily accessible to, those with a clear interest in the policy in question.[226]

Given this legal context, the DoT's decision to consult all stakeholders, coupled with the tariffs' potential effect upon BT's business, would likely establish an expectation of BT's consultation. As such, the exclusion of BT from the process would appear to be a significant oversight. The rationale for distinguishing BT from other providers in this case remains ambiguous and it is difficult to see how such a decision would be justified.

With regards the second issue surrounding information gathering, there is a general expectation that decisions should stem from a thorough comprehension of the issue at hand, which involves considering all relevant information. Lord Diplock's

[218] Government Legal Department, 'The Judge Over Your Shoulder' (6th edn, Assets Publishing Service 2022 40, <https://assets.publishing.service.gov.uk/government/uploads/system/uploads/attachment_data/file/1105680/The_Judge_Over_Your_Shoulder_JOYS_6th_edition_2022.pdf> accessed 23 November 2024.

[219] [1986] 84 LGR 168, 189.

[220] [2014] UKSC 56, [2014] 1 WLR 3947.

[221] Government Legal Department, 'The Judge Over your Shoulder' (n 218).

[222] *Council of Civil Service Unions v Minister for the Civil Service* [1985] AC 374.

[223] [2007] EWHC 311.

[224] [2020] EWCA Civ 1577.

[225] [2013] UKSC 38.

[226] UK Cabinet Office's *Consultation Principles* (2018) https://assets.publishing.service.gov.uk/media/5aafa4f2e5274a7fbe4fbacb/Consultation_Principles__1_.pdf accessed 23 November 2024

comments in *Secretary of State for Education and Science v Tameside MBC*[227] underscored the need for decision-makers to consider information relevant to their decision, aligning with the principle established in *Associated Provincial Picture Houses Ltd. v Wednesbury Corporation.*[228] Making clear that the pertinent judicial question is whether the decision-maker took reasonable steps to familiarize itself with the necessary information to make an informed decision?[229]

To summarize, in *R (Moseley) v LB Haringey*,[230] Lord Wilson, drawing on *R (Osborn) v Parole Board*[231] underscored the essential objectives of consultation: to underpin informed decision-making, to prevent the perception of injustice, and to uphold democratic values. The exclusion of BT from the tariff consultation process appears to undermine all these objectives. Therefore, whilst in this scenario the court could theoretically uphold the tariffs despite the noted procedural issues, considering that the outcome would not have been materially different had the alleged misconduct not occurred,[232] it is perhaps more likely that the court would intervene to set aside the tariffs after identifying significant procedural improprieties. See *R (Greenpeace Ltd) v Secretary of State for Trade and Industry*[233] where the courts found the government's consultation process to be flawed and procedurally unfair. Whilst declaratory relief was considered a more appropriate remedy in that matter, it highlights the courts' apparent willingness to intervene when consultation processes are flawed. Similarly, see *R (Article 39) v Secretary of State for Education*[234] where the court granted a declaration that the secretary of state had acted unlawfully, taking issue with selective consultation. Further, see *R v Liverpool Corporation, ex p. Liverpool Taxi Fleet Operators' Association*,[235] whilst the last case surrounded a specific promise of consultation that was not adhered to, the courts emphasized the requirement for fairness in policy decisions, issued an order of prohibition and displayed a willingness to ensure interested parties would be consulted. Given BT's absence from the tariff-setting consultation process, which directly influences its operations, it is likely the courts would hold such conduct unfair and side with BT in any potential judicial review. Perhaps the most likely course of action, contingent on the case details, is setting aside of the tariffs due to the procedural failings identified.

Finally, regarding compensation, a judicial review claim can include damages claim (section 31(4) of the Senior Courts Act 1981), but it cannot be the sole claim. Unlawful decisions or public law breaches don't inherently entitle one to financial compensation, as seen in *R (Quark Fishing Ltd) v Secretary of State for Foreign and Commonwealth Affairs.*[236] There is only an entitlement to damages when a claimant could have made a private law claim, perhaps under section 8 of the Human Rights Act 1998 as a result of the violation of rights under Article 1 of Protocol 1 of the European

[227] [1977] AC 1014.
[228] [1948] 1 KB 228.
[229] See further M Fordham, *Judicial Review Handbook* (7th edn, Hart Bloomsbury 2020) 649
[230] [2014] UKSC 56, [2014] 1 WLR 3947.
[231] [2013] UKSC 61.
[232] Government Legal Department (n 218) 42. See further s 31(2A), (3C), and (3D) of the Senior Courts Act 1981.
[233] [2007] EWHC 311.
[234] [2020] EWCA Civ 1577.
[235] [*1972*] 2 QB 299.
[236] [2005] UKHL 57.

Convention on Human Rights 1950 (the right to peaceful enjoyment of possessions), possible in this matter but perhaps unlikely.

M. United States of America

Jeffrey Lubbers and Giacinto della Cananea

In our view, if the tariff applying to BT was based on BT's individual circumstances, then BT should have a due process right to a hearing before DOT to contest the tariff since its impact would be individualized to BT. If, however the tariff applied similarly to all three railway companies, then BT's argument would be that it should have been consulted before the rate was set. Under the APA, this form of administrative action would be rate-making, which is a form of rulemaking. There has been discussion about rate-making from two points of view. The first concerns the inclination of agencies, in particular the (former) Interstate Commerce Commission, to allocate traffic on a 'fair share' basis, without taking into account the operational costs of competing services. Reasonableness, again, applies. The second point of view, which is more direct concern for the case at hand, regards the procedure followed by these agencies. This aspect is of paramount importance because, unless the procedure provides for the requirements that are traditionally associated with procedural due process of law, 'one's rights are circumscribed' and 'administrative action is likely to become arbitrary and oppressive'.[237] In this respect, what matters is whether and how a hearing should be conducted by the agency, which findings of fact should be made to support the conclusions it reaches and, last but not least, how the process as a whole should be construed in order to meet the demands of a fundamental fairness.

In our view, in this case, if it is a rate-making of particularized applicability (which the APA allows for), with the rates assigned to each market participant in relation to their particular circumstances, then due process would apply and a fair hearing would have to be given. A distinction should, however, be made. If the tariffs applied to all three railways equally (and there were not factors specifically pertinent to each), the action would be a rate-making of general applicability and there would be no due process right to a fair hearing. But, even if it were a rate-making of general applicability under the APA, there would be a right to public notice and comment. That would mean that BT (and the public) should have been given a right to comment on the proposed tariff before it was finalized, and the matter would be remanded to the DOT for a reopening of the comment period. This conclusion is consistent with the conclusion reached by the Supreme Court in *Permian Basin Area Rate Cases*,[238] where the Court did not make objections to the rates because they had been defined through 'group or class proceedings'.

[237] PM Berkson, 'Due Process Requirements of a Fair Hearing in a Rate Proceeding' (1938) 38 Columbia L Rev 978.

[238] 390 US 747, 769 (1968).

VI. Case 5—'Parents for School Preservation' and Closing Down a School (Duty to Consult Users; Duty to Give Reasons)

A. Austria

Stefan Storr and Sophie Praniess

In this case, there are no specific procedural rights for the issuance of an ordinance or a decision ordering the closure of a (state) school. If such an ordinance is contested, the Austrian Constitutional Court will examine whether the school's closure is compatible with the principle of objectivity and the prohibition of arbitrariness. When deciding whether or not to close a school, the legislature and the competent creator of the respective ordinance have a wide margin of discretion. However, the Austrian Constitutional Court will not examine whether the school closure is reasonable (*zweckmäßig*).[239]

If the law requires it, the municipality should publish ordinances and other orders, including notices of hearings, on their homepage.

In this case, there are no statutory obligations concerning specific procedural rights in relation to issuing an ordinance to close a school.

School closures do not have to comply with the principle of objectivity and can be arbitrary if there is no objective reasoning for closure. In Austria, when making assessment-based decisions (*Abwägungsentscheidung*), the authority must provide objective reasoning for its decisions. Several factors play a role in this, such as the need for an educational offer, the number of students, service by other schools, and the distance between the school and the student's place of residence.[240] In the case at hand, the local administrative body must give a reason why the school in question is not needed in order to provide compulsory education. It is not sufficient to claim that the number of students is decreasing across the country. In order to justify school closures, there must be an actual, and not merely potential, decrease in the number of students who need compulsory education in a specific school district.

This example demonstrates quite well that general procedural requirements for an ordinance are not necessary. Requirements can arise from specific statutes or general substantive requirements, such as the necessity of fact-finding before an ordinance is issued.[241]

As far as the hearing is concerned, it should be noted that, in principle, a hearing is not required for issuing an ordinance. However, it may be necessary if the purpose of the hearing is to determine the facts of the case. In this case, the consultation period must be appropriate. If this is too short, the Austrian Constitutional Court will annul the ordinance on the grounds of arbitrary decision-making.

[239] VfSlg 16580/2002.

[240] See s 41 Styrian Compulsory School Maintenance Act (*Steiermärkisches Pflichtschulerhaltungsgesetz 2004—StPEG 2004*), Orig Vers: LGBl No 71/2004.

[241] HP Rill, 'Article 18' in B Kneihs and G Lienbacher (ed), *Rill-Schaeffer-Kommentar zum B-VG* (1st edn, Verlag Österreich 2001) rec 87.

B. China

Xiaowei Sun

The court may agree with PSP's argument that the decision to close a school would not be considered a regulatory document but rather a concrete administrative act affecting a right. In this case, the court would quash the contested decision for lack of adequate consultation.

There has been a debate in Chinese administrative litigation about the possibility of challenging an act that delimits school districts. Before the 2014 amendment of the Administrative Litigation Law, courts were unsure of whether any given act was concrete or abstract. Some local courts accepted challenges to this kind of decision, while others did not.[242] As stated in the introduction, the 2014 amendment of this law abandoned the distinction between concrete and abstract administrative acts. The new criterion is to determine whether the act is a regulatory act or not, which is necessary so that the act can be reviewed either by way of exception or directly. The Judicial Interpretation of the Supreme People's Court relating to the application of the Administrative Litigation Law defines regulatory acts as 'acts issued by administrative authorities for unspecified persons that can be applied repeatedly'.[243] Recent cases have shown that courts are to regard the delimitation of school districts as a 'concrete administrative act having an impact on the rights and duties of interested parties'.[244]

A decision to close a school will be deemed to be similar to a decision that delimits a school district, and it will therefore be reviewed as an individual act. The court may use the concept of 'due process', and examine whether the fundamental procedural rights under the Judicial Interpretation of the Supreme People's Court have been respected.

As a reminder, an intermediate people's court declared that when a decision is likely to affect the rights and duties of the interested party, the participation of that person in the proceedings is a fundamental element in ensuring the fairness of the administrative procedure. Being heard is an essential condition for the participation of the interested person.[245]

C. Czech Republic

Daniel Burda

First of all, it must be said that the action would not succeed in the Czech Republic, simply because it was brought before the court by the parents of the students (or rather

[242] See H Zhou (周慧蕾), 'Practice Comments on the Judicial Review of Delimitation of School District' (我国学区划分的司法审查实践评析) (2020) 8 Law Science (法学) 147.

[243] ibid: 行政机关针对不特定对象发布的能反复适用的规范性文件.

[244] 对利害关系人的权利和义务产生实际影响. See Intermediate People's Court of Wenzhou, Zhejiang Province (浙江省温州市中级人民法院), 2017, case No 03-230 (浙03行终230号).

[245] Intermediate People's Court of Nantong, Jiangsu (江苏省南通市中级人民法院), 2015, case No 00169 (通中行终字第00169号) (n 66).

by the parents' association), whose right to education is not at issue in this case; only their children, the students themselves (or potential students), have that right. For this reason, the parents (or their association) cannot defend such a right in court on their own behalf. They could only act in court as legal representatives of their children (students)[246] on whose behalf the action would be brought. The Supreme Administrative Court has reached the same conclusion on several occasions.[247]

Nonetheless, even if we modified the scenario so that it was the students themselves who brought the action, we would probably conclude that the action could not succeed, particularly if it was brought directly against the decision to close the school. The issue is that public schools are neither opened nor closed by administrative decisions. Instead, they rely on an act by an administration that does not perform public power prerogatives. In this case, a so-called welfare administration secures the provision of certain public services. These acts may follow from both public and private law.[248]

Just a short digression here on how state schools (except for public universities) are normally established in the Czech Republic. Public schools are mainly established by municipalities (in the case of kindergartens and primary schools) and regions (which play a key role in establishing secondary schools; however, they can also establish other types of schools)[249] within what is known as their autonomous capacity. Municipalities and regions establish schools either as 'educational legal entities' or as their own budget-funded organizations.[250] It is the municipal Council[251] or Regional Council[252] that decides on their establishment and closure.

Although the act is rooted in public law, it is not an administrative act, as previously stated. This is because it is not used to directly determine the specific rights and duties of individuals to public services, such as education. Instead, it is solely used to ensure the provision of such services. For this reason, it would not be possible to challenge it independently within administrative justice with no further ado. The scope of Act No 500/2004 Sb, the Code of Administrative Procedure, as a basic law regulating administrative procedures and processes, should be mentioned here. Section 1 of the Code provides for its scope only in the field—with some simplification—of the administration performing public power prerogatives. The courts' jurisdiction within administrative justice is subsequently derived from said definition (or rather from similar criteria) (see section 4 of the Code of Administrative Justice). Therefore, it can be concluded that a decision to close a school cannot be directly challenged in court. As a result, the arguments put forward in the scenario described above, such as that

[246] See s 35(1) of Act No 150/2002 Sb, the Code of Administrative Justice.

[247] Cf the judgment of 27 July 2011, File Ref No 1 As 53/2011-109 and that of 31 March 2016, File Ref No 4 As 281/2015-32.

[248] Case law also refers to the category of acts of a non-interventive nature (ie acts of an administration not performing public power prerogatives). On this issue, see the resolution of a special panel dealing with conflicting jurisdiction (a so-called conflict panel) of 21 May 2008, File Ref No Konf 31/2007-82, or the judgment of the Supreme Administrative Court of 19 June 2018, File Ref No As 152/2016-47.

[249] On this issue, see s 177 ff of Act No 561/2004 Sb, the Education Act. However, they may also be established by some ministries. In addition to public schools, so-called church schools, as well as other private schools, can be established.

[250] See s 8 of the Education Act.

[251] See s (2)(d) and (e) of Act No 128/2000 Sb, on the establishment of municipalities.

[252] See s 35(2)(i) and (j) of Act No 129/2000 Sb, on the establishment of regions.

the decision was not supported by evidence or that the affected individuals were not consulted beforehand, would not apply either.

This conclusion also follows from the construction of the right to education as enshrined in Act No 561/2004 Sb, the Education Act. The right does not depend on the existence of specific educational establishments but is conceived more generally to mean that a student/pupil must be guaranteed a place in an appropriate educational establishment (in which they then have the right to study). At the level of primary education, the primary responsibility lies with the municipalities, which are obliged to secure primary education for their citizens by establishing their own schools or by ensuring that children can attend a school established by another municipality (and therefore in another municipality) or a school established jointly by several municipalities.[253] Municipalities thus have relatively wide discretion in terms of how to ensure the fulfilment of this duty (and the implementation of the students' right to education). Therefore, calling for the continued existence of a particular school is generally not possible as there is no right to do so. Moreover, the Supreme Administrative Court has concluded in the past that it is usually not possible to claim directly that municipalities fulfil their general obligation to bring an action against a municipality directly so that it secures sufficient capacity in schools, for example. In standard practice, individuals can only defend themselves against a municipality's failure to fulfil its obligation by bringing an action against an administrative decision not to admit a child to a particular school.[254] However, it is conceivable that if a municipality completely abdicated its duty to protect a person (and that protection could not then be sought by contesting the specific administrative act), then a direct action against the municipality would probably be admissible.[255]

D. European Union

Edoardo Chiti

It is not easy to reformulate this hypothetical case and to adapt it to the EU context. One way to do this is to set aside the substantive issues, such as the EU's lack of competence in this specific field, and focus on the structural elements of the case. From this perspective, we may refer to a situation of indirect execution, where the proceeding public authority is a local administration of a Member State, subject to legal principles and rules established at least in part by EU sources. It is not clear from the

[253] See s 178 of the Education Act.

[254] See the judgment of 4 April 2013, File Ref No 7 Ans 21/2012-22. The thing is that, in line with the principle of subsidiarity, protection in administrative justice is primarily provided (if this is possible) against a resulting administrative act which 'absorbs' the unlawfulness into itself. Only if there is no such act is it possible to defend oneself in court against an administrative intervention other than a decision; see s 85 of the Code of Administrative Justice.

[255] See the conclusions in the Constitutional Court judgment of 23 January 2018, File Ref No I. ÚS 2637/17, and the subsequent judgment of the Supreme Administrative Court of 9 May 2019, File Ref No 3 Ads 151/2016-117. In this case, an action was admitted against a region which allegedly failed to fulfil its obligation to secure social services for persons with disabilities, while the choice of the specific means to do so was at the discretion of the region.

formulation of the hypothetical case whether the proceeding authority is required by the applicable rules to grant consultation or whether the decision to consult is free and unilateral. Even assuming the existence of a legal obligation to consult, the way the hypothetical case is presented suggests that local bodies are not required to carry out consultation for a specific number of days.

In this adaptation of the case to the EU system, the measure adopted by the local authority would be challenged before the competent national court, but the ECJ might be asked to provide a preliminary ruling on interpretation, with a view to assessing whether the measure is in violation of EU law.

When discussing the possible outcome of such litigation, it is appropriate to distinguish between two different situations. In the first, the decision to consult has been freely taken by the proceeding authority, outside any positive law obligation. In this case, the ECJ would not consider the specific consultation procedures, including the short period of time given to send comments and documents, as a violation of EU law. As has been recalled in relation to some of the previous hypothetical cases, the general premise of EU courts is that consultation must be envisaged by a positive law provision (Treaty article, regulation, directive, or decision), in the absence of which the ECJ will not monitor the fairness of a procedure of consultation afforded by a proceeding authority. Such a premise implies that the ECJ would not assess whether the ways consultation has actually been carried out by the local authority breach the principles of good administration, which EU courts regard as general principles of EU law applicable to Member States when they implement EU law. Accordingly, the applicants' claim that consultation, even when undertaken in the absence of a positive law obligation, should be fair and respect a number of minimum standards, including an adequate time for participation, would be rejected. It should be added that the ECJ might assess whether the national measure breaches the obligation to give reasons, which is not only envisaged by Article 296 TFEU and Article 41 of the Charter of Fundamental Rights of the European Union but is also part of the above-mentioned principles of good administration. However, the reasons given by the local authority would probably satisfy the requirements laid down by the EU courts: while their case law is demanding where the challenged measure is of an individual nature, the EU courts have consistently held that in the case of general measures it is not necessary to provide a complete evaluation of the relevant points of fact and law, but it might suffice to indicate the situation addressed by the rulemaking measure and the objective that it intends to achieve.[256]

In the second possible scenario, the decision to consult has been taken by the proceeding authority on the basis of an obligation established by a provision of EU positive law, although such a provision does not require the implementing national authority to afford consultation for a specific number of days. The main difference between the previous and the current situation is that the ECJ would accept the task of monitoring the fairness of the procedure. Moreover, it might also refer to standards that are not explicitly laid down by the relevant source of EU law but are anyway necessary to ensure an effective consultation procedure. These include providing sufficient

[256] See eg Case C-122/94, *Commission v Council*, ECLI:EU:C:1996:68, § 29.

time to participate and giving a reasoned explanation of how the comments received were taken into account in the final text of the rulemaking measure. If the ECJ were to take this approach, the national measure would certainly be subject to criticism.

E. Germany

Lilly Weidemann

The court would probably accept PSP's argument that the decision to close the school had not been preceded by adequate consultation, but it would not follow its reasoning that the decision was not justified.

When deciding which school locations to close, the school board can exercise its discretion with regard to planning, which the courts can only review to a limited extent.[257]

Whereas in the past it was essentially a matter of whether the school organizational decision would lead to unreasonable results for the parties involved, later, based on the principles generally developed in planning law, the weighing process as such was also taken into account in addition to the result of said process.[258]

The organizational decision can only be reviewed to a limited extent and in relation to unreasonable impairments and gross planning errors in terms of whether all the interests that needed to be taken into account had actually been considered according to the circumstances, whether the weight of the affected public and private interests had been misjudged, or whether the balance between the interests had been assessed in a way that was disproportionate to the objective importance of the interests, in addition to whether obvious planning alternatives have been evaluated. This restricted degree of examination is due to the weight of the state-established right to education and proper upbringing laid down in Article 7 of the Basic Law,[259] which presupposes corresponding organizational powers of action.

[257] See Federal Administrative Court, Judgment of 31 January 1964—VII C 65.62–, BVerwGE 18, 40; Order of 23 October 1978—7 CB 75.78–, DVBl 1979, 352; Order of 7 January 1992—6 B 32.91–, DVBl. 1992, 1025; Judgment of 8 April 2015—2 KN 351/13–; Judgment of 22 April 2013—2 KN 57/11–, juris.

[258] Higher Administrative Court of Lower Saxony, Order of 14 August 2015—2 LA 92/15–, para 13 et seqq.

[259] Art 7 Basic Law provides: (1) The entire school system shall be under the supervision of the state. (2) Parents and guardians shall have the right to decide whether children shall receive religious instruction. (3) Religious instruction shall form part of the regular curriculum in state schools, with the exception of non-denominational schools. Without prejudice to the state's right of supervision, religious instruction shall be given in accordance with the tenets of the religious community concerned. Teachers may not be obliged against their will to give religious instruction. (4) The right to establish private schools shall be guaranteed. Private schools that serve as alternatives to state schools shall require the approval of the state and shall be subject to the laws of the Länder. Such approval shall be given when private schools are not inferior to the state schools in terms of their educational aims, their facilities or the professional training of their teaching staff and when segregation of pupils according to the means of their parents will not be encouraged thereby. Approval shall be withheld if the economic and legal position of the teaching staff is not adequately assured. (5) A private elementary school shall be approved only if the education authority finds that it serves a special educational interest or if, on the application of parents or guardians, it is to be established as a denominational or interdenominational school or as a school based on a particular philosophy and no state elementary school of that type exists in the municipality. (6) Preparatory schools shall remain abolished.

The state's obligation to provide schools, stemming from Article 7 of the Basic Law, stands independently alongside parental educational rights under Article 6, paragraph 2 sentence 1 of the Basic Law;[260] it is not subordinate, but equal, to it. The situation of the associated right to organize a school is another matter, however. In order to adequately implement the state's responsibility for education, the state, or the school authority, depends on economic planning that takes into account the school's (educational) requirements. In the planning decision, what is decisive is not the individual interest of individual pupils in maintaining their school in particular but whether, in view of the overall situation of the school system in the area, such a (previous) educational offer can continue to be provided.

To a certain extent, the school authority may also pursue its 'own school policy'. It is therefore incumbent upon it to find the decisive priorities in the political debate. Due to the considerable degree of liberty in matters of planning, the decision under school organization law can therefore only be reviewed with regard to unreasonable consequences for pupils/parents (such as the length of the journey to and from school or the condition of the new school) or for gross planning errors (planning errors if significant concerns have been disregarded or inadequately balanced).

It would also constitute a planning error if the decision was based on an incorrect factual basis.[261] However, in the present case, PSP did not establish that the authority's assumption that the birth rate is falling is, in fact, incorrect.

Regarding the alleged breach of the obligation to consult, if the law stipulates a consultation requirement for the enactment of a standard, it aims to ensure that the result of the consultation is included as an informative basis in the legislator's decision on how to weigh up the results. The consultation requirement is therefore not properly complied with if the consultation is only carried out 'pro forma' without the possibility or readiness to take the result into account in the legislator's decision on the weighing of interests. However, a lack of openness to advice cannot be assumed on the basis of mere speculation, but only on the basis of tangible facts.[262] Such facts have not been presented by PSP.

However, the court would probably consider the time allowed for consultation too short to allow public consultation, which consists above all in the full identification and correct assessment of the interests affected by the planning.[263] The consultation must not be so long as to preclude a weighing up of the interests to the required extent. Effective public participation means that the public must first be given the opportunity to obtain sufficient information and then have sufficient time to formulate a substantiated statement.[264] What is an appropriate length of time cannot be determined in general terms as it depends on the circumstances of the individual case,

260 Art 6 para 2 sentence 1 Basic Law stipulates that the 'care and upbringing of children is the natural right of parents and a duty primarily incumbent upon them'.

261 See Administrative Court Cologne, Judgment of 19 July 2016—14 K 7394/13–, para 63, juris.

262 Federal Constitutional Court, Order of 12 October 2010—2 BvF 1/07–, BVerfGE 127, 293–335, para 105.

263 See Higher Administrative Court Baden-Württemberg, Judgment of 28 November 2012—3 S 2313/10–, para 43, juris (concerning the shortening of the consultation period after an amendment of a development plan).

264 See Higher Administrative Court of Bavaria, Judgment of 26 May 2023—9 N 19.699–, para 25, juris (concerning the shortening of the consultation period after an amendment to a development plan).

including the complexity and scope of the plan in question.[265] Bearing this in mind, 10 days will arguably not be considered reasonable for carrying out the consultation.

F. Hungary

Lilla Berkes and Balázs Szabolcs Gerencsér

If the validity of the decision of the local body is not subject to consultation, the legality of the procedure is not affected whether or not consultation is carried out. In such a case, public access to the decision will facilitate knowledge of the decision. If the public authority is not under a statutory obligation to hold a consultation, the court will tend to dismiss the plaintiff's claim, as the decision is a matter for the public body's authority alone. The authority did not deprive the PSP of any rights by not taking into account its arguments, as it had no normative obligation to take them into account.

However, if this were a statutory obligation, the authority would also have a duty to state reasons. The decision would become unlawful in this case if the authority failed to provide written reflection on the arguments received during the commenting process.

G. Italy

Leonardo Parona

In order to analyse this case, some preliminary words on the organization and functioning of the school system in Italy are necessary. Within the framework of Italy's regional structure, administrative responsibilities in the field of education are distributed over various institutional levels:

1. The state establishes the criteria and parameters for organizing the school network, evaluates the school system, and determines the allocation of financial resources;[266]
2. Regions are responsible for various functions, including planning the syllabus for both education and vocational training; planning the school network, subdividing the regional territory into school districts based on proposals from local bodies, and approving the school calendar;[267]
3. Provinces (for upper secondary education) and Municipalities (for lower levels of school institutions) handle tasks such as establishing, merging, or closing

[265] See Higher Administrative Court Baden-Württemberg, Judgment of 28 November 2012—3 S 2313/10–, para 47, juris (concerning the shortening of the consultation period after the amendment of a development plan).

[266] The functions are exercised by the Ministry for Instruction, University and Research in consultation with a Unified Conference, in accordance with art 137 Legislative Decree 112/1998.

[267] Art 138 Legislative Decree 112/1998.

schools, as well as developing organizational plans for the school network, including designating school buildings, and forming and supervising school collegiate bodies at the local level.[268]

Under the Italian legal system, the decision to close the school in the case at issue would therefore be issued by a Municipality (*Comune*) or by a Province—provided that the prior assent of the Region is obtained.

According to Article 34 Const, which guarantees the right to education, students (represented by their parents) are afforded legal protection, in the form of a legitimate interest, concerning administrative decisions that significantly affect how educational services are organized and provided.[269] Recognizing such an interest (which can, of course, be enforced judicially in the competent courts under Article 24 Const) does not, however, imply that public administrations are obliged to consult the potentially affected parties before adopting general acts that affect the provision and organization of the school system. There is no requirement to allow time for the submission of observations, nor, consequently, to provide reasons and respond to any comment received. Acts such as closing a school affect a potentially indeterminate number of individuals due to their impact on the provision and organization of a public education service. As general acts, the relevant legal framework differs from that regarding the adoption of individual acts (such as, for instance, refusal to admit students or their expulsion from school, as well as other disciplinary measures).

The earlier discussion on the legal framework governing general administrative acts should therefore be reiterated, particularly in relation to the exclusion from procedural guarantees laid down in Article 13 Law No 241/1990, particularly in relation to the obligation to notify the commencement of proceedings and ensure opportunities for public participation.[270] Also, the usual caveat concerning the possible introduction of additional safeguards by sector-specific legislation applies to this type of act.

Furthermore, Article 8(2) of Legislative Decree No 267/2000 (Consolidated Code on Local Bodies) stipulates that 'procedures relating to the adoption of acts that affect individual legal positions must incorporate forms of participation by interested parties, as established by statute, in compliance with the principles of Law No 241 of 7 August 1990'. The provision, however, is more symbolic than prescriptive, since, on the one hand, it generically refers to 'forms of participation', and, on the other (and more significantly) it delegates the actual regulation of such forms of participation to local bodies, principally through their statutes. As a consequence, it is up to the latter to determine the form, time, and scope of application of public participation they choose

[268] Art 139 Legislative Decree 112/1998. These competences are exercised according to DPR 233/1998 (a regulation, ie an act of secondary law). Art 4(2) of the DPR establishes that '[l]ocal authorities are granted all powers regarding the abolition, establishment and transfer of offices, complexes and units of educational institutions which have obtained legal personality and autonomy. This competence is exercised upon proposal and, in any case, after agreement, with the educational institutions involved.' No mention is made, as is clear from the wording, to the involvement of citizens or consultation with them.

[269] Calabria Administrative Court, Catanzaro, Sec II, No 119/2012, and, in a similar vein, Veneto Administrative Court, Venice, Sec III, No 747/2011.

[270] Lombardy Administrative Court, Brescia, Sec I, No 35672022; Campania Administrative Court, Naples, Sec III, No 3654/2020; Tuscany Administrative Court, Sec II, No 218/2019; Veneto Administrative Court, Sec III, No 1057/2018.

to implement. Indeed, the objective to 'ensure that educational institutions have the necessary capacity for discussion, interaction and negotiation with local authorities, institutions, social organizations, associations operating in the relevant territorial area and the related services' is sometimes established by local bodies in the discretionary exercise of their normative and administrative functions.[271] Even with this clarification, however, it must be pointed out that within the procedures leading to the adoption of general acts concerning the organization of schools, the interests of the public (including the school children) are generally represented through the mediation of the (democratically elected) local authorities, often within bodies such as provincial conferences, that ensure sincere cooperation among the institutions involved.[272]

On the basis of these preliminary considerations, it important to recognize that in the absence of a legal requirement to consult, a decision to close a school can only be challenged on grounds of substantial unlawfulness. PSP can in fact dispute—and prove—that the decision exhibits some illogical elements or manifest contradictions. For instance, if a school were to be closed one year after having enlarged the school building due to an increase in student numbers. It should however be recalled that, given the wide discretion granted to public administrations in this area, the merits of these kinds of decisions cannot typically be challenged.[273] This conclusion is consistent with the position of the Council of State, whereby 'reorganisation plans for the school network, as an expression of general organisational authority, do not require specific justification beyond rationalisation criteria'.[274] As a consequence, the request of PSP to obtain evidence of the allegedly decreasing number of students requiring education within the local community might be excessive.

Lastly, this case raises an issue that recalls in part some of the considerations made in the answer to Case 4. In the case at hand, the court would recognize that before closing the school, the local body was under no statutory obligation to ensure participation, wait for comments, or to justify its decision in the light of these. However, since the local body originally decided—at its discretion—to gather comments, leaving a 10-day period for stakeholders to submit them, it should have respected its prior decision, acting in a consistent, and therefore lawful, way. The court could therefore deem the conduct of the administration procedurally illegitimate; this, however, would not automatically lead it to the conclusion that the decision to close the school is substantially unlawful and to be annulled. In an administrative court, the local authority could demonstrate that, despite the lack of a time for comments, the investigation phase had nonetheless been completed, that comprehensive information had been gathered, and that it had fully and adequately ascertained the facts and weighed

[271] The quotation is taken from guidelines (ie non-binding acts) adopted by the Campania Region, which were relevant in a case decided by Campania Administrative Court, Naples, Sec VIII, No 5237/2014.

[272] As clarified in case law: the powers of local authorities regarding the suppression, establishment, transfer of offices, complexes, and units of educational institutions provided for by art 4(2) of Presidential Decree No 23318 June 1998, are exercised within the provincial organizational conference, which constitutes the only procedural instrument provided for by art 3, for the involvement and composition of the relevant public interests in the matter in question and pertaining to the various subjects. Sardinia Administrative Court, Cagliari, s I, No 386/2012, quoting Abruzzo Administrative Court, No 453/2006).

[273] Calabria Administrative Court, Catanzaro, Sec II, No 119/2012.

[274] Council of State, Sec VI, No 6820/2003 (later confirmed, for instance, by Sec VI, No 7248/2003 and No 2325/2004)

the various interests before reaching the decision to close the school. Considering that, as already mentioned, the decision to close a school is highly discretionary, the court could only annul the action in cases of manifest illogicality or unreasonableness due to an abuse of power.

H. Netherlands

Jacobine van den Brink, Louise Verboeket, and Veerle van Waarde

It should be noted that schools in the Netherlands are governed by a special type of law and may not necessarily adhere to the rules of general administrative law. The case will therefore regard a parent–teacher association that brought the case because associations of students' parents are not common in the Netherlands. Parent–teacher associations, however, have legal rights and obligations under Dutch law.

The Participation in School Decision-Making Act (*Wet medezeggenschap op scholen*) lays down the procedure for consulting parent–teacher associations when closing down a school, as required by Dutch law. According to Article 11 (1)(c) of the Participation in School Decision-Making Act, the parent–teachers association (*medezeggenschapsraad*) needs to be consulted before a decision to close a school is reached. Under Dutch law, it would not be possible to close a school on the assumption that the number of students requiring education is steadily decreasing. Article 139 of the Primary Education Act (*Wet op het primair onderwijs*) states that a state-run primary school can only be closed down when, after three consecutive years, the number of students is fewer than the minimum number (*opheffingsnorm*) applicable to the municipality in which it is located has been reached.[275] According to Article 4.24 of the Secondary Education Act (*Wet voortgezet onderwijs 2020*), the same procedure applies with regard to closing a state-run secondary school.[276] Article 17 of the Participation in School Decision-Making Act states that the opinion of the parent–teachers association needs to be sought when their advice can still have a substantial effect on the decision whether or not to close the school. In addition, if the advice is not (fully) followed, the parent–teacher association needs to be given the opportunity to meet with the local authority before a definitive decision is made.

In the case at hand, the parent–teacher association asked the local body to review its intention to close the school. Under Dutch law, this would mean that the parent–teacher association advised against closing the school. Due to the fact that the local body decided not to act in line with the advice of the parent–teacher association, the decision to close the school will not be enforced for another six weeks.[277] In addition, the parent–teacher association can submit a dispute to the National Committee for

[275] A privately run primary school (*bijzondere school*) can never be closed under Dutch law, but funding can be ended when the minimum number of pupils is reached. The effect would most probably be the same, as no funding probably means the school will have to be closed.

[276] A privately run secondary school (*bijzonder school*) can never be closed under Dutch law, but the funding can be ended when the termination norm is reached. The effect would most probably be the same, as no funding probably means the school will have to be closed.

[277] Art 34(1) Participation in School Decision-Making Act.

Disputes on the Participation in School Decision-Making Act (*Landelijke Commissie voor Geschillen WMS*) in accordance with Article 34(1) of the Participation in School Decision-Making Act. Furthermore, Article 34(5) of the Participation in School Decision-Making Act obliges the Committee to review the reasonableness of the decision of the local body not to act in line with the advice of the parent-teacher association and the decision to close the school. Due to the fact that the local body did not close the school in line with either the procedure of Article 17 of the Participation in School Decision-Making Act or the termination norms, the Committee will probably order the local authority not to close the school.[278] Appeal against decisions by the Committee may be lodged with the Court of Appeal in Amsterdam (*Gerechtshof Amsterdam*).[279] The Committee would thus endorse the PSP's argument, insofar as the decision to close the school was not justified, at least by not adhering to the procedural norms mentioned above.

I. Norway

Eivind Smith

Provided that the relevant school belongs to the local authority (municipality), the decisions are not of a rulemaking nature. Every part of the activities of the public administration falls under the APA regime regarding general requirements of administration (conflict of interests, and so on) (chapters II and III). By contrast, it is not governed by the norms in chapters IV (consultation of individual parties) or chapter VI (on public hearings).

As for the substance, the question of 'rationalizing' the school structure in a municipality, the assessment of the number of future students etc would normally fall within the discretion of the relevant body, acting, of course, under the supervision of its electorate.

J. Portugal

Rui Guerra da Fonseca

In the Portuguese administrative system, and considering doctrinal and jurisprudential positioning,[280] it is unclear whether the decision to close a school is an administrative rule or an administrative act. Administrative rules are abstract, meaning they consist of norms that are applicable in many situations that might materialize in real life and fulfil their predictions. Administrative acts, on the other hand, are extinguished after a single application (in theory). Nevertheless, it is possible that the

[278] Art 34(6) Participation in School Decision-Making Act.

[279] Art 36 Participation in School Decision-Making Act. See eg Gerechtshof Amsterdam 28 December 2022, ECLI:NL:GHAMS:2022:3696.

[280] P Otero, *Direito do Procedimento Administrativo*, I (Almedina 2016) 314 ff.

creation or opening of the school had taken place in the past through an administrative regulation which also encompassed its rules of functioning. In the latter case, closing the school would have to be done through an administrative regulation.[281] This is the hypothesis assumed from here on (notwithstanding marginal references).

In this case, it seems that the procedure was properly publicized and that students and parents were given the opportunity to participate. As pointed out in a previous case,[282] public notice of the beginning of the procedure must be given on the authority's website so that any stakeholder can come forward and be recognized as an interested party, which will then give them the right to make suggestions (Article 98 CPA). Moreover, since this regulation directly and immediately affects the rights and legitimate interests of individuals, a preliminary version must be submitted for prior hearing for no fewer than 30 working days. In addition, all those who have qualified as an interested party may participate (Article 100/1 and 2 CPA).

The deadline for stakeholders to give their reasons is a dilatory one, meaning it cannot be interrupted. Therefore, the public authority can only make its final decision after that time. In fact, until the deadline expires, other stakeholders can still forward information, and even those who have already done so may present additional information. It is important to remember that a prior hearing is not only a (fundamental) right but also a demonstration of the principle of collaboration between public authorities and citizens (Article 11 CPA).

But what if the final administrative decision[283] comes right after the deadline, with no significant interval between the two stages (such as, for the sake of argument, the next day)? The CPA does not directly regulate this aspect by imposing a specific interval. Therefore, it is necessary to resort to principles for the reasoning. The problem is to know whether the reason for the prior hearing[284]—as it was envisaged by the legislator as a mandatory part of procedure—is maintained and respected when the final administrative decision happens so quickly. The issue is not, however, whether this decision was swift,[285] but whether it was taken after due consideration of all the elements collected from the stakeholders during the prior hearing. If the decision was not swift enough to allow time to consider all the reasons given during this procedural step, then it is possible to say that it is not objectively impartial[286] as it only considers the previously reached opinion of the public authority in question (Article 9 CPA). In addition, the stakeholders' right to participate has been substantively violated (Article 12 CPA and Article 267/5 CRP): the procedural stage was respected, but no one was listening. Moreover, the opening of this step of the procedure certainly led

[281] The revocation of one legislative norm necessitates the enactment of another legislative norm, even if the latter solely entails the revocation of the previous one without introducing any new provisions for the future. Indeed, art 142 CPA specifies that an administrative regulation cannot be derogated by an administrative act; *a fortiori*, nor cannot it be revoked.

[282] See 'Portugal—Case 2', section III.J in this chapter.

[283] This decision—ie the approval of an administrative rule or regulation—is not an administrative act: see M Aroso de Almeida, *Teoria Geral do Direito Administrativo* (7th edn, Almedina 2021) 246 and other references found there.

[284] Or public consultation, or any other procedural stage for that matter.

[285] As it might even be considered urgent, though not urgent enough to waive a prior hearing (which is a possibility: art 100/3 al. *a)* CPA).

[286] See 'Portugal—Case 4', section V.J in this chapter.

the stakeholders to believe that the public authority was listening to them, but as this was not the case, there is a violation of the principle of good faith (Article 10 CPA).

All this will all depend on the courts' assessment of the circumstances, as the CPA does not require (or even mention) public authorities to give reasons for their when deciding differently from suggestions made by the stakeholders. Yes, this obligation exists as far as administrative acts are concerned. The reasons given by a public authority in its final decision must address the objections or suggestions that were raised in the prior hearing (Articles 152 and 153 CPA), but there is no such demand in relation to regulations.

It is true that regulations are approved based on a project that must contain a grounded justification (which must include a cost–benefit analysis of the measures: Article 99 CPA). But this project is made available to stakeholders during the participation phase, and there is no legal obligation to amend it at the end before the approval of the regulation, nor to include or provide any reasons at this final stage in response to stakeholder involvement if the public authority makes decisions different from those suggested or sought.[287]

Public authorities have a wide range of discretion to choose the contents of regulations, as long as they remain within the limits of the law that is being regulated. In the case of independent regulations[288] this discretion is even wider, which is why it would be very difficult to challenge the public authority's argument regarding the reduced birth rate and its significance. If this is a proven fact, the only counterargument would have to be about the rationality and proportionality of the measure, namely closing the school, as it affects fundamental rights, such as the right to education. However, it is unlikely that administrative courts would overturn the regulation unless closing the school was clearly disproportionate and could not be rationally justified in terms of public governance.

Therefore, it is likely that this regulation would only be overturned in the event of a violation of the above-mentioned principles regarding a 'staged' prior hearing, as has been addressed in previous cases.

K. Sweden

Patricia Jonason and Björn Forssén

In situations such as the one described, the decision to close the school would be challenged through a special kind of appeal known as municipal appeal (*kommunalbe svär*).[289] This appeal is open to all residents of the municipality (similar to an *actio popularis*). However, the court can only determine whether the decision was made in accordance with the law and will not examine the appropriateness of the decision.

[287] The CPA does not provide further regulation for the elaboration of the project, so it must be considered as coming under the general principles of administrative law (see Aroso de Almeida, *Teoria Geral do Direito Administrativo* (n 283) 241).

[288] Portugal—Case 3—IV.J in this chapter.

[289] Then chapter 1 § 9 RF below can arise, as mentioned in Holmberg and others (n 48) 74.

When reviewing the legality of a decision, the municipality certainly has an obligation to consult, as mandated by the Local Government Act.[290] Indeed, according to its section 3, chapter 8, '[t]he boards must work to ensure that consultation takes place with those who use their services'. However, according to the *travaux préparatoires*, '[a] lack of consultation in a certain matter ... does not mean that the decision becomes invalid'.[291] In the case at hand, the court will therefore not overturn the decision. There are no legal penalties, only political ones.

L. United Kingdom

John Morison and David Mark

Under UK law, consultations, whether mandatory or voluntary, 'must be conducted properly to satisfy the requirements of procedural fairness'.[292] Lord Wilson in *R (on the application of Moseley) v Haringey London Borough Council* [2014][293] endorsed the well-known criteria for fairness in consultations put forward by Lord Justice Sedley as counsel in the case of *R v Brent London Borough Council ex p Gunning*[294] (a case notable in this instance for its similarities to the given scenario, in Gunning a decision to close two schools was quashed as the consultation process, especially with the parents, was held to be unlawful). These criteria state that consultation must:

1. Occur at a 'formative stage', allowing it to genuinely influence the outcome.
2. Provide 'sufficient reasons' for proposals, enabling intelligent consideration and response.
3. Allow 'adequate time' for consideration and response.
4. Ensure that the consultation 'product' is 'conscientiously taken into account' in the final decision.

These criteria are reinforced in 'The Judge Over Your Shoulder' guidelines and the government's own consultation principles, which underline the necessity for clarity, adequate duration, and responsiveness in consultations.[295]

In this scenario, the consultation's timing, duration, and response consideration seem deficient. The consultation was held after the local body's decision to close the school, suggesting it wasn't at a 'formative stage' and the duration of 10 days (or possibly three days, as the question perhaps intends) appears inadequate for a matter of this significance, potentially impeding effective participation. Whilst the local administrators argue that no set duration for consultations is mandated by national legislation, UK precedent and government principles clearly demonstrate that 'consultations should last for a proportionate amount of time'.[296] Moreover, a consultation's adequacy

290 *Kommunallagen* (2017:725).
291 Prop 1986/87:91, p 60.
292 Government Legal Department (n 218).
293 [2014] UKSC 56, [2014] 1 WLR 3947.
294 [1986] 84 LGR 168, 189.
295 Government Legal Department (n 218) 41. See also UK Cabinet Office (n 226).
296 UK Cabinet Office (n 226).

depends on more than just duration; it also hinges on its timing and thoroughness. Which leads us to the response consideration of the local body, if a decision-maker ignores any provided feedback, which is alluded to in the scenario, this further undermines the fairness of a consultation. See for example *The Queen (on the Application of Mr Lionel Morris) v Newport City Council*[297] in which the court quashed the decision of a local council where it had failed to take account of, and reference feedback received from its consultation process. See also *R (WX) v Northamptonshire County Council.*[298]

In reference to the other point raised by the association of students' parents, the lack of supporting evidence or reasoning provided by the local body for its decision. Decisions by public bodies must be rational and evidence-based, a principle rooted in the *Associated Provincial Picture Houses v Wednesbury Corporation*[299] case. Echoing this, the government's consultation principles state that 'consultations should be informative [and] give enough information to ensure that those consulted understand the issues and can give informed responses'.[300] The Court is likely to expect a public authority to provide reasons for its decisions, especially in cases affecting rights, or cases in which there is a deviation from established practices, or when decisions are made that appear contrary to evidence. Whilst the detail required in decision-making varies per case, the reasons should be intelligible and adequate, showing the decision-maker considered the parties' submissions and the basis of their decision.

Also note the comparisons that can be drawn with *R (Law Society) v Lord Chancellor*,[301] in that matter a decision was challenged on the basis that the decision-maker had failed to disclose, as part of the consultation process, certain analysis relevant to the justification of the proposal. The court found that there was no good reason for the non-disclosure of the information and the failure to disclose it caused prejudice to consultees, as without that information they could not have made an intelligible assessment of the proposal.

With all this being said, it is somewhat difficult to answer this question generally, given that the type of school being closed determines the procedural requirements around such a closure. If one is to assume this scenario refers to a maintained school in England or Wales, overseen by the applicable local authority and therefore not private or independent in any way. Then there is a statutory procedure that has not been applied in this scenario[302] (see further section 30 of the School Standards and Framework Act 1998, and section 15 of EIA 2006 and indeed with reference to Wales, School Standards and Organisation (Wales) Act 2013). For comparison, see for example, *Bradbury v Enfield London Borough Council*,[303] where the court ruled against

[297] [2009] EWHC 3051. See Welsh government 'Making Good Decisions: Guidance for Public Authorities' –38 https://www.gov.wales/sites/default/files/publications/2019-02/making-good-decisions.pdf accessed 23 November 2024.

[298] [2018] EWHC 2178.

[299] [1948] 1 KB 228.

[300] [2009] EWHC 3051.

[301] [2018] EWHC 2094.

[302] See generally Department for Education, 'Opening and Closing Maintained Schools – Statutory Guidance for Proposers and Decision Makers', January 2023 <https://assets.publishing.service.gov.uk/government/uploads/system/uploads/attachment_data/file/1131568/Opening_and_closing_maintained_schools_Jan_2023.pdf> accessed 23 November 2024.

[303] [1967] EWCA Civ J0823-1

a school reorganization decision due to inadequate consultation that was required by statute (the Education Act 1944). The courts held this failure to give notice denied parents and schools the opportunity to object to the proposal.

In conclusion, generally if the court finds a decision was based on weak evidence and the consultation process was flawed, the decision may be deemed unlawful due to procedural impropriety and/or unfairness. In a scenario like this, the courts will look to a decision's evidence basis and the consultation's adequacy in terms of timing, duration, and response consideration. In this matter concerning the school, these standards do not appear to have been met, as such the court is likely to rule in PSP's favour, potentially overturning the school's closure and requiring an adequate consultation to take place over such a decision.

Furthermore, it is perhaps pertinent to point out that in this scenario, it appears as though the legislation around school closures and consultations has clearly *not* been followed and a court would be highly unlikely to side with the local body in this scenario (see *Bradbury 1967*).

M. United States of America

Jeffrey Lubbers and Giacinto della Cananea

In the United States, education policy (including school closings) is a matter of state or local law—including state and local APAs and other procedural statutes. And local law is governed by the state constitutions or the laws passed by the state legislature. So, whether the described procedure would be legal would depend on state law.

The objectors may not have a due process right to a hearing, even though the school board apparently had made its decision to close the school and only sought post-closure comments. Although the students have a right to free public education somewhere in the jurisdiction, they may not have the right to go to a particular school. Therefore, if the government is applying neutral criteria for its school closing policy, they may not have a right to any process under the Fourteenth Amendment's due process clause. See for example *O'Bannon v Town Court Nursing Center*,[304] where the Supreme Court held that the government may close a publicly funded nursing home without hearing from the residents (who then have to move to another home) on the ground that their property interest based on the government entitlement is the right to be housed in a government nursing home, but not a specific one. In a previous case, which involved the direct relationship between a publicly owned utility and its customers; the utility had provided its customers with a legal right to receive continued service as long as they paid their bills, the Court held that 'the utility's customers had a constitutional right to a hearing on a disputed bill before their service could be discontinued'.[305]

[304] 447 US 773 (1980).
[305] *Memphis Light, Gas & Water Division v Craft, 436 US 1 (1978).*

Nevertheless, applying US administrative law principles, the decision may be vulnerable to a challenge on other grounds. It appears that the school board offered the public a ten-day comment period and then short-circuited it after three days. If so, the board violated its own procedure. The state or local APA may also require longer comment periods for such an action. Finally, the state's rationale for the closing seems arbitrary and capricious. It cited general demographic statistics, but made no effort to analyse the actual demographics of the area around the school.

If the action did violate the state or local APA's procedure, then it would be remanded for a new notice-and-comment period. If the state or local APA allowed a judicial review challenge on arbitrary/capricious grounds, the court should require the local body to analyse the demographic facts on the ground before making a decision.

VII. Case 6—Ms Rand and the Legal Effects of Partially Unpublished Administrative Rules (Duty of Publication)

A. Austria

Stefan Storr and Sophie Praniess

Under Austrian law, the determination of the type of legal act that the Minister's order constitutes is essential as the prescribed way of publication depends on it. In this case, the order is not a decree (*Erlass*), as it is not intended to be limited to intra-administrative application. The order in this case is a general norm issued by an administrative authority within the scope of public administration. It is intended to apply to recipients determined by genre characteristics, as the price rules are intended to apply to pharmacists like Ms Rand. As such, the order constitutes an ordinance and must be published as such.[306]

According to Article 89 paragraph 1 B-VG, ordinances that have not been published in the prescribed manner are considered to have no legal effect whatsoever (*absolute Nichtigkeit*). Therefore, the courts will not apply them, even without being challenged, as the Constitutional Court has determined.[307] Under Austrian law, ordinances have to be published in the Federal Law Gazette in order to come into force. Since only a portion of the order was published on the Health Department's website, and furthermore, it was published there instead of in the Federal Law Gazette, it has not been published in the correct manner and therefore has no legal effect.

Ms Rand's being sanctioned by the local administration for selling masks at a price that does not comply with the Minister's order is unlawful since there is no legal basis for the sanction. Ms Rand will therefore be successful in her attempt to challenge the penalty imposed on her and will be repealed.

B. China

Xiaowei Sun

The court would endorse Ms Rand's arguments based on the failure to publish. It would invalidate the order and nullify the penalty inflicted on the plaintiff.

According to Chinese law, publication is one of the requirements for an administrative rule to be valid.[308] The first question is whether the authorities have the faculty to determine the form of publication of a regulatory document. As such, the relevant rules provide three ways to publish a regulatory document: the official journal, the official website, and the local public press.[309] Even if the form of publication is diverse

306 S 4 BGBlG.

307 VfSlg 14457/1996.

308 Art 71 of the Legislation Law, art 28 of the Regulations on Procedures for the Formulation of Administrative Regulations, art 31 of the Regulations on Procedures for the Formulation of Rules, and art 23 of the Open Government Information Regulation (政府信息公开条例).

309 ibid.

and flexible, authorities do not have discretionary power to decide which form of publication will be issued.

In this sense, the decision made by an intermediate people's court provides an illustration.[310] In this case, a local market supervisory authority imposed a penalty on a company based on a regulatory document that could be consulted on the intranet of the State Administration for Industry and Commerce and in the *Compendium of Rules Applicable to the Industrial and Commercial Administration*. The document could also be found through the Baidu search engine. The court recognizes that there is no general rule governing the publication procedure of regulatory documents and considers that in this situation, the principle of due process must be respected. The way in which the authority published its document was not sufficient to prove that the document had been duly published through official channels. This document cannot be used as the legal basis for the sanctioning act.

Furthermore, the pertinent rules require timely and accurate publication.[311] The court would consider an incomplete publication to be inaccurate and therefore unlawful under these provisions.

C. Czech Republic

Daniel Burda

An administrative court (which is a regional court of first instance, part of an undifferentiated system of courts, and the Supreme Administrative Court as appellate court) would uphold Ms Rand's arguments. As a result, it would annul the administrative decision imposing the fine, or rather the decision on the administrative contravention.

In the Czech legal system, the proper publication of a piece of legislation is a condition for its validity and effect, as well as for its binding force. This applies to both statutes and administrative regulations. The publication of ministerial regulations (or regulations of central administrative authorities) is regulated by the Act on the Collection of Laws,[312] which enshrine the above-mentioned rule.[313] This Act, which has come into effect in 2024, provides for an electronically maintained Collection of Laws. This Act also provides an alternative method of publication if a piece of legislation cannot be published in the Collection of Laws due to technical issues with the electronically maintained system. However, no such situation arose in the scenario presented here.

In the scenario described, Ms Rand would only be bound by the part of the ministerial regulation that was properly published. The part of the regulation that was only

[310] Beijing Intermediate People's Court No 2 (北京市第二中级人民法院), 2019, No 02-1743 (京02行终1743号).

[311] Art 6 of the Open Government Information Regulation, art 2, para 8, of the Circular of the State Council on strengthening the formulation, supervision, and management of administrative regulatory documents (国务院办公厅关于加强行政规范性文件制定和监督管理工作的通知) and some local relevant regulations.

[312] This is the Collection of Laws in which this type of administrative regulations is published. Act No 222/2016 Sb.

[313] See s 9 of the Act on Collection of Laws.

published on the Ministry's website, which defined the specific prices of face masks and respirators, would not bind her in any way. In fact, it could be said that in such a case there is no administrative regulation at all. The Ministry of Health cannot specify in a ministerial regulation that the regulation is to be published in an informal manner, thereby circumventing the formal publication of a related administrative regulation (or a part of it). Within the judicial review of an administrative decision which imposed a fine on Ms Rand (or in which she was found guilty of an administrative contravention), an administrative court would refuse to apply the rules (tariffs) laid down in the document published on the Ministry's website. Consequently, the court would conclude that Ms Rand had not breached any valid and effective legislation and would therefore quash the decision as unlawful.[314]

The Ministry of Health's efforts to raise awareness of the prices set by the ministerial regulations are commendable and in line with the principles of good administration. These efforts contribute to legal awareness. Although informal publication may have a greater impact than formal publications in the Collection of Laws, they cannot replace formal publication. In other words, they cannot bring about the same legal effect as correctly carried out publication.

D. European Union

Marco Lunardelli

It can be inferred from the reformulation of this hypothetical case, to adapt it to the EU legal system, that the EU Commissioner for Health and Food Safety, who corresponds to the Minister of Health at the national level and is a member of the EU Commission with a personal cabinet and administrative services,[315] only partially fulfilled an obligation. The obligation at issue was to publish an order establishing both the prices of various types of face masks during a pandemic and the pecuniary penalties in the event of noncompliance. By failing to include those prices in the published order and by publishing it in the EU Commission department's website instead of the official journal, the Commissioner is responsible for a twofold violation.

First, the prices of masks are one of the elements that Member State administrations, whether at the national or local level, have to oversee to ensure compliance by pharmacies. In this case, pricing is also relevant to the application of pecuniary penalties. Since the penalties referred to in this hypothetical case appear to have 'a quasi-punitive quality', despite their administrative nature, affected persons must be provided with such guarantees as severe as those put in place by criminal law, namely those deriving from the principle *nulla poena sine lege certa*.[316] In other words, the

[314] See s 78(1) of the Code of Administrative Justice.

[315] See N Nugent and M Rhinard, *The European Commission* (2nd edn, Palgrave 2015) 155–56.

[316] See J Schwarze, *European Administrative Law* (revised 1st edn, Sweet & Maxwell 2006) cxxv–cxxvi and N Lazzerini, 'Fundamental Rights as Constraints to the Power of the European Union to Impose Sanctions' in S Montaldo, F Costamagna, and A Miglio (eds), *EU Law Enforcement. The Evolution of Sanctioning Powers* (Giappichelli Routledge 2020) 103.

price of face masks is a structural element of the order and—consequently—of the sanctioning power vested in national administration bodies.

Secondly, the ECJ has pointed out that Article 297(1) TFEU, when interpreted in the light of the principle of legal certainty, requires that legislative acts may enter into force and produce legal effects after they have been published in the Official Journal of the European Union. Persons who may be affected by such an act must have had a chance to learn about the obligations it establishes before those obligations are enforced.[317]

Even though it may not be recognized as being of a legislative nature, the order at issue is an act of general character. As such, it does not specify the persons or classes of persons to whom it is addressed and it is therefore subject to publication in the EU Official Journal under Article 297(2) TFEU. This type of publication is sometimes mandatory for decisions that are specific to certain recipients, such as communication and notification requirements.[318] In this case, however, the order is a prerequisite for the penalty to be adopted, and publication in its entirety in the official journal is a means of ensuring transparency. The close relationship between the order and the penalty shows that transparency 'is required for EU citizens to effectively exercise their right to challenge an administrative decision adversely affecting them'.[319] In this case, adapted to the EU legal system, the Commissioner for Health and Food Safety published face mask prices on its department's official website. However, there is no element in the case, from which it may be inferred that the administration has been granted discretion to establish the measure of knowledge required to fulfil the obligation to publish. Publication on the department's official website may only be an additional option. Therefore, Ms Rand's argument that the order cannot restrict her economic freedom, as the local administration failed to publish the entire order in the way prescribed by EU legislation, should allow her to win the case. The situation does indeed seem analogous to cases where certain standards or thresholds for conducting specific business activities by individuals are contingent upon the requirement of public notification in the official journal.[320]

E. Germany

Lilly Weidemann

The court would probably endorse Ms Rand's arguments based on the failure to publish the order.[321]

[317] See Case C-161/06, *Skoma-Lux sro v Celní ředitelství Olomouc*, EU:C:2007:773, §§ 33 and 37 and Case C-345/06, *Heinrich*, EU:C:2009:140, §§ 42–44.

[318] See Schwarze (n 316) 1417–18, esp. 1418.

[319] A Buijze, 'Transparency in the Multi-Jurisdictional Setting of the EU' in M Scholten and A Brenninkmeijer (eds), *Controlling EU Agencies* (Edward Elgar 2020) 158.

[320] See Case C-160/20, Grand Chamber, *Stichting Rookpreventie Jeugd and Others*, ECLI:EU:C:2022:101, §§ 49–51.

[321] The determination of pecuniary penalties by way of an 'order' is unconstitutional in Germany. Art 103 para 2 of the Basic Law states that an act may be punished only if it was defined by a law as a criminal

Even if the pecuniary penalties for disregarding the set prices of face masks were determined by statute, but only the details were set out in a statutory instrument, the latter could still not serve as a valid basis for imposing a penalty in the present case, as the statutory instrument was published in a way that is incomplete and therefore non-compliant.

Publication is a constitutional formal requirement for all legal acts and a mandatory prerequisite for validity, which, however, only comes into being upon entry into force.[322] Acts must be published in the official journal, and only then does the respective provision become 'legally extant'. The importance of publication under the rule of law requires the entire legal instrument to be published and not just an incomplete partial version (the so-called principle of completeness).[323]

Under Article 80 paragraph 1 sentence 2 of the Basic Law, statutory instruments must be published in the Federal Law Gazette in the same way as laws, unless there is a special provision to the contrary. Thus, there exists not only the alternative of the Federal Law Gazette or the Federal Gazette, but also other options if a federal statutory provision permits it. However, since statutory instruments must be formally made known to the public in the same way as laws, such a different regulation can only designate a different official publication organ. Forms of publication other than one of these (eg in mass media such as newspapers, radio, or television) are not permitted.[324]

Concerning administrative regulations, prevailing opinion, in particular in jurisprudence, recognizes no general obligation to publish.[325] The Federal Administrative Court holds that the obligation to publish as a general prerequisite for the effectiveness of legal norms does not apply to administrative regulations as they are only binding on public authorities.[326] As a point of principle, administrative regulations do not require

offence before the act was committed. The purpose of the provision is to define the conditions of criminal liability in such specific terms that the scope and application of the offences can be recognized and determined by interpretation. This obligation serves a dual purpose. On the one hand, it is about the protection of the addressee of the norm under the rule of law. Everyone should be able to foresee what conduct is prohibited and threatened and sanctionable. In connection with this, on the other hand, it should be ensured that the legislature alone decides on criminal liability: leaving the decision on whether specific conduct is punishable to the executive or judicial power would be incompatible with the principle enshrined in the Basic Law that the decision on the restriction of fundamental rights or on the prerequisite for a restriction is incumbent on the legislature and not on the other state powers (Federal Constitutional Court, Order of 17 January 1978—1 BvL 13/76–, BVerfGE 47, 109–28, para 38). This strict legal reservation prevents the executive and judicial authorities from determining the normative requirements for punishment or the imposition of fines (Federal Constitutional Court, Chamber's Order of 15 September 2011—1 BvR 519/10–, para 35). Therefore, a formal legal basis for the pecuniary sanction is compulsory, whereas the details might be determined by statutory instrument (Remmert, 'GG Art. 103 Abs. 2' in Dürig, Herzog, and Scholz (n 20) para 103).

322 SU Pieper, 'GG Art. 82' in V Epping and C Hillgruber, *BeckOK Grundgesetz* (56th edn, CH Beck 2023) para 21.1.

323 H Butzer, 'GG Art. 82' in Dürig, Herzog, and Scholz (n 20) para 237. Since the content of art 82 para 1 sentence 2 Basic law refers to para 1 sentence 1, the same applies, *mutatis mutandis*, to the promulgation of statutory instruments and the promulgation of laws. This correspondence applies in particular to the validity of the principle of completeness; Butzer (n 323) para 271.

324 ibid para 268.

325 H Schmitz, 'VwVfG § 1' in Stelkens, Bonk, and Sachs (eds) (n 78) para 212 with further references.

326 Federal Administrative Court, Judgment of 25 June 1964—VIII C 23.63–, BVerwGE 19, 48–61, para 22 et seq.

general publication; there is no general obligation in this respect.[327] Rather, the administration must decide at its own discretion whether to publish administrative regulations or merely to make them known to the subordinate authorities. However, if the administration is bound by a specific administrative regulation in one sense or the other, this administrative regulation can provide a degree of confidence that the administration will proceed accordingly.[328]

Even though there is no general duty to publish administrative regulations, if they have a direct external effect on third parties then they are obliged to published them under rule of law obligations.[329] The duty to publish administrative regulations with direct external effect on third parties is based on the principle of the rule of law (Article 20 paragraph 3 Basic Law; Article 28 paragraph 1 sentence 1 Basic Law) and the guarantee of effective legal protection (Article 19 paragraph 4 Basic Law).[330] Given this obligation to publish administrative regulations, publishing of a part of their content is not sufficient.[331]

In the present case, regulation of the prices of various types of face masks, and imposing pecuniary sanctions for those who do not conform, would probably be considered as having a direct external effect, since regulations directly affect the rights of addressees. Thus, the obligation to publish would arise in this case, which, as the notice was published only in part, has not been complied with.

F. Hungary

Lilla Berkes and Balázs Szabolcs Gerencsér

In relation to legislation, administrative courts only have jurisdiction over local government decrees and normative decisions and instructions (the Curia can annul them or, in the event of failure to adopt a decree, grant the county government office[332] the right to adopt them).[333] Therefore, only the Constitutional Court can make a decision about the ministerial decree. However, the court may initiate proceedings before the Constitutional Court if it finds that it should apply a rule of law that is unconstitutional in an individual case.[334]

[327] Concerning administrative regulation, there is no provision similar to art 80 para 1 sentence 2 of the Basic Law requiring the publication of statutory instruments.

[328] Federal Administrative Court, Judgment of 8 April 1997—3 C 6/95–, BVerwGE 104, 220–30, para 28.

[329] Federal Administrative Court, Judgment of 25 November 2004—5 CN 1/03–, BVerwGE 122, 264–71, para 31 with further references.

[330] Federal Administrative Court, Judgment of 25 November 2004—5 CN 1/03–, BVerwGE 122, 264–71, para 31.

[331] ibid.

[332] Fundamental Law of Hungary, art 17(3): 'The capital or county government offices shall be the territorial state administration organs of the Government with general competence.'

[333] Fundamental Law of Hungary, art 25(1): 'Courts shall administer justice. The supreme judicial organ shall be the Curia. (2) Courts shall decide on criminal matters, civil disputes, the lawfulness of administrative decisions, the conflict of local government decrees with any other law and their annulment, the establishment of omission by a local government of its obligation based on an Act to legislate, and on other matters specified in an Act.'

[334] Act CLI of 2011 on the Constitutional Court, s 25 (1): 'If a judge, in determining a specific case in progress is bound to apply a legislation that he or she perceives to be contrary to the Fundamental Law, or

Promulgation in the official gazette is a constitutional obligation derived directly from the Fundamental Law.[335] Only the text of the norm thus promulgated or published will be binding on all under the Fundamental Law.[336] Since the ministerial decree has not been published in the official gazette, it cannot be valid; the judge needs to submit a petition to the Constitutional Court to declare that the legislation in question is contrary to the Fundamental Law, the Constitutional Court would declare it invalid, and the presiding judge could then annul the sanction.

G. Italy

Leonardo Parona

The requirement that an administrative act be known (or, rather, that it *can be* known) by the individuals it will affect is common to both general administrative acts and individual administrative acts. However, the methods by which this requirement is met, differ significantly. In the Italian legal system, various forms of communication and notification are prescribed for individual administrative acts to ensure their specific addressees are informed.[337] Conversely, when the number of addressees is particularly large,[338] or when the act is general or normative (applying to an indefinite and unknown number of individuals), various forms of publicity—and publication rules—are established.

The need for the content of an act to be made public is even greater when the act is a normative one. In fact, both primary and secondary sources of law produce their effects only after publication, and—more precisely—only after an established period has expired. No source of law can produce its effects if it is not published.[339] Consequently, and with limited exceptions, the moment an act is formally completed (*perfezione*) and the moment it begins to produce its effects (*efficacia*) do not coincide, as publication is a necessary prerequisite.

which has already been declared contrary to the Fundamental Law by the Constitutional Court, the judge shall stay the judicial proceedings and, in accordance with Article 24(2)(b) of the Fundamental Law, submit a petition to the Constitutional Court for declaring that the legislation in question or any provision thereof is contrary to the Fundamental Law, and/or the exclusion of the application of the legislation that is contrary to the Fundamental Law. (2) Based on the petition, the President shall take measures to put the case on the agenda at a time considered appropriate for reasons of compliance with the time limit prescribed under Article 24(2)(b) of the Fundamental Law.' <https://hunconcourt.hu/act-on-the-cc/> accessed 23 November 2024.

[335] Article T)(1) Generally binding rules of conduct may be laid down in the Fundamental Law and in laws adopted by an organ having legislative competence specified in the Fundamental Law and promulgated in the official gazette.

[336] CC Decision 33/2008 (III. 20.)

[337] Personal notifications follow the rules established by the Code of civil procedure at arts 137 ff, see also art 21-*bis* Law No 241/1990.

[338] Art 8(3) Law No 241/1990.

[339] As will be clarified later, for administrative acts, the rule is not as strict as for normative acts, in relation to which a *vacatio legis* period applies; see art 73(3) Const for statutes and art 10(1) of the 'Provisions of the law in general', preliminary to the civil code, for regulations (and statutes as well). The latter provision, in fact, establishes that 'laws and regulations become mandatory after fifteen days from publication'.

The latter observation clarifies that, in the case at issue here, regardless of whether the act establishing prices is classified as a general administrative act or as a regulation, the solution would not differ significantly.

Having clarified these preliminary remarks, it is important to point out that the case poses two relevant issues from the perspective of the Italian legal system: on the one hand, the adequacy and eventual equivalence of the various forms of publication; on the other hand, the issue of partial publication and its consequences.

Regarding the first issue, as previously mentioned, in the case of general administrative acts, publication can take many forms. For national and regional statutes and regulations, the publication of certain administrative acts (such as those setting tariffs or prices) traditionally took place through the Official Journal of the Italian Republic and regional bulletins. Physical publication through the posting of bills on public notice boards was also a common practice for many administrative acts and is still compulsory for the deliberations of local bodies, as laid down in Article 124 Legislative Decree No 267/2000.

Nonetheless, from 2009, 'the obligations to publish administrative acts and decisions that have the effect of legal publicity are considered fulfilled with their publication on the official websites'.[340]

As a direct consequence of this provision, the first issue presented by our case should be resolved in the sense that publication solely on the Minister of Health's website makes the order perfectly valid and effective.

However, this is only part of the answer, as the second issue (namely partial publication) remains unresolved. To address this, it should be noted that an act such as the one adopted in this case by the Minister of Health, which fixes prices for face masks, could be seen as a restriction on the freedom of economic enterprise and the contractual autonomy of pharmacists. Consequently, the rule prescribed by Article 21-*bis* of Law No 241/1990 (or at least the general principle underlying it) would apply. This provision concerns the effectiveness of administrative acts affecting private individuals and establishes that

> a measure restricting the legal sphere of private individuals becomes effective towards each recipient upon communication ... If personal communication is not feasible due to the number of recipients or is particularly burdensome, *the administration will proceed through suitable forms of advertising established by the administration itself on a case by case basis* ....

Publication on the website, as already clarified, is certainly a 'suitable form of advertising'; publication, however, must be complete. Partial publication, on the other hand, should be understood as the non-publication of the part of the act that is not reproduced[341]—unless the act, instead of reproducing already published acts, refers

[340] Art 32(1) Law No 69/2009.

[341] A distinct but related issue concerns the consequences of partial publication at the legally established 60-day deadline for challenging administrative acts. Incomplete publication could delay the start of the statutory deadline for submitting an annulment action until the act is published in full, as full knowledge of the act, or, at least, of its harmful aspects and grounds for unlawfulness may not have been attained (see art 41 CAP). On this issue see TRGA Bolzano, No 273/2016; Tuscany Administrative Court, Sec I, No 1422/2015; Calabria Administrative Court, Sec II, No 540/2014; Veneto Administrative Court, Sec I, No 1060/2012; Piedmont Administrative Court, Sec I, No 2265/2009.

to documents already accessible to the general public, which is not the case here. This conclusion, drawn from the cited provision, actually stems from the general unwritten principle that administrative acts (unless urgent) must be made known or published before they can have legal effect, thereby presuming that they are known.[342] If part of an act remains unpublished, that part cannot be presumed to be known and cannot, therefore produce legal effects. The issue, therefore, would not concern the validity of the act, but rather its effectiveness.

H. Netherlands

Jacobine van den Brink, Louise Verboeket, and Veerle van Waarde

The order of the Minister of Health setting the prices of various types of face mask, together with the pecuniary sanctions for not applying them, qualifies as a ministerial regulation (*ministeriële regeling*) under Dutch law. The only formal elements during the drafting stage of a ministerial regulation are (i) enactment by the Minister, and (ii) the publication of the ministerial regulation. According to Article 89(3) of the Dutch Constitution in conjunction with Articles 5(a) and 8 of the Publication Act (*Bekendmakingswet*), the ministerial order needs to be published in the Government Gazette (*Staatscourant*) in order to take effect. The fact that the Minister of Health decides to publish the ministerial regulation on the Ministry's website would, under Dutch law, have no legal effect, because the ministerial regulation has not been published in the Government Gazette.

In the case at hand, we have a single-case decision (*beschikking*) under Dutch law because Ms Rand has been sanctioned by the local administrative authority (*bestuursorgaan*) for selling face masks at a different price.[343] A single-case decision is defined in Article 1:3(2) GALA as a decision which is not of general scope, and also the rejection of a request for such a decision. According to Article 8(1) GALA, a single-case decision can be challenged in an administrative court through judicial review (*beroep*). This means Ms Rand can lodge a claim for judicial review against the sanction in the administrative court. The Explanatory Memorandum of the Publication Act states that failure to publish in accordance with Articles 4 and 5 of the Publication Act does not lead to general binding regulations becoming nonbinding if they are published in another adequate manner.[344] Whether or not the court would uphold Ms Rand's arguments based on the failure to publish the ministerial regulation thus depends on the question of whether the ministerial regulation has, according to

342 Another application of this principle is found in art 39 of Legislative Decree 33/2013 ('Reorganisation of the regulations concerning the obligations of publicity, transparency, and dissemination of information by public administrations'). As clarified, for instance, by the Lombardy Administrative Court, Milan, Sec II, No 2341/2014, under this provision (entitled 'Transparency of territorial planning and governance activities'), public administrations are required to publish all acts related to urban planning and their amendments. Publication of these acts is a prerequisite for their effectiveness.

343 This case thus differs from Case 1 (Parliament and administrative procedures concerning asylum seekers).

344 *Kamerstukken II* 1985/86, 19583, no 3, p 10.

the court, been published in another adequate manner. On the basis of the facts of the case, there is no reason to conclude that Ms Rand has been notified of the content of the ministerial regulation by dispatching it to her—for example, by sending a letter in which the new prices of face masks, as well as the pecuniary sanctions in case of disregard of such prices, are stated.[345] This means the ministerial regulation has not been published in another way that Ms Rand would find adequate. Since the case at hand deals with a sanction, which is an unfavourable decision (*belastende beschikking*), and the ministerial regulation is only partly published, and not in the Government Gazette, it is likely that the court will declare the regulation non-binding and endorse Ms Rand's arguments.

I. Norway

Eivind Smith

According to APA section 38, regulations must (*inter alia*) be published in the Norwegian Law Gazette. According to section 39, they

> cannot be invoked against any person until they have been published as prescribed in section 38, unless it is established either that the administrative agency has in some other manner made the regulations known to the public or to the enterprises, professions or skilled trades or interest groups concerned, or to the person against whom the regulations are invoked, or that such person has been [made] acquainted with the regulations.

In the present case, the incomplete publication can be remedied at a later stage, and the regulations are not necessarily invalid as such. Because the publication on the ministry's website did not mention the specific prices for the various types of face masks, however, Ms Rand cannot be submitted to pecuniary sanctions (provided, of course, it is not proven that she knew from other sources which prices were legal).

J. Portugal

Rui Guerra da Fonseca

In Portugal, as in many other countries, the prices of medicines, medical devices, medical technology, and treatment can be subject to a ceiling established by the

[345] Compare with ABRvS 4 July 2007, ECLI:NL:RVS:2007:BA8692 and Rb Utrecht 10 January 2008, ECLI:NL:RBUTR:2008:BC2759. Both these cases deal with benefits and therefore refer to favourable decisions (*begunstigende beschikking*). The case in question is about a sanction and thus refers to an unfavourable decision (*belastende beschikking)*.

government (with the possible involvement of other public authorities with health-related functions).[346] Laying aside the exact definition of facial masks for this purpose (as it is beyond the scope of what is relevant for the current case) and other details relating to specific competences, it would be possible for the Minister of Health to make this decision within the framework of the Portuguese system. The existence of a pandemic does not, by itself, bring any extra legal justification for such a governmental measure, unless it would justify the declaration of a constitutional state of exception (emergency).[347] In the latter case, the presidential decree that determines the state of emergency could have special rules on the matter, simplifying it and possibly making it clearer and more specifically refer to masks.

It is possible to determine sanctions administratively within the framework and the limitations that have already been established.[348]

To take effect, the order of the Minister of Health, qualifying as an administrative regulation, must be published in the Official Journal of the Republic (*Diário da República*). It may also be published on the Ministry website.[349] There can be no doubt that uploading the regulation on a website is not enough, as publication in the Official Journal is an absolute requirement, with no exceptions.[350]

Therefore, Ms Rand has a legitimate claim. If the order was not duly published in the Official Diary, it produced no legal effect either on her or in general. Not only was she under no legal duty to sell masks respecting price, but she also could not be sanctioned because of it, as both the maximum prices and the sanctions were in the same (unpublished) regulation. So, the problem with the order is one of efficacy or production of effects. But the problem with the sanctions applied to Ms Rand is one of illegality and thus of validity, as the corresponding execution act had no normative basis (since the regulation never came into effect).

This illegality, due to the lack of normative basis, would normally allow the possibility of annulling the act imposing sanctions (an administrative act).[351] But in this case, since a sanction is involved, the solution could be different. The principle of legality establishes that a given conduct can only be punished if it was considered illegal and sanctioned at the time it occurred.[352] This is a situation where constitutional

346 See Decree-Law 97/2015 of 1 June (last amended by Decree-Law 115/2017, 7 September).

347 See art 19 CRP.

348 See the answer to question 2 in Part I, .

349 See art 139 CPA, and art 119/1 al. *h)* CRP. Also arts 1 and 3/2 of Law 74/98, 11 November (last amended by Law 43/2014, 11 July).

350 Interestingly, Government Decree 2-A/2020, issued on 20 March, executed Presidential Decree 14-A/2020 of 18 March, which declared the state of emergency in 2020, introducing an exception. Under art 31, the regulations for the execution of the aforementioned Decree took effect only through publication on the websites of the relevant administrative authorities. This was particularly contentious in the light of arts 119 and 19 of the Portuguese Constitution.

351 Art 163 CPA. In the Portuguese system, invalid administrative acts can be categorized as null (void) or subject to annulment. The former represents a more severe form of invalidity, rendering the administrative act totally devoid of effects, and nullity can be declared indefinitely. The cases of illegality that determine this type of invalidity are standard (arts 161 and 162 CPA). On the other hand, an act that is subject to annulment will remain effective as usual until it is annulled by a court, with the usual deadline for challenging such acts set at three months. Beyond this, in principle, the act can no longer be challenged on these grounds.

352 Art 2 of Decree-Law 433/82, 27 October (see the answer to question no 2 in Part I, Chapter 11, II).

guarantees regarding criminal law might apply, specifically the fundamental right to not be criminally convicted if the conduct was not considered a crime at the time of the fact, nor be subjected to a sentence that had not been expressly stated in previous law (Article 29/1 and 2 CRP). The Constitution does not mention administrative sanctions, but its nature—as a sanction, with similar aspects to criminal sanctions—can determine the extension of those constitutional guarantees, particularly when the principle of legality is involved as in the present case.[353] Therefore, the act that determined the sanction could be considered null because it violates the essential core of a fundamental right (Article 161/1 al. *d)* CPA). The courts would certainly uphold Ms Rand's claim.[354]

K. Sweden

Patricia Jonason and Björn Forssén

The provisions taken by the government shall be published in the official gazette, which can be accessed online. Publication is a requirement for promulgation (section 5, Act (1976:633) on the Publication of Acts and Other Statutes).[355] The court would endorse Ms Rand's arguments and not apply the penalty.

This assessment is supported by case law. In the two cases described below, which concerned rules ranked lower than government orders, the court decided that failure to publish rules containing penalties led to the non-application of the challenged rules.

In a decision regarding technical standards for laser pointers, which were only published in English, the Supreme Court determined that the failure to only publish the standards in this language violated the penal principle of legality. As a result, the contested rule could not be applied.[356]

In a decision concerning local traffic regulations, which did not state the date of entry into force, the court of appeal (*Hovrätten över Skåne and Blekinge*), referring to the Act on the Publication of Acts and Other Statutes, assessed that '[a] provision on the entrance into force constitutes a necessary and integrated part of the regulations' and did not apply the contested rule'.[357]

353 See JJ Gomes Canotilho and V Moreira, *Constituição da República Portuguesa—Anotada*, I (4th edn, Coimbra Ed 2007) 498.

354 In this case, application of the sanction should be challenged in the judicial rather than administrative courts. Although the sanction has been applied through an administrative act, this is the traditional solution in the Portuguese system, which reserves the jurisdiction of administrative courts to the review of some specific sanctions (namely infringements of rules regarding urban planning and tax/fiscal regulations: Art 4/1 al. *l)* of the Statute of Administrative and Tax Courts of Law—Law 13/2022, 19 February, last amended by Law 114/2019, 12 September).

355 *Lag om kungörande av lagar och andra författningar.*

356 NJA 2019 s 577, 27 June 2019.

357 RH 2002:32, 15 September 2002.

L. United Kingdom

John Morison and David Mark

The issues in the scenario involving Ms. Rand and the partially unpublished administrative order by the Minister of Health, reflect principles requiring legal authority to be accessible and foreseeable to the public.

R (Bridges) v Chief Constable of South Wales[358] in the Divisional Court, subsequently reviewed by the court of appeal,[359] discussed these principles of 'accessibility' and 'foreseeability', echoing the precedents established in *The Sunday Times v The United Kingdom*,[360] *Silver v United Kingdom*,[361] and *Malone v United Kingdom*,[362] which underscore the requirement that laws are fair, predictable, and clear. Indeed, it is perhaps appropriate to note that the three European cases noted above were the basis for the ECHR establishment of a dual test of accessibility and foreseeability for any measure which is required to have the quality of law, see *Huvig v France*[363] at paragraph 26, and *Kruslin v France*.[364] That test has continued to be cited by the Strasbourg court as the authoritative statement of the meaning of 'law' in subsequent cases: see, for example, the more recent case of *Catt v United Kingdom*.[365]

To expand upon these concepts somewhat, the noted *Sunday Times* case, heard by the European Court of Human Rights, emphasized the importance of the public's ability to access and understand the law. It framed this within the broader principle of legality in Article 7 of the European Convention on Human Rights. The Court articulated that 'firstly, the law must be adequately accessible ... Secondly, a norm cannot be regarded as a "law" unless it is formulated with sufficient precision to enable the citizen to regulate his conduct.' To clarify further, in *Re Gallagher* the court helpfully addressed the accessibility aspect of these principles by noting that, 'for a measure to have the quality of law, it must be possible to discover, if necessary with the aid of professional advice, what its provisions are. In other words, it must be *published and comprehensible*' (emphasis added). Moreover, with regards foreseeability, using the Strasbourg formulation, this means the relevant provision must be formulated with sufficient precision to enable the citizen to regulate his conduct and foresee to a degree that is reasonable in the circumstances, if need be, with appropriate advice, the consequences that may result from an action, see *Perinçek v Switzerland*.[366]

As such, these precedents suggest that in Ms Rand's case, noting the long-standing legal tradition emphasizing the necessity for clear, accessible, and foreseeable laws, the court would be likely to find the Minister's order either invalid or unenforceable

358 [2019] EWHC 2341.
359 [2020] EWCA Civ 1058.
360 (1979) 2 EHRR 245.
361 (1983) 5 EHRR 347.
362 (1984) 7 EHRR 14).
363 (1990) 12 EHRR 528.
364 (1990) 12 EHRR 547.
365 *Catt v United Kingdom* App No 43514/15 (ECtHR, judgment 24 January 2019).
366 *Perinçek v Switzerland* App no 27510/08 (ECtHR, judgment 10 October 2015) para 131.

due to its failure to meet the established standards of accessibility and foreseeability, with the main issue being the partial publication of the order.

M. United States of America

Jeffrey Lubbers and Giacinto della Cananea

In our view, in this case the court would endorse the claimant's arguments and would quash the administrative rule, because it has infringed an important legal requirement.[367]

Two preliminary points should be mentioned. First, under section 552(a) of the APA, the agency must publish essential information about final rules in the *Federal Register* (the equivalent of the official journal in European countries). Second, many rules can be effective only after the expiry of a minimum of 30 days after they are published in the *Federal Register.*[368]

This allows those who would be affected by the rule to have time to prepare for its effects. However, there can be a reduction of this minimum requirement, if the agency demonstrates 'good cause', in the sense that immediate effectiveness is in the public interest. Conversely, for 'major' rules (ie, those with over $100 million impact on the economy, the Congressional Review Act provides that they must wait 60 days to become effective.

Finally, it is only if administrative agencies have published their rules that the APA—sections 552(a)(1) and (2)—permit them to rely upon such rules in their dealings with the public.

That said, under the case law interpreting the US APA, the agencies must follow the requirement that they publish their proposed and final rules in the *Federal Register* and that simply publishing these items on the internet (including agency websites) does not suffice. The reviewing court would quash the sanction against Ms Rand and the agency would be required to follow the prescribed publication procedure before it could enforce the prices.

[367] See PL Strauss, 'Publication Rules in the Rulemaking Spectrum: Assuring Proper Respect for an Essential Element' (2001) 53 Admin L Rev 803 (for whom this is an 'essential' requirement).

[368] See <https://www.govinfo.gov/content/pkg/USCODE-2011-title5/pdf/USCODE-2011-title5-partI-chap5-subchapII.pdf> accessed 23 November 2024.

VIII. Case 7—Bellevue and Hastily Reviewed Taxi Licence Standards (Protection of Procedural Expectations)

A. Austria

Stefan Storr and Sophie Praniess

The statement issued by the City Board serves solely as official information and does not immediately entail any legal consequences. It does not confer rights or obligations upon those under the jurisdiction of the law.

Even if the promise to give notice or conduct consultation before changing its licensing policy itself constitutes an ordinance and thus has some legal effects, it should be noted that the legislator may—in principle—regulate *pro futuro*. The Austrian Constitutional Court is therefore rather restrictive in accepting the protection of legitimate expectations.

In this context, the Austrian Constitutional Court distinguishes between three categories of cases. First, it imposes strict requirements on retroactively burdening legislation. Retroactivity of an ordinance is only allowed if the retroactivity is explicitly granted by statute.[369]

Secondly, *pro futuro* restrictions of properly acquired rights (*wohlerworbene Rechte*) are unconstitutional if legal positions, in which those subject to the law have put legitimate trust, are seriously and trenchantly changed. However, being able to simply rely on the uninterrupted continuation of the legal framework at a specific moment in time is not constitutionally protected in any specific manner. The legislator has the right to change a legal position once it has been created, even to the detriment of those affected and contrary to their expectations.[370]

Thirdly, a certain, albeit limited, protection of legitimate expectations is also afforded to dispositions factually made by private individuals. A prerequisite for any such protection is that decisions be made based on the (ongoing) existence of specific legal provisions. In this case, the legislator is only obliged to modify the legal framework with regard to these decisions.[371]

In the present case, it is to be assumed that the taxi companies have made considerable investments (ie the acquisition and maintenance of their vehicles) assuming the (ongoing) existence of certain legal norms. This trust was reinforced in particular by the information provided by the City Board (which in itself did not trigger any legal consequences). The sudden specification of just one colour significantly affects the discretion of certain taxi companies, as it potentially renders all non-white cars useless or triggers high adaptation costs.

A proportionality test must be carried out to determine whether the abrupt change in the licensing regime (with effect not only for new but also existing licences) can be justified. To provide justification, transitional solutions (*Einschleifregelungen*) might be necessary for taxi companies licensed under the 'old' regime. As the recognition

369 VfSlg 8946/1980.
370 T Öhlinger and H Eberhard, *Verfassungsrecht* (13th edn, Facultas 2022) 366.
371 ibid 367.

value of only white vehicles cannot outweigh the high cost of adapting them, an abrupt change in the licensing regime without transitional solutions constitutes a violation of the principle of proportionality. However, the obligation to use only white cars is not equally disadvantageous for the licensing of new taxi businesses. They are not covered by the protection of legitimate expectations, which is why the regulation would not be deemed to constitute a violation of the principle of proportionality with regard to them.

If the licensing policy is issued through an ordinance, the taxi companies concerned can appeal to the Austrian Constitutional Court. If a taxi company has been penalized for disregarding the licensing regime (ie continued commercial use of vehicles of a different colour), it can appeal to the competent administrative court, which will then refer the matter to the Austrian Constitutional Court. The court will repeal the ordinance for the above-mentioned reason.

B. China

Xiaowei Sun

The court would endorse Taxi Drivers' arguments, declare the new policy unlawful, refuse to use it as a legal basis, and send the authority a recommendation to remedy the irregularity.

As a regulatory act, *Bellevue's* new policy can be reviewed by the court in the light of Articles 53 and 64 of the Administrative Litigation Law by way of exception. Two situations of illegality could arise under the Judicial Interpretation of the Supreme People's Court of 13 November 2017 relating to the application of the Administrative Litigation Law:

- The regulatory act has no legal basis, and illegally increases obligations or restricts rights of citizens, legal persons, or other organizations;
- The administrative authority failed to comply with legal approval procedures and publication procedure or committed a serious procedural breach.

Regarding the first case, the Judicial Interpretation can be seen as imposing additional costs on taxi drivers who are required to change the colour of their vehicles. As established by the guiding case mentioned in Case 3 concerning the rejection of medical payment by the Social Insurance Office,[372] the court would declare unlawful a regulatory document that increases obligations or restricts the rights of citizens, legal persons, or other organizations, and would refuse to use it as a legal basis.

Regarding the second issue, the local rule stipulates that the authority must provide notice or engage in consultation before changing its policy regarding taxi licensing. This consultation would be considered a legal procedural duty according to the Judicial Interpretation. Moreover, the obligation to consult is mentioned in many texts, such as

[372] Intermediate People's Court of Rizhao, Shandong Province (日照市中级人民法院), 2016, case No 2016-11-9, (鲁11行终9号) (n 118).

the Legislation Law (Article 67), the Regulations on Procedures for the Formulation of Administrative Regulations (Article 13), the Regulations on Procedures for the Formulation of Rules (Article 16), and the Circular on Strengthening the Formulation, Supervision, and Management of Administrative Regulatory Documents (Article 2, section 5).[373] As previously stated, courts are typically very reluctant to review regulatory documents on procedural grounds. However, given the explicit mention of the duty to notify and consult before changing the policy in this case, the court would have no choice but to note the lack of notification and consultation.

C. Czech Republic

Jiří Rajchl

In this response, we do not address the issues relating to the existence of multiple municipal bodies (particularly the distinction between a representative body and an executive body), and we further assume that the body referred to above as the City Board has the authority and competence to deal with taxi-service issues (in the Czech Republic, municipalities cannot currently determine the uniform colour of taxi vehicles). A change in the City Board's policy may be possible in two potential forms. First, the policy may be reflected in the form of a municipal bylaw, which would be necessary in a situation where there is a legal entitlement to obtain a licence. Secondly, if there is no legal entitlement to be awarded a licence even having satisfied the requirements, and the decision to issue one is at the discretion of the administrative body, it is also possible that an internal standard could be created and, despite not being a legal regulation, it will be followed by the City Board when making licensing decisions. We infer from the scenario and from the term 'policy' that the latter situation is more likely; that is, a document which is not generally binding but which is determinative for further official actions of the city's governing bodies. That is to say, working with the construction that there is no legal entitlement to be awarded a taxi licence (though, in the Czech Republic, the right to a licence takes the form of a legal claim if the statutory conditions are met).[374]

The city's assurance that it will give notice of possible changes in advance or even consult with the persons concerned before making changes is a logical and correct expression of goodwill that increases the participation of those involved. Allowing space for feedback and objections is important to ensure that future decisions are fair and appropriate, but it is not a legal requirement. Such a right cannot be successfully invoked by the persons concerned, whether or not the intention of the prior consultation has been announced in advance. If the City Board made such an assurance prior to accepting licence applications and granting licences, it could influence applicants to consider whether or not they should seek a taxi licence. However, based on the scenario presented here, it seems that the assurance was given after the licences were granted. In such a case, the assurance has no legal effect, although possible changes

[373] ibid.

[374] See Act No 111/1994 Sb, on road transportation.

may have a negative economic impact on the persons concerned. In this regard, it is reasonable to assume that the court would not accept Taxi Drivers' arguments based on the prior assurance. More precisely, an action against the policy itself would be found inadmissible. If there was an action for damages caused by maladministration, the arguments would probably be found to be unreasonable, given that the necessary causal link between an omission by the City Board and the costs incurred by Taxi Drivers was not established.

However, the effects of the new policy would not, in and of themselves, be reflected in administrative decisions that have already been made or in other procedures. There are several administrative procedures that apply to taxi services in the Czech Republic. These include trade permits for carriers, licences for taxi drivers, and the registration of taxi vehicles. For our purposes, it is not necessary to analyse exactly which procedures would be affected by the change or in what manner. For the sake of simplicity, we shall discuss licences. The bottom line is that a non-binding document expressing a new policy could not, by itself, have any effect on existing circumstances. The first step would be to change the contents of the licences of the individuals. Changing the contents without it being requested by a taxi driver—that is, by virtue of office—can only be done based on a legal provision which allows for such a change. As a rule, this could only happen for compelling reasons, such as compliance with other legislation or ensuring proper operation in the public interest. In any case, interference with decisions that have attained legal effect is very limited; it must be supported by a law, and there must be sufficiently compelling legitimate reasons. A decision that has attained legal effect should not be changed based solely on a change in a municipal policy. In practice, regulators tend to regulate changes gradually, particularly when tightening practice, and only in connection with making a change requested by the operator themselves, as conditions for use of the granted licence. Such a situation is hard to imagine in this line of business.

If a new policy were to be implemented in a municipal bylaw, it would be necessary to analyse other circumstances, particularly the extent to which the bylaw would explicitly conflict with the content of the licences. If the bylaw conflicted with the explicit content of the licences issued, the licences would first have to be amended. The behaviour of taxi drivers who comply with the licences may be interpreted as legally permissible conduct and as a circumstance that excludes the unlawfulness of the conduct in relation to the new municipal bylaw.

If the taxi licences issued did not contain provisions regulating the colour of a vehicle or the maximum daily working hours, the new municipal bylaw might bind the taxi drivers as of the date of its entry into force. However, it could be argued, within the framework of subsequent proceedings for the imposition of remedial measures or administrative penalties for non-compliance with the new rules, that there is impermissible interference with the legal certainty of licence holders. Where a body belonging to the same municipality has granted licences under certain conditions and over a period of several years, the municipality itself should not change the regulations immediately thereafter in a way that leads to the devaluation of the investment of the taxi drivers. It is not necessary to let the full term of the licence under the original conditions expire, but it is necessary to preserve at least the time necessary to get a return on the taxi drivers' investment and a reasonable profit, which they could have legitimately expected in such circumstances. What is important is how long before the policy change the licences were issued. If it was, for example, already five years earlier, this is a sufficient period of time. However, if a licence was issued only a few months before a significant change in policy, this period may seem too short. The term of the licences validity must be weighed against the cost of the impacts the new policy will have on taxi drivers. At the same time, it would not be possible to provide for the transition to the new regime on an individual basis; in other words, each taxi driver at a different point in time with respect to the term of effect of their licence. It would be more appropriate to determine a common transition period that ensures equal treatment for all persons with a valid licence. If someone's licence expires during the transition period, they must apply for a new one under the new conditions. Such a dual regime may create some difficulties for consumers. However, it is possible that even taxi drivers with old licences would try to adapt to the new policy in order to be competitive and credible with customers.

Therefore, all legally relevant arguments must relate to the area of the principle of legal certainty and the protection of rights acquired in good faith. They should not relate merely to the breach of the assurance of prior notification or consultation. On the other hand, providing sufficient notice in advance would be beneficial for the municipality. This would allow affected individuals to prepare for the changes, such as purchasing a vehicle of the required colour if necessary or planning their business activities more accurately in view of the restrictions on working hours. It would then be impossible for Taxi Drivers to use the argument of legitimate expectations to preserve the original conditions.

D. European Union

Marco Lunardelli

This hypothetical case is quite similar to the one discussed in Case 3 of the questionnaire as it is concerned with a limited number of licences, the granting of which is affected by a change in policy, and both occurred in the indirect enactment of EU law. Therefore, in either case, the new policy adopted by a Member State's administrative body, namely a local one in the case at issue here, leads to the question of whether the stakeholders should have been consulted and the protection of legitimate expectations ensured. According to the solution given for Case 3, a duty of consultation has not been deemed to exist, as it was not provided for by the national administrations, which had been assigned the power to draft their own licensing proceedings. As far as the latter issue is concerned, it has been argued that, provided that equal treatment and fair competition among applicants in the licensing proceedings are ensured, the ECJ may hold that the public interest underlying the new rules prevails. In the case at issue here, too, the ECJ may consider the change in policy legitimate and thus unable to adversely affect Taxi Drivers' legitimate expectations. However, the case description underlines that the competent municipality board, which may be deemed to have been delegated to act by EU law, had released a statement assuring that any change to the policy on taxi licensing would be subject to notice or consultation with stakeholders. The protection of legitimate expectations is closely related to legal certainty,[375] and not only are they both general principles of EU law, they have also been defined as 'sub-concepts of the rule of law'. The former requires the existence of a legislative act or an administrative decision capable of producing 'justifiable reliance'—respectively—on its validity and on the rights and benefits it confers upon its recipients.[376] Such reliance may derive from specific assurances contained in that act or decision.[377]

The issue here is whether the municipal board's statement, released in the course of the indirect enactment of EU law, may equate to an official act capable of generating legitimate expectations. In other words, the issue is whether or not that statement may be considered similar to a scenario in which the EU Commission has to comply with the principle of 'self-commitment', since it has set standards, normally by adopting guidelines, to limit the exercise of its own discretionary powers, as is usually the case with EU law on state aid.[378] In this area, national legislation on revocation or annulment measures cannot be used to justify a Member State's refusal to return legitimate aid.[379] Nevertheless, the decision to grant state aid must have been published in the official journal, or the affected persons must have had adequate knowledge of the decision and the underlying policy.[380] A similar argument may be used in the case at issue. In general, indeed, the ability of 'a consistent administrative practice or individual statements' to cause legitimate expectations and thus to have individuals act according to good faith may not be ruled out.[381] From a comparative perspective, if the statement released by the City Board were published in the official journal or on the municipality's institutional website, it could be considered a public policy, and this would be the case regardless of its general applicability.[382] If this is the case, then argument based on the need to protect the Taxi Drivers' legitimate expectations would appear to be sound. However, the case description does not specify this aspect. Therefore, it can be assumed that the statement made by the City Board does not have a high level of formality. Additionally, EU law does not address the aforementioned distinction between different policy statements in terms of applicability. Instead, it provides for a notice-and-comment procedure when this is determined by EU executive agencies in rulemaking, especially if technical issues are involved.[383] Although technical assessments and purely discretionary considerations and assessments are often closely intertwined, making it more

[375] See Joined Cases C-177-181/99, *Ampafrance SA v Directeur des services fiscaux de Maine-et-Loire* (C-177/99) and *Sanofi Synthelabo v Directeur des services fiscaux du Val-de-Marne* (C-181/99), ECLI:EU:C:2000:470, § 67.

[376] See HCH Hofmann, 'General Principles of EU law and EU Administrative Law' in C Barnard and S Peers (eds), *European Union Law* (OUP 2014) 208–211.

[377] See Case T-283/02, *EnBW Kernkraft GmbH v Commission*, ECLI:EU:T:2005:101, § 89.

[378] See Schwarze (n 316) cxxxvi–cxxxix.

[379] See R Noguellou, 'L'influence du droit communautaire sur le régime des décisions administratives' in J-B Auby and J Dutheil de la Rochère (eds), *Droit administratif européen* (Bruylant 2007) 927.

[380] See Case C-180/88, *Wirtschaftsvereinigung Eisen- und Stahlindustrie v Commission*, ECLI:EU:C:1990:441, §§ 24–26.

[381] See Schwarze (n 316) cxliii–cxliv.

[382] The reference is to the federal Freedom of Information Act in the US legal system. See 5 USC § 552(a)(1)(D) and (2)(B) (2018 edn).

[383] For an example of a notice-and-comment procedure carried out by the European Aviation Safety Agency, see L Mustert and M Scholten, 'Controls in the Case of the EU Civil Aviation Safety Rules' in Scholten and Brenninkmeijer (n 319) 255–56.

difficult to understand the decision-maker's logical path,[384] the municipality clearly exercised administrative discretion in this case.

Therefore, even if the City Board's statement is interpreted as falling within guidelines capable of restricting administrative discretion, the solution to the case may be found at the EU level, where it is not easy to establish when guidelines are capable of producing a binding—here, more accurately, a self-binding—effect.[385] In the description of the case, the local authority pinpointed the reason for changing the policy on taxi drivers by referring to an international event, which would take place six months after the new policy was adopted It may also be argued that the taxi drivers were adversely affected by the administrative decision, without having the opportunity to be consulted beforehand. Furthermore, if it is ascertained that the the decision brought about an unexpected change in the taxi drivers' legal position, they may even bring a claim for damages.[386] However, since the binding effect of the statement is not clear, and adopting a notice-and-comment procedure is not mandatory under EU law although it would be according to the ReNEUAL model of administrative rulemaking,[387] the local authority may well win the case. In general, the more serious the adverse effects determined by an administrative measure not ensuring legitimate expectations are, the greater—the more compelling—the public interest should be.[388] Here, the public interest underlying the change in policy is explicitly stated and the adverse effects the decision brings about do not seem to be serious enough to render it illegitimate (if the ECJwas preliminarily asked to assess the compliance of the decision with EU law) or to direct the national court to award damages to Taxi Drivers. The duty to give reasons may be cited in resolving the dispute.[389]

E. Germany

Lilly Weidemann

The court would probably uphold Taxi Drivers' arguments concerning the binding effect of the unequivocal assurance that a consultation would take place before any change of policy.

384 See J Mendes, 'Discretion, Care and Public Interests in the EU Administration: Probing the Limits of Law' (2016) 53(2) CML Rev 425.

385 See J Mendes, 'Executive Rule-Making: Procedures in Between Constitutional Principles and Institutional Entrenchment' in C Harlow, P Leino, and G della Cananea (eds), *Research Handbook on EU Administrative Law* (Edward Elgar 2017) 378–79.

386 See P Craig and G de Búrca, *EU Law* (7th edn, OUP 2020) 633.

387 The reference made here is to Book II of ReNEUAL Model Rules on EU Administrative Procedure, namely to art II-4(2) and (3). Indeed, the case under discussion here appears to be suited both a generalized notice-and-comment procedure open to all, and to a targeted one, where only the affected persons —ie the taxi drivers—may be invited to participate by submitting a comment. See D Curtin, HCH Hofmann, and J Mendes, 'Book II—Administrative Rulemaking' in G della Cananea, D-U Galetta, HCH Hofmann, J-P Schneider, J Ziller (eds), *ReNEUAL Model Rules on EU Administrative Procedure* (ReNEUAL 2014-) § 44, 61 <http://www.reneual.eu/images/Home/BookII-AdministrativeRulemaking_individualized_final_2014_09_03.pdf> accessed 23 November 2024.

388 See P Boymans and M Eliantonio, 'Europeanization of Legal Principles? The Influence of the CJEU'S Case Law on the Principle of Legitimate Expectations in the Netherlands and the United Kingdom' (2013) 19(4) EPL 719.

389 Pursuant to the 2006 directive on services in the EU internal market, discharging this duty is also a prerequisite for subjecting a service activity to an authorization scheme, See art 9(2) of Directive 2006/123/EC of 12 December 2006, [2006] OJ L376/36, 54.

The Municipality of Bellevue's policy for issuing taxi licences would constitute administrative regulations, which are binding only internally on the administration and have no external binding effect, generally speaking. As mentioned above, they only have an indirect external effect mediated by the principle of equality and administrative practice.[390]

In principle, a change with respect to administrative regulations and deviation in individual cases is always possible for objective reasons. However, the principle of ensuring legitimate expectations (*Vertrauensschutz*) must be observed when changing previous administrative practice.

As seen above,[391] an administrative authority is generally bound by its own acts (*Selbstbindung der Verwaltung*) in the sense that it may not deviate from established practice without an objective reason for doing so. In general, no specific number of cases is required to justify an administrative practice; rather, the announcement of a planned procedure by administrative regulation (anticipated administrative practice, *antizipierte Verwaltungspraxis*) or an initial decision in conjunction with the principle of equality, can lead to the administration being bound by itself. This applies above all when the authority has already announced its future practice by means of announcements,[392] as is the case here.

The Federal Administrative Court holds that since directives and the corresponding established practice can have a binding effect on discretionary decisions, this is not to the extent that it must have an unrestricted effect on all future cases. A later deviating exercise of discretion is generally permissible if it is appropriate and does not subsequently interfere with facts pertaining to the past. Where discretionary considerations have an effect on facts and legal relationships that have not yet been finalized for the future, they can only be impugned if the protection of legitimate expectations in an individual case sets limits on the deviating exercise of discretion. This is not the case if the expectations of the person concerned have merely been disappointed. In addition, the person concerned must have made decisions with regard to the continuation of the discretionary commitment and may reasonably trust that it will endure in the long term. These principles do justice to the tension between the necessary adaptation of the administration to new circumstances on the one hand and the interest of the individual in maintaining administrative practices that are favourable to him on the other. They take sufficient account of the principle of ensuring legitimate expectations.[393]

The Municipality of Bellevue was, therefore, in principle free to change its policy for the future. It is assumed that the uniform colour for taxis constitutes an objective reason that would justify a change in policy. The same would apply to restricting working hours, if reasonably motivated. However, Taxi Drivers could argue that they reasonably trusted that Bellevue's policy would not change in this regard. This is

390 HA Wolff, 'VwGO § 114' in H Sodan and J Ziekow, *Verwaltungsgerichtsordnung: VwGO* (5th edn, CH Beck 2018) Rn 103.

391 See 'Germany—Case 3', section IV.E in this chapter.

392 Higher Administrative Court Bavaria, Order of 4 December 2023—22 ZB 22.2621–, para 14, juris.

393 Federal Administrative Court, Order of 20 March 1973I WB 217.72 –, BVerwGE 46, 89-95.

especially true since Bellevue issued an unequivocal assurance that no policy change would occur without prior consultation.

Bellevue bound itself by issuing this assurance regarding the procedure it would adopt if it changed its policy (namely consulting stakeholders first), so the municipality cannot now change policy. Consequently, the lack of prior consultation would constitute a procedural flaw.

F. Hungary

Lilla Berkes and Balázs Szabolcs Gerencsér

In cases where 'unequivocal assurance' means a local regulation on how legislation is to be made, or the rules of organization and operation (ie decree) contain conditions for participation in decision-making and that the subjects of the regulation must be involved in decision-making, Taxi Drivers' claim will be upheld by the court. In this case, the judge would examine the criteria that the local body should take into account when making its decision.

However, if the guarantee is 'only' a political declaration, the court will dismiss the action, as a political declaration cannot in itself be a legal basis for rights and obligations.

G. Italy

Leonardo Parona

To address the legal issues raised by the current case and explain the solution that an Italian court would reach, it is necessary to clarify that general statements and resolutions by the City Board concerning future conduct or policies, such as the assurance that the Municipality would ensure consultation before altering taxi-licensing policies, do not carry legal consequences. Unless issued in the form of regulations, they do not bind administrations, nor do they immediately or directly affect the rights or legitimate interests of the addressees (taxi licence holders in this case). Statements of this kind, rather, primarily have political implications for local administrations and give rise to mere expectations with no legal protection.

As a consequence, the City Board's initial statement would have no consequences in the legal analysis and solution of the current case. Thus, the subsequent policy change introduced by the Municipality (and potentially enacted through a general administrative act[394] or a municipal regulation) should be considered—in legal terms—as

[394] For qualification in terms of the general administrative act, refer to a similar case concerning the reorganization of permits for the transit of tourist buses in the historic centre. In this case, the Council of State observed that 'the number of stakeholders involved meant that the City Board's act was a provision of a general nature, and there is no doubt that when the interested parties are numerous, the act qualifies as a general administrative act', adding that, regardless of the essentially programmatic and non-preceptive nature of the provision, art 13 of Law 241 of 1990, an indisputably primary rule with respect to the Municipal

a stand-alone action, evaluated on its own procedural and legal merits. From this point of view, in a similar case involving the amendment of municipal regulations in Bologna concerning taxi licences and chauffeured car rental services, the Council of State qualified them as general administrative acts, the content of which is left to the discretion of the administration, and do not give rise to specific private interests during the adoption process.[395] Consequently, procedural safeguards, such as prior consultation, do not apply.[396]

In cases like the one analysed here, the protection of the parties affected by the new policy is ensured at a later stage through judicial review. In fact, 'a subject authorised to carry out a specific activity ... [such as a taxi licence holder] can indeed challenge the general administrative act which regulates the authorised activity and affects its performance and convenience without the need for an implementing act'.[397]

However, it is one thing to acknowledge that taxi licence holders have standing to challenge the new policy (either directly or together with the enforcement act, through the previously mentioned mechanism of the dual challenge). It is quite another to assess the potential success of the legal action they initiate.

As previously indicated, general administrative acts characterized by broad discretion can only be considered unlawful if they exhibit manifest unreasonableness or introduce patently disproportionate obligations. In our scenario, both the newly imposed costs under the regulation, and the limits it introduced on maximum working hours are justified by the need to accommodate the upcoming international sailing yacht competition. Thus, neither the grounds nor the content of the act itself appear manifestly unreasonable. As a consequence, it is improbable that a court would accept Taxi Drivers' arguments.

The outcome of the case could be slightly different if the initial statement issued by the City Board was legally binding and produced effects (this quite implausible scenario would depend on the legal basis, competence, and procedure followed in its adoption). In such a case, the act could qualify as a general administrative act, and the subsequent policy change would be incompatible with the former. When a subsequent

Statute, is directly applicable in this case, given that the obligations relating to participation referred to in the general law on administrative procedures do not apply to the activity of the public administration aimed at issuing administrative regulatory, general, planning, and programming acts (Council of State, Sec V, No 1858/2018, which annulled the judgment at first instance of the Tuscany Administrative Court, Florence, No 214/2017, which instead affirmed that, considering that the economic operators ought to have been consulted as they belonged to a specific category).

[395] Council of State, Sec V, No 1182/2015 (and in similar terms Sec IV, No 1349/2013).

[396] See also the Campania Administrative Court, Naples, Sec III, No 3654/2020, adjudicating a case similar to the one at issue, and concerning the adoption of a new general act impacting on the rights of enterprises already authorized to install billboards on public streets. These enterprises argued that they should have been consulted, but the administrative court affirmed that given the general nature of the act, procedural guarantees such as participation and the duty to give reasons did not apply. Also, with reference to another sector strictly related to the one at issue, the case law has clarified that acts concerning urban traffic are the product of broad discretionary choices that surely need to ensure the 'balancing of conflicting interests according to criteria of reasonableness' but that do not need to allow participation (Lombardy Administrative Court, Milan, Sec III, No 1596/2022; TRGA Trento, No 91/2022; Campania Administrative Court, Salerno, No 431/2020).

[397] Council of State, Sec V, No 5840/2014, also referring to Sec V, No 960/2002.

act contradicts or is inconsistent with previous administrative acts, it could be considered to constitute an abuse of power and, therefore, unlawful. However, departing from the content of prior acts might be justified depending on the grounds put forward by the administration and any objective reasons, such as the urgency to address an upcoming sailing competition. Even in this case, therefore, it would be difficult for a court to accept Taxi Drivers' arguments: it would not change the solution with regard to the lack of consultation but might bear greater weight in terms of the substantial lawfulness of the policy change.

H. Netherlands

Jacobine van den Brink, Louise Verboeket, and Veerle van Waarde

The case does not make clear whether the new policy is laid down in a general binding regulation (*algemeen verbindend voorschrift*) or a policy rule (*beleidsregel*). Therefore, both alternatives will be discussed. A claim for judicial review cannot be directly lodged against a decision containing a general binding regulation or a policy rule, as laid down in Article 8(3)(a) GALA. Therefore, an action against a general binding regulation or a policy rule should be brought before civil courts. Even assuming that Taxi Drivers fulfils the general standing requirements for interest groups under Article 3:305a of the Dutch Civil Code (*Burgerlijk Wetboek*), standing in an appeal against general binding regulations and policy rules before civil courts is limited. Appeals are inadmissible if a general binding regulation or a policy rule can be reviewed incidentally (*exceptieve toetsing*) before the administrative court.[398] In this case however, the new policy has direct effect, meaning the policy rule applies immediately without the intermediary of an appealable decision. This would mean that the individual taxi drivers would need to act in breach of the general binding regulation or policy rules. This is an unreasonable burden on taxi drivers, so an appeal may be made against the new policy rule to the civil courts.

In the Netherlands, there is, in principle, no obligation for public authorities to consult the parties concerned (*belanghebbenden*) prior to the establishment of policy rules unless the uniform public preparatory procedure (*uniforme openbare voorbereidingsprocedure*) is applicable. This procedure is described in Division 3.4 GALA. The Explanatory Memorandum of the GALA states that the uniform public preparatory procedure is used in drafting a decision which affects a large number of parties concerned, or other persons unknown to the administrative authority (*bestuursorgaan*).[399] This procedure is usually applicable to the preparation of single-case decisions but can also be used in drafting general binding regulations[400] or policy rules. In such a case, the application of the general binding regulation or the policy

[398] See HR 9 July 2010, ECLI:NL:HR:2010:BM2314 (*Staat/Vreemdelingenorganisaties*), HR 22 May 2015, ECLI:NL:HR:2015:1296 (*Privacy First/Staat*) and HR 3 June 2016, ECLI:NL:HR:2016:1049 (*SCAU/Universiteiten*).

[399] *Kamerstukken II* 1999/2000, 27023, 5, p 6.

[400] See eg art 43(1)(a)(b) Fertiliser Act (*Meststoffenwet*) and art 4 Water Authority Act (*Waterschapswet*).

rule must be deposited by the administrative authority, as laid down in Article 3:11(1) GALA. To this end, the application or the draft will be published in a government-issued gazette and will set out who will have the opportunity to state their views and how this can be done.[401] Article 3:15(1) GALA states that the uniform public preparatory procedure is generally used for the parties concerned. However, according to Article 3:15(2) GALA, statutory regulation or the administrative authority may provide other individuals with the opportunity to express their views. The time limit for expressing a view will normally be six weeks.[402] The above shows that a claim based on the lack of consultation of the taxi drivers will only be likely to succeed if a statutory regulation or an order of the municipality of Bellevue declares that the uniform public preparatory procedure is applicable.

The facts of the case show that there is no such statutory regulation or order by the municipality of Bellevue. However, the Municipality of Bellevue provided unequivocal assurance by means of a statement delivered by the City Board that it would give notice or embark upon consultation before changing its policy concerning taxi licensing. If this unequivocal assurance by means of a statement qualifies as a decision, in the Netherlands, the uniform public preparatory procedure will be applicable.[403] The court will then rule that the municipality must follow this procedure, but it will not express an opinion on the content of the general binding regulation or policy rule.

If the unequivocal assurance by means of a statement cannot be qualified as a decision, it must be established whether the statement has given rise to the legitimate expectation that Taxi Drivers would be consulted. If it is found to be a decision, weighing the interests involved may lead to the conclusion that adopting a general binding regulation or policy rule would violate the principle of legitimate expectations. In order for an appeal on the principle of legitimate expectations to succeed, a set of conditions must be met.[404] First, there has to be a statement (step 1). In the case at hand, this condition is satisfied, namely an unequivocal assurance by means of a statement. In its statement, the City Board declares that it will provide notice or engage in consultation before changing its taxi-licensing policy. From this statement, Taxi Drivers could reasonably conclude that the City Board would have given notice or start consultation before changing its policy concerning taxi licensing. This statement is delivered by the Municipality of Bellevue, which means that it can be attributed to the administrative authority, namely the City Board (step 2). Due to the fact that this statement can be attributed to the administrative authority, legitimate expectations (*gerechtvaardigd vertrouwen*) exist. The third step entails a balancing of interests in which the question is answered as to whether the legitimate expectation should be accepted. Taxi Drivers has a great interest in consultations before changing the policy concerning licensing, because the new policy causes higher and unforeseen costs for Taxi Drivers. We expect that under Dutch law the court will rule that the interest of the municipality in organizing an international sailing yacht competition in six months does not outweigh the interests of Taxi Drivers. If the administrative court rules that the general binding

[401] Art 3:12 GALA in conjunction with art 12 Publication Act (*Bekendmakingswet*).
[402] Art 3:16(1) GALA.
[403] Art 3:10(1) GALA.
[404] See ABRvS 29 May 2019, ECLI:NL:RVS:2019:1694 (*Amsterdams dakterras*).

regulation or the policy rule has no legal effect due to a violation of the principle of legitimate expectations, the basis for administrative enforcement will cease too. The court is not obliged to give an opinion on the content of the general binding regulation or policy rule but can decide to do so and thereby declare that the municipality should take this decision into consideration when adopting a new general binding regulation or policy rule after consulting Taxi Drivers.

I. Norway

Eivind Smith

The court would rule in favour of the taxi drivers as far as the absence of prior consultation is concerned (cf APA section 37). Moreover, the 'revised' regulations also seem sufficiently burdensome to make it likely that the outcome could have been affected by the arguments provided by Taxi Drivers. A period of six months is likely to be deemed sufficient to carry out a reasonable consultation and evaluation process.

J. Portugal

Rui Guerra da Fonseca

Bellevue Municipality's administrative regulation has an immediate and direct impact on the rights and interests of taxi drivers and/or owners. The regulation imposes obligations on them that require no further administrative implementation act, and some drivers would be required to change the colour of their vehicles and limit their working hours. Therefore, the Municipality should have publicized the procedure (Article 98 CPA) and opened a period of prior hearing no less than 30 working days beforehand (Article 100/1 CPA). The number of taxi drivers/owners in Bellevue would not be so high as to make the hearing incompatible and justify the Municipality opting for a public consultation (Articles 100/3 al. *c)* and 101 CPA).

However, the Municipality may be able to dispense with the hearing in urgent cases (Article 100/3 al. *a)* CPA),[405] and the proximity of the yacht competition (six months) could justify such an exception. From the legal point of view, the Municipality's option is legitimate. Even so, is there any relevance in its declarations 'that it will give notice or embark upon consultation before changing its policy concerning taxi licensing'? Certainly, this kind of declaration would have created a sense of trust, which is relevant in the context of the principle of good faith (Article 10 CPA). But since the law

[405] Administrative bodies may also qualify a certain situation as representing a 'state of administrative necessity', allowing them not to follow the procedural rules enshrined in the CPA and still maintain the validity of their acts, even if those who suffer damages have the right to be compensated according to the general rules of administrative civil responsibility (art 3/2 CPA). But the situation in hand does not seem to meet the criteria for this, as the administrative courts tend to associate 'urgency' in this particular case with 'exceptional circumstances of clear and present danger or risk' (see Ac Supreme Administrative Court 03478/14.1BEPRT, 07/04/2022).

allows for urgency as a justification to dispense with a hearing, the Municipality could always claim that trust could not be created outside of the existing legal framework. On the one hand, those declarations could be seen as a self-binding way to interpret clauses subject to interpretative discretion such as 'urgency'. On the other hand, urgency always introduces an element of unpredictability, which is rather difficult to define. The taxi drivers/owners would not have much success with this kind of argument. Urgency could be justifiable, and its justification would depend, in no small part, on administrative discretion. The court would probably not consider dispensation from the hearing illegal.

However, the taxi drivers and owners have made substantive claims that they refer to as 'economic'. These claims are of a legal nature, although they are not procedural. The case does not mention any negative consequences arising from non-compliance with the new regulation, but it is reasonable to assume that there would be some. For example, taxis and drivers that do not respect the demands relating to colour and working hours would be prohibited from circulation.

The colour of the taxis rises several issues. First, if the Municipality has 'issued numerous taxi licences over the years', regardless of the colour of the vehicle, this change in policy may contradict the principle of good faith, as it led drivers/owners to believe that the colour of their vehicle was irrelevant and would remain so (Article 10 CPA and Article 266/2 CRP). They made their investments in an environment of trust, but now that trust is being betrayed, and they are facing serious financial consequences. Secondly, we must consider whether changing the colour to white was the most appropriate way to achieve the desired outcome of recognition. Was there no other way to achieve the same result without imposing such a heavy burden on drivers and owners, taking into account the public interest (Article 7 CPA and Article 266/2 CRP)? Thirdly, if most taxis are already white, then this means that the drivers/owners of taxis with different colours are the only ones who will be forced to adapt and incur extra costs. Leaving aside the issue of discretion regarding the choice of the colour, this clearly contradicts the principle of equality (Article 6 CPA and Article 266/2 CRP) with respect to the equitable distribution of public burdens for the satisfaction of public interests.

This case does not reference any previous legal precedent for this regulation. Therefore, since it interferes with a fundamental right, namely private economic initiative and property (Articles 61 and 62 CRP), there would be a problem regarding encroachment on Parliament's legislative powers (Article 165/2 al. *b)* CRP).[406]

In any case, if the courts do not endorse this view and still consider the regulation lawful, then the special burden or sacrifice placed upon drivers and owners of

[406] This calls for a more detailed explanation. Private economic initiative and property (arts 61 and 62 CRP) are systemically located in a part of the CRP dedicated to economic, social, and cultural rights and not under civil and political rights, which are the only ones reserved to parliamentary legislation (albeit with the possibility of legislative authorization for the government to issue decree-laws: art 165/1 CRP). Nevertheless, private companies and property are considered safeguarded by civil and political rights (art 17 CRP), benefiting from the constitutional guarantees of the latter. This analogy is firmly established in Portuguese legal doctrine as well as in constitutional and general case law.

non-white taxis could sustain administrative liability for damages arising from a lawful act that imposes particular sacrifice (Article 16 of Law 67/2007, 31 December).[407]

There is also a legal issue regarding the maximum number of driving hours. In fact, this matter is the subject of legislation that contemplates a different system for organizing working hours for drivers, which may allow for a longer maximum of daily hours of work (Decree-Law 237/2007, 19 June), in line with Directive 2002/15/EC of the European Parliament and of the Council of 11 March 2002 on the organization of the working hours of persons performing mobile road transport activities. Portuguese law does not grant municipalities the authority to regulate this matter, and so the regulation would be unlawful. It could also be questioned whether this restriction violates the right to freely choose a profession and how to exercise it, as well as the right of private economic initiative (Articles 47 and 61 CRP).[408]

K. Sweden

Patricia Jonason and Björn Forssén

In the case at hand, we assume that the municipality made the decision within its jurisdiction. Taxi Drivers have the right to appeal the decision as municipal residents. As the appeal takes the form of a municipal appeal (*kommunalbesvär*), the county administrative court cannot examine the appropriateness of the decision, but only its legality. As previously noted in Case 4, municipalities are obliged to consult in accordance with section 3, chapter 8 of the Local Government Act. The *travaux préparatoires* indicate however that the non-fulfilment of the duty to consult does not invalidate the decision.[409]

L. United Kingdom

John Morison and David Mark

In the Bellevue Municipality case concerning the abrupt change in taxi licensing policy, the scenario engages the doctrines of legitimate expectation and procedural fairness.

Simply put, legitimate expectation can arise when a public body suggests through its actions or statements that it will act in a certain manner, leading individuals to rely on this projected behaviour. Whilst noting that within UK law there is no general right to consultation, what is clear is that 'a legal duty to consult may … arise from a

[407] On this matter, and especially administrative responsibility arising from legal regulations, see J Valle, 'Artigo 16.º—Indemnização pelo sacrifício' in C Amado Gomes, R Pedro, and T Serrão (eds), *O Regime da Responsabilidade Civil Extracontratual do Estado e Demais Entidades Públicas: Comentários à Luz da Jurisprudência* (AAFDL 2017) 799. Also, Ac Central Administrative Court-North 0219/05.8BEPRT, 23-03-2012.

[408] For the measures available to administrative courts, see 'Portugal—Case 2', section III.J in this book.

[409] Prop 1986/87:91, p 60.

legitimate expectation, for example if there has been a promise to consult in a statement or guidance'.[410] The promise or representation should be clear, unambiguous, and made by someone with the legal authority. It should be targeted at those directly affected and come from the authority now being challenged. Detrimental reliance on this promise by the individual or group may also be a factor. This concept is rather succinctly summarized by Laws LJ in *R (Bhatt Murphy) v Independent Assessor*,[411] 'the power of public authorities to change policy is constrained by the legal duty to be fair (and other constraints which the law imposes). A change of policy which would otherwise be legally unexceptionable may be held unfair by reason of prior action, or inaction, by the authority. If it has distinctly promised to consult those affected or potentially affected, then ordinarily it must consult (the paradigm case of procedural expectation).'

See for example *R (Greenpeace Ltd) v Secretary of State for Trade and Industry*,[412] this case revolves around a white paper which provided that the government would not produce nuclear power stations without full public consultations, however the government then sought to construct such a power station, with minimal consultation. The court intervened stating that 'there was procedural unfairness, and a breach of the claimant's legitimate expectation that there would be the fullest public consultation'. Similarly, in *R v Liverpool Corporation, ex p. Liverpool Taxi Fleet Operators' Association*[413] the Liverpool city council had a statutory power to set the number of taxi licences in Liverpool. However, it made a public undertaking that it would not increase the number without consultations, before attempting to do so anyway. The courts intervened to ensure that the council acted fairly in deciding the policy, with Denning LJ stating with reference to the promise of consultation that 'so long as the performance of the undertaking is compatible with their public duty, they must honour it'.

Against this legal backdrop, in the scenario at hand the UK courts would likely find the 'unequivocal assurance' by the City Board amounts to a legitimate expectation of a promised consultation before undertaking changes to taxi licensing.

However, it should be noted that an established legitimate expectation can still be overridden if there is a compelling public interest. Courts will look at the importance of the promised benefit, how specific and firm the promise was, the extent of detrimental reliance, and the public interest in deviating from the promise. In this scenario whether there is a compelling public interest justifying the deviation from a promised notice or consultation depends on several key factors. The urgency and importance of the international sailing yacht competition, the necessity of the policy changes for the event, and perhaps their impact on public safety and traffic management would be considered. If these changes are essential for the event and significantly benefit the public, they might constitute a compelling public interest. However, I find this to be unlikely and when held against the detrimental impact on the taxi drivers and

410 Government Legal Department (n 218) 40.
411 [2008] EWCA Civ 755.
412 [2007] EWHC 311.
413 [1972] 2 QB 299.

the possibility of less intrusive means to achieve the Municipality's objectives, it is doubtful that a court would support such a policy.

The courts will attempt to uphold a concept of fairness in these decisions. Effectively, where the decision-maker fails to undertake a consultation that is required as a result of a promise it has made or its prior practice, and there are no overriding public interest reasons to justify defeating the legitimate expectation, the Court may invalidate any decision.[414]

See, for example, cases like *Bradbury v Enfield London Borough Council*,[415] where the court ruled against a school reorganization decision due to inadequate consultation. A failure to give notice denied parents and schools the opportunity to object to the proposal, leading to the decision's invalidation. Similarly, in *Bank Mellat v HM Treasury (No 2)*,[416] the Supreme Court declared the Treasury's restriction of Bank Mellat's access to the UK financial markets unlawful due to the lack of prior notice. The bank wasn't given a chance to contest the allegations before the policy change was enacted. Highlighting a legal principle that entities should be given notice and an opportunity to respond before significant policy changes affecting them are implemented.

In addition to the above, it would perhaps be ill advised not to mention in this matter the European Convention on Human Rights, particularly Article 1 of Protocol No 1 concerning the protection of property, which arguably enters the frame here. The taxi drivers could argue that the abrupt policy changes, like colour standardization and working hour limits, interfere with their ability to use their taxis effectively, necessitating a justification for such interference. (Noting section 6 of the Human Rights Act 1998 requires public authorities act in a manner compatible with convention rights.)

In summary, the Bellevue case's resolution will hinge upon balancing the expectations and rights of the taxi drivers against the Municipality's reasons for policy change and any overriding public interest. Perhaps the most likely option would be the overturning of these policies on the basis of legitimate procedural expectation and fairness. Particularly given the similarities with precedent such as *R v Liverpool Corporation, ex p. Liverpool Taxi Fleet Operators' Association*;[417] more recently see *R (Buckingham) v NHS Corby Clinical Commissioning Group*.[418]

M. United States of America

Jeffrey Lubbers and Giacinto della Cananea

In our view, the courts would endorse the argument of Taxi Drivers. Explaining why they probably would do so requires, first, a quick look at the case law and, second, a distinction between process and substance.

414 See Welsh Government (n 297) 37.
415 [1967] EWCA Civ J0823-1.
416 [2013] UKSC 38.
417 [1972] 2 QB 299.
418 [2018] EWHC 2080.

In the United States, the issue whether taxicab licences should be subject to regulation by local authorities (city councils) is an issue that is decided at a state or local level. Several major cities, such as New York, issue licences (called medallions). Taxicab licensing systems may include decisions about capping. Thus, for example, city councils may either decide to amend the licensing structure to allow more participants (newcomers) in the market[419] or order that no more licences should be issued, except for renewals.[420]

That said, under the federal APA, and most if not all state or local APAs, the policy change envisaged in the hypothetical case would be rules, and would be required to be issued after notice and comment (unless it was some sort of emergency—which it doesn't appear to be). If that were true, even without the fact that the municipality reneged on its pledge to use notice and comment—it should do so anyway. Substantively, the change in the rules could be challenged as arbitrary and capricious.[421] The board may be able to justify the changes, but it would have to provide adequate reasoning for them, including that it had taken into account the additional costs imposed on the taxi owners and that it could show an adequate basis for why the changes in policy were necessary.

If, for some reason, no APA applied to the municipality, the taxi drivers could invoke due process concerns and argue that the government must provide fundamental fairness before it can require new expenditures by the licensees or reduce their income, when the licensees had relied on rules in effect at the time they were provided the licence.

419 See *Minneapolis Taxi Owners Coalition, Inc. v City of Minneapolis*, 572 F3d 502, 507-08 (8th Cir 2009).
420 See eg *United States v Yellow Cab Co.*, 332 US 218 (1947).
421 See *FCC v Fox Television Stations*, Inc, 556 US 502 (2009).

IX. Case 8—Sun City: Urban Planning, Private Property, and Procedural Fairness (Duty of Consideration)

A. Austria

Stefan Storr and Sophie Praniess

In this case, there is an important aspect to be emphasized. A plan is not a conditionally defined but a result-oriented form of state action, a legal act aimed at reaching specific goals. The authority is responsible for planning, so also for defining the goals to be attained, and it has extensive discretionary powers in this respect. Under Austrian administrative law, this specificity leads to two fundamental issues. The first to be addressed is the specificity of the statutory basis (*Bestimmtheit der gesetzlichen Grundlage*, cf Article 18 para 2 B-VG), which determines the scope of the authority's discretion in planning.

The second aspect to be taken into account is compliance with the legally defined procedure for issuing a plan.[422] Procedural correctness is of particular importance if its purpose is to determine the factual basis for planning and goal setting.[423] For this reason, section 2 paragraph 1 of the building regulations for Vienna,[424] for example, expressly mandates that preparing a spatial plan initially requires an assessment of the natural, ecological, economic, infrastructural, social and cultural conditions.

In Austria, zoning plans (*Flächenwidmungspläne*) are issued by municipalities as regional laws (*Landesgesetze*).[425] Accordingly, each region has its own zoning act. However, as all nine regional zoning acts are very similar, it is sufficient to refer to one of them for analysis in this case.

Section 38 of the Styrian zoning act[426]—exemplary for all—specifies that the draft for the preparation or modification of a zoning plan must be made accessible, and an opportunity to provide feedback must be provided. The decision is to be publicly announced through posting on the official notice board. Furthermore, the specific authorities, interest groups, and landowners concerned must be individually notified.

In practice, there is no legal requirement to engage in dialogue with stakeholders. Nevertheless, the municipal council must discuss objections promptly and take them into account as far as possible when considering the local regional planning interests. After a resolution has been adopted, those who have raised objections must be notified as to whether their objections have been accepted or not; if they have not been accepted, reasons must be given.

However, there is no general rule providing for a consultation with persons concerned or affected. This is due to the fact that the zoning plan is issued as an ordinance

422 Antoniolli and Koja (n 3) 174.

423 VfSlg 17161/2004.

424 Building Regulations for Vienna (*Wiener Stadtentwicklungs-, Stadtplanungs- und Baugesetzbuch (Bauordnung für Wien—BO für Wien)*), OrigVers: LGBl. No 11/1930.

425 Arti 15 para 1 B-VG.

426 Styrian Regional Planning Act (*Gesetz vom 23. März 2010 über die Raumordnung in der Steiermark (Steiermärkisches Raumordnungsgesetz 2010 – StROG)*), Orig Vers: LGBl. No 49/2010.

and—as explained above—there is no general law to regulate the procedure for issuing an ordinance in this respect.

Based on the Styrian zoning act, the Austrian Constitutional Court would likely overturn the ordinance due to its procedural flaws.

B. China

Xiaowei Sun

The court would judge the case based on 'fundamental principles of fair procedure' and would rule in favour of Suburbia.

Urbanization plans are generally considered regulatory acts under Article 13 of the Administrative Litigation Law and therefore cannot be challenged in court.[427] Otherwise, courts will allow interested persons to challenge detailed urban plans if their interests are concretely affected. Sun City's local plan would be regarded as a detailed plan affecting the plaintiffs' rights.

Regarding the procedural lawfulness of the decision relating to a detailed urban plan, two cases adjudicated by the High People's Court of Guangdong Province in 2018[428] and 2019[429] may provide some clarifications. In these two cases, the local urban authority made a detailed urban plan without consulting the interested persons, on the grounds that the local regulations did not specify a procedure for making such a decision. The court rejected the argument of the urban authority. It considered that even if there were no clear procedural rules for making detailed urban decisions, this did not mean that there were no procedural restrictions. It confirmed that the legality of the detailed urban plan depended on whether this decision was made in compliance with the 'fundamental principles of fair procedure',[430] especially the principle of Due Process.[431] The High People's Court of Guangdong Province declared the detailed urban decision unlawful. Since the annulment of this decision was likely to harm the public interest of an entire neighbourhood, the decision was not quashed, but compensation was ordered for the applicants.

C. Czech Republic

Daniel Burda

A response to this question requires some clarification regarding the mode of regulation of procedural issues in the Czech Republic. The scenario itself raises only a hypothetical situation in the Czech legal system, namely that the process of adopting a local

[427] Supreme People's Court, 30 March 2020, No 2019-10407 (2019最高法行申10407号).
[428] High People's Court of Guangdong Province, 5 March 2018, No 2017-1544 (2017粤行终1544号).
[429] High People's Court of Guangdong Province, 27 June 2019, No 2018-378 (2018粤行终378号).
[430] 最基本公正程序原则.
[431] 正当程序原则. Concerning the concept of 'due process', see 'China—Case 2', section III.B in this chapter.

development plan is not in principle regulated by laws, and its basic limits must therefore be inferred from more general legal rules or principles. However, this is not the case in the Czech legal system, and such a situation is generally not inherent to it. Legal regulation adopted in the form of a statute at the national level provides for the process of adopting a local development plan in detail.[432] In addition, various administrative processes and procedures are generally regulated in the Code of Administrative Procedure,[433] which applies subsidiarily; or alternatively, there are provisions regulating the basic principles of the activity of administrative authorities enshrined in the same Code. If—quite hypothetically—there were no regulation of the basic principles, it is possible that the courts would infer similar rules from the constitutionally enshrined right to a fair trial; nevertheless, it would be difficult to predict a court's decision in this respect. In our opinion, it is therefore useful to structure the answer to the question into several hypotheses, so that we can describe as comprehensively as possible both what the Czech administrative law is like (ie highlighting the current legal situation) on the one hand, and, on the other, and more generally, on what principles it operates (ie how it would respond to the hypothetical situation outlined in this scenario).

First of all, it should be noted that the local development plan is adopted in the form of a general measure, that is, in the form of a so-called mixed act. It is of a regulatory nature, directed outside of the public administration and, first and foremost, it is concrete in terms of the subject of regulation but abstract in terms of the determination of its addressees—it is not personalized (for more information on this issue, see the general part). This legal form is for one established formally, that is, directly by a statute,[434] and for another it might also be inferred from the essential elements of the local development plan, which is also significant.

1) Here we come to a kind of subsidiary (middle) hypothesis, which would apply if the Czech legal system did not contain special rules for the adoption of a local development plan in the Planning and Building Regulations Act. The Code of Administrative Procedure, as a basic and general regulation of administrative processes and procedures, regulates, in its individual parts, procedures (procedural regimes) leading to the issuance or adoption of various types of acts within the framework of administration performing public power prerogatives (irrespective of whether they are issued by state administration bodies, local or professional self-government, or other public administration which represents a kind of residual category). In Part Six, the Code of Administrative Procedure regulates the procedure for issuing general measures. There are two basic principles which are essential for the application of the Code of Administrative Procedure; as a result of the general subsidiarity of the Code of Administrative Procedure, the procedural rules set out there are always applied unless a special law provides for its own regulation (or rather to the extent to which a special law does not provide for special regulation)[435] and, at the same time, unless a special law explicitly excludes the application of the Code of Administrative Procedure or

[432] Act No 283/2021 Sb, the Building Act

[433] Act No 500/2004 Sb, the Code of Administrative Procedure.

[434] See s 73(1) of the Building Act.

[435] Which is the manifestation of the legal principle of *Lex specialis derogat legi generali.*

its individual parts. The other principle is closely related to the previous one and allows its full implementation. The Code of Administrative Procedure perceives various forms of administrative acts as to their functions (based on their essential elements), so if, for example, it defines the concept of a administrative decision[436] using certain features, then any act of public administration provided for by a special law which satisfies these features is subject to the relevant procedural regime set out in the Code of Administrative Procedure. This, of course, applies if a law does not expressly prescribe that an act in question takes a different form (eg it does not prescribe that the act must take the form of an administrative regulation instead of a general measure).

This general regulation also presupposes the participation of various persons whose legal sphere could be affected by the issuance of a general measure in the issuance procedure. The Code of Administrative Procedure specifically grants certain procedural rights to persons whose (substantive) rights, obligations, or interests may be directly affected by a general measure.[437] This group of persons is then further subdivided into those who may potentially be affected directly in terms of their right to real property ownership and other directly affected persons. The former group may submit (in writing and within a statutory period) their 'objections to a draft measure of a general nature', which is to be published as a public notice on an official notice board (ie not in a personalized way). It would include reasoning. Other directly affected persons may submit their 'comments on the draft'. The objections are—in the theory—a more powerful procedural instrument, as the administrative body must decide on them; decisions on individual objections then become a part of the reasoning of the measure of a general nature; however, such decisions must have all the elements of a administrative decision (ie be of an individual nature, contain the statement and reasoning). The administrative body is also obliged to deal with the comments, which are a weaker procedural instrument. It is the duty of the administrative body to deal with them in the reasoning of a general measure, but they are not decided on individually.

Therefore, if the court in the case at hand applied the general regulation to the procedure for issuing a general measure as regulated in the Code of Administrative Procedure, it would rule in favour of the applicants (Suburbia) because it would find that their objections (but not the objections of other persons—they would have to defend themselves) or comments (it is not possible to determine exactly from the scenario what procedural position the applicants would have in the procedure of adopting the local development plan) are not contained in the reasoning of the local development plan, which runs contrary to the law. For this reason, the court would quash the local development plan in question.

2) In the case of a hypothesis based entirely on the current legal regulation, it would also be necessary to take into account the special procedural regulation for adopting a local development plan contained in the Building Act. It regulates the process for adopting a local development plan (as a general measure) in much greater detail, while also dividing it into several stages (with a possibility for the public to be involved at various stages). At the same time, unlike the general regulation in the Code of Administrative Procedure, the Building Act simplifies the modes of participation of

436 See s 9 and s 67 of the Code of Administrative Procedure.

437 See s 172(4) and (5) to the Code of Administrative Procedure.

the public. It allows to everybody (there is no condition of direct affection in rights) to make comments to the proposal of local development plan. The real property owners concerned have not the special regime.[438]

3) The third hypothesis is probably closest to the scenario at hand. In this case, we would assume that there is no special regulation for the adoption of a local development plan in the Planning and Building Regulations Act. At the same time, the Act excludes the application of the Code of Administrative Procedure in such cases, including the general regulation of the procedure for the issuance of a measure of a general nature contained in Part VI thereof. Even in such a case, of course, we would not find ourselves in a legal vacuum; this would be contrary to the principle of legality, ie, contrary to the constitutionally enshrined principle that public authority may be asserted only in cases, within the bounds, and in the manner provided for by a statute;[439] it is inconceivable that the procedure for the adoption of the local development plan would be left to the arbitrariness of the Sun City bodies. In such a case, at least the basic principles governing the activities of administrative bodies, which constitute the introductory part of the Code of Administrative Procedure[440] and which provide the basic procedural framework—largely derived from the values protected by the Constitution and international treaties (the principle of fair trial, and the like) and from the principle of good administration—for any acts of administration performing public power prerogatives, would apply. These principles are directly applicable.

In the case at hand, the rule under section 4(4) of the Code of Administrative Procedure would apply, according to which an administrative body is obliged to allow persons potentially affected by an administrative act under preparation to assert their rights and legitimate interests. This would imply, in our case, an obligation on the part of the competent body of Sun City municipality to consult the local plan with the persons concerned (including the applicants) prior to its approval.[441] Therefore, the court would probably endorse the first plea in part. However, the question is whether it would also infer that the administrative body must respond to (deal with) the comments made by those persons in an explicit way (in the reasoning)—that is to say, whether it would also endorse the other plea. The answer to this question would be decisive in the case at hand. The applicants' (Suburbia's) issue is not that they had not the possibility to raise their comments, but that they believe their comments were not taken into account. While no such obligation is explicitly set out in the basic principles, we believe that the administrative courts would likely infer an obligation on the part of the competent Sun City's body to justify the local plan (a measure of a general nature) and to adequately respond in reasoning to comments raised in the consultations. In the past, the administrative courts followed a similar approach in relation to administrative decisions where the application of the Code of Administrative

[438] See s 97 of Building Act.

[439] See art 2(3) of the Constitution along with art 2(2) of the Charter of Fundamental Rights and Freedoms.

[440] See ss 2–8. They are, to some extent, of a quasi-constitutional nature because they apply even when a special law completely rules out applying the Code of Administrative Procedure to the course of action of the administrative body but does not itself establish a regulation comparable to the basic principles of the Code. This rule is contained in s 177(1) of the Code of Administrative Procedure.

[441] Compare with the resolution of the expanded panel of the Supreme Administrative Court of 22 October 2014, File Ref No 8 As 55/2012-62 (count 108).

Procedure had been excluded. According to the courts, the obligation to state reasons for administrative decisions arose from fundamental principles and, in a broader sense, from the right to a fair trial (or rather the right to a judicial review). If the persons concerned (ie the applicants—Suburbia in our case) have the right to judicial review,[442] the courts 'must have something to review'; in other words, the court must have sources capable of being reviewed—that is, also the considerations which have led the administrative body to adopt a particular solution (reasoning), including how the comments made were dealt with.[443] Thus, we believe that the court would side with the applicants' (Suburbia's) arguments.

D. European Union

Marco Lunardelli

As the case at issue concerns planning law, a subject matter that does not fall within EU competences, it might appear difficult to adapt it to the EU legal system. However, EU institutions have the power to intervene and adopt policies on the environment. Since the two subject matters are closely related, Member States' urban planning laws have long been influenced by EU environmental law.[444] Therefore, as EU law is at least indirectly involved, the main issue here is whether the consultees' participation in the decision-making process, which, according to a group of residents, was disregarded in the final version of the plan adopted by the municipality, is relevant only from a procedural perspective or also from a substantive one. The duty of care appears to be capable of keeping these two perspectives together. First, this duty is essentially conceived of as a procedural guarantee for the private (and public) parties involved in proceedings, and, so understood, it has been referred to as 'the principle of careful and impartial examination' of all relevant aspects in a specific case.[445] Intended as an application of the principle of good administration, established by Article 41(1) of the Charter of Fundamental Rights of the European Union, it has usually been recognized by the ECJ and the Tribunal in proceedings different from those devoted to rulemaking and planning, such as public procurement proceedings to ensure competition.[446] This

[442] Under art 36(2) of the Charter of Fundamental Rights and Freedoms, 'a person who claims that their rights have been curtailed by a decision of a public administrative authority may turn to a court to have the legality of the decision reviewed, unless the law provides otherwise'.

[443] On the issue, see eg the Supreme Administrative Court judgment of 4 February 2010, File Ref No 7 Afs 1/2010-53 and of 11 June 2020, File Ref No 7 As 28/2019-41.

[444] See J-B Auby, 'The Influence of European Law on Planning' (1998) 4(1) EPL 49–50.

[445] See Mendes, 'Discretion, Care and Public Interests' (n 384) 426. As for case law, see Case T-31/99, *ABB Asea Brown Boveri Ltd v Commission*, ECLI:EU:T:2002:77, § 99.

[446] See Case T-54/99, *max.mobil Telekommunikation Service GmbH v Commission*, ECLI:EU:T:2002:20, §§ 48–51. The case was appealed before the ECJ, which laid down substantially the same arguments in this regard. See Case C-141/02 P, Grand Chamber, ECLI:EU:C:2005:98, §§ 16–18. In this judgment, the ECJ also held (§§ 67–70) that, even if an individual may have a specific interest in the annulment of a decision of general scope but theoretically capable of affecting that interest (§§ 64–65), it does not mean that this individual is always entitled to bring an action for annulment. Indeed, it has to be ascertained whether the decision at issue is a 'challengeable measure'. This principle—the ECJ added—'is not at variance with the

way, the principle also has substantive importance, as the EU Commission, in making a discretionary assessment of the EU's (sole) interest, has to properly take into account 'all the relevant matters of law and fact in order to decide what action to take in response to a complaint'.[447] The same holds true in the domain of state aid.[448] However, given the close relationship between urban planning and environmental law, the precautionary principles require that the careful and impartial of all relevant aspects in a specific case also be understood to demand the scientific objectivity of the measures adopted, thus avoiding the risk of arbitrariness; that is, an abuse of discretion. In other words, an accurate scientific risk assessment must be carried out.[449]

Therefore, the ECJ considers the duty of care capable of restricting administrative discretion, and, as such, it does not apply only to individual proceedings but also to those that will conclude with the adoption of an act of general character.[450] The principle of good administration has a twofold meaning, as it may be seen both as an overall concept encompassing all the rights and principles good administration implies for any administrative proceedings carried out and as the expression of procedural guarantees in specific proceedings.[451] The ECJ also considers the duty of care (or diligence) in proceedings resulting in the adoption of measures of general application to be similar but not tantamount to a procedural guarantee to be applied to individual proceedings, ie, a guarantee that may be enforced before the ECJ by an affected person bringing an annulment action or a claim for damages in the exercise of their own right of defence.[452] In individual proceedings, the duty of the competent authority to thoroughly and impartially examine all the relevant aspects of the individual case gives the affected person the right to express their view and obtain an adequately reasoned decision.[453] In proceedings where the authority has to assess candidates or compare multiple participants' legal positions, such a duty, being a procedural guarantee, falls

principle of sound administration or with any other general principle of Community law' (§ 72). See M Eliantonio and F Grashof, 'Types of Administrative Action and Corresponding Review' in C Backes and M Eliantonio (eds), *Judicial Review of Administrative Action* (Hart 2019) 131–32.

[447] Case C-449/98 P, *International Express Carriers Conference (IECC) v Commission*, ECLI:EU:C:2001:275, § 45.

[448] See Case T-95/96, *Gestevisión Telecinco SA v Commission*, ECLI:EU:T:1998:206, § 53.

[449] See Case T-13/99, *Pfizer Animal Health SA* v *Council*, ECLI:EU:T:2002:209, §§ 170–172, concerning the authorization of antibiotics used as additives in food stuff, esp. §§ 170–172. See HCH Hofmann and M Tidghi, 'Rights and Remedies in Implementation of EU Policies by Multi-Jurisdictional Networks' (2014) 20(1) EPL 150 n 17, referring to these paragraphs of the judgment as an example of the application of the duty of care to risk regulation. The judgment at issue has also been mentioned to highlight the strict interpretation of the 'manifest error of assessment' test traditionally adopted by the ECJ in reviewing the completeness and accuracy of the information contained in the evidence on which complex assessments are based and the consistency of the conclusions drawn from that information. See H Pünder and A Klafki, 'Grounds of Review and Standard of Review' in Backes and Eliantonio (eds), *Judicial Review* (n 446) 463 n 72.

[450] See Mendes, 'Discretion, Care and Public Interests' (n 384) 430–33.

[451] See L Azoulai, 'Le principe de bonne administration' in Auby and Dutheil de la Rochère (n 379) 495.

[452] See Case T-369/03 (order), *Arizona Chemical BV and Others v Commission*, ECLI:EU:T:2005:458, §§ 86–89. This order, issued by the Court of First Instance, was upheld by the ECJ. See Case C-150/06 P (order), ECLI:EU:C:2007:164, esp §§ 45–48 and 50.

[453] See Case C-269/90, *Technische Universität München v Hauptzollamt München-Mitte*, ECLI:EU:C:1991:438, § 14.

within the scope not only of the aforementioned principle of good (or sound) administration but also of the principle of equal treatment, which requires that similar situations be treated in the same way but different ones in a different way.[454]

There appears to be no specific provision in the EU legal system to solve the case at issue. However, it involves an urban plan adopted by a municipal administration, and plans may have—potentially at least—different external effects, as they may concern an indefinite number of addresses, not only in national legal systems but also at EU level.[455] The group of residents challenging the local administration's new urban policy, namely the final statement that did not take into account their representations, allege that they may be adversely affected by that policy without having a real opportunity to express their views. In the EU legal system, the ECJ's review on compliance with the duty of care, understood in the manner explained above, is fundamental when the Commission or another administrative authority is assigned broad discretion, as the exercise of the latter 'is only subject to a limited judicial review of the merits'.[456] Therefore, the violation of a fair procedure alleged by the group of residents also seems to be relevant from the substantive perspective. Indeed, when adopting urban plans, authorities usually enjoy a wide margin of discretion. Although—as observed—the review of compliance with the duty of care in these cases is not as strict as it is when an authority carries out individual proceedings, since no individual guarantees may be judicially enforced, the ECJ may still detect a violation of EU law, especially of the duty of care as a component of the principle of good administration, should it be asked to provide a preliminary ruling on interpretation. In the light of all the considerations mentioned above, a potential violation can be viewed from either a procedural or a substantive perspective.

E. Germany

Lilly Weidemann

The court would probably endorse Suburbia's arguments regarding the breach of the obligation to consult stakeholders.

Even without an explicit statutory requirement to engage in debate with consultees,[457] the requirement to consult means having to consider statements and

[454] See Case T-410/03, *Hoechst GmbH v Commission*, ECLI:EU:T:2008:211, §§ 128–130. For such a content of the principle of equal treatment, albeit specifically referred to the duty of impartiality imposed upon the public administration by art 97 of the Italian Constitution, see already P Barile, 'Il dovere di imparzialità della pubblica amministrazione' in *Scritti giuridici in memoria di Piero Calamandrei* (vol IV, Cedam 1958) 37. See also G della Cananea and C Franchini, *I principi dell'amministrazione europea* (3rd edn, Giappichelli 2017) 74, arguing that to apply the principle of equality—*rectius*, of equal treatment—does not require 'the equalizing' of any individual position. On the principle of good (or sound) administration, see n 446.

[455] See Curtin, Hofmann, and Mendes (n 387) § 20, 51.

[456] Case T-333/10, *ATC and Others v Commission*, ECLI:EU:T:2013:451, § 84. This was an interlocutory order, ie, an interim measure, as the Eighth Chamber of the GC subsequently pointed out. See Order of 17 September 2014, ECLI:EU:T:2014:842, §§ 2–3.

[457] For so-called procedures for planning approval, the German APA actually does provide for a duty to discuss objections of persons affected by the project (s 73 para 6 APA: 'Following the closing date for lodging objections, the hearing authority shall *discuss* those objections made to the plan in good time, and

ponder them appropriately during the decision-making process. The participation procedure must not be merely pro forma.[458]

Although there are no abstract rules on how a participation process must be conducted, those affected by the standard must be placed in such a position as to present their specific concerns in the standard-setting process in an appropriate manner.[459]

With regard to the consultation procedure concerning planning permission, it is generally acknowledged that it serves a variety of purposes.[460] It ensures that the project is publicized by informing other authorities and interested members of the public; that is, it serves to ensure the transparency of official actions. It serves the right to a fair procedure, in particular the substantive consultation of those whose interests may be affected by the project. The hearing procedure constitutes a form of protection of fundamental rights through proceedings by means of legal safeguards in the administrative procedure. The consultation should take account of the public interest in gathering as much information as possible about the relevant facts and the legal situation. The opinions of other authorities and associations to be involved, as well as the objections of privately affected parties, improve the planning authority's overview of the actual and legal effects of the project. They expand the decision-making material for the final planning decision and are grounds for initiating a revision of the plan. The consultation procedure can optimize planning and help to pacify conflicts between divergent interests.[461]

To adequately protect the individual rights of those affected by the norm, the concerns raised must not only be addressed formally but they must also be discussed in factual and legal terms in order to clarify the issues raised and find a solution to the concerns that arise which is able to balance the interests concerned.[462] This has not been the case here, as Sun City has not even referred to the representations made by the consultees.

F. Hungary

Lilla Berkes and Balázs Szabolcs Gerencsér

The substantive rules on building and urban planning strictly separate the scope and means of political, professional, and legal decisions. The political decision is the first phase in which the involvement of the stakeholders is possible. The professional phase is the engineering and design work, while the legal decision is the drafting of the actual local regulation for the site. Since the rights and position of Suburbia are

the opinions of the authorities with regard to the plan, with the project developer, the authorities, the persons affected by the plan and those who have lodged objections to it' (emphasis added).

458 Higher Administrative Court Lower Saxony, Judgment of 14 November 2018—13 KN 249/16, BeckRS 2018, 30397 Rn 43.

459 Hufen and Siegel (n 78).

460 W Neumann and C Külpmann, 'VwVfG § 73' in Stelkens, Bonk, and Sachs (n 78) para 7.

461 ibid.

462 T Weiß, 'VwVfG § 73' in Schoch and Schneider (eds) (n 80) para 329.

clearly affected by the proposed regulation, its involvement in the development of the plan would have been necessary. (In the relationship between the capital of Hungary, Budapest, and its agglomeration, there have been several attempts to create a joint urban plan. At present, it is the 'Danube coastal building code', which is created in co-operation with several local self-governments as districts of Budapest.)

G. Italy

Leonardo Parona

The case concerns a procedure leading to the adoption of a local plan: a typical example of general administrative act which, in the Italian legal system, has long been regulated by sector-specific legislation. More precisely, the subject is concurrently regulated by state and regional law, with Law No 1150/1942 representing the general normative framework. Essentially, once urban planning projects are adopted (*adozione*) and published by the Municipality, the law allows all citizens to submit written observations, ensuring even greater participation (in the form of oppositions) for parties possibly affected in a direct and individual way by specific provisions of the planning act (eg if the plan establishes that a state-run school will be built in a certain area, resulting in expropriation). Once observations are collected and addressed (perhaps through the publication of a general act in response, and potentially amending the initial plan), the plan is approved by the regional government (*approvazione*) and published again. It then becomes effective. Regional laws establish mechanisms to ensure greater public participation, also prior to the initial adoption of the plan.

In the case of the local planning procedure conducted by Sun City, consultation was actually ensured, with citizens allowed to submit representations. The residents of Suburbia, however, were not convinced that the consultation was meaningful or effective. In fact, when the Municipality finally adopted the plan (which is a broadly discretionary general act), it did not refer to the representations, nor did it provide reasons for disregarding them. The residents of Suburbia requested something more from the administration, seeking an actual debate that would require the Municipality to specifically consider each position and address the requests made by the residents in the motivation of the final act. Framed in these terms, the request advanced by the residents of Suburbia is indeed quite burdensome.

The issues concerning the contested fairness of the procedure therefore regard two related aspects: meaningful participation on the one hand, and adequate consideration of the consultees in the reasoning of the final act, on the other.

As far as the first aspect is concerned, besides the specifics of regional legislation, which cannot be addressed here,[463] it should be recognized that Italian law does not

[463] On this topic, see A Simonati, 'La partecipazione dei privati al governo del territorio nella legislazione regionale fra tradizione e sperimentazione. Per una nuova urbanistica 'reticolare'' (2016) 3 Rivista giuridica dell'edilizia 268 ff; A Simonati, 'La partecipazione dei privati alla pianificazione urbanistica: il modello dell'inchiesta e le suggestioni provenienti dai sistemi europei' (2012) 1–2 Rivista giuridica dell'urbanistica 312 ff.

require an actual debate during local planning procedures, but only that written observations be submitted before final adoption of the plan.[464] Further procedural guarantees, akin to the participation rights established by the general Law No 241/1990, are however excluded, since the latter 'does not apply, in fact, to procedures for the adoption of urban planning instruments (in compliance with the letter of Article 13, Law No 241[/1990])'. This is because 'on the ontological level, the need for cross-examination between the public and private parties is already safeguarded within the current regulations on the formation of primary urban planning instruments (publication, submission of observations, examination, counterarguments, approval)'.[465] According to the case law, therefore, the way procedural safeguards are established by Italian law with regard to local planning procedures is not incompatible with the principle of procedural fairness. As a consequence, the claim by the residents of Suburbia that a debate should have been allowed, could not be accepted by the court. In fact, as observed by the administrative court: 'The rules governing the approval process of the urban planning instrument ... do not impose any obligation to 'convene' the private individuals involved in an urban planning procedure.'[466]

Coming now to the second issue, it is necessary to begin with the premise that—according to Article 3(2) Law No 241/1990—reasons need not be given for general administrative acts. As a consequence, administrative jurisprudence has clarified that observations formulated by owners affected by municipal planning merely constitute collaborative contributions to the formation of the urban planning instrument; their rejection, therefore, does not require detailed justification, as it is sufficient that they have been examined and considered in a serious and reasonable manner, and deemed in incompatible with the considerations of general public interest underlying the plan.[467] Conversely, 'should a specific response to private individuals' observations be required, then the planning activity would lose its general character and would result in the sum of an inextricable number of specific situations'.[468] Although this solution has been criticized in part, since it arguably renders public participation in urban planning procedures quite ineffective and meaningless,[469] the case law is unanimous and consolidated on this point. Therefore, it would be extremely improbable that the residents of Suburbia's arguments would be endorsed by the court.

For a court to judicially impose the requirement to provide reasons on the Municipality, it would be necessary for the plan to contain provisions specifically affecting the differentiated and individualized positions of particular citizens.[470] This, however, does not occur in our case, since the policy not to permit the construction of new buildings applies to the territory of the whole municipality. A different solution could be reached if, for instance, the policy only applied to the neighbourhood

[464] Arts 9–10, Law No 1150/1942, see on this Council of State, Sec IV, No 5547/2013, No 1236/2005.

[465] Lombardy Administrative Court, Milan, Sec II, No 477/2021.

[466] Lombardy Administrative Court, Milan, Sec II, No 879/2021.

[467] See eg Council of State, Sec IV, No 1316/2023; No 6803/2020; No 874/2017; No 3643/2016; No 2973/2014.

[468] Piedmont Administrative Court, Turin, Sec II, No 824/2022, referring on this point to Council of State, Sec II, No 2378/2020.

[469] On this debate, see A Cassatella, 'La motivazione dei piani urbanistici: aspetti evolutivi' (2016) 3 Rivista giuridica dell'edilizia 289 ff.

[470] Council of State, Sec IV, No 811/2009.

of Suburbia, while in the rest of the municipality the construction of new buildings would still be allowed.[471]

H. Netherlands

Jacobine van den Brink, Louise Verboeket, and Veerle van Waarde

According to Article 3.8(1) of the Spatial Planning Act (*Wet ruimtelijke ordening*), a zoning plan (*bestemmingsplan*) in the Netherlands must be prepared using the uniform public preparatory procedure (*uniforme openbare voorbereidingsprocedure*).[472] The public preparatory procedure is described in Division 3.4 GALA and ensures that everyone concerned (*belanghebbenden*) can state their opinion (*zienswijze*) regarding a (draft) decision.[473] To this end, the application or the draft will be published in a government-issued gazette and will set out who has the opportunity to state their views and how this can be done.[474] Article 3:15(1) GALA states that the uniform public preparatory procedure is generally used for the interested parties concerned. However, according to Article 3:15(2) GALA, statutory regulation or the administrative authority (*bestuursorgaan*) may provide other individuals with the opportunity to express their views. The time limit for expressing a view will normally be six weeks.[475] The definitive decision is adopted taking into due consideration the opinions. Article 3:44(2) GALA states that the decision will be made available for inspection with the documents relating to the case, including the opinions brought forward. In addition, Articles 3:46 and 3:47 GALA require administrative authorities to take the opinions into consideration when giving proper reasons for the zoning plan. Taking the above into account, the municipality of Sun City must prepare the zoning plan by using the uniform public preparatory procedure. The municipality should consider the opinions when the draft zoning plan is adopted and also explain why the opinions do not lead to adjustments to the zoning plan.

If the uniform public preparatory procedure is not applicable, the principle of due care (*zorgvuldigheidsbeginsel*), as laid down in Article 3:2 GALA, requires the municipality to adopt a fair procedure before reaching a decision that may adversely affect a group of persons. Under Dutch law, this principle is only set out in the more concrete requirements for single-case decisions. Before taking a single-case decision that affects a party concerned who has not applied for it, Article 4:8(1) GALA requires administrative authorities to give these parties a chance to state their views if the decision is based on information about facts and interests relating to the party concerned that

[471] Even in this latter case, however, the plan would be subject to 'the scrutiny typical of discretionary acts reviewable ab external (according to the canons of manifest unreasonableness, arbitrariness and/or obvious misrepresentation of the conditions)' (Council of State, Sec IV, No 8429/2019).

[472] It should be noted that this text was written before the Environment and Planning Act (*Omgevingswet*) was enacted. This law has replaced the Spatial Planning Act (*Wet ruimtelijke ordening*).

[473] See art 3:15 GALA and C Backes and M Eliantonio (eds), *Cases, Materials and Text on Judicial Review of Administrative Action. Maastricht Edition* (Hart Publishing 2019) 109 and 297.

[474] Art 3:12 GALA in conjunction with art 12 Publication Act (*Bekendmakingswet*).

[475] Art 3:16(1) GALA.

was not supplied by the party concerned itself. This Article can be applied in the same way as other decisions in single-case decisions.

In conclusion, assuming that Suburbia has standing under Article 1:2(3) GALA,[476] the court would side with Suburbia.

I. Norway

Eivind Smith

If the relevant local plan is legally binding, but of a general nature only, Norwegian law does not require specific formal reasons (unlike the requirement to give reasons when it comes to individual acts). In practice, the necessary 'justification' of which the final plan is a product is supposed to appear in the plan itself.

J. Portugal

Rui Guerra da Fonseca

The residents of Suburbia are making a procedural claim, but they risk potential substantive damage: the prohibition of new buildings. Before addressing the procedural issue, let us contextualize it by looking briefly at the substantive aspect.[477]

The classification and reclassification of land is a planning option that defines its use (Article 10/3 and 4 of the Law of Public Policy for Land, Planning and Urban Planning— 'LPPSPU')[478] at the intermunicipal and/or municipal levels (Articles 20/1 and 43). In Portuguese law, as in many other legal orders, urban plans are municipal.[479] There are three kinds of municipal urban plans: main municipal plans, urbanization plans, and detailing plans. These plans are all mandatory for both public authorities and private parties (Article 46).

According to Article 17/1 of the LPPSPU, the relinquishing of pre-existing legally sound rights can only occur if the law or plans (which are administrative norms or regulations) allow it, and compensation is paid. Although the technical meaning of 'pre-existing rights' and 'legally solid' rights may be open to discussion, Article 17/3 makes it very clear that compensation is due for any sacrifice with the equivalent effect

[476] Suburbia advocates in particular for the interests of the residents most affected by municipal polices, as evidenced by its objectives outlined in their statutes and factual activities. See ABRvS 1 October 2008, ECLI:NL:RVS:2008:BF3911 (*Stichting Openbare Ruimte*).

[477] The case bears many similarities to the one addressed in R Guerra da Fonseca, 'IV. Case 3: Participation and Due Process in Urban Planning' in M Conticelli and T Perroud (eds), *Procedural Requirements for Administrative Limits to Property Rights* (OUP 2022) 131 ff, so we will refer to many of the points covered there on this occasion.

[478] See Law 31/2014, of 30/05.

[479] This is actually a 'European common': see R Guerra da Fonseca, 'Sobre uma hipotética harmonização europeia ao nível dos campos de aplicação da descentralização territorial' in AM Cordeiro and others (eds) *Estudos em Homenagem ao Professor Doutor Paulo de Pitta e Cunha—Volume I—Assuntos Europeus e Integração Económica* (Almedina, Coimbra 2010) 1215 ff.

to an expropriation ('sacrifice expropriation') imposed on land owners, regardless of any technicalities.

Planning and programming the use of land is a public obligation (Article 8/2 al. *a)* LPPSPU). For reasons of general interest, public authorities must make decisions regarding the uses of land (public and private), and these decisions often limit the possibilities that a certain piece of land offers at a given moment. In other words, private owners are sometimes faced with changes regarding the possible use of their land. For instance, a portion of land that could be used for building might lose this option because the public authorities suddenly consider that it is part of a natural reserve or is due to be used for a public infrastructure. These possibilities must be accepted as the price or risk of living in a society. Accordingly, indemnities for these changes tend to be subject to strict (if not exceptional) conditions and time limits.[480] The restrictions imposed by plans have an effect equivalent to expropriation. They do not transfer ownership of the land to a third party, but they deprive or diminish the owner's ability to use the land. This is why they are called 'expropriations of sacrifice', 'plan expropriations', or 'substantial expropriations',[481] which are all perfectly admissible in Portuguese law and recognized by the Constitutional Court[482] and the Administrative Supreme Court.[483]

Turning to the procedural aspect, participation in procedures regarding uses of land, planning and urban planning is a general right guaranteed under Articles 6/2 and 49 of the LPPSPU, along with access to information held by the public authorities. However, in the field of urban planning, there are specific rules regarding participation before new planning rules (which have the nature of administrative rules) are adopted.[484]

The Land Planning Instruments Law[485] (LPIL) establishes a complex network of participatory rights when public authorities want to introduce changes to these plans (Articles 118, 119). Many aspects depend on the type of change. In any case, the public authorities must initiate the procedure and provide public information to citizens, allowing suggestions and other interventions (Article 88). There is a period

[480] See arts 171/4 and 5 LPPSPU.

[481] See F Alves Correia, *Manual de Direito do Urbanismo*, II (Almedina 2010) 132; FP Oliveira, *Regime Jurídico dos Instrumentos de Gestão Territorial* (Almedina 2012) 484.

[482] See Decisions of the Constitutional Court 341/86, 131/88, 184/92, 262/93, and—most relevantly to the situation in question—329/99 and 517/99. On this case law, see Alves Correia (n 481) 137–38.

[483] See Decision of the Supreme Administrative Court, Pr 0996/06, 15/10/2014. This issue is related to an important debate on whether the *ius aedificandi* (the right to build) is inherent to the right of property, or if it is attributed by public authorities through plans (regulations) and other administrative decisions (the latter is the thesis supported by constitutional and administrative case law and is the one most widely accepted in scholarship): see Oliveira (n 481) 484. An example of the minoritary thesis: see J Reis Novais, 'Ainda sobre o ius aedificandi (... mas agora como problema de direitos fundamentais)' in Faculdade de Direito da Universidade de Lisboa (ed) *Estudos Jurídicos e Económicos em Homenagem ao Prof. Doutor António de Sousa Franco* (Coimbra Ed 2006) 493 ff. Considering when building rights have already been attributed not only in general terms by a plan but also adjudicated by a licence — an administrative act or concrete decision, see Guerra da Fonseca, 'IV. Case 3 (n 477) 133.

[484] Even though the CPA rules about prior hearing and public consultation (arts 98 ff CPA) are subsidiary: see the answers to the cases mentioned above for more detailed information and analysis of these norms.

[485] See Decree-Law 80/2015, of 14/05.

of public discussion that is duly publicized. It lasts no less than 20 or 30 working days depending on the type of plan.

Subsequently, according to Article 89/3, the Town Hall must consider all claims, observations, suggestions, and requests for clarification brought to its attention by participants. It is obliged to answer and give proper reasons to all those who claim, 'namely' (i) disconformity or incompatibility with programmes, plans, and projects that must be considered, (ii) disconformity with legal and administrative rules, or (iii) damage to subjective rights. The use of the adverb 'namely' clearly means that other equivalent claims might be subject to the same duty of specified response. These specified responses must be communicated in writing to the claimants, and whenever necessary or convenient, clarifications by the town or other technicians must be provided (Article 89/4 and 5). Furthermore, after public consultation/discussion, the Town Hall must weigh up and publish the results, including in the media and on the internet/electronic platforms before presenting the final version of the proposed plan for approval (Article 89/6).

The residents of Suburbia would thus have standing, and the courts would certainly endorse their arguments.

K. Sweden

Patricia Jonason and Björn Forssén

The competent court (the Land and Environment Court (*Mark och miljödomstolen*)), for examining the appeal of a decision to adopt a detailed plan must, according to section 17, paragraph 1, chapter 13 of the Plan and Building Act (2010:900)[486] (PBL), only examines whether the appealed decision contravenes any rule of law in the manner stated by the appellant or otherwise apparent from the circumstances.

The duty to consult for the carrying out of local plans (detailed plans), as set out in the Plan- and Building Act, includes, *inter alia*, the residents affected as well as associations and individuals who have a significant interest in the proposal (section 11, chapter 5, PBL), which doesn't seem to include consultees. Strictly speaking, therefore, the municipality is not required to listen to the opinions of the consultees.[487]

Moreover, the duty of the municipality to 'report the views that have come to light in the consultation, as well as the comments and proposals that the municipality makes in relation to the views' (section 17, chapter 5, PBL) does not include consultees.

It would therefore be difficult for the appellant to argue that the above-mentioned provisions had been violated.

Perhaps the court could consider that the municipality violated the requirement of objectivity (*saklighet*) laid down in section 1, chapter 9 of the Instrument of Government, which, according to the doctrine, requires administrative authorities

[486] *Plan- och bygglagen.*

[487] It is nevertheless interesting to note that the goals for the consultation mentioned in the law are 'to produce as good a basis for decision as possible' as well as to 'provide the opportunity for transparency and influence' (s 12, Chapter 5, PBL).

to 'ensure that there is a sufficient factual basis for making decisions'.[488] However, the Supreme Administrative Court rarely grants leave to appeal in cases regarding the evaluation of evidence, which makes it difficult to find adequate case law in that matter.[489]

However, if the stakeholders mentioned in the PBL are not consulted, and their comments and reports are not taken into account, the decision will probably be overturned, as was the case in a Land and Environment Court of Appeal judgment concerning a detailed plan.[490] In this case, the court decided that the municipality's failure to send the affected owners the collection of comments received during the consultation and its own proposals in response to the comments constituted a procedural error that justified the cancellation of the plan.

In the context mentioned above, the rationale presented in this judgment is particularly interesting: referring to the court's review limited to the legality of the decision, the court states:

> Since the scope for material review of a detailed plan is limited, there is reason to place relatively strict requirements on the formal processing that precedes the decision. This concerns especially the parts of the processing which aim to enrich the basis of the decision (*beslutsunderlaget*) with the views from relevant stakeholders concerning the type of questions that cannot be subject to any actual review in court.

Thus, the consultation procedure is of the utmost importance.

L. United Kingdom

John Morison and David Mark

It is implied in this scenario that some form of consultation has engendered responses from consultees, who feel that their representations to the administrators of Sun City have largely been ignored. The administrators, the decision-maker in this scenario,

[488] Wenander p 36 who quotes T Bull, 'Objektivitetsprincipen' in L Marcusson (ed), *Offentligrättsliga principer* (4th edn, Iustus 2020) 113. See also Holmberg and others (n 48) 74–75 and Eka and others (n 48) 41–46.

[489] The general requirement of leave to appeal to the Supreme Administrative Court has been introduced in the early 1970s. The goal was 'to transform the Supreme Administrative Court to a pure court of precedent', where leave to appeal is given 'only when a decision by the Supreme Administrative Court is expected to be a precedent or when a serious error has occurred in the handling of the case in lower instances. In 2010, for instance, leave to appeal was only 'granted in 2 to 3 percent of the cases appealed to the Supreme Administrative Court'. See
Rune Lavin and Lars-Göran Malmberg, 'Administrative Law' in M Bogdan (ed), *Swedish Legal System* (Norstedts Juridik 2010) 66–94, 88. Thus, a matter strictly regarding evidence is unlikely to reach the Supreme Administrative Court, unless it is a matter of serious error, and even then, experience speaks against leave to appeal. See also, '*Förvånansvärt mycket oklarheter kring bevisfrågor och processrättsliga principer*' (English translation, 'Surprisingly many uncertainties about evidence issues and procedural principles'), an article in the Internet paper 'Legally Yours' on 4 March 2022 by Stefan Wahlberg, in which he interviews Helena Jäderblom, chairwoman of the Supreme Administrative Court.

[490] MÖD 2019:4.

have responded that there is no express statutory requirement to engage in a 'debate' with consultees.

UK law is clear that consultations, whether mandatory or voluntary, 'must be conducted properly to satisfy the requirements of procedural fairness'.[491] Lord Wilson in *R (on the application of Moseley) v Haringey London Borough Council*[492] endorsed the well-known criteria put forward by Lord Justice Sedley as counsel in the case of *R v Brent London Borough Council ex p Gunning*[493] that consultation must:

1. Occur at a 'formative stage,' allowing it to genuinely influence the outcome.
2. Provide 'sufficient reasons' for proposals, enabling intelligent consideration and response.
3. Allow 'adequate time' for consideration and response.
4. Ensure that the consultation 'product' is 'conscientiously taken into account' in the final decision.

As such, a 'debate' may not be legally mandated, but there is a requirement of fairness and that such consultations, when undertaken, genuinely influence the decision and be conscientiously taken into account.

Indeed, expanding upon the fourth requirement, that the consultation 'product' is 'conscientiously taken into account' in the final decision, the Suburbia residents have argued that the report produced by Sun City has ignored their representations. In UK administrative law, decisions by public authorities must be reasonable and proportionate, encompassing a duty to consider all relevant factors while disregarding irrelevant ones.[494] See for example *R (WX) v Northamptonshire County Council*[495] when the court held a decision to close libraries after a public consultation was unlawful, with Justice Yip noting that whilst the consultation itself was fair, the product of the consultation was not conscientiously taken into account.

That is not to say that decision-makers are without discretion, however, the courts have made it clear that this does not negate the decision-makers responsibility to ensure they consider obviously material and relevant matters; see *R. (on the application of Friends of the Earth Ltd.) v Heathrow Airport Ltd*[496] with regards to relevant and irrelevant considerations.

In conclusion, considering the principles of UK administrative law, particularly the emphasis on procedural fairness and stakeholder consultation, the decision of Sun City appears legally vulnerable. The lack of consultation with the Suburbia group, coupled with the failure to provide reasons for the decision, undermines the principles of procedural fairness and stakeholder engagement in significant policy changes. The cases *of R (Greenpeace Ltd) v Secretary of State for Trade and Industry*,[497] *and Bank Mellat v HM Treasury (No 2)*,[498] among others, suggest a judicial inclination

[491] Government Legal Department (n 218) 40.
[492] [2014] UKSC 56, [2014] 1 WLR 3947.
[493] [1986] 84 LGR 168, 189.
[494] Government Legal Department (n 218) 14, 20.
[495] [2018] EWHC 2178.
[496] [2020] UKSC 52.
[497] [2007] EWHC 311.
[498] [2013] UKSC 38.

towards inclusive and effective consultations, particularly when decisions significantly impact certain groups. Furthermore, cases such as R *(WX) v Northamptonshire County Council*[499] and *R (Kohler) v Mayor's Office for Policing and Crime*[500] indicate a requirement to ensure the product of a consultation is conscientiously taken into account. Note, whilst public bodies must be able to demonstrate that the outcome of the consultation has been taken into consideration that does not necessarily mean that they have to disclose the internal workings of their decision-making processes or the information used to assess the responses to the consultation. Given these factors, it is certainly possible that a court would find the decision-making process of Sun City procedurally flawed and, as a result, could potentially determine the decision unlawful for failing to meet the legal standards of fairness and consultation in administrative law.

M. United States of America

Jeffrey Lubbers and Giacinto della Cananea

Land use (zoning) regulations and individual development permit decisions are mostly governed by state and local law. When the federal government engages in decisions about federal lands, it has to follow the APA and various land use laws as well as consultation and environmental laws such as the National Environmental Policy Act (requiring environmental impact statements) and the Endangered Species Act.

As to state and local land use laws, the general zoning requirements are either determined by legislative statutes or by zoning agency regulations (through rulemaking). The early (pre-APA) outline for how to do this derives from the 1926 Model Act drafted by the US Department of Commerce, 'A Standard State Zoning Enabling Act—Under Which Municipalities May Adopt Zoning Regulations'.[501]

Once such an act is enacted, individual development permits can be adjudicated. There is a model act for such procedures as well, the American Bar Association's, Model Statute on Local Land Use Process.[502]

So applying this to the question, Sun City should follow the rulemaking procedures applicable to rulemaking in that jurisdiction—presumably notice-and-comment procedures. Under the federal APA, even though, by its terms, it does not require an agency to respond to comments on the proposed rule when it issues a final rule, reviewing courts have required that as an aid to their judicial review. The theory is that the court would need to see the response to comments to know whether the agency was arbitrary/capricious in formulating the final rule.

Therefore, the court would likely invalidate the rule and remand it to Sun City for further proceedings.

[499] [2018] EWHC 2178.
[500] [2018] EWHC 1881.
[501] See <https://planning-org-uploaded-media.s3.amazonaws.com/legacy_resources/growingsmart/pdf/SZEnablingAct1926.pdf> accessed 23 November 2024.
[502] See <https://cpb-us-w2.wpmucdn.com/voices.uchicago.edu/dist/4/640/files/2017/11/ModelLandUseCode-253epgk.pdf> accessed 23 November 2024.

X. Case 9—Old Park and the New Tram Route (Cost-Benefit Analysis)

A. Austria

Stefan Storr and Sophie Praniess

The legal requirement to make the decision 'feasible and prudent' is a question of expediency. The lawfulness of non-expedient measures is subject to debate in legal scholarship.[503] The Austrian Constitutional Court, however, does not review the expediency of a measure, and it can only consider unlawfulness in cases of obvious inexpediency. The question of expediency also includes economic efficiency, in particular, a cost-benefit analysis.

However, a distinction must be made between the question of whether the measure under consideration is economically feasible and the question of whether it has been tested and/or analysed for economic feasibility. So far, this analysis is a procedural requirement provided for by law. A measure is in any case unlawful if no review of economic expediency has been carried out by the issuing authority. The court would annul the authority's decision for this reason.

However, it should be noted that the possibility of bringing an action to court depends on the infringement of the complainant's subjective public right. The inexpediency or inefficiency of a decision does not, in principle, violate any subjective rights of a citizen.

B. China

Xiaowei Sun

The court would probably be satisfied with Moderna's position.

The decision to construct a tram line would not be regarded as a regulatory document but a concrete administrative act likely to affect a right. In this sense, the authority must respect its duty to give reasons for an administrative decision. There is no general rule establishing the obligation to state reasons for administrative decisions. The law-maker specifically mandates such an obligation in certain areas of administrative action. For example, administrative penalties,[504] administrative authorizations,[505] public information,[506] and, more particularly, penalties relating to national security.[507] Judicial doctrine distinguishes three types of error related to the reasons for administrative acts: lack of reason, erroneous reason, and insufficient reason, as does the case law. Any of these may result in a decision being annulled.

503 For example K Lachmayer, 'Effizienz als Verfassungsprinzip. Eine Maxime für staatliches Handeln in Österreich' in M Bungenbergand others (eds), *Recht und Ökonomik* (2004 CH Beck) 135 ff.
504 Administrative Penalty Law (行政处罚法).
505 Administrative Authorisation Law (行政许可法).
506 Open Government Information Regulation (政府信息公开条例).
507 Public Security Administration Punishment Law (治安处罚法).

In this case, both national and local rules require any new transportation project to be assessed for feasibility and prudence. The question is whether Moderna's position would be considered an insufficient reason.

In a guiding case published by the Supreme People's Court in 2014, a local court quashed a decision for inadequate reasoning.[508] In fact, the administration merely cited the legislative provisions in its decision without providing any evidence or justification. The court relied on Article 32 of the Administrative Litigation Law, which places the burden of proof on the administration for individual administrative acts. Mere mention of the legislative provisions cannot be considered sufficient proof within the meaning of the law, which requires the rationale for the decision to be set out.

However, courts limit themselves to verifying the existence of the proof. There has been no precedent for ascertaining that they would examine the appropriateness of any such demonstration.

C. Czech Republic

Daniel Burda

Implementing new transport project would require approval at two levels. First, the conditions for the tramline would have to be set out in a local development plan, which would need to be adopted by the municipal council within legal limits and based on political discretion. The corridor through which it would run would have to be incorporated into the plan. The construction itself would subsequently require individual permission. In this case, incorporation of the project into the local development plan would be crucial. If the project were incorporated into the plan, it would probably be impossible to prevent a building permit being issued by suggesting an alternative route for the tramline. On the other hand, even in such a case, it would probably be possible to point to alternative solutions that would respect the local development plan, such as running a part of the tramline under or above ground.

Regarding the above procedures, it must be said that for the preparation of a local development plan and in deciding to issue a building permit, the basic procedure is that the building authority examines whether the draft local development plan or building project complies with all legal requirements. These obligations primarily arise from public law (eg compliance with the local development plan, compliance with general requirements for development, various technical standards, etc) but also from private law, such as rules relating to nuisance caused to adjacent affected land, etc.[509] In this assessment, there will normally be no legal obligation to analyse various options and look for the one that is the most economical, socially responsible, and the most protective of various public and private interests (and therefore best suited to

[508] District People's Court of Kecheng, Quzhou, Zhejiang (浙江省衢州市柯城区人民法院), 2003, No 8 (柯行初字第8号). Supreme People's Court, 2014, Guiding case No 41.

[509] Compare eg the Supreme Administrative Court judgment of 30 April 2020, File Ref No 6 As 171/2019-37.

an analysis involving several such criteria—see, for example, cost-benefit analysis). A statute usually determines relatively certain requirements (a sort of a basic or minimum standard). A local development plan or building project either meets them or not; or, as the case may be, certain restrictive conditions for the implementation of the building project (or for the use of a certain area in the development plan) may be imposed. Even if another option, for example, one that is better in terms of protecting the public interest, could be envisaged, it would be irrelevant if the current options meet the requirements. A criterion for the proportionality of the local development plan as a general measure could be an exception to the rule. It follows from the case law of administrative courts that a general measure must, *inter alia*, satisfy the proportionality criterion when subjected to judicial review. However, administrative courts are rather self-restrained in this respect and primarily review whether the relevant administrative authorities have addressed objections or comments[510] regarding disproportionality at all (eg an objection to competing private or even public interests) if any were raised during the adoption of a general measure. In other words, the courts examine whether the objections were taken into account at all. However, when reviewing how the objections were dealt with, the courts are usually restrained and do not replace the administrative authorities' consideration of how various interests should be balanced. Instead, they focus on eliminating extremes, particularly when dealing with violations of private rights. In this respect, it would be appropriate to consider various options, albeit in a respectful manner.

There are, of course, some explicit exceptions to this construction, most typically in the context of environmental protection where a local development plan or development project is subject to an EIA.[511] In such cases, there is, to a certain extent, an obligation to consider alternative solutions for building projects and choose the least intrusive one.

Let us assume that in the scenario present here, the project for the new tramline has satisfied all the standard legal requirements to be incorporated into the local development plan. However, in addition to the standard legal requirements for the approval of transportation projects, there is also a rather atypical criterion, namely the criterion of prudence in the scenario. This criterion is relatively vague. The question is, what exactly does it entail? What should a building authority examine in relation to it? We therefore believe that a judicial review of such a criterion would probably be relatively deferential. The courts would be reluctant to replace the political discretion of the municipal council with their decision based on a vague statutory criterion, especially in the case of a local development plan. Indeed, it is important to emphasize that a local development plan is a reflection of the municipality's self-governance and is subject to political discretion. This includes deciding which public interests will be prioritized.

We therefore believe that in the case of a local development plan this criterion would probably be assessed in a similar way to the general criterion of proportionality when reviewing measures of a general nature (as described above). The administrative courts would, therefore, probably focus on whether the administrative authorities have reasonably weighed various public and private interests (and whether they have

510 Henceforth 'objections'.

511 On this issue, see Act No 100/2001 Sb on the environmental impact assessment.

failed to take any of them into account, and the like). In this respect, they might require that something like a cost-benefit analysis be carried out, in the sense of 'take into account' (but it is not very likely, because it is not an explicit statutory requirement). In this case, it appears that the administrative authorities considered the public interest in preserving Old Park, although this is not entirely clear from the scenario. However, they prioritize the public interest in saving public funds. It is hard to imagine that the courts would substitute their decision for the consideration of the competent authorities where various interests have been reasonably accounted for.

If there is a problem with the location of a construction in a corridor that has already been determined, the question is not whether the tramway line should run through the park but *how* it should do so. If the local development plan does not address these issues, the courts could infer, based on the 'prudence' criterion (mentioned in the scenario), that various options should be considered. These include running the line underground, aboveground, or in a standard ground-based manner, but as considerately as possible. In such a case, the courts would no longer be encroaching upon political discretion and would therefore have greater autonomy in interpreting the 'prudence' criterion.

D. European Union

Marco Lunardelli

This hypothetical case concerns a municipality's failure to conduct a thorough cost-benefit analysis before approving the construction of a new means of communication, namely a tram line, in a central area of the town. To propose a solution from the EU law perspective, it would be apposite to follow a two-pronged approach. First, the decision to approve the public work should be considered as a new policy formulated by the Commission. Since the 2002 communication on Impact Assessment (IA),[512] the Commission has laid down some criteria for policy-making. These include identifying policy options, evaluating the potentially irreversible nature of a given measure, and the possibility of applying the precautionary principle when appropriate to the context. The 2009 guidelines on better regulation[513] led to increasing use of cost-benefit analysis (CBA), underlining that, even though the formulation of policies may apply multiple criteria, it should include 'a quantitative/monetary estimate of expected benefits and costs' when feasible. The 2015 Communication on better regulation agenda went in the same direction.[514] The guidelines clarified that the CBA is the best instrument to assess a draft policy only when direct costs and benefits may be readily monetized and the impact of the policy is significant enough to justify the effort made and time spent on conducting a CBA itself. Otherwise, a Cost-Effectiveness Analysis

[512] European Commission, COM(2002) 276 final, 5 June 2002, <https://eur-lex.europa.eu/LexUriServ/LexUriServ.do?uri=COM:2002:0276:FIN:EN:PDF> accessed 23 November 2024.

[513] European Commission, COM(2009) 15 final, 28 January 2009, <https://eur-lex.europa.eu/LexUriServ/LexUriServ.do?uri=COM:2009:0015:FIN:en:PDF> accessed 23 November 2024.

[514] European Commission, COM(2015) 215 final, 19 May 2015, <https://eur-lex.europa.eu/legal-content/EN/TXT/PDF/?uri=CELEX:52015DC0215&from=EN>.

(CEA) or an assessment based on multiple criteria should be preferred as a policy review method.[515] In 2019, the Commission issued a new communication on better regulation, which confirmed that the Impact Analysis (IA) of legislative acts proposed at EU level must be carried out from the economic, social, and environmental perspectives and must also be proven to be useful for assessing administrative measures in the indirect execution of EU law. Indeed, it pointed out that an IA must include not only EU delegated and implementing acts but also the implementation of EU law by Member States at the national, regional, and local levels.[516] Furthermore, this communication observed that since simplification is one of the main objectives, benefits are sometimes easier to evaluate qualitatively than quantitatively.[517] Therefore, the first approach referred to above requires that the decision at issue in the present case be considered as if it were an actual regulation or, in any case, an act adopted at the end of a rulemaking proceedings. This way, the IA, in the form of a CBA, may integrate the technical standards of interoperability that the 2016 EU directive established in the railway sector and appear to apply to the means of communication considered in this case.[518] The second approach is a comparative one. It is based on the assumption that the situation here is modelled on a famous US case, known as *Overton Park* and decided by the Supreme Court in 1971. In particular, the Supreme Court held that judicial review, conducted on matters of law and fact contained in the administrative record of the case, consisted in ascertaining whether the decision was rational, namely whether 'a "feasible and prudent" alternative route exist[ed]', and whether the planning activity carried out was capable of minimizing the harm caused to the park.[519]

The description of the case at issue underlines that, pursuant to relevant legislation and local rules, any new transportation project is lawful provided it meets the conditions established by the Supreme Court in the aforementioned decision. An association of residents and other persons challenged the decision approving the construction of the tramway line as it did not meet the required conditions. The association claims that the decision was not based on an actual CBA. The municipal administration, in fact, merely stated that the chosen route was the least expensive solution. From an examination of the two approaches described above, it is clear that there is a difference in the frequency of use of IAs. While most types of regulations are subject to IAs, conceived of as an instrument of *ex ante* review, in the United States, a combination of IAs and *ex-post* evaluations is usually the way legislative acts in the EU legal system are reviewed. It has also been pointed out that, unlike in the United States, where performing an IA is a structural element of rulemaking proceedings, IAs are more informal in the EU legal system, even though they apply to EU legislation

515 See A Renda, 'Cost-Benefit Analysis and EU Policy' in S Garben and I Govaere (eds), *The EU Better Regulation Agenda* (Hart 2020) 55–57.

516 See European Commission, COM(2019) 178 final, 15 April 2019, respectively, 7 and 9 <https://eur-lex.europa.eu/legal-content/EN/TXT/PDF/?uri=CELEX:52019DC0178&from=EN> accessed 23 November 2024.

517 ibid 11.

518 Directive (EU) 2016/797 of 11 May 2016 on the interoperability of the rail system within the European Union (recast), [2016] OJL 138/44, as amended by Directive (EU) 2020/700 of 25 May 2020, as regards the extension of their transposition periods, [2020] OJL 165/27.

519 See *Citizens to Preserve Overton Park v Volpe*, 401 US 402, 405 (1971).

and regulatory acts.[520] Accordingly, in the latter, legislative, implementing, and delegated acts, together with new policies in general, are seldom subject to a CBA alone.[521] A traditional example of the influence of the US experience on the EU legal system is the use of CBAs—or IAs, in a broader sense—in environmental issues.[522] In this regard, the municipality did not carry out a comprehensive CBA, as it manifestly considered only the economic aspects of the policy, thus overlooking the environmental perspective, as well as the social one. Therefore, whether deemed to be subject to a CBA or, more generally, to an IA, the administrative decision appears to be unlawful as the municipality did not demonstrate that it had explored all feasible alternatives. In other words, since it had disregarded—or, at least, underestimated—both the environmental and social implications of the decision about the route singled out for the new tram line, the municipality did not carry out an IA that would appear to be in conformity with EU law. When the Commission adopts acts subject to IA, they have to be based on an integrated approach, thus taking into account all the aspects mentioned above. In this way, those acts are sustainable, ie, compatible, with all EU policies and objectives.[523] In the present case, the administrative decision cannot be considered as such.

Since the municipality failed to conduct—either entirely *ex ante* or partly *ex post*—a comprehensive CBA, or even any IA, the administrative decision turns out to be illegitimate. The same conclusion may also be reached from a different perspective. The decision in question may be considered a violation of the principle of proportionality. This perspective is useful here, as it is perceived in the light of a possible judicial review by the ECJ, which might occur if the administrative decision were deemed to be subject to a CBA or a more general IA, as an indirect execution of EU law in a broad sense. Reference to the proportionality principle comes to serve as a further reason to argue that the residents' association has standing to challenge the administrative decision before a national court, which in turn may bring the matter before the ECJ pursuant to Article 267 TFEU. From this perspective, the ECJ may determine whether an EU institution or another decision-making authority, in exercising its discretion, has taken into account 'all the relevant factors and circumstances' by opting for a given solution.[524] Although it was created especially for use in legislative or regulatory proceedings, to conduct an IA may help the ECJ review the legality of an act or measure of general applicability from a substantive perspective, including compliance with the general principles of subsidiarity or proportionality in order to limit the broad discretion assigned to the decision-maker,[525] or from a procedural perspective, for instance

[520] See ACM Meuwese and S van Voorst, 'Regulatory Impact Assessment in Legal Studies' in CA Dunlop and CM Radaelli (eds), *Handbook of Regulatory Impact Assessment* (Edward Elgar 2016) 22–24.

[521] See Renda, 'Cost-Benefit Analysis' (n 515) 58–61.

[522] See G Majone, *Regulating Europe* (Routledge 1996) 52–53.

[523] See A Alemanno, 'A Meeting of Minds on Impact Assessment' (2011) 17(3) EPL 489.

[524] See Case C-310/04, *Spain v Council*, ECLI:EU:C:2006:521, § 133. The case originated from an application submitted by Spain to get the annulment of some provisions of a 2003 Council regulation concerning direct support schemes under the common agricultural policy, namely in the sector of cotton production. In this judgment, the ECJ also pointed out (§ 98) the limited scope of the proportionality principle with respect to measures of general applicability. In such cases, it consists in the review of whether those measures are 'manifestly inappropriate'. The quotation can be found in Pünder and Klafki (n 449) 478 n 136.

[525] See Case C-176/09, *Luxemburg v European Parliament and Council*, ECLI:EU:C:2011:290, §§ 61–62.

to verify whether a notice-and-comment procedure was carried out.[526] It may also be argued that a comprehensive CBA or another type of IA justifies the ECJ's deferential approach to a discretionary decision adopted at the regulatory level.[527] However, this is not a solution for the case at issue, where the CBA was incomplete. Overall, the residents' association will most likely win the case.

E. Germany

Lilly Weidemann

The court would share Citizens to Preserve Old Park's point of view that an adequate cost-benefit analysis has to be carried out before deciding to construct a new tramway line.

Under section 28 of the Passenger Transportation Act,[528] operating facilities for streetcars may only be built or modified if the plan has been approved in advance. The public and private interests affected by the project, including its environmental impact, must be taken into consideration in the planning approval process. Sections 72–78 of the Administrative Procedure Act apply to the planning approval procedure within the framework of the Passenger Transportation Act.

The principle of balancing the legally protected interest (*Abwägungsgebot*) laid out in sentence 2 of the provision requires all public and private interests relevant to the planning project to be balanced and the allocation of these interests in the balancing process in relation to their importance, as well as an appropriate, proportionate planning decision resulting from the balancing process.[529] This includes the obligation to consider planning alternatives.[530]

The requirement to balance the public and private interests affected by planning fairly against each other and among each other arises from the nature of planning in accordance with the rule of law, irrespective of any legal positivity, and accordingly applies generally.[531] The Federal Administrative Court explained in this respect that planning is always a matter of balancing varyingly numerous interests, whose interrelationships are complex, and which, moreover, are usually intertwined in a specific way so that nothing can be conceded to one interest without affecting numerous other interests in a kind of chain reaction. Private interests must be protected in accordance with rules that are appropriate to the nature of planning. These rules include, first and foremost, fair balancing of the public and private interests affected by the planning.[532]

526 See A Alemanno, 'Courts and Regulatory Impact Assessment' in Dunlop and Radaelli (n 520) 131–32.

527 See J Nowag and X Groussot, 'From Better Regulation to Better Adjudication? Impact Assessment and the Court of Justice's Review' in Garben and Govaere (n 515) 190–91. As for case law, see Case C-176/09 (n 525) §§ 65–72, esp §§ 70–71.

528 Personenbeförderungsgesetz (PBefG) in the wording of 8 August 1990 (Federal Law Gazette I s 1690).

529 C Heinze, 'PBefG § 28' in C Heinze, M Fehling, and LH Fiedler (eds), *Personenbeförderungsgesetz* (2nd edn, CH Beck 2014) Rn 10.

530 Federal Administrative Court, Judgment of 14 November 2002—4 A 15/02–, BVerwGE 117, 149–62, para 45.

531 Federal Administrative Court, Judgment of 30 April 1969—IV C 6.68–, para 17, juris.

532 ibid.

According to the jurisprudence of the Federal Administrative Court concerning the Federal Building Act, but, in principle, applicable to planning in general, the requirement to balance demands that first, a balance is actually found; secondly, that the balancing of interests includes everything necessary for the situation; andthirdly, that neither the significance of the public and private interests concerned is misjudged and the balance between them is not disproportionate to the objective weight of the interests.[533]

Within this framework, however, the principle of balancing is not breached if the planning authority decides to give priority to one interest and thus sets aside another in the conflict between them. On the contrary, the weighting of the public and private interests affected by the planning is essential to freedom of planning and, as such, is not subject to review by administrative courts. In the context of the balancing requirement, this is therefore limited to the question of whether the planning approval authority has correctly determined the legally and factually relevant aspects to be balanced and whether—on the basis of the material thus correctly determined for balancing—it has complied with the limits of the balancing process as indicated.[534]

In the present case, Moderna has not even determined all the public and private interests affected by the plan to construct a new tramway line, let alone balanced them. Thus, a breach of the requirement to balance the public and private interests affected by planning fairly against each other and among each other is certain.

F. Hungary

Lilla Berkes and Balázs Szabolcs Gerencsér

Local bodies must consider environmental, economic, social and urbanization aspects in the urban planning process. The framework for this is set out in the Built Environment Protection Act[535] (the substantive law of urban planning and building). A procedure brought by a civil party may be successful if the municipality of Moderna has failed to apply these requirements set by law.

In Budapest, one of the most popular public parks (*Városliget*) faced a similar problem after 2014. The project, which started as a government investment, consisted of the comprehensive renovation of an otherwise neglected but much-visited site and the creation of a cultural centre. However, the documentation for the project was not made public, and there was considerable public opposition. The court issued a binding new decision on some serious procedural issues in the initial stages of the project, but the substance of the project was not subject to court proceedings. Later, as the project progressed and the actual content of the improvements became known, social tensions eased. However, the project is still going on, and after the demolition of

[533] Federal Administrative Court, Judgment of 14 February 1975—IV C 21.74–, BVerwGE 48, 56–70, para 37.

[534] ibid.

[535] Act LXXVIII of 1997 on the development and protection of the built environment <https://njt.hu/jogszabaly/1997-78-00-00> accessed 23 November 2024 (no official English translation available).

the old buildings and the construction of new ones, the park is now one of Budapest's most visited tourist hubs.

G. Italy

Leonardo Parona

In general terms, decisions concerning whether and where to build public infrastructures such as a new tram line are left to the discretion of the competent public administrations.[536] Discretion on these decisions is wide and concerns the evaluation of both the various public and private competing interests that must be considered in planning and localization and the appreciation of the technical details relating to the infrastructure, as well as its potential alternatives.

The Italian legal system does not require, in either statutory law or judicial interpretation, that public administrations carry out a prior cost-benefit analysis when making this kind of discretionary decision.[537] Localization is the outcome of a process that entails the discretionary weighing of various interests and objectives.

With specific regard to environmental interests, a prior evaluation of the potential impact of public infrastructures (and any public and private activity or work) is a required by EU law, which introduced the fundamental requirement to conduct an environmental impact assessment within the Member States' legal systems.[538] Besides this requirement, which does not seem to lie at the core of the hypothetical case, and which will anyway be addressed in greater detail in the answer to the next case, the discretion of public administrations concerning infrastructure localization decisions has long been widely unfettered in the Italian legal system, both in substantial and procedural terms.

Only recently have specific rules that might be invoked by Citizens to Preserve Old Park been introduced in Italian law. In particular, we recall the rules on public debate, which were introduced in our legal system by a 2018 government decree (a secondary source of law), enacted on the basis of the previous Code of Public Contracts.[539] Of relevance to our case is the fact that those rules required the public authorities and private bodies responsible for building public infrastructures to make their projects public if they might have a significant impact on the environment, cities, and the territory. This requirement allows public debate before a final decision on the issue is

536 Depending on the dimensions, relevance, and type of infrastructure, as well as on the eventual presence of landscape or architectural constraints in the interested area, competence is split among various public authorities, established at different institutional levels (including both local and state, even though decentralized bodies).

537 A sort of cost-benefit analysis is envisioned according to a sector-specific ministerial regulation (DM No 226/2011), concerning tender criteria and rules for evaluating the offer for awarding of contracts concerning natural gas distribution services.

538 The analysis carried out within environmental impact assessments also extends to assessing other competing interests, as clarified later. On the topic, see E Frediani, 'Dibattito pubblico, inchiesta pubblica e valutazioni ambientali: una 'relazione' problematica' (2020) 2 Diritto amministrativo 399 ff.

539 Decree of the President of the Council of Ministers No 76/2018, adopted under art 22(2) Legislative Decree No 150/2016.

adopted, the outcome of which must be made public, including through access to the minutes of discussion with stakeholders[540]. This rule was confirmed by the new Code of Public Contracts enacted in 2023, which, however, only makes the requirement mandatory in a limited number of cases, leaving discretion to the proceeding authority for the remaining ones.[541] The infrastructure at issue in our case (ie a tram line) does not fall within the cases enlisted as mandatorily requiring a public debate, which, therefore, would be left to Moderna's discretion.

As a consequence, a decision on the case would depend, once again, on the discretion of Moderna city council and its interpretation of the wording 'feasible and prudent'. In Italian case law, it appears to be quite permissive, being interpreted as granting ample leeway to the administration and, in turn, requiring a certain deference on the part of reviewing courts as long as the decision taken by the administration is not manifestly unreasonable. In fact, according to the Council of State:

> the merit of the decision relating to the location of public infrastructure lies, in principle, outside the control of administrative courts, with the sole exceptions of illogicality, misrepresentation, and decisions of a contradictory nature. Nevertheless, administrations are required to provide an account, in their decisions, of the assessment and consideration of all the interests involved, particularly those sacrificed, and to adequately take into account the positions affected by the location of the infrastructure.[542]

Also with regard to the argument that Moderna should have weighed the costs and benefits of alternative solutions, the Italian administrative courts tend to be quite deferential to the decisions of the authorities. In very clear terms, the Council of State affirms in fact that 'the public authorities are not required to provide in this regard specific reasons for the selection of one location rather than another' since it is 'an aspect that pertains to technical discretion and, therefore, to the merit of the administrative act'.[543] The Council of State has gone even further, asserting that simply arguing that an administrative act establishing the location of public infrastructure does not consider alternative solutions does not, in itself, constitute a lack of justification.[544]

In brief, an Italian court would probably accept Moderna's position and permissible interpretation of the feasible and prudent requirement, as a more thorough judicial analysis would risk substituting its own discretionary evaluations for those of the administration, thereby violating the principle of the separation of powers.

[540] On this topic, see G della Cananea, 'Exit or Voice? *Debat Public* Goes to Italy' (2019) 2 European Public Law 157 ff, especially 163.

[541] See art 40 and Annex I.6 of Legislative Decree No 36/2023. The latter provides a table listing the infrastructures for which (above certain thresholds) public discussion is mandatory, namely airports, ports, infrastructures for the defence of the sea and shoreline, railways for long-distance transportation, and roads with at least four lanes.

[542] Council of State, Sec V, No 3009/2021.

[543] Again, Council of State No 3009/2021, quoting on this point Sec IV, No 5492/2012.

[544] Council of State, Sec IV, No 2094/2015, quoting on this point its previous judgment No 2246/2006.

H. Netherlands

Jacobine van den Brink, Louise Verboeket, and Veerle van Waarde

The decision of the municipality of Moderna to construct a new tram route would, under Dutch law, be set out in a zoning plan (*bestemmingsplan*). According to Article 3.8(1) of the Spatial Planning Act (*Wet ruimtelijke ordening*), a draft zoning plan in the Netherlands is prepared by using the uniform public preparatory procedure (*uniforme openbare voorbereidingsprocedure*).[545] The uniform public preparatory procedure is described in Division 3.4 GALA and guarantees the possibility for parties concerned (*belanghebbenden*) to state their opinion regarding a draft decision.[546] Article 6:13 GALA states that claims for judicial review are not permitted if the claimant has not delivered an opinion as defined in Article 3:15 GALA. If Citizens to Preserve Old Park qualify as a party concerned, a claim for judicial review can be lodged regardless of whether the association has delivered an opinion. According to Article 1:2(3) GALA, Citizens to Preserve Old Park will qualify as a party concerned if the association, according to its statutes and activities, has a particular role in looking after a collective interest directly affected by the challenged decision.[547] If, according to their statutes, the scope of the activities of Citizens to Preserve Old Park is not too broad and general, and if their activities do not consist of only opposing decisions in court, the association will most probably qualify as a party concerned. If, however, Citizens to Preserve Old Park does not qualify as a party concerned, the association should, (i) have delivered an opinion regarding the draft zoning plan, or (ii) should not be held accountable for not delivering an opinion regarding the draft zoning plan in order to have standing in a claim for judicial review, as confirmed in the *Varkens in Nood* judgment of the Court of Justice of the European Union.[548]

Assuming Citizens to Preserve Old Park indeed qualifies as a party concerned and has delivered an opinion regarding the draft zoning plan or cannot be held accountable for not doing so, the court would most likely rule that an adequate cost-benefit analysis must be carried out before deciding. Article 3.1.6(1)(f) of the Spatial Planning Decree (*Besluit ruimtelijke ordening*) requires zoning plans to have explanatory notes in which the feasibility of the zoning plan is discussed. A ground for appeal regarding the feasibility of the zoning plan, including financial-economic feasibility, can only lead to the annulment of the zoning plan if Moderna Town Council was supposed to state in advance that the zoning plan was not feasible.[549] Given the facts of the case, the zoning plan seems to be feasible. However, when adopting a zoning plan, Moderna is also obliged to weigh all the interests and consider all the alternatives, including those that may avoid the destruction of Old Park. Due to the fact that Moderna has not considered these alternatives and/or has not given reasons why these alternatives are not feasible, the draft zoning plan will be annulled due to violation of the principle of due

[545] It should be noted that this text was written before the Environment and Planning Act (*Omgevingswet*) was enacted. This law has replaced the Spatial Planning Act (*Wet ruimtelijke ordening*).

[546] See art 3:15 GALA and Backes and Eliantonio (eds), *Cases, Materials...* (n 473) 109 and 297.

[547] ABRvS 2 October 2008, ECLI:NL:RVS:2008:BF3911 (*Stichting Openbare Ruimte*). See Backes and Eliantonio (eds), *Cases, Materials...* (n 473) 236–38.

[548] CJEU 14 January 2021, ECLI:EU:C:2021:7 (*Varkens in Nood*).

[549] See ABRvS 26 October 2022, ECLI:NL:RVS:2022:3090.

care (*zorgvuldigheidsbeginsel*) or the duty to give reasons (*motiveringsbeginsel*), as laid down in Articles 3:2 and 3:46 GALA.[550]

I. Norway

Eivind Smith

According to APA section 37 § 1, the administration 'shall ensure that the case is clarified as thoroughly as possible before an administrative decision is made'. The provision reflects a general norm for handling administrative cases, but must, of course, be applied with due consideration of the specific case.

Some leeway is normally left to the administration's political considerations when deciding on regulations, and even more so when the decision-making power is left with an administrative body led by a directly elected assembly, like a municipality. Even municipalities are bound by national legislation and must, at the very least, adhere to requirements such as those applicable in this case ('feasible and prudent'). Under the conditions outlined here, this specific project is clearly 'feasible'. The other condition ('prudent') is far less clear. Whatever the outcome may be, however, the administration is bound to consider the main arguments and be seen to have affectively done so. If Citizens to Preserve Old Park were right in assuming that the costs and benefits to determine whether alternatives existed have not been weighed altogether, the association would have a fair chance of winning the case.

J. Portugal

Rui Guerra da Fonseca

It is questionable whether the decision to construct the new tram route can be qualified as an administrative rule, as it is a specific decision which in itself does not consist of a rule for subsequent general application. This would certainly be one of the first issues that the residents' association (Citizens to Preserve Old Park) would have to argue in court to determine the correct procedure (although the administrative courts would have jurisdiction in any case). The process would certainly involve passing administrative regulations, and the essential considerations of discretion or binding nature is not radically different, so we will assume there is an 'administrative rulemaking environment'.

Public authorities with powers to approve regulations have very wide discretion in choosing their contents.[551] They are, of course, bound by the laws they mean to regulate, but these laws are so often vague and establish little more than the allocation of the powers to pass the necessary regulations.[552] In the Portuguese system, this comes

[550] Compare with ABRvS 17 October 2018, ECLI:NL:RVS:2018:3363 and ABRvS 20 May 2020, ECLI:NL:RVS:2020:1264.

[551] Aroso de Almeida, *Teoria Geral do Direito Administrativo* (n 283) 240.

[552] Regarding the category of independent regulations, see 'Portugal—Case 3' and 'Case 5', sections IV.J and VI.J in this chapter.

from a certain lack of definition as to which subjects are a matter of law and which of regulations (at least which the legislative body does not appropriate to itself, and if it is not a subject of parliamentary reservation).[553]

Weighing costs and benefits in a decision like this is absolutely essential. First, it is the only way to guarantee the principle of pursuing the public interest while respecting citizens' rights and interests (Article 4 CPA and Article 266/1 CRP). Secondly, it is the only way to guarantee that administrative decisions are objectively impartial or non-biased;[554] otherwise, it would simply reflect the administrative representatives' 'political passion' for doing something and not a rational option (Article 9 CPA and Article 266/2 CRP). Thirdly, the law seems to demand that requirements of being 'feasible and prudent' be met. Failure to do so would amount to an illegality in itself. But, even if this were not the case, such requirements would be the consequence of the first two points and would derive from a non-written principle of rationality or a 'prohibition of arbitrariness' and an obligation to balance as an implication of the rule of law.[555]

Moreover, public interest is not a category that is detached from fundamental rights. It takes the latter into consideration and weighs different rights and interests. In a republic, all public activity must be considered within this framework as a consequence of a substantive principle of the rule of law. Both transport problems and the enjoyment of a public park are matters tied in with fundamental rights (the right of freedom of movement, the right to leisure times and places, and the right to a decent quality of life or adequate standard of living). The procedure in question seems to completely ignore this and thus to eliminate any chance of applying proportionality tests: were there any alternatives that would not imply the complete elimination of one of the positions? If it is not possible to apply such a test, arbitrariness becomes apparent. This is why Article 99 CPA stipulates that regulations are approved subject to a project that must include a substantiated justification, with a cost–benefit analysis of the proposed measures.

Citizens to Preserve Old Park would certainly have standing (Article 9/2 CPTA). However, the specific procedural requirements to bring this claim to the administrative courts depend on aspects that are not clear in this case. But it is reasonable to assume that the courts would accept Citizens to Preserve Old Park's argument and deem the regulation invalid (Articles 143/1 and 144 CPA).

K. Sweden

Patricia Jonason and Björn Forssén

If the municipality's decision is subject to the special kind of judicial review for municipal decisions known as municipal appeal (*kommunalbesvär*), then the court may only examine the legality of the decision, but not its appropriateness.

553 Otero, *Direito do Procedimento Administrativo* (n 280) 299 ff.
554 See 'Portugal—Case 4', section V.J in this chapter.
555 Otero, *Direito do Procedimento Administrativo* (n 280) 240 ff.

The question is whether the court would deem that the decision of the municipality 'has not been legally established' (section 8, paragraph 1.1, chapter 13, Local Government Act) since the decision had not been prepared correctly. If the court comes to this conclusion, then it would overturn the decision and send it back. One may nevertheless observe that, under section 9, chapter 13 of the Local Government Act 'if an error has no significance for the outcome of the case, the decision does not need to be overturned'.

If the municipality's decision is subject to the ordinary judicial review called *förvaltningsbesvär*, then in a situation such as the one described in the above-mentioned case, the court would probably find that there is a lack of sufficient factual basis (*tillräckligt faktaunderlag*) for taking the decision. This is based on a requirement to investigate that is laid down in the special applicable statutes or, if the special statutes do not content such an investigation requirement, based on the general investigation requirement laid down in the Procedure Administrative Act, section 23. If the statutes do not contain such an investigation requirement, then the court would base its decision on the general investigation requirement laid down in the Administrative Procedure Act, section 23.

The court has the power to overturn the decision or send it back to the municipality. Alternatively, it could make its own decision in place of the municipality's decision, conducting a cost-benefit analysis when making its decision.

L. United Kingdom

John Morison and David Mark

Within the United Kingdom, decisions by public authorities must be reasonable and proportionate, encompassing a duty to consider all relevant factors whilst disregarding irrelevant ones,[556] see *Secretary of State for Education and Science v Tameside MBC*.[557] Indeed, even where a statute sets out matters which a decision-maker *must* take into account, this does not necessarily mean that these are the *only* factors which should (or may) be considered.[558] To expand upon this, the Supreme Court in *R. (on the application of Friends of the Earth Ltd.) v Heathrow Airport Ltd*[559] succinctly categorized considerations into three types, namely

1. those which statute expressly or impliedly identifies as considerations to which regard must be had;
2. those which statute expressly or impliedly identifies as considerations to which regard must *not* be had; and
3. considerations to which the decision-maker may have regard if in their judgment and discretion they consider it right to do so.

[556] Government Legal Department (n 218) 14, 20.
[557] [1977] AC 1014.
[558] Government Legal Department (n 218) 14, 22.
[559] [2020] UKSC 52.

From this it does appear as though the courts will allow a significant amount of discretion to the decision-maker. However, the 'feasible and prudent' requirements noted in this scenario as part of national and local rules, perhaps call for a more practical and cautious approach by Moderna. Such terminology could be interpreted by the court as necessitating an exploration of viable alternatives and their impacts. In Moderna's tramway project, the court would likely examine whether the municipality adequately considered all relevant factors, including the environmental impact on Old Park, social implications for local residents, and feasible alternatives. A decision focusing solely on cost savings, neglecting these factors, could be deemed unlawful. Further, it is perhaps important to note that the apparent disregard for environmental considerations could cause difficulties for Moderna. Cases such as the noted *R. (on the application of Friends of the Earth Ltd.) v Heathrow Airport Ltd*[560] and *R (on the application of Mott) v Environment Agency*[561] indicate a balancing exercise between environmental and economic considerations is often expected by the courts. Similarly, *R (on the application of Morge) v Hampshire County Council*,[562] while centred around the protection of a species, reflects the broader EU ethos of environmental stewardship, pertinent to Moderna's decision. See also the recent establishment of the office for environmental protection who exist to protect and improve the environment by holding government and other public authorities to account.[563]

Moderna's scenario is not just a test of legal compliance but also of fairness and balance, a concept exemplified in the noted *R v North and East Devon Health Authority, ex parte Coughlan*.[564] Though primarily focused on legitimate expectation, the Coughlan case subtly notes that economic considerations, while important, should not overshadow other critical interests. The court would be likely to require Moderna to demonstrate that its decision to construct the tramway through Old Park was made following a comprehensive and balanced consideration of all relevant factors, including environmental and social impacts, and an exploration of feasible alternatives. Decisions made in a vacuum, devoid of consideration for less intrusive options run the risk of being considered unreasonable. Indeed, government guidance in Wales specifically notes that 'decision-makers should consider and document possible alternative decisions fully. The courts are more likely to find that the objective could have been achieved in a less intrusive way if the public authority has failed to even consider the alternatives.'[565]

Given the apparent disregard for some arguably significant issues, accompanying apparent failings with regards to a consultation or notice. The courts would be likely to side against Moderna's argument which appears to focus solely on lower costs, given that it would appear they have not fully considered the 'feasible and prudent' requirements.

560 [2020] UKSC 52.
561 [2018] UKSC 10.
562 [2011] UKSC 2.
563 https://www.theoep.org.uk/node/17 accessed 23 November 2024.
564 [2001] QB 213, [108].
565 See Welsh Government (n 297) 63.

M. United States of America

Jeffrey Lubbers and Giacinto della Cananea

The court would most probably not be satisfied with how the municipality acted. A landmark decision in this area in the early 1970s was *Citizens to Preserve Overton Park, Inc. v Volpe*, 401 US 402 (1971).[566] The case involved the US Secretary of Transportation's decision to authorize federal funds for the construction of a highway that would traverse an important municipal park, called Overton Park, in Memphis, Tennessee. A citizens group, who intended to contest the decision because of its adverse impact on the park, argued that a federal statute, the Highway Act of 1968, prohibited the use of Department of Transportation funds to build highways through parks unless no other route was 'feasible and prudent' and that the Secretary had failed to make such a finding. The Highway Act did not require the Secretary to make formal findings, as asserted by the citizens group, but it required him to carry out 'all possible planning to minimize harm'. The Supreme Court began by reiterating the old dictum according to which the Secretary's decision was 'entitled to a presumption of regulalarity', butit ended with overturning the decision. As a first step, it noticed that the Act contained no indication that Congress intended to limit judicial review. Next, it observed that the case was about adjudication and, with regard to section 701 of the APA, that the exemption for action 'committed to agency discretion' did not apply, as the Secretary did have 'law to apply', rather than wide-ranging discretion. On the merits, the Court held that:

> The reviewing court must consider whether the Secretary properly construed his authority to approve the use of park land as limited to situations where there are no feasible alternative routes or where feasible alternative routes involve uniquely difficult problems. And the reviewing court must be able to find that the Secretary could have reasonably believed that, in this case, there are no feasible alternatives, or that alternatives do involve unique problems. Scrutiny of the facts does not end, however, with the determination that the Secretary has acted within the scope of his statutory authority. Section 706(2)(A) requires a finding that the actual choice made was not 'arbitrary, capricious, an abuse of discretion, or otherwise not in accordance with law'. 5 U.S.C. § 706(2)(A). To make this finding, the court must consider whether the decision was based on a consideration of the relevant factors and whether there has been a clear error of judgment.[567]

Thus, in our view, courts would likely interpret the 'feasible and prudent' requirement as implying that the agency should do a cost-benefit analysis before proceeding (as the Supreme Court did in interpreting the Occupational Safety

[566] 401 US 402 (1971).
[567] 401 US at 416. For further remarks, see PL Strauss, *Administrative Justice in the United States* (3rd edn, Carolina Academic Press 2016) 503 (discussing later cases).

and Health Act in Industrial Union Department, *AFL-CIO v American Petroleum Institute*.[568]

In a recent environmental law case, the Court specifically applied the arbitrary and capricious test to require the agency to give sufficient consideration to the costs and benefits of taking a particular regulatory approach.[569]

568 448 US 607 (1980).
569 *Michigan v EPA*, 576 US 743 (2015).

XI. Case 10—A Gold Mine Plan with No Environmental Impact Assessment (Environmental Impact Assessment)

A. Austria

Stefan Storr and Sophie Praniess

The answer to both questions concerns the scope of decision-making by the administrative court. If a licence (in this case the permission to build and operate a gold mine) is the object of appeal, a court would determine whether the authority disregarded or violated statutory provisions in its decision-making and licensing process. If an environmental impact assessment was not performed, disregarding statutory provisions, the competent administrative court can—under certain circumstances—make up for the faulty administrative procedure because, in principle, the administrative court has to resolve the case with a ruling.[570] In a case like the one at hand, the administrative court itself is compelled to adjudicate the case on the merits of the appeal against the administrative decision if the pertinent facts have already been established, or if the determination of the relevant facts by the administrative court itself would expedite the proceedings or lead to considerable cost savings.[571] If the prerequisites for rendering such a decision on the merits are not met, the competent administrative court must invalidate the initial decision and remand the case to the administrative authority for further review.

B. China

Xiaowei Sun

The court would declare the contested action unlawful, refuse to use it as a legal basis, and recommend that the authority remedy the irregularity.

There are two ways to contest an urban plan as a regulatory document. Citizens or legal persons can contest it directly by way of exception if their interests are actually affected. Alternatively, they can challenge an administrative authorization under Article 53 of the Administrative Litigation Law.

There has been no precedent for ascertaining that the likely impact before mining actually commences can be considered as actually affecting the interests of the plaintiffs. They have to wait until the authority makes a decision authorizing mining activity in the area in question.

By way of exception, the court would review Terranova's plan in light of Article 148 of the Judicial Interpretation in relation to the application of the Administrative Litigation Law. More precisely, it would verify whether Terranova's action was in conformity with the 'legally approval procedures', as defined in that text.

[570] S 28 para 1 Administrative Court Procedure Act (*Bundesgesetz über das Verfahren der Verwaltungsgerichte (Verwaltungsgerichtsverfahrensgesetz—VwGVG)*) Orig Vers: BGBl I No 33/2013.

[571] S 28 para 2 VwGVG.

Article 19 of the Environmental Protection Law[572] states:

> An environmental impact assessment shall be conducted as legally required in the preparation of a relevant development and utilisation plan or the construction of a project impacting the environment.
>
> A development and utilisation plan that has not undergone environmental impact assessment as legally required may not be implemented. The construction of a construction project that has not undergone environmental impact assessment as legally required may not be commenced.[573]

This law imposes a duty to carry out an environmental impact assessment for all development plans likely to affect the environment. In this case, the authority 'failed to comply with legal approval procedures', which is a clear lack of compliance with their duty.

C. Czech Republic

Jiří Rajchl

As with the previous questions, the legal nature of the plan for the development of economic activities will be of great importance. The term 'plan' is more indicative of belonging to a group of non-binding acts. In the Czech Republic, there are regional development plans adopted at the regional level that set out the basic requirements for the efficient and economical setup of the region's territory.[574] These documents are already legally binding general measures. They straddle the line between legal regulation and administrative decision, as they concern a specific territory or issue, and they affect an indefinite number of addressees. In addition to a state planning policy at the state level, and a local development plan at the municipal level, a regional development plan, as a type of planning documentation, represents a broader regulation than the document specified in the scenario because it also incorporates non-economic issues. On the other hand, it is narrower in some respects as it does not address economic development that does not affect the territory. Despite these differences, the regional development plan is the best fit for the scenario, so we will build on that.

A regional development plan should include an assessment of the impacts on the sustainable development of the territory, including an assessment of the territorial conditions for the favourable environment, economic development, and cohesion of the community of inhabitants of the territory.[575] The environmental impact

572 环境保护法.

573 编制有关开发利用规划，建设对环境有影响的项目，应当依法进行环境影响评价 未依法进行环境影响评价的开发利用规划，不得组织实施；未依法进行环境影响评价的建设项目，不得开工建设。

574 S 36 of Act No 183/2006 Sb, the Planning and Building Regulations Act. As of 1 July 2024, s 77 of Act No 283/2021 Sb, the Building Act.

575 S 6 and attachment 3 of Regulation No 157/2024 Sb, on planning analytical data, planning documentation, and uniform standard.

assessment should describe and evaluate any environmental impact of the regional development plan that has been identified and is anticipated to be significant. Anyone may submit comments when the plan is being drafted. The usual procedures under the Environmental Impact Assessment Act have been replaced by special arrangements. The Ministry of the Environment issues an opinion on the environmental and public health impact assessment.[576] General measures can be challenged through administrative justice. Claims can be made for violations of procedural rules that may have affected the legality of the measure or for direct contravention of laws. The failure to attempt to incorporate an environmental impact assessment, as indicated in the scenario, would be a direct contravention of the law. The contested general measure would be quashed.

It is difficult to imagine a situation where a legal regulation does not require an environmental impact assessment, as the legal system is already heavily focused on the environment. In fact, general requirements for environmental protections are expressed in several laws. In addition to the Building Act, the Environment Act,[577] the Environmental Impact Assessment Act,[578] and the Act on the Protection of Nature and Landscape are applicable.[579] Additionally, there are various laws that apply to specific areas, such as air, water, forests, etc. The Charter of Fundamental Rights and Freedoms, which is part of the constitutional system, also provides, in Article 35, that everyone has the right to a healthy environment.[580] This provision, along with the right to information about the environment,[581] falls within the scope of those constitutional rights that can only be invoked within the limits of laws implementing said provisions.[582] The same regime applies to the right to the protection of health, enshrined in Article 31 of the Charter of Fundamental Rights and Freedoms. It is therefore questionable to what extent the quoted substantive provision regarding the right to a favourable environment would be applicable without further statutory regulation. However, the complete absence of a statute cannot completely negate the existence of the constitutional provisions in question.[583] Especially now, when people are becoming more aware of how important it is to protect the environment, we can assume that this provision will be applied directly. The provision in question is rather vague, which could pose an obstacle. However, land-use planning without regard for the environment may be considered unconstitutional. The existing case law of the Constitutional Court in this area is scarce, and it is not possible to reach the unequivocal conclusion that direct application as indicated in the case study is possible.

[576] S 10i in conjunction with s 21 Act No 100/2001 Sb, on the environmental impact assessment.

[577] Act No 17/1992 Sb, on the environment.

[578] Act No 100/2001 Sb, on the environmental impact assessment.

[579] Act No 114/1992 Sb, on the protection of nature and landscape.

[580] The Charter of Fundamental Rights and Freedoms, promulgated by the Board of the Czech National Council on 16 December 1992 as a part of the constitutional system of the Czech Republic (Act No 2/1993 Sb).

[581] Art 35(2) of the Charter of Fundamental Rights and Freedoms is implemented by Act No 123/1998 Sb, regulating the right to information about the environment.

[582] Art 41(2) of the Charter of Fundamental Rights and Freedoms.

[583] Under art 4 of the Fundamental Rights and Freedoms, when applying provisions concerning limitations on fundamental rights and freedoms, the essence and significance of those rights and freedoms must be preserved.

D. European Union

Edoardo Chiti and Marco Lunardelli

In this hypothetical case, which does not need to be adapted to be analysed from the EU perspective, a regional authority failed to conduct an EIA before adopting a plan for the exploitation of economic activities, namely a number of gold mines, located on the territory under its jurisdiction. According to the case description, some groups of residents and other persons, concerned about the impact of mining on the environment, bring an action, whereby they challenge the legitimacy of the plan. Not only is the latter not based on an EIA, but, in more general terms, the regional authority adopting it did not include environmental considerations in its policy, even though the harm pollution in that area may cause to the ecosystem and—consequently—to human beings is documented in scientific studies. In the current EU legal order, legislation on this subject matter may be considered to be divided into two main directives. A 2001 directive addresses the strategic environmental assessment (SEA) of plans and programmes,[584] while the directive identifying the types of projects subject to a mandatory EIA was enacted in 2011[585] and amended in 2014.[586] However, no environmental assessment requirement is established for the formulation of policies or for legislative acts.[587] The 2001 and 2011 directives (the latter in the consolidated version currently in force) are similar as they both substantially provide for a mandatory EIA whenever—respectively—a plan, programme, or a project is deemed to produce significant effects on the environment. Indeed, the regional plan at issue might fall within the scope of either directive, depending on the interpretation followed. If one stresses the fact that the plan was adopted by a regional administration as required by national legislation, and it is considered to come under land use, the 2001 directive applies.[588] If emphasis is placed on the primary purpose of the plan, ie, the arrangement and regulation of gold mines, which, as economic activities, may later be assigned to private businesses through concessions adopted on the basis of projects they submit, the 2011 directive may be deemed to apply.[589]

Therefore, in the case at issue, the plan adopted by the municipality has to be considered unlawful because it lacks a mandatory requirement, the EIA, which is not carried out before mining licences are released, a conclusion that may be reached from

[584] Directive 2001/42/EC of 27 June 2001 on the assessment of the effects of certain plans and programmes on the environment, [2001] OJL 197/30.

[585] Directive 2011/92/EU of 13 December 2011 on the assessment of the effects of certain public and private projects on the environment, [2012] OJL 26/1.

[586] Directive 2014/52/EU of 16 April 2014, [2014] OJL 124/1.

[587] See A García-Ureta, 'Environmental Impact Assessment in the EU: More than only a Procedure?' in M Peeters and M Eliantonio (eds), *Research Handbook of EU Environmental Law* (Edward Elgar 2020) 168–69.

[588] Respectively, arts 2(a) and 3(2)(a), Directive 2001/42/EC. As for case law, see Case C-473/14, *Dimos Kropias Attikis*, ECLI:EU:C:2015:582, §§ 5–8 and 24–27.

[589] In particular, Annex 1 to Directive 2011/92 contains a list of projects concerning works and facilities, the realization of which requires an EIA under art 4(1) of the directive. The list encompasses (No 19) quarries, 'open-cast mining', and peat bogs, as long as they have a predetermined minimum size. Even though there is no express reference to gold mines, and the description of the case does not provide details on their size, it may be assumed that the gold mines in question meet the requirement.

different perspectives. First, even if the plan in question was not intended to be subject to a mandatory EIA (or Single European Act), the ECJ has played a fundamental role over time in interpreting those directives, and its decisions therefore provide valuable insights. Not only did it do so by addressing the relevant definitions, such as the meanings of 'plan' and 'project', but it also identified projects that require the performance of an EIA. This imposes an obligation upon Member States' administrations when they implement the directives, namely in the indirect execution of EU law.[590] It also held that the authority adopting a decision serving as the prerequisite for authorizing activities that will have an impact on the environment has to take into account all potential environmental effects at the earliest possible stage in the decision-making process and certainly before individual authorizations are released.[591] Accordingly, the ability of Member States to exclude projects from the EIA requirement has to be interpreted strictly, and in any case entails the burden of accurately assessing all factors that may have a notable impact on the environment.[592]

Secondly, the plan does not appear to be lawful when considered in the light of the Århus Convention,[593] especially because it does not ensure participation rights. The reference is, especially, to Articles 6 and 7 of the Convention, which establish obligations that aim to ensure transparency and fairness in the decision-making process on environmental issues.[594] As far as those rights are concerned, the Convention's provisions were implemented by a 2003 directive, imposing on Member States the obligation to give individuals 'early and effective opportunities' to participate in the decision-making process.[595] The 2001 and 2011 directives mentioned above prescribe

[590] See García-Ureta, 'Environmental Impact Assessment in the EU' (n 587) 171–75. In the Italian legal system, for instance, urban implementing plans adopted at municipal level are traditionally deemed not to be subject to an SEA, as the latter is requisite in the proceeding for the formation of the urban general plan, and thus it was already carried out. See F Salvia, C Bevilacqua, and N Gullo, *Manuale di diritto urbanistico* (4th edn, Wolters Kluwer 2021) 349. By applying such a rule to the hypothetical case at issue, the unlawfulness of the municipal plan for failing to conduct an accurate EIA or SEA—which has to consider all types of relevant factors, and not only economic ones—is more evident, to the extent that such an assessment did not occur at regional level.

[591] See Case C-201/02, *The Queen, on the application of Delena Wells v Secretary of State for Transport, Local Government and the Regions*, ECLI:EU:C:2004:12, §§ 50–52. As has been underlined, the *Delena Wells* judgment also identified (§§ 55–58) the requirement for an individual to legitimately rely on direct effects produced by EU directives. The failure to fulfil the obligations established by those directives is capable of affecting a third party, thereby causing some harm or disadvantage to it. See Pünder and Klafki (n 449) 527–28, esp 528.

[592] See Case C-404/09, *European Commission v Spain*, ECLI:EU:C:2011:768, § 80.

[593] United Nations, Convention on Access to Information, Public Participation in Decision-Making and Access to Justice in Environmental Matters, signed in Aarhus, Denmark, on 25 June 1998, <https://treaties.un.org/doc/Treaties/1998/06/19980625%2008-35%20AM/Ch_XXVII_13p.pdf> accessed 23 November 2024.

[594] See L Squintani and G Perlaviciute, 'Access to Public Participation: Unveiling the Mismatch between What Law Prescribes and What the Public Wants' in Peeters and Eliantonio (eds) (n 587) 139–43.

[595] Art 2(2) of Directive 2003/35/EC of 26 May 2003 providing for public participation in respect of the drawing up of certain plans and programmes relating to the environment and amending with regard to public participation and access to justice Council Directives 85/337/EEC and 96/61/EC, [2003] OJL 156/17, 18. This directive was amended first by Directive 2011/92, already mentioned, and then by Directive (EU) 2016/2284 of 14 December 2016 on the reduction of national emissions of certain atmospheric pollutants, [2016] OJL 344/1, which—respectively—repealed art 3 and added point (g) in Annex I of Directive 2003/35.

that participatory rights should be recognized at an early stage of that process.[596] If they were not ensured early enough—in the course of the comprehensive planning proceeding—to allow interested persons an effective participation, thus the ability to affect at least some contents of the plan, such as those an EIA should address, the ECJ would most likely consider the plan itself unlawful.

E. Germany

Lilly Weidemann

The court would probably do no more than check whether there is a particular obligation to carry out an environmental impact assessment of this particular project and, if there is not, dismiss the action concerning the second argument, ie the lack of an environmental impact assessment. It would, however, probably uphold the residents' argumentation in that environmental considerations have to be taken into account.

The Environmental Impact Assessment Act[597] stipulates whether, and under which circumstances, a project is to be subjected to an environmental impact assessment. The EIA Act distinguishes between the unconditional EIA obligation for new construction projects (Section 6 EIA Act), modification projects (section 9 paragraph 1 and 2; sections 10 et seq EIA Act), the preliminary EIA obligation for new construction projects (section 7 EIA Act), and modification projects (section 9 paragraphs 3, 4 EIA Act). With regard to the preliminary EIA assessment, a distinction must be made between general preliminary assessments (section 7 paragraph 1 EIA Act) and site-specific preliminary assessments (section 7 paragraph 2 EIA Act). The general preliminary assessment examines whether the project might have a significant adverse environmental impact (section 7 paragraph 1 EIA Act). When carrying out a site-specific preliminary assessment, the first step is to apply specific criteria to examine whether there are any conditions specific to the local context; only if this is the case does the authority then examine whether the project may have a significant adverse environmental impact on the particular conservation objectives of the area (section 7 para 2 EIA Act). Section 5 EIA Act provides for a special procedure to determine whether or not an EIA obligation exists (screening procedure).

If the court were to find a statutory obligation to conduct an EIA in the present case, it would probably block Terranova's plan. According to section 4 of the Environmental Appeals Act[598] (EAA), action can be taken to block a plan if the necessary EIA has not been carried out.[599]

[596] Arts 6(2) of Directive 2001/42/EC and 6(4) of Directive 2011/92/EU. As for case law, see—respectively—Case C-474/10, *Department of the Environment for Northern Ireland v Seaport (NI) Ltd and Others*, ECLI:EU:C:2011:681, §§ 7, 14, 31, and 45; and Case C-411/17, *Inter-Environnement Wallonie ASBL and Bond Beter Leefmilieu Vlaanderen ASBL v Conseil des ministers*, ECLI:EU:C:2019:622, §§ 14, 26, 58, and 163–166, even though the latter deals with a Member State's—namely, Belgium's—national legislation.

[597] *Gesetz über die Umweltverträglichkeitsprüfung* in the wording of 18 March 2021 (Federal Law Gazette I p 540), amended by art 10 of the Law of 22 December 2023 (Federal Law Gazette 2023 I No 409.

[598] *Gesetz über ergänzende Vorschriften zu Rechtsbehelfen in Umweltangelegenheiten nach der EG-Richtlinie* 2003/35/EG (*Umwelt-Rechtsbehelfsgesetz*—UmwRG) in last version of 23 August 2017 (Federal Law Gazette I p 3290).

[599] S 4 para 1 No 1 lit a) Environmental Appeals Act.

Even without a statutory obligation to conduct an environmental impact assessment, Terranova would have to consider the environmental impact that adopting the plan might have. First of all, as seen in Case 9, the authority has to balance the public and private interests affected by the planning fairly. Secondly, the provision in Article 20a of the Basic Law[600] obliges the state—also assuming responsibility for future generations—to protect the natural foundations of life. The addressees of the protection requirement include executive power 'in accordance with law and justice'. This means that the state objectives of Article 20a of the Basic Law are generally relevant to the administration where the laws allow for some leeway; this is the case, for example, with planning decisions.[601]

F. Hungary

Lilla Berkes and Balázs Szabolcs Gerencsér

This is a fairly clear situation in Hungarian law, in which the relevant legislation—the Mining Act,[602] the Government Decree on Environmental Impact Assessment[603]—provides in detail for the obligation to prepare an environmental impact assessment for mining activities, and it must be attached to the application, so without it the permit will not be granted.

If this were not an impact assessment but some kind of opinion, if the legislation requires the authority to request another body (authority) as a condition for the decision (eg an involvement of the specialist authority),[604] failure to do so would mean that the decision is unlawful.

The court would in any case examine whether any legal provision been breached. In the absence of such legal provisions, especially in cases where environmental protection is involved, the court is also inclined to refer to international treaties, since they are part of Hungarian law and may therefore impose an express obligation on the parties, which are legal entities. In addition, the Mining Act itself stipulates as a basic requirement that mining activities must be carried out in a manner that protects human life, health, the environment, land, and property, and ensures that mineral and geothermal energy resources are managed in accordance with the requirements of the law.[605] Consequently, the court also has the possibility to assess, in the context of the

[600] Art 20a of the Basic Law stipulates: 'Mindful also of its responsibility towards future generations, the state shall protect the natural foundations of life and animals by legislation and, in accordance with law and justice, by executive and judicial action, all within the framework of the constitutional order.'

[601] Federal Administrative Court, Judgment of 4 May 2022—9 A 7/21–, BVerwGE 175, 312–38, para 61 with further references.

[602] § 26/A (3) of the Act XLVIII of 1993 on mining <https://njt.hu/jogszabaly/1993-48-00-00> accessed 23 November 2024 (no official English translation available).

[603] Government Decree 14/2005 (XII. 25) on the environmental impact assessment and the single authorization procedure for the use of the environment <https://njt.hu/jogszabaly/2005-314-20-22> accessed 23 November 2024 (no official English translation available).

[604] §§ 55–57, § 123 (1)b), (2)c) of the Act CL of 2016 on the Code of General Administrative Procedure <https://njt.hu/jogszabaly/en/2016-150-00-00> accessed 23 November 2024.

[605] § 2 of the Act XLVIII of 1993 on mining.

clarification of the facts, whether granting the licence complied with this principle, which also gives the opportunity to apply international and constitutional requirements to the specific case.

G. Italy

Leonardo Parona

The Italian legal system, like those of the other Member States, is profoundly shaped by EU law regarding the subject of the present case (ie the approval of plans and projects potentially affecting the environment) and the issues it poses. Before addressing the answer to this hypothetical case, it seems therefore necessary briefly to outline the supranational, international, and national normative framework.

With a 2001 directive, the EU mandated that an SEA of plans and programmes be conducted before their adoption.[606] The types of projects subject to a mandatory EIA were identified in a directive enacted in 2011[607] and amended in 2014.[608] These directives have been transposed into the Italian legal system by the Environment Code, enacted by Legislative Decree No 152/2006 and subsequently amended several times.[609] The most relevant provisions, from our perspective, are contained in Part II, Titles I–III of the Code (Articles 4–29). Lastly, thanks to the ratification of the Aarhus Convention through Law No 108/2001, comprehensive participatory rights have been introduced into the Italian legal system. Specifically, Articles 6 and 7 of the Convention establish general obligations to ensure transparency and fairness in decision-making processes concerning environmental interests.

Coming to the facts of the case, when adopting a plan concerning the exploitation of commercial activities such as gold mines, upon which individual licences were subsequently issued, the regional authority of Terranova allegedly acted unlawfully. The alleged unlawfulness pertained to both procedural and substantive aspects of the plan, since Terranova did not carry out a prior EIA. Procedurally, Terranova did not incorporate any environmental considerations, specifically failing to demonstrate whether, to what extent, and with which consequences, environmental interests had been taken into consideration.

In very clear terms, Article 29(1) of the Environment Code establishes that 'authorisations for a project adopted without verification of eligibility for EIA or without EIA, where required, shall be annulled for violation of the law'. The subsequent paragraphs also introduce administrative sanctions for such violations, and further legislative provisions also add criminal sanctions.

[606] Directive 2001/42/EC. See E Boscolo, 'La valutazione ambientale strategica di piani e programmi' (2008) 1 Rivista giuridica dell'edilizia 3 ff.
[607] Directive 2011/92/EU.
[608] Directive 2014/52/EU.
[609] Moreover, Legislative Decree No 195/2005, implementing Directive 2003/4/EC, introduced rules regulating environmental information and the public's right of access. Environmental information that must be published is also subject to civic access legislation (art 40 of Legislative Decree No 33/2013).

The unlawfulness of an individual measure issued without an EIA is, therefore, unequivocal under this provision. However, the act issued by the regional authority in our case is a plan, ie a general administrative act, and not an individual one. This distinction does not alter the substance of the outcome: conducting an EIA remains a mandatory requirement according to Article 6 of the Code,[610] and a violation of applicable law still constitutes grounds for unlawfulness under Article 21-*octies*(1) of the General Law No 241/1990.

As a consequence, the plan adopted by Terranova would be considered unlawful, and it could be challenged in court by associations of residents working to protect the environment,[611] although its discretionary nature might complicate judicial review and not necessarily lead to the act being annulled.[612]

Even beyond statutory law, a decision like the one reached by the regional authority of Terranova in the present case would also contradict established case law according to which, concerning general administrative acts, it is necessary to uphold 'compliance with the criterion of sustainable development and the principle of proportionality between consumption of natural resources and the benefits for the community, which must govern the balancing of contradictory needs'.[613] The solutions established

610 Moreover precisely for the purposes for which the environmental impact assessment is intended, the law has structured the procedural investigation phase (*istruttoria*) to be open to the participation of those with public and private interests involved in the project. As a result, the justification provided by the competent authority in its decision-making becomes more substantial when the investigation, informed by participatory contributions from public and private entities, including community interests, reveals potential negative impacts on the environmental and urban context affected by the initiative (Council of State, Sec II, No 2949/2021; see also Sec V, No 2234/2012).

611 The case law has clarified that the protection of environmental interests can also be asserted through the challenge of general administrative acts of urban planning, as well as planning and programming acts, if they have adverse effects on the aforementioned environmental aspects due to their instrumental role in evaluating the impact on the landscape and the environment of the planned interventions (Lombardy Administrative Court, Milan, Sec II, No 2500/2019; referring to Council of State, Sec V, No 3109/2018; Sec IV, No 2329/2011. See also Lombardy Administrative Court, Brescia, Sec I, No 439/2020; Campania Administrative Court, Salerno, Sec II, No 1420/2019; Veneto Administrative Court, Sec II, No 50/2017). Regarding this matter, and in addition to the special standing of environmental associations, it is pertinent to recall the established orientation of administrative jurisprudence, which considers general administrative acts to be independently contestable only in mandatory cases. This stance represents an exception to the general rule that such acts do not, as a rule, contain provisions immediately detrimental to the legal sphere of the associates, since the impact on their legal situations is deferred to the subsequent stage constituted by the adoption of subsequent implementing measures (Lazio Administrative Court, Rome, Sec III, No 6325/2021).

612 Mention should also be made to the circumstance that an action for annulment should be submitted within the short deadline of 60 days. In our case, this deadline might already have expired, since individual mining licences have been issued; in this case, the issuance of a licence might be challenged (within 60 days), and then the unlawfulness of the plan might be challenged indirectly, which is a solution similar to the double challenge mechanism we referred to in relation to the judicial review of general administrative acts and enforcement (individual) measures.

613 Council of State, Sec V, No 4928/2014 (see also Sec IV, No 4246/2010; Sec VI, No 933/2007). Moreover, as clarified by the Council of State: 'The case law has repeatedly affirmed ... that, in accordance with community and national principles, as well as its own specific purposes, environmental impact assessment does not consist of a mere technical verification of the abstract environmental compatibility of the work, but implies a complex and in-depth comparative analysis aimed at evaluating the environmental sacrifice imposed with respect to socio-economic utility, also taking into account the possible alternatives and the repercussions on the so-called zero-option.' (Council of State, Sec II, No 2949/2021). At times, administrative courts also interpret the EIA requirement as mandating a thorough cost-benefit analysis to be carried out in a 'coordinated and comprehensive manner' (see Sardinia Administrative Court, Cagliari, Sec II, No 439/2018).

by this case law now carry even greater weight in the Italian legal system in the light of the recent constitutionalization of environmental protection.[614]

Lastly, it should be added that, although a court would find Terranova's actions unlawful, it still might decide not to annul the plan but rather to order a retrospective EIA be carried out.[615]

H. Netherlands

Jacobine van den Brink, Louise Verboeket, and Veerle van Waarde

The administrative court would first of all check whether the administrative authority (*bestuursorgaan*) should have carried out an EIA (*milieueffectenrapportage*) according to EU Regulations 2014/52 and 2001/42. If an EIA was indeed required, the administrative court will quash the plan. If there was no obligation to carry out an EIA, the court will reject the claim as unfounded. The administrative court would not consider *ex officio* whether an obligation to carry out an environmental impact assessment in accordance with constitutional values, principles, or international law, such as Article 8 ECHR, exists. These values, principles, and the ECHR[616] do not regard public order and are therefore not reviewed *ex officio*. It can be claimed before the administrative court that even though there is no legal obligation to do so, the administrative authority's failure to carry out an EIA is a violation of Article 3:2(1) GALA. As far as we are aware, such a ground for appeal has never been accepted in the Netherlands. Furthermore, it can be argued that not carrying out an EIA is a breach of international law, such as Article 8 ECHR.[617] If this is the case, both options (annulment or imposition of an adequate EIA) are open.

I. Norway

Eivind Smith

In all probability, the court would verify the validity of the argument regarding the absence of any pertinent EIA. If the argument is proved to be true, the licence would have been issued in manifest breach of the requirements to carry out the assessments prescribed in the relevant sector legislation and might entail the invalidation of the licence. This outcome would be even more probable considering that no mining have actually commenced.

[614] Art 9(3) Const was amended in 2022, requiring the Italian Republic to 'safeguard the environment, biodiversity, and ecosystems, also in the interest of future generations'.

[615] See Lombardy Administrative Court, Brescia, Sec I, No 141/2023. This solution was allowed also by the ECJ, Case C-117/17, *Comune di Castelbellino v Regione Marche and Others* [2018] ECLI:EU:C:2018:129. For an analysis, see G Mannucci, 'La VIA postuma all'esame della Corte di Giustizia' (2018) 6 Giornale di diritto amministrativo 757 ff.

[616] See ECtHR 15 November 1996, 18877/91 (*Sadik/Greece*).

[617] Compare with Supreme Court 20 December 2019, ECLI:NL:HR:2019:2006 (*Staat/Urgenda*).

J. Portugal

Rui Guerra da Fonseca

Urban and territorial plans and programmes, like other similar instruments concerning land use that establish the framework for future projects, which are themselves subject to environmental assessment, must usually be submitted to such (previous) assessment too. The complex web of legal regulations on this matter probably already justifies referring to such a general principle.[618]

In this case, Terranova is a 'regional' authority which, by itself, does not allow a clear-cut classification of the plan at hand due to the intricacies of Portugal's administrative structure and competences in this regard. But assuming we are at the municipal level, even certain plans that might be exempt from environmental assessment may, after all, be subject to it if they could have a significant impact on the environment or if they establish the framework for future projects that will be subject to environmental assessment.[619]

According to the legal framework concerning environmental impact assessment (AIA),[620] the mining projects in question would necessitate evaluation, and the absence of any such an assessment can be challenged in the administrative courts (Articles 1, 37, and Annexes I and II of the AIA). Thus, in principle (and not considering exceptions), the plan and later projects requiring licences would be subject to environmental assessment.

If the procedural requirements are not met, the courts will certainly uphold the residents' claim and deem the plan illegal. This will happen regardless of what might happen in the future in relation to potential licences.

K. Sweden

Patricia Jonason and Björn Forssén

If Terranova is considered a public authority and the plan is mandatory, then it must comply with the rules in chapter 6 of the Environmental Code (*Miljöbalken*, MB). According to the provisions of this chapter, Terranova must investigate whether the implementation of the plan may have a significant environmental impact. After the investigation, the public authority must decide, through a special decision, whether the plan is expected to have a significant environmental impact. If the investigation shows that there will be a significant environmental impact, an EIA must be carried out, as laid down in section 9, chapter 6 of the MB.

618 See Decree-Law 232/2007, 15 June (last amended by Decree-Law 58/2011, 4 May), namely art 3/1; and, in close relation to this, Decree-Law 80/2015.

619 These are specific urbanization and detailing plans (see art 78 of Decree-Law 80/2015, and also 'Portugal—Case 8', section IX.J in this chapter).

620 Decree-Law 151-B/2013, of 31 October (last amended by Decree-Law 152-B/2017 of 11 December).

In other words, if an EIA is not required, the court would dismiss the case. It is important to note that the decision on whether a significant environmental impact can be assumed cannot be appealed separately (section 8, chapter 6, of the MB).

The Mineral Act requires an EIA only at the stage of the concession of exploitation (section 2, chapter 4, Mineral Act) but not during the exploration stage. Nevertheless, the Mineral Act shows some concerns for the environment even in the stages prior to the exploration phase: it states that '[t]he (exploration) work shall be carried out in such a way as to cause the least possible damage to, and encroachment on, any other person's property and the natural and cultural environment' (section 3, paragraph 4, chapter 3, Mineral Act).

L. United Kingdom

John Morison and David Mark

Important to this scenario involving Terranova's plan to develop gold mines, is the legal framework governing EIAs in the United Kingdom.

The UK's environmental legislation has been greatly influenced by EU law, notably through the implementation of EU Directive 85/337/EEC, which requires comprehensive EIAs for projects with significant environmental impact. With recognition of the changes brought by Brexit, this directive's legacy continues to shape UK environmental policy. Specifically, the Town and Country Planning (Environmental Impact Assessment) Regulations 2017, under the Town and Country Planning Act 1990, which are crucial for determining whether Terranova's project, necessitates an EIA. Cases like *R (on the application of Barker) v London Borough of Bromley*[621] and *R v Secretary of State for the Environment, ex parte Berkeley*[622] highlight the courts' apparent insistence on strict adherence to EIA regulations. Furthermore, *R (Swire) v Secretary of State for Housing, Communities and Local Government*[623] (leading on from *Gillespie v First Secretary of State*)[624] emphasized the 'precautionary principle,' particularly relevant in situations of environmental uncertainty. This principle was clarified in *Champion v North Norfolk District Council*[625] when Lord Carnwath advised that, 'application of the precautionary principle, which underlies the EIA Directive, implies that cases of material doubt should generally be resolved in favour of EIA.' Terranova's move to exploration without such an environmental assessment is certainly at risk of judicial intervention. Furthermore, the regional authority will not be able to get away with substituting the EIA with any other form of environmental statement. In *Berkeley*, the House of Lords ruled an EIA cannot be substituted by other enviromental documents, thereby reinforcing the need for a formal EIA.

621 [2006] UKHL 52.
622 [2000] UKHL 36.
623 [2020] EWHC 1298.
624 [2002] EWCA Civ 400.
625 [2015] UKSC 52.

In this context, given the UK courts' tendency to prioritize environmental protection in the face of potential harm, it is likely that the court would consider Terranova's plan unlawful in response to non-compliance with EIA regulations.

Even in the event that an EIA is deemed unnecessary, the Office for Environmental Protection, created by the Environment Act 2021, underscores a growing legal commitment to environmental stewardship, balancing environmental and economic interests. Cases such as the noted *R. (on the application of Friends of the Earth Ltd.) v Heathrow Airport Ltd*[626] and *R (on the application of Mott) v Environment Agency*[627] indicate a balancing exercise between environmental and economic considerations is often expected. *R (on the application of Morge) v Hampshire County Council*,[628] while centred around the protection of a species, mirrors the wider European commitment to environmental care, relevant to this discussion.

In addition to this, it is important to note, in the context of mining, that various mining-related activities necessitate an environmental permit.[629] Moreover, several conservation laws are relavent here, such as the Wildlife and Countryside Act 1981 and the Conservation of Habitats and Species Regulations 2017 (which consolidated and updated the Conservation of Habitats and Species Regulations 2010).

To conclude, given the judicial trend towards prioritizing environmental protection, it is highly probable that a failure to conduct an EIA would lead to the courts consideringTerranova's mining plan unlawful. UK courts have repeatedly shown that environmental considerations are paramount in any decision with such a potentially large ecological impact.

M. United States of America

Jeffrey Lubbers and Giacinto della Cananea

In the United States, the courts would not enforce an environmental treaty, unless the Senate has ratified it, but there are domestic rules that could be applied.[630]

To begin with, in the United States, there is no federal constitutional right to a clean environment, so if this were on federal land or required a federal licence, any challenge to this action would have to be based on a statute. There are a few states—Alaska, Hawaii, Illinois, Massachusetts, Montana, and Pennsylvania—that have

626 [2020] UKSC 52.
627 [2018] UKSC 10.
628 [2011] UKSC 2.
629 See further ICLG 'Mining Laws and Regulations United Kingdom' 2023 <https://iclg.com/practice-areas/mining-laws-and-regulations/united-kingdom> accessed 23 November 2024.
630 For further analysis, see RB Stewart, 'A New Generation of Environmental Regulation?' (2001) 29 Capital U L Rev 21 (illustrating the changes occurred in environmental regulation); DC Esty, 'Next Generation Environmental Law: A Response to Richard Stewart' (2001) 29 Capital U L Rev 183 (arguing that heightened attention to information is necessary); and JB Wiener, 'Global Environmental Regulation: Instrument Choice in Legal Context' (1999) 108 Yale L J 677 (discussing the choice between various instruments from a global perspective).

constitutionally based environmental rights protections, but challengers in the other states would have to cite state statutes.

Fortunately, at the federal level, the 1970 National Environmental Policy Act (NEPA) does require the government to undertake either an environmental assessment or a more substantial environmental impact statement for all 'major federal actions affecting the quality of the human environment'. The courts have enforced this requirement by enjoining such actions if the requisite assessment or statement is not done. Normally these are prepared by the agency in charge of the action after consultation with other affected agencies and an opportunity for public comment.

On the state level, 20 states have 'little NEPAs',[631] but if the jurisdiction does not have such a constitutional or statutory obligation, the action would be likely to be dismissed. Courts would not enforce an applicable international treaty unless the US Senate had ratified it.

631 <https://ceq.doe.gov/laws-regulations/states.html> accessed 23 November 2024.

PART IV
COMPARATIVE ANALYSIS

The fourth part compares the solutions identified by the experts from the national legal systems—and their reasoning. The section begins with a chapter discussing the importance and implications of general legislation on administrative procedures adopted in the majority, but not all, of the legal systems included in our comparison. Additionally, there are two chapters dedicated to comparing the approaches to rulemaking and planning, respectively.

16
A Comparative Analysis of Administrative Procedure Legislation on Rulemaking

Angela Ferrari Zumbini

I. Introduction

This chapter will carry out a comparative analysis of the administrative procedure legislation on rulemaking in the various legal systems examined in this volume. The analysis will therefore be based on the answers provided by the national experts to the general questions concerning the distinction—whether at the legislative level or in judicial doctrine—between adjudication and rulemaking, and the general principles governing the latter form of administrative action.

The purpose of the comparison is to highlight commonalities and distinctive features concerning the procedural requirements imposed on administrations when adopting rulemaking. In pursuit of this objective, our analysis will not be limited to examining the legal texts of those legal systems that have adopted a general law on rulemaking procedures. It will also consider the procedural requirements imposed by courts applying general principles in countries with no general rulemaking law.

In this way, an attempt will be made to outline the legal framework of procedural constraints in the different legal systems, highlighting transparency requirements and the rights of the interested parties to participate in decision-making.[1] The comparative analysis will make it possible to assess the legal relevance and significance of having—or not having—a general act on administrative rulemaking procedures.

In the concluding remarks, beyond highlighting commonalities and distinctive features, some considerations on the institutional level will be drawn.

Finally, some words about definitions are necessary. As this chapter will show, different legal systems adopt different terms to refer to rulemaking. The differences are not merely nominal; the range of administrative acts that can be subsumed under this category can vary deeply depending on whether it is interpreted narrowly or broadly, and the criteria used to define the category itself also have important implications. Thus, the concept of administrative rulemaking is viewed more broadly here, so as to include administrative procedures for issuing generally applicable rules and acts.

[1] On the importance of ensuring more accountable rulemaking procedures, especially in terms of participation and transparency, see, among many, SG Breyer and others, *Administrative Law and Regulatory Policy* (9th edn, Aspen 2022); for a practical overview, see CM Kerwin and SR Furlong, *Rulemaking: How Government Agencies Write Law and Make Policy* (5th edn, CQ Press 2018). On a general and theoretical level, J Barnes calls for what he refers to as 'third generation procedures', which should be more collaborative, non-hierarchical and decentralized, 'Towards a Third Generation of Administrative Procedure' in S Rose-Ackerman and PL Lindseth, *Comparative Administrative Law* (Edward Elgar 2010) 336 ff.

Angela Ferrari Zumbini, *A Comparative Analysis of Administrative Procedure Legislation on Rulemaking* In: *Administrative Rulemaking and Planning in European Laws*. Edited by: Giacinto della Cananea and Angela Ferrari Zumbini, Oxford University Press. © Angela Ferrari Zumbini 2025. DOI: 10.1093/oso/9780198867616.003.0016

II. Constitutional Provisions Regulating Administrative Rulemaking

Some constitutions clearly reference general acts adopted by the public administration, thus endowing them with rulemaking authority, albeit with different terminology, definitions, requirements, content, and degree of detail.

The Austrian Federal Constitutional Act empowers public authorities to issue general acts in Article 18 paragraph 2: 'Every administrative authority can issue ordinances on the basis of law within its sphere of competence.' In its settled case law, the Austrian Constitutional Court has clarified that an ordinance is a general legal act issued by an administrative authority in the exercise of public law, regardless of its designation.

Article 79(3) of the Constitution of the Czech Republic clearly states that 'Ministries, other administrative agencies and territorial self-government bodies may issue on the basis and within the scope of a law legal regulations, if they are authorised to do so by law'. Moreover, Article 78 allows the government, as the head of the executive branch, to enact regulations for implementing the laws without requiring explicit authorization. Thus, governmental regulations are limited to purposes of implementation. The situation is different regarding territorial self-governing entities, endowed by Article 104(3) with the general authority to adopt 'generally binding ordinances' within their competences, provided they are not in conflict with the law. They are not, therefore, limited to mere implementation purposes; they can also be innovative and autonomous.

The German Constitution contains an article devoted to rulemaking, detailing the constraints, procedures, requirements, and oversight applicable to the adoption of statutory instruments. Article 80 of the *Grundgesetz* (GG) states that

> (1) The Federal Government, a Federal Minister or the Land governments may be authorized by a law to issue statutory instruments. The content, purpose and scope of the authority conferred shall be specified in the law. Each statutory instrument shall contain a statement of its legal basis. If the law provides that such authority may be further delegated, such sub-delegation shall be effected by statutory instrument. (2) Unless a federal law otherwise provides, the consent of the Bundesrat shall be required for statutory instruments issued by the Federal Government or a Federal Minister regarding fees or basic principles for the use of postal and telecommunication facilities, basic principles for levying of charges for the use of facilities of federal railways or the construction and operation of railways, as well as for statutory instruments issued pursuant to federal laws that require the consent of the Bundesrat or that are executed by the Länder on federal commission or in their own right.

Hence, delegated legislation in Germany must be rooted in a parliamentary act; the executive does not possess autonomous and inherent rulemaking power, and Parliament keeps control over rulemaking, as its consent is required for issuing statutory instruments in sensitive and important matters. The need for parliamentary control was subject to scrutiny by the German Federal Constitutional Court, which found it constitutional. Indeed, the *Grundgesetz* grants Parliament legislative power, so it is legitimate for it to retain 'decisive influence on the enactment and content of the regulations to itself'[2] when it opts to delegate this power.

The Portuguese Constitution contains several provisions devoted to administrative rulemaking, which is considered a standard approach to conducting administrative action. Administrative regulations can be issued by the central government in the form of regulatory decrees, the governments of the Azores and Madeira regions, as well as all the municipalities. In addition to this explicit endowment of regulatory authority in the constitutional text, Portuguese legal doctrine unanimously[3] asserts that public administrations may establish administrative regulations in performing their duties even in the absence of any clear rule attributing such powers. Furthermore, the Constitution guarantees individuals 'the right to challenge administrative norms which have external force and harm those of their rights or interests that are protected by law' (Article 268(5)). This article specifically focuses on ensuring citizens' rights vis-à-vis public bodies, including the right to notification, the requirement to give reasons, and setting deadlines for authorities to respond to citizens' requests for information.

The Swedish Constitution does not expressly mention administrative rulemaking. However, it imposes obligations on the government regarding consultation when 'preparing Government business', which has been interpreted as applicable to all administrative activities including rulemaking. Specifically, section 2, chapter 7 stipulates that the necessary information and opinions must be obtained from the relevant public authorities. It also states that information and opinions must be obtained from local authorities as required. Organizations and individuals must also be given the opportunity to express their opinions as necessary.

Section 1, chapter 9 of the Swedish Constitution requires public authorities to 'observe objectivity and impartiality'. These principles are also considered generally applicable to administrative actions producing rules.[4]

At the European level, the Treaty on the Functioning of the European Union (TFEU) clearly confers on EU institutions the power to adopt delegated rulemaking measures (Article 290 TFEU) and general implementing acts (Article 291 TFEU). Moreover, several treaty provisions dedicated to sector-specific subject matter empower EU institutions to adopt regulations in a specific sector.

The Chinese Constitution uses various terms to describe the activities of administrative bodies. Specifically, Article 89 grants the State Council the authority to 'adopt administrative measures, enact administrative regulations, and issue decisions and orders'. Additionally, Article 90 authorizes the ministries and commissions under the State Council to 'issue orders, directives, and regulations'. As for local authorities, local people's assemblies have the power to adopt resolutions, plans, and local regulations, while local governments 'conduct administrative work' and 'issue decisions and orders'.[5]

[2] Federal Constitutional Court, Order of 12 November 1958; see L Weidemann, 'Germany' in this book.
[3] See R Guerra da Fonseca, 'Portugal' in this book.
[4] See P Jonason and B Forssén, 'Sweden' in this book.
[5] See X Sun, 'China' in this book.

III. Rulemaking and the Separation of Powers

In many legal systems, public law scholarship has tried to solve the issue of reconciling the adoption of general acts containing rules by public administrations with the principle of the separation of powers. Hungary, Italy, and Germany are the main examples.

In Germany, Article 80 of the Basic Law (GG) is regarded as a fundamental expression and implementation of the principles of the separation of powers and the rule of law. This provision clearly delineates the legislative and executive powers in the law-making process, ensuring that the executive's legislative actions are bound by the legislature's guidelines. The fact that the executive cannot issue statutory instruments independently not only limits its legislative power but also ensures that this power is subject to parliamentary requirements. Statutory instruments, as derived legal sources, are always subordinate to parliamentary acts, which means that they cannot, at least in principle, amend or override these acts; they cannot contradict or override laws.

In Hungary, until very recently, the Constitutional Court declared the Act on law-making unconstitutional because it allowed the adoption of legal guidelines and 'public law regulatory instruments', asserting that 'other legal instruments of State governance cannot assume the function of legislation'.[6]

On the contrary, in many legal systems, the power of public administrations to adopt rules is undisputed and expressly provided for in broad terms in national constitutions. This is evident not only in the case of China, where the executive enjoys broad discretion, but also in Austria, the Netherlands, Portugal, and Sweden, among others.

IV. The Legal Relevance and Significance of Administrative Rulemaking

A. Legal Definitions

The American Administrative Procedure Act (APA) is perhaps the best-known legislation on rulemaking, and it clearly differentiates between rulemaking and adjudication. It also contains a strong definition of what a 'rule' is in section 2(c):

> the whole or any part of an agency statement of general or particular applicability and future effect designed to implement, interpret, or prescribe law or policy or to describe the organisation, procedure, or practice requirements of any agency and includes the approval or prescription for the future of rates.

In contrast, the American APA defines an 'order', which is the result of administrative adjudication, as the final disposition 'other than rule making'.

6 See L Berkes and BS Gerencsér, 'Hungary' in this book.

The Norwegian APA of 1967 explicitly and clearly distinguishes between rulemaking and adjudication. Section 2 of the APA defines an administrative decision as 'a decision made in the exercise of public authority which generally or specifically determines the rights or duties of private persons'. It goes on to specify that an individual decision is 'an administrative decision relating to the rights or duties of one or more specified persons', while regulation should be understood as 'an administrative decision relating to the rights or duties of an indefinite number or an indeterminate group of persons'.

The Dutch General Administrative Law Act (GALA) contains a very broad definition of administrative decision, stating that '[d]ecision means a written decision of an administrative authority constituting a public-law juridical act' (Article 1.3, §1). This definition includes both adjudication and rulemaking. Interestingly, individual decisions are defined by what they are not: they do not have general application, but the law does not provide a comprehensive list or definition of decisions of general scope. Among those, only 'policy rules' are defined in Article 1.3 §4 as 'general rules, not being a generally binding regulation, established by decision, concerning the balancing of interests, establishment of facts, or interpretation of legislation in the exercise of a power of an administrative authority'. Consequently, the concepts of generally binding regulations and other decisions of general scope have been further developed by case law.

The Portuguese Code of Administrative Procedure contains detailed procedural rules for administrative regulation procedure in Articles 97 and following. Article 135 defines administrative regulations as 'general and abstract legal rules which, in the exercise of legal-administrative powers, aim to produce external legal effects'.[7]

The German APA does not explicitly regulate administrative rulemaking, nor do the APAs of the *Länder*, with the notable exception of Schleswig-Holstein. Under the *Verwaltungsverfahrensgesetz*, the only general acts considered are general orders, which are considered administrative acts 'directed at a group of people defined or definable on the basis of general characteristics or relating to the public law aspect of a matter or its use by the public at large' (Article 35). Despite the lack of explicit statutory regulation, rulemaking has been theorized and categorized by judicial doctrine, as we will see in the next paragraph.

The Italian general law on administrative procedure explicitly excludes rulemaking from the scope of application of most of its guarantees and provisions, including, first of all, those on participation and the obligation to give reasons. In particular, Article 13 of the Italian APA specifies that the rules concerning participation do not apply 'to the activities of public administration for the issuance of regulatory, general, administrative, planning, and programming acts for which specific rules governing the formation of the act remain'. However, the law does not provide a clear definition of these acts. The procedure for adopting general acts is, instead, established by the various sectoral rules, leading to significant fragmentation and heterogeneity. While participatory rights are generally guaranteed, the level of participation can vary greatly, depending on the sector-specific regulations in place.

[7] There is no official tradition in English of the Portuguese Code of Administrative Procedure. Translations are therefore my own.

Although there is a general aversion to administrative rulemaking in Hungary, so much so that the Constitutional Court ruled in 2009 that other legal instruments of state governance assuming legislative functions were unconstitutional, there is a legislative reference to 'administrative acts of general scope'.[8] This reference was introduced in a 2017 amendment to the Code of Administrative Court Procedure. These acts are 'to be applied in a specific case, and not falling under the scope of the Act on law-making'. What is particularly interesting is the justification provided for the introduction of this new category of acts, which seemingly contradicts Hungarian legal doctrine opposing such acts. Indeed, according to the explanatory memorandum to the amendment, the Court of Justice of the European Union has applied this concept in several decisions, so this type of act must be classified as an administrative act.[9] This category includes, for example, regulations issued by public bodies.

B. Judicial Doctrines

In some legal systems, the distinction between individual and general acts, adopted as the outcome of rulemaking procedures, is relevant and has consequences, although the two types of acts are not defined in any law. In Italy, the distinction has been developed and refined in legal scholarship over time. The distinction is grounded in the differing nature, functions, and effects of those acts and bears significant consequences for the procedures that must be followed for their adoption and judicial protection against them, both in terms of standing and the remedies available.[10] However, the difference between regulations (normative acts and sources of law) and general administrative acts (simple administrative acts, even if they are addressed to many people or to all citizens) is not always clear cut.[11]

In China too, although the Constitution lists a series of acts that can theoretically be categorized into two types, namely regulations, resolutions, directives, and plans on the one hand, and decisions and orders on the other, no legal text clearly establishes such a distinction. Moreover, some administrative actions referred to in the Constitution, such as administrative measures and actions relating to administrative work, cannot be classified so neatly.[12]

Czech doctrine has developed two distinctive criteria for categorizing administrative acts into concrete and abstract forms. The first criterion pertains to 'the degree of generality from the point of view of the subject of the regulation (abstract/concrete)',[13] and the second considers the degree of personalization of the act, so personalized acts are directed at specific persons, while non-personalized acts are directed at an indeterminate group of people. Thus, regulations are abstract and non-personalized, while decisions are concrete and personalized.

[8] See Berkes and Gerencsér (n 6).
[9] ibid.
[10] G della Cananea, *Atti amministrativi generali* (Cedam 2000).
[11] BG Mattarella, 'Participation in Rulemaking in Italy' (2010) 2 It J Publ L 339.
[12] See Sun (n 5).
[13] See J Rajchl, D Burda, and G Blahoudková, 'Czech Republic' in this book.

In Germany, rulemaking has been categorized into three main typologies. The first is statutory instruments (*Rechtsverordnungen*), which have traditionally been considered from the substantial point of view as subordinate and generally binding legal provisions issued by the executive (the substantive concept of a statutory instrument). However, recent scholarship has increasingly favoured a formal definition of the term. This formalized concept depends on the legislative body involved, as well as the form and procedure by which the statutory instrument is issued, particularly its designation as such, and the promulgation and citation of the authorizing law.

The second category is that of administrative regulations (*Verwaltungsvorschriften*), defined by the Constitutional Court as regulations that 'make binding statements for an abstract variety of administrative matters without being aimed at a direct external legal effect'.[14] They are issued to subordinate authorities by a higher authority or by a superior to their subordinate administrative staff and are used to set a uniform interpretation of undefined legal terms or uniform standards.

The third category consists of bylaws (*Satzungen*), legal provisions established by a public law entity within its legal remit. They are binding on individuals who are part of, or subject to, that entity. They stem from the constitutional principle of decentralization.[15] Local government authorities or recognized autonomous bodies, such as universities or professional associations, issue bylaws to independently regulate their own affairs without needing specific statutory authorization. Like statutory instruments, bylaws are generally abstract and apply within a specific locality or to the organs and individuals associated with the relevant autonomous bodies.

The Swedish Supreme Administrative Court has developed some additional criteria for distinguishing normative decisions from individual ones. In addition to the criterion of general applicability, it also takes into account a temporal criterion (rules should not concern only a short time period) and one regarding the geographical area where the decision will be implemented.[16]

V. Rulemaking Legislation

The best-known legislation on rulemaking is probably the American APA, which clearly distinguishes between rulemaking and adjudication.

The Norwegian APA contains a section dedicated to regulation (chapter VII), which is much shorter and less constraining than those concerning adjudication (chapters IV–VI).

The Swedish APA clearly states which provisions apply to rulemaking and which do not. For example, the obligation to give prior notice that a measure will be issued to the parties concerned, allowing them to intervene and express their opinion, does not apply to the adoption of administrative rules. The same holds for the requirement to give reasons.

[14] Federal Constitutional Court, Order of 2 March 1999.
[15] See Weidemann (n 2).
[16] See Jonason and Forssén (n 4).

The Portuguese Code of Administrative Procedure contains detailed rules regarding administrative regulations in Articles 97 et seq which are devoted to 'Administrative Regulation Procedure'. Numerous aspects are defined and regulated, including the procedure for their adoption, their effects, validity, and procedural guarantees.

Italy has a law on the regulation of government activity. Article 17 of Law No 400/1988 addresses government rulemaking, establishing its general legal regime the procedures that must be followed for their adoption, distinguishing among various types of regulation. In particular, rulemaking may be issued for (i) the execution of laws; (ii) the implementation and integration of laws and legislative decrees containing rules of principle, excluding those relating to matters reserved for regional competence; (iii) matters for which there is a lack of regulation by laws, provided these are not matters reserved to the law; (iv) the organization and functioning of public administrations according to the provisions dictated by law. However, this law only concerns executive regulations. There is no general law on administrative rulemaking procedure.[17]

China has 'Regulations on Procedures for Making Administrative Regulations', and, as of 1983, legal doctrine has developed a dogmatic distinction between 'concrete administrative action' and 'abstract administrative action'.[18] The 1989 legislation concerning administrative litigation transposed this dichotomy into a normative text, confining the possibility of judicial review to 'concrete administration', but without providing any definition. In any case, section 13 of the law excluded direct appeal against four categories of administrative acts: 'administrative regulations, rules, decisions, and orders with general binding force'. These acts could only be subject to judicial review in conjunction with an individual implementing act.[19]

Surprisingly, Austria, which was the first country to enact an APA in 1925, which served as a model for *Mitteleuropa*, does not have a general law regulating rulemaking procedure. Germany too, which has one of the best-known and most studied APAs, has a regulatory gap regarding the procedural regulation of rulemaking. The Czech APA establishes no procedure for adopting regulations, nor does it explicitly distinguish between abstract and concrete acts as found in administrative doctrine.

VI. The Legal Effects of Rulemaking

In all the legal systems considered—with the sole exception of Hungary—administrative rulemaking may, and does, have binding effects. In the United States, administrative rules can have the same force and effect as law if they have been properly issued and have withstood judicial review.[20] In Austria, the Czech Republic, the Netherlands, Norway, and other countries, ordinances/regulations are legally binding.

Of course, the principle of hierarchy must be taken into consideration, as regulations must comply with the law and the Constitution.

17 See L Parona 'Italy' in this book.
18 M Wang, *Administrative Law Outline* (Law Press China 1983).
19 See Sun (n 5).
20 See J Lubbers and G della Cananea, 'United States of America' in this book.

Not all administrative rules have binding effects. All the legal systems considered have a varied and heterogeneous multitude of general non-binding measures. Even the names given to them vary, including such terms as 'official advice' and 'recommendations'. Non-binding rulemaking is especially important in the EU legal system, also in terms of contributing to the smooth functioning of the various policy sectors.[21]

The distinction between binding and non-binding administrative rules may appear very clear on paper, but it often turns out to be rather blurred in reality. Sometimes, the distinction between binding and non-binding administrative rules is confused and tenuous even in abstract terms. For instance, the distinction between non-legislative interpretative rules and statements of policy is not always as clear-cut in the United States.[22] Similarly, the UK Guidances have proven influential in court decisions, as even if there is no general right to consultation, 'a legal duty to consult may ... arise from a legitimate expectation, for example if there has been a promise to consult in a statement or guidance'.[23]

VII. General Duties Imposed on Authorities for Rulemaking

In examining the procedural obligations that administrations are bound to comply with, it may be appropriate to divide the analysis according to a fundamental legal criterion, namely the existence or otherwise of a general rulemaking procedure law. This approach will make it possible to compare the results obtained and assess the legal relevance and significance of having a general rulemaking procedure regulation or not.

As previously stated, 'it is not true that administrative procedure exists only insofar as it is regulated by legislation'.[24] Indeed, administrative procedure may be subject to self-regulation by administrative bodies (through general principles, or on a case-by-case basis), or it may be regulated in the courts. In any case, 'the source of regulation is not only important; it is crucial'.[25] The question arises whether the same can be said of the administrative rulemaking procedure.

Of course, the concept of a general law on rulemaking procedure[26] includes not only standalone regulatory texts specifically dedicated to this subject matter but also sections or parts of a regulatory act with a broader subject matter that, however, specifically establish general procedural rules for the adoption of regulations.

[21] See E Chiti, 'European Union' in this book.

[22] See W Funk, 'A Primer on Non-legislative Rules' (2001) 53 Administrative Law Review 1321, examining how courts determine when a rule is legislative or non-legislative.

[23] UK Government Legal Department, *The Judge Over Your Shoulder* (6th edn, Assets Publishing Service 2022) 40, <https://assets.publishing.service.gov.uk/government/uploads/system/uploads/attachment_data/file/1105680/The_Judge_Over_Your_Shoulder_JOYS_6th_edition_2022.pdf> accessed 23 November 2024.

[24] S Cassese, 'La disciplina legislativa del procedimento amministrativo. Una analisi comparata' (1993) 116(1) Il Foro Italiano 27ff, my translation.

[25] ibid.

[26] For a comparative perspective, see S Rose-Ackerman and PL Lindseth, *Comparative Administrative Law* (Edward Elgar 2010).

Furthermore, among the countries that do not have a general law on rulemaking procedures, we will try to distinguish between systems that make up for this absence by relying on general principles and systems where there is a lacuna, and the participatory rights of interested parties, as well as the principle of transparency, do not seem to be adequately protected in all rulemaking procedures.

A. Legal Systems with a General Rulemaking Procedure Law

In the United States, constitutional due process requirements apply only to individual rather than general determinations. The procedural requirements for rulemaking are set out in paragraphs 553, 556, and 557 of the APA. The most widely used type is informal rulemaking, where the agency must publish a 'notice of proposed rulemaking' and provides an opportunity for anyone to file written comments. The much less frequent formal rulemaking procedure requires a trial-like oral hearing process for deliberation on proposed rules.

However, the American APA contains some exemptions that allow agencies to promulgate rules without following the notice and comment procedure. These exemptions cover 'rules of agency organization, procedure, or practice' and rules related to 'public property, loans, grants, benefits or contracts'. These are very broad exemptions that allow many rules of great public interest to be issued without notice and comment.[27]

Over time, courts have imposed additional procedural requirements on the authorities beyond those prescribed by law. In the landmark *Vermont Yankee* ruling in 1978, the Supreme Court condemned this judicial activism and upheld the opposite principle, that courts should not impose additional procedural requirements beyond those prescribed by law.[28]

In Norway, the 1967 APA contains several obligations that the administration must adhere to when exercising its power of 'delegated legislation', although these obligations are less restrictive than those for individual acts. Chapter VII of the APA specifically requires administrative bodies to investigate cases, provide a motivated draft regulation for all public and private parties that will be affected by the regulation, and allow them to submit comments that the administration will have to take into consideration. Lastly, the APA establishes an obligation to publish the regulation. In contrast to the provisions for individual acts, the Norwegian APA does not generally grant the right to have access to relevant documents, the duty to state reasons, or judicial review. However, the general principles of due process, fairness, and transparency apply to all administrative activities, including regulation.[29]

The Portuguese Code of Administrative Procedure contains several procedural requirements for adopting administrative regulations. Individuals even have a right

27 For an overview of the many different procedural constraints on rulemaking deriving from decisions taken by courts, Congress, and presidents, see J Lubbers, *A Guide to Federal Agency Rulemaking* (6th edn, ABA 2019).

28 See Lubbers and della Cananea (n 20).

29 See E Smith, 'Norway' in this book.

of initiative, as interested parties may submit petitions to the competent bodies requesting the creation, amendment, or repeal of regulations (Article 97). The start of a procedure must be publicized on the Internet, providing details such as the public authority that initiated the procedure, the date of commencement, the purpose of the regulation, and how to submit comments to the draft (Article 98).

Furthermore, the draft regulation must be accompanied by a reasoned justification, which must include an assessment of the costs and benefits of the proposed measures (Article 99). In addition to the consultation obligations, there is a substantive right for interested parties to be heard in cases of a 'regulation containing provisions that directly and immediately affect citizens' legally protected rights or interests' (Article 100). Interested parties must be heard in written or oral form, which may be waived if 'the number of interested parties is so large that the hearing would be impractical, in which case a public consultation shall be held' (Article 100(3)(c)).

In China, public authorities must comply with several legal obligations, including assessing and appraising the necessity, feasibility, and reasonableness of their actions, hearing opinions from the public, making decisions collegially, and informing the public in good time. As for administrative rules and regulations, their respective regulations require 'a public hearing for drafting regulations or rules which significantly affect a public interest or for which a major disagreement remains and have an important impact on an individual's rights and duties'.[30] Publication is another legal requirement necessary for an administrative rule to be valid. Some general principles of law apply to all administrative actions, including regulations. These principles are (i) lawfulness, (ii) fairness, (iii) due process, (iv) efficiency, (v) honesty and trustworthiness, (vi) responsibility.[31]

B. Legal Systems Without a General Rulemaking Procedure Law

A significant dichotomy can be observed among legal systems that lack a general framework for the rulemaking process. In some countries, even in the absence of specific regulatory provisions, a series of procedural safeguards are in place to guarantee the participation of interested parties and ensure transparency through the application of general principles. In other countries, on the other hand, procedural safeguards, understood as generally applicable to any rulemaking procedure, irrespective of sectoral disciplines, appear deficient.

1. General principles applied to rulemaking

In Austria, despite the lack of a general law on rulemaking proceedings, administrations must comply with a number of important requirements, either laid down by law or derived from general principles. The law expressly regulates the publication of

[30] Art 22 of the Regulations on Procedures for Making Administrative Regulations; art 16 of the Regulations on Procedures for Making Administrative Rules; art 16 of the Provisional Regulations on Major Administrative Decision-making Procedures, see Sun (n 5).

[31] These principles are listed in Article 5 of the decision of 22 March 2004 of the State Council on the programme for the general implementation of the principle of legality in the administrations.

federal and regional ordinances, and the Constitutional Court has extended the scope of the publication requirement to other public authorities based on the principle of legal certainty. Moreover, sectoral laws establish a set of procedural requirements for the adoption of administrative ordinances (*Verwaltungsordnungen*) adopted by a hierarchically superior authority to regulate the organizational aspects of a subordinate authority. The requirements are diverse, but all ensure the participation of the authority that will be affected by the order in the procedure.[32]

In addition to legal constraints, the Austrian Constitutional Court has derived other important obligations for public authorities from general principles of law when adopting regulatory acts. First, the principle of the rule of law requires authorities to clarify the factual and legal prerequisites for the adoption of an ordinance expressly, allowing for judicial scrutiny on this point. Secondly, when an ordinance interferes with fundamental rights, the requirement becomes more stringent, demanding greater specificity even with regard to all the circumstantial details. Lastly, the Court has frequently applied the principles of objectivity and the prohibition of arbitrariness in its judicial review on rulemaking.

The Austrian Constitutional Court attributes considerable importance to the violation of procedural rules, in line with the case law of the *Verwaltungsgerichtshof* (Administrative Court), which was among the first to elaborate and give importance to the concept of administrative procedure by annulling administrative acts that disregarded the essential procedural forms. The Constitutional Court too, in its case law, states that non-compliance with procedural rules, such as the right to be heard, is 'significant' and results in the annulment of general acts.[33]

In the United Kingdom, the fundamental concept is embodied in the 'no fettering rule', which means that administrative rulemaking discretion should be free, of course within its legal boundaries, allowing administrations to reach the best solution in a given context. However, this is a much-debated principle and has been re-elaborated over time, resulting in a more flexible interpretation, and its role has 'changed from being a doctrine which preserves administrative discretion to one which regulates the development and application of administrative rules'.[34]

Nonetheless, several important constraints are imposed on administrative rulemaking. First of all, in accordance with its historical tradition of parliamentary sovereignty, there is almost always parliamentary oversight over how rulemaking power is exercised by administrations. Acts of Parliament that delegate rulemaking powers generally require rules to be presented before one House of Parliament for approval. Moreover, although there is no general duty to consult in rulemaking procedures, courts have identified four circumstances in which consultation is required: (i) if the relevant statute mandates consultation; (ii) if an administration promised to consult; (iii) if there is an established practice of consultation; and (iv) if avoiding consultation would 'lead to conspicuous unfairness'.[35]

[32] See S Storr and S Praniess, 'Austria' in this book.
[33] ibid.
[34] A McHarg, 'Administrative Discretion, Administrative Rule-making, and Judicial Review' (2017) 70 Current Legal Problems 267, 271.
[35] See J Morison and D Mark, 'United Kingdom' in this book.

In addition to applying the general principles of protecting legitimate expectations and the duty to act fairly, the courts have also specified the requirements for a consultation to be considered adequate. These requirements are known as the Gunning Principles, whereby (i) consultation must take place when rulemaking is still in the formative stage; (ii) the proposal must be explained in order to allow for intelligent consideration and response; (iii) people should be given adequate time to submit their considerations and responses; and (iv) the administration must take into due account the outcomes of the consultation.[36]

In Sweden, although the APA does not require public consultation before the adoption of administrative rules, legal and judicial doctrine derives such an obligation from the general constitutional duty of the government to consult stakeholders when 'preparing government business'. This provision only applies to the government and not to other public bodies. However, under the Municipal Act, municipalities must consult, although 'the lack of consultation on a certain matter ... does not mean that the decision becomes invalid'.[37] It is interesting to note that the Swedish APA does not apply to the government itself, which, however, usually follows and voluntarily complies with its provisions.

In the Netherlands, the law does not impose a general obligation to consult stakeholders before adopting a general binding rule. However, there is an established practice of doing so, and the principle of transparency is also applied to such proceedings.[38]

2. General principles not applied to rulemaking

In Italy, the general law on administrative procedure explicitly excludes rulemaking from the scope of application of most of its guarantees and provisions, including those on participation and the duty to give reasons.[39] Consequently, rulemaking procedures do not follow the principles of administrative procedure as codified in the 1990 general law. Rather, each rulemaking procedure is governed by its specific sectoral laws, which leads to a high degree of fragmentation in terms of requirements.

In the Czech Republic, many aspects of rulemaking are directly regulated by the Constitution. However, neither the Constitution nor the law provide requirements or constraints regarding the procedures to be followed when adopting regulations. As a result, rulemaking 'often takes place *in camera*'.[40] A new law enacted in 2024 concerning executive regulations has introduced greater transparency and allows certain public institutions and some private law organizations to make comments on draft regulations. However, individuals still lack the right to intervene and can only passively observe the comments procedure on the government information portal.[41] More transparency and participation rights are ensured at the municipal and regional

[36] ibid.

[37] Prop 1986/87:91, p 60. See Jonason and Forssén (n 4).

[38] See J van der Brink, L Verboeket, and V van Waarde 'The Netherlands' in this book.

[39] Art 13, para 1 of Law No 241/1990 establishes that '[t]he provisions of this Chapter shall not apply to the activities of the public administration for the issuance of regulatory, general, administrative, planning and programming acts for which the specific rules governing the formation of training remain'. Art 3, para 2 of the same law also establishes that the requirement to give reasons does not apply to normative and general administrative acts.

[40] See Rajchl, Burda, and Blahoudková (n 13).

[41] ibid.

levels. These local entities adopt regulations within their self-government powers by discussing drafts in public sessions of the municipal/regional council, where citizens can present their viewpoints. Additionally, acts known as 'measures of a general nature', which are neither regulations nor individual decisions (since they regulate specific cases without being personalized) follow a different procedure. The individuals involved are guaranteed the right to present observations and raise objections, which public authorities must consider and address with a reasoned response.[42]

In Germany, the procedural requirements and guarantees in rulemaking proceedings are deficient. One part of the doctrine argues that rulemaking, being inherently part of the general concept of administrative procedure, should adhere to the general principles established by the Administrative Procedure Act (APA). However, this view is not universally accepted, and there are opposing perspectives. 'Generally speaking, a procedural doctrine of administrative rulemaking does not exist, although some scholars advocate for its creation.'[43] Moreover, the prevailing opinion holds that participation and consultation of the affected parties in rulemaking proceedings is unnecessary unless expressly provided for by law. Case law has repeatedly held that such a requirement cannot be inferred by analogy: neither from Article 28 of the APA, which clearly imposes an obligation to hear the affected parties only for individual acts, nor from Article 103(1) GG, which establishes the right to be heard before a court, or from the general principle of rule of law arising from Article 20(3) GG. According to the prevailing opinion, individuals' rights are adequately protected by their ability to seek judicial protection against statutory instruments that adversely affect them.[44] Sector-specific legislation imposes consultation duties in various forms, resulting in a highly heterogeneous framework.

Lastly, Hungary has no rules on administrative rulemaking, as its legal system views such acts with extreme disfavour. The Constitutional Court has supported this stance by sanctioning the constitutional illegitimacy of general acts of a normative nature. Moreover, public participation is generally considered an opportunity rather than a right for interested parties, and failure to consult produces no legal effects.[45]

VIII. Judicial Review of Rulemaking

In Austria, judicial review on rulemaking is centralized, as ordinances must be challenged before the Constitutional Court rather than the administrative or ordinary courts.[46]

In many legal systems, rules adopted by public authorities cannot be challenged immediately and directly before the courts. Individuals may, however, challenge administrative acts of adjudication adopted on the basis of a regulatory act. This provides a form of 'deferred protection' and is necessarily linked to the negative effects produced

[42] ibid.
[43] See Weidemann (n 2).
[44] ibid.
[45] See Berkes and Gerencsér (n 6).
[46] See Storr and Praniess (n 32).

by an individual act implementing rulemaking. This approach is envisaged in many legal systems, such as those of China, Italy, and the Netherlands. When courts must assess the legality of an individual act implementing a general rule laid down in a general act, they must assess the legality or legitimacy of the general act upstream of the individual act as the primary source of the rule to be applied.

In the Netherlands, in addition to this incidental review, general binding regulations with direct effect—without the need for an implementing act—can be directly challenged in civil courts.[47]

In China, in addition to the deferred protection and the impossibility of directly challenging general administrative acts in court, there is another important difference regarding the judicial review of both individual and general acts. A 2014 amendment to the Administrative Litigation Law introduced the notion of 'manifestly inappropriate' administrative action, allowing courts to annul an individual administrative act in whole or in part if deemed manifestly inappropriate. However, courts can only assess the legality of a regulatory act, not its appropriateness.[48]

An interesting mixed solution is adopted in the Czech Republic. Direct challenges to regulations are centralized in that they are subject to review by the Constitutional Court, which can only be initiated by public institutions and public officers. The Constitutional Court can repeal regulations, 'should they contravene the constitutional order or the law', as stated in Article 87(1)(b) of the Constitution. Individuals may only challenge the legality of administrative regulations together with—and as the legal basis of—an implementing act. If the Court considers that the regulation to be applied in a given case conflicts with the Constitution or the law, it does not in fact apply it. Indeed, in these cases of diffused control over regulation, the courts can disapply a regulation in specific cases but cannot annul it *erga omnes*.[49]

Another interesting mixed solution is adopted in Germany, where the invalidity of a statutory instrument can be challenged in court using several methods. Individuals may request an indirect review of a statutory instrument through an annulment action if it serves as the basis for an individual administrative act that affects them. Alternatively, they can initiate an (atypical) declaratory action under Article 43(1) of the Code of Administrative Court Procedure which states that 'the nullity of an administrative act may be requested by means of an action if the plaintiff has a justified interest in a prompt solution (action for a declaratory judgment)'. Lastly, an abstract judicial review by the Federal Constitutional Court is available under Article 93(1)(2) of the Basic Law, which can be initiated by the federal government, a *Land* government, or a quarter of the Members of the Bundestag.[50]

In Portugal, there exists a wide-ranging judicial review on rulemaking in terms of standing and timing.[51] Article 144 of the Portuguese Code of Administrative Procedure is dedicated to invalidity with regard to administrative regulations. The invalidity of a regulation may be invoked at any time by any interested party, and it may

[47] See van der Brink, Verboeket, and van Waarde (n 38).
[48] See Sun (n 5).
[49] See Rajchl, Burda, and Blahoudková (n 13).
[50] See Weidemann (n 2).
[51] See Guerra da Fonseca (n 3).

also be declared invalid by the competent administrative bodies at any time. However, regulations that suffer from formal or procedural flaws that do not result in their unconstitutionality may only be challenged or declared invalid by the administration of its own motion within six months from the date of their publication, unless there is an absolute lack of legal form or there has been a failure to consult the public as required by law.

IX. Concluding Remarks: Commonalities and Distinctive Features

A. The Ontological and Constitutional Levels

At the ontological level—regarding the nature of existence or 'being' as such—a primary commonality emerges: the very existence of rulemaking power in the hands of public bodies. This power is abstractly and concretely provided for in all the legal systems analysed, with the sole exception of Hungary. However, Hungary was compelled to include a provision concerning the 'administrative acts of general scope'[52] in its Code of Administrative Court Procedure in 2017, as mandated by numerous judgments of the Court of Justice of the European Union.

At the constitutional level, on the other hand, we encounter a wide range of scenarios. The first major dichotomy concerns the very existence or non-existence of constitutional rules on rulemaking.

Some constitutional texts expressly provide for the adoption of acts of general scope by administrative bodies, establishing the prerequisites, limits, and procedures on each occasion (Austria, the Czech Republic, Portugal). In some instances, this regulatory power of the executive is considered general and autonomous (the Czech Republic but only with regard to the government, and Portugal), while in other cases, it must be expressly authorized and delegated by Parliament (the Czech Republic with regard to any administration apart from the government, and Germany). Legislative bodies sometimes retain the power of control over approved legislation, as the text must be submitted for approval (Germany) or they only have the power of veto, or the delegating law provides on a case-by-case basis for some kinds of parliamentary control (United Kingdom). In Sweden, parliamentary authorization is only required for regulations imposing obligations on private individuals or otherwise affecting their personal or economic situation.

Other constitutional texts do not expressly permit administrations to adopt acts of general application or, if they do mention them, they do not establish procedural requirements for their adoption.

In these cases, we encounter a second important dichotomy. In some legal systems, the absence of any such explicit reference prevents the application of the general principles laid down for individual administrative activity to administrative

[52] See Berkes and Gerencsér (n 6).

acts of general scope (Germany, Italy, United States) by analogy. Thus, for example, the principle of due process, of the right to be heard, although it is provided for in the Constitution, is not considered directly applicable to rulemaking if there is no legislative act explicitly providing for it. On the contrary, in other legal systems, the absence of an explicit constitutional provision is not seen as an impediment to subjecting administrative rulemaking activity to the general principles that constitutions or legal systems impose for administrative activity *tout court* (Sweden, Norway).

B. Distinctive Features

In terms of judicial review, there is a great commonality, again at the ontological level: namely the possibility of submitting general administrative acts to judicial review. However, once beyond the sphere of what we might consider the fundamental right to judicial protection, practical aspects, such as implementation, standing, time frame, the instruments available, and the forms of protection that courts can provide resemble a tree with many intricately intertwined branches.

First of all, there is diversity among the courts that have jurisdiction, as judicial control may be centralized in a constitutional court, but in most cases, control is mostly devolved to ordinary and/or administrative courts.

Another major difference lies in the possibility of immediately and directly appealing against a general administrative act, or the requirement to challenge an individual act implementing one. In this case, protection is deferred and incidental, since it takes place during an action against the individual act that implements the rule.

And again, in cases of deferred protection, the court may rule on the lawfulness of the general act, but the instruments at its disposal may vary from the mere non-application of the general act in the specific case to its total annulment *erga omnes*.

Three more differences might be highlighted concerning rulemaking.

First, the criteria used to distinguish between adjudication and rulemaking vary. Typically, two main criteria are used: generality and abstractness, albeit with different interpretations. Generality is assessed both with regard to the subject matter regulated and in relation to the group of persons affected by the act.

Secondly, the interplay and sometimes the antinomy between general principles and sector-specific rules can lead to very different solutions in countries with special rules for the subject matter of the case that differ significantly from the general norms, for instance in the case concerning rail transport in countries where a state monopoly still exists.

Third, there is a great diversity of terminology used to designate acts adopted through rulemaking. For example, in Austria, they are referred to as 'ordinances' (*Verordnungen*). In China, Norway, and the Czech Republic they are known as 'regulations'. Germany uses terms such as 'statutory requirements' (*Rechtsverordnungen*), 'administrative regulations' or 'directions' (*Verwaltungsvorschriften*), and 'bylaws' (*Satzungen*). In the Netherlands, they are further subdivided into general binding regulations (*algemeen verbindende voorschriften*), policy rules (*beleidsregels*), and other decisions of general scope (*overige besluiten van algemene strekking*).

C. Concluding Remarks at the Institutional Level

Four final remarks can be drawn from our comparative analysis at the institutional level.

First, one of the legal systems where rulemaking is most extensively regulated by the Constitution is that of the Czech Republic. However, neither its Constitution nor its legislation establishes principles or rules regarding procedures for their adoption. Nor are general principles applied by the courts to detect procedural breaches, which means that due process, transparency, and fairness are not fully ensured. Thus, despite the detailed constitutional provisions on substantive requirements, limitations on jurisdiction, and the judicial reviewability of rulemaking, in the absence of statutory law and/or the application of general principles on administrative action, the procedural rights of individuals might not be fully guaranteed.

Secondly, even in cases of apparent convergence, this apparent similarity may not be entirely reflected in practice. For instance, in China, the Supreme People's Court has developed the principle of due process since 2017, defining 'fundamental procedural rights, such as the right to be heard, the right to make observations, and the right to defend oneself'.[53] However, in the practical resolution of cases, there is no certainty that courts will consider the lack of consultation a 'serious procedural breach'. The due process principle was developed for individual acts, not regulatory acts. Moreover, courts are very hesitant to annul regulatory acts for procedural breaches because it would entail annulling the entire act. In practice, therefore, courts allow public authorities to correct procedural breaches *ex post facto*. Indeed, in China, 'there is no precedent for the court to review a regulatory act ... on procedural grounds'.[54] Thus, despite apparent textual similarities, it becomes clear that a rule must always be considered within the legal system to which it belongs, bearing in mind not only the wording itself but the broader constitutional framework and legal practices.

Thirdly, as we saw in the sections discussing the general obligations placed on authorities for rulemaking, the participatory rights of stakeholders and the principle of transparency are found to be safeguarded not only—and not always—in legal systems with specific laws on rulemaking. In fact, among the countries lacking such legislation, several do protect participatory rights and transparency very adequately by applying the general principles of administrative action, even though they were originally formulated for adjudication. Moreover, in some cases, relying on general principles ensures higher levels of protection than a narrow regulatory framework would.

[53] Supreme People's Court, Judicial Interpretation of 13 November 2017, see Sun (n 5).
[54] See Sun (n 5).

Lastly, in contexts where there exists a general law governing rulemaking procedures, expressly establishing extensive procedural and participatory rights for the interested parties alongside the obligations on administrative bodies—as is in Portugal—the level of protection afforded to interested parties is not only high but also uniformly and consistently applied.

17

Commonality and Diversity in Administrative Rulemaking

Giacinto della Cananea

I. Introduction

The previous two Parts of the book provided a general view of the legal systems included in our comparative research and illustrated the solutions they would adopt for the hypothetical cases central to our 'factual analysis'. This and the following chapter discuss these solutions, with this one focusing specifically on administrative rulemaking.

This form of administrative action holds twofold importance from the common core perspective. On the one hand, the procedural issues that it poses are, at least to some extent, distinct from those encountered in administrative adjudication.[1] Whereas adjudication is based on the paradigm of judicial proceedings, underpinned by the principles of due process rooted in European law, rulemaking is more akin to legislation. On the other hand, there is the question of whether the factual analysis confirms the diversity—emphasized in the previous chapter—that characterizes administrative procedure legislation in this regard.

The chapter is structured as follows. The first section briefly illustrates the context. The second section provides a concise description of our 'factual analysis' and outlines the questions we aim to answer. The subsequent three sections discuss the constraints that the various legal systems impose on rulemaking, categorized depending on whether they are based on political oversight, consultation, or general principles. The section to follow touches on the relevance and significance of this analysis to our broader enquiry into the common core of European administrative laws. The chapter then concludes with some closing remarks.

II. Context

The present discussion will consider some general features of the legal systems examined as they emerge from Part II of this book. Moreover, a brief historical perspective is necessary for a proper understanding of present-day laws, as it was asserted in the past that the law governing administrative rules showed a profound divergence, a sort of divide, between common law systems and civil law systems. After that, our

[1] For this line of reasoning, see R Fuchs, 'Procedure in Administrative Rule-Making' (1938) 52 Harvard L Rev 259; P Craig, *Administrative Law* (5th edn, Sweet & Maxwell 2003) 457.

Giacinto della Cananea, *Commonality and Diversity in Administrative Rulemaking* In: *Administrative Rulemaking and Planning in European Laws*. Edited by: Giacinto della Cananea and Angela Ferrari Zumbini, Oxford University Press.
 DOI: 10.1093/oso/9780198867616.003.0017

discussion turns to a description of current trends before examining the implications of different contexts from a dual angle: that of consultation and judicial review.

A. The Rejection of Administrative Rules

In the past, the existence of administrative rules was a contested issue. This opposition took two main forms. In continental countries, earlier administrative law scholarship, including that of Mayer, was based on a clear-cut distinction between regulations and individual decisions. Collective orders, such as a police order requiring everyone in a town square to evacuate it for security reasons, were regarded as an aggregate of individual orders.[2] Even today, German public law considers general orders (*Allgemeinverfügungen*) as directed at a group of people in a specific situation, distinct from regulations and ordinances.[3] For the same reason, until the 1960s, Italian public law scholarship refused to acknowledge the existence of '*atti amministrativi generali a contenuto non normativo*', that is, administrative acts of general application.[4]

In England, more pragmatically, the existence of administrative rules was acknowledged, but they were kept within strict limits. At the turn of the twentieth century, the courts demonstrated their reluctance, if not their outright refusal, to give much weight to policies or rules defined by public authorities. Thus, in *Corrie*, the secretary of an association applied for permission to sell pamphlets in London parks.[5] The permission was refused because of a council bylaw that prohibited any sales in parks. The judicial reaction was that this prohibition was excessive as each application ought to be considered on its merits. A general policy or rule was thus permitted, provided it was *intra vires* and did not fetter discretion.

Some decades later, this judicial doctrine was overemphasized by an Italian observer, Massimo Severo Giannini. He promoted the translation of William Wade's treatise on administrative law and wrote the preface, where he regarded the non-fettering doctrine—discussed by Wade in the context of judicial review of administration[6]—as exemplary. He did so for two reasons, one of which was explicitly stated, while the other was implied. Giannini took a positive view of this doctrine because it allowed public administrations considerable leeway.[7] He did so also on broader ground, considering this an opportunity to criticize the administrative laws of Italy, France, and other continental European countries. The underlying idea was still that England had no formal administrative law system and did pretty well without one.[8] Whatever the intellectual soundness of this idea, the least that can be said is that he took this argument too far, because—as we observed earlier—the solution envisaged by the courts

[2] O Mayer, *Deutsches Verwaltungsrecht* (1894), French translation by the author, *Droit administratif allemand* (Giard et Brière 1903) I, 130.

[3] See E Chiti, 'European Union' Chapter 5 in this book.

[4] G della Cananea, *Gli atti amministrativi generali* (Cedam 2000).

[5] *R v LCC ex p. Corrie* (1918). For further details see Craig (n 1) 532.

[6] W Wade, *Administrative Law* (2nd edn, Clarendon 1967) chapter 2, Italian translation *Diritto amministrativo inglese* (Giuffrè 1969) 91.

[7] MS Giannini, 'Prefazione' in W Wade, *Diritto amministrativo inglese* (Giuffrè 1969) xv–xvi.

[8] Giannini (n 7) xix (affirming that English law was 'more advanced' because continental administrative law was a 'hindrance').

in the United Kingdom was not that administrative authorities were precluded from adopting a policy or a rule. As Anthony and Leyland observe, the case law could 'become much more complex than this, as the courts have to determine the extent of discretion and also whether an authority has actually fettered its powers'.[9]

This complexity emerges in the case of *British Oxygen*.[10] When the Board of Trade exercised the discretion it was given under primary legislation, deciding not to provide grants for expenditure below a certain amount of money, this policy was challenged as unlawful by a potential recipient. However, Lord Reid, speaking for the House of Lords, disagreed. He stated that if 'the Act read as a whole indicate[s] any policy which the Board is to follow or even give[s] any guidance, ... then the Board must exercise its discretion in accordance with such policy or guidance'. But, he added, he could find nothing in the Act to guide the Board in circumstances such as those for which the Board had drawn up its policy. Apart from the two general grounds on which the exercise of unqualified discretion could be challenged, namely bad faith and unreasonableness, Lord Reid stated that 'if the Minister thinks that policy or good administration requires the operation of some limiting rule, I find nothing to stop him', provided that the authority was willing to listen to anyone who had something new to say.[11] Legal scholarship, too, has shown more openness towards administrative rules. According to Craig, a public authority is entitled to have a policy, and this could become so precise that it could be called a rule, provided that it would not be deaf to those who had something to say about it.[12] In their analysis of UK law in this book, Morison and Mark adhere to the view that there has been a change from a 'doctrine which preserves administrative discretion to one which regulates the development and application of administrative rules'.[13]

Thus considered, the doctrine is not so distant from that defined by some continental courts. In the mid-twentieth century both German and Italian administrative courts held that if legislation did not establish standards for exercising discretion in individual cases, the public authority was required to predetermine the canons of conduct. Otherwise, there was a risk that discretion could be used very inconsistently from one case to another and thus fall into arbitrariness. The phrase coined by German jurists, '*Selbsbindung der Verwaltung*', expresses the idea that the administrative authority must adopt a rule governing its action and adhere to it. Unlike legislative or regulatory provisions, this type of rule is not strictly binding. In her report, Weidemann adeptly explains that a deviation from the self-imposed rule must be justified by compelling reasons.[14] Interestingly, in France the traditional dichotomy between discretionary power and bound administrative action ('*administration discretionnaire ou liée*') has been enriched by the definition of a third type of action, called '*ligotée*', that is, tied in such a way as to allow for some measure of reasonable discretion.[15] There is, therefore, at least potentially, some common ground.

[9] G Antony and P Leyland, *Textbook on Administrative Law* (8th edn, OUP 2016) 295.
[10] House of Lords, *British Oxygen Co Ltd v Board of Trade* [1971] AC 610.
[11] ibid 625. For further remarks, see Anthony and Leyland (n 9) 297.
[12] See P Daly, *Understanding Administrative Law in the Common Law World* (OUP 2022) 151.
[13] See J Morison and D Mark, 'United Kingdom' Chapter 13 in this book.
[14] L Weidemann, 'Case 4—Germany' Chapter 15.V.E in this book.
[15] On this distinction see L Di Qual, *La compétence liée* (LGDJ 1964) 368.

B. Increasing Administrative Rules

When discussing rulemaking in contemporary legal systems, it is easy to lose sight of the fact that what matters is not only its foundation but also its extent or scope. In this respect, two observations soon emerged from national reports. Over time, administrative rules have multiplied for various reasons, raising some concerns and, in turn giving rise to various reactions, ranging from attempts to rationalize the plethora of rules to, in extreme cases, deeming them unlawful.

Previous comparative studies, though limited to just a few legal systems,[16] already revealed the increase of administrative rules, and the same phenomenon is now attested in other legal systems.

Thus, for example, Smith observes that in the Norwegian legal system, there is a 'proliferation of general statements' from national departments, including comments, guidance, and so forth.[17] Interestingly, this trend is common to non-state legal entities, such as the European Union, where the Commission adopts a range of acts, including guidelines, instructions, and codes, often generically called soft law, with the aim of guiding national authorities.[18]

Interestingly, the reasons that explain this phenomenon are more or less the same. First, as observed by public law scholarship a century ago,[19] the subject matter may be technically complex, making it difficult for parliaments and governments (in the narrow sense) to adopt legislation. Secondly, the subject matter may require frequent updates due to either the rapid obsolescence of rules or to the inadequacy of parliamentary legislation because of its slow pace of change. Thirdly, when a public authority formulates a policy relevant to its exercise of powers, it delineates key considerations and priorities that will guide its decisions in individual cases. Fourthly, there is increasing pressure from global regulatory regimes, particularly in banking, insurance, and environmental protection.

This does not mean, however, that everyone agrees on the general need for administrative rulemaking. Legal literature across many nations abounds in criticism, often echoing concerns about the multitude of rules, adopted by public authorities, their uncertain legal effects, and the difficulties that arise with regard to accessibility. On the eve of the adoption of the US Administrative Procedure Act (APA), an American observer pointed out that not only were individuals no longer able to keep abreast of the numerous rules governing their conduct but even government officers were 'unable to find their way in the labyrinth of regulations accumulated in different bureaus

[16] See F Cammeo, 'Della *manifestazione* della *volontà* dello Stato nel campo del diritto amministrativo: Legge ed ordinanza (decreti e regolamenti)' in VE Orlando (ed), *Primo trattato completo di diritto amministrativo italiano*, vol III (Società editrice libraria 1901) 121 (examining Italy, France, Belgium, Germany, the United Kingdom, and the US) and one century later T Ziamou, *Rulemaking, Participation and the Limits of Public Law in the United States and in Europe* (Ashgate Publishing 2001) (comparing the United States with Germany, Greece and the United Kingdom).

[17] See E Smith, 'Norway' Chapter 10 in this book.

[18] See Chiti (n 3).

[19] See Cammeo (n 16) 126. For a recent reappraisal, see M Cartabia and N Lupo, *The Constitution of Italy. A Contextual Analysis* (Hart 2022) 111.

without adequate systematic registration or publication'.[20] Some years ago in France, a legislative action established that all circulars and instructions were unlawful. More recently, in Hungary—as discussed by Berkès and Balasz in this book—the practice of issuing circulars, directives, and interpretative documents was declared unconstitutional.[21] In a different vein, the US APA of 1946 laid down norms governing administrative rulemaking in both formal and informal procedures. Other legal systems, such as those of Italy and the Netherlands, followed the same pattern, albeit with some differing norms. For example, the latter requires reasons to be given, while the former does not. This blend of commonality and diversity makes this matter so interesting that it is the subject of one of our first hypothetical cases.

C. Constraints on Rulemaking

The increasing significance of administrative rulemaking has prompted various legal systems to implement constraints and control mechanisms. These include political oversight, particularly by parliamentary bodies, as well as through consultation and judicial review.[22] A few words of explanation may be helpful to shed light on these various forms of constraint.

Political control varies considerably between the legal systems included in our survey. Firstly, the role of parliamentary institutions in the legal systems examined differs. These include not only parliamentary democracies—for instance, the United Kingdom and Germany—and presidential systems, such as the United States, but also a very different form of government, that of China. Secondly, even within the former, there may be no general requirement that executive rules be laid before parliamentary bodies.[23] When this must be done, there are numerous ways in which this can occur.

The second constraint is ably encapsulated in the German concept of *Grundrechtsschutz durch Verfahren*, namely 'the protection of basic rights through procedures'. Consultation and participation are topics which have been subjects of considerable discussion in recent years. There is, however, little point in merely invoking the mantra of participation, as the effectiveness of participatory rights depends significantly on the type of constitutional order in which public authorities operate and the underlying theories that inform such orders. Thus, the purposes and incidence of procedural rights vary, as will be seen, between pluralist democracies and more authoritarian governments, such as the United States and China, respectively. Differences may also be said to emerge in Europe, albeit to a lesser extent, where procedural rights extend not only to individuals but also to groups, and where the more

[20] AK Kuhn, 'The Administrative Procedure Act and the State Department' (1946) 40 Am J Int L 784. See also LA Jaffe, 'Publication of Administrative Rules and Orders' (1936) 24 Am Bar Ass J 393, at 394 (same remark).

[21] L Berkes and B S Gerencsér, 'Hungary' Chapter 17 in this book.

[22] Of course, some legal systems have a more differentiated pattern of mechanisms for the control of executive rule-making, eg for the United Kingdom, Craig (n 1) 367 examines consultation, publication, legislative scrutiny and judicial review.

[23] For further analysis see S Rose-Ackerman, *Democracy and Executive Power. Policymaking Accountability in the US, the UK, Germany, and France* (Yale UP 2021).

particular administrative rights diverge as a consequence of both the legislative and judicial formants. Two rationales underpin consultation or participation. They can provide decision-makers with a better understanding of the relevant facts and thus allow better outcomes. Moreover, they can strengthen the legitimacy of administrative decisions (this is called '*legitimation durch verfahren*' in Germany).[24] Whatever the rationale, when there is a duty to consult, failure to comply will render the administrative rule voidable before the courts.

Beneath this apparent uniformity, however, lies a pronounced heterogeneity. First, in some legal systems, such as in the United Kingdom, there is no general duty to conduct consultations. Secondly, even where general legislation exists, it does not necessarily impose a duty to consult in all circumstances. Thus, for example, in the Italian APA, in a seeming paradox, the only general norm concerning planning (and rulemaking) is that there are no general norms. The underlying reason is that consultation and participation with regard to rulemaking need to be tailored to each sector. Thirdly, the same idea may justify a different solution. For example, in Norway, the APA provisions are often supplemented by higher standards concerning public hearings.[25] Fourthly, even when consultation is mandated by law, it may not *always* be obligatory, being merely directory.

In another respect, there is not simply a common trend but a common constitutional tradition requiring the possibility of judicial review of administrative rules. In other words, there is no cloak of immunity or general exemption from judicial review. After all, the exclusion of review would be irreconcilable with Article 6 of the European Convention of Human Rights, as the Committee of Ministers of the Council of Europe remarked two decades ago.[26] However, a distinction must be drawn between standing (or *locus standi*, in Anglo-Saxon systems) and justiciability. The latter concerns the suitability of resolving a particular type of dispute through judicial process, regardless of intends to bring it to court.[27] In this respect, in Europe, the United States, and elsewhere, any clause excluding judicial review on executive action must be considered out of date. The rules on standing, on the other hand, determine whether a particular claimant has the right to challenge a particular act or measure, or a failure to act in court. In this respect, there are policy arguments that may induce legislators to either limit or exclude the possibility to challenge administrative rules directly. Moreover, the same recommendation of the Council of Europe's Committee of Ministers specified that judicial review 'may be direct or by way of exception'. Thus, for example, in both the Czech Republic and Italy, direct challenges to rules are not permitted as a matter of principle. In Italy, an exception to this is when a regulation or an administrative act of general content infringes the principles of equality and reasonableness, as would be the case of a provision excluding a certain category of persons from access to

[24] N Luhmann, *Legitimation durch Verfahren* (Suhrkamp 1969).

[25] Smith, 'Norway' (n 17).

[26] Council of Europe, Committee of Minister, 'Recommendation (2004(20) to Member States on Judicial Review of Administrative Acts', <https://rm.coe.int/09000016805db3f4#:~:text=All%20administrative%20acts%20should%20be,impropriety%20and%20abuse%20of%20power> accessed 24 November 2024 (recalling art 6 ECHR and defining some principles, the first of which is 'all administrative acts should be subject to judicial review').

[27] See Craig (n 1) 717.

a benefit without an adequate reason (eg those who have red hair cannot have access to a position in the public sector).[28] In contrast, in Hungary, recently adopted norms now allow acts of soft law to be challenged.

It is with this caveat that we may better appreciate the Chinese report, which ably explains that while there is no conceptual difference between individual decisions and acts of general applicability, judicial review is allowed for the former but is excluded for the latter. Notwithstanding the recent changes that have taken place in the legislative framework concerning administrative litigation,

> Administrative regulations, rules and most decisions with general binding force are still *excluded from the scope of judicial review*. Judicial review of a regulatory document is permissible only during a lawsuit against an administrative action based on this regulatory document.[29]

To use different terminology, it may thus be said that there are two general norms. The first is general in the sense that it is distinct from a series of legislative clauses that purport to render various acts of a general nature watertight, excluding any direct attack against executive rules. Judicial review in this form is, therefore, wholly ruled out. The second norm does not derogate from the first but operates in a different way, allowing what may be called either a collateral or indirect challenge. This is the only circumstance in which individual litigants may challenge the legality of executive rules. Within these limits, it is possible to state a case, potentially opening up the field for more extensive judicial review. The adverb 'potentially' indicates that not only the availability of judicial review but also the conditions to which it is subject and the willingness of judges to allow it must be considered. A factual analysis may be helpful in this context.

III. Factual Analysis

Before we discuss the outcomes of our factual analysis, it might be helpful to prepare the ground by briefly revisiting the ideas underlying it and the nature of the questions that will be discussed.

Rudolf B Schlesinger, in his often-cited essay on the common core in the formation of contracts, provides a well-explained foundation for the ideas underlying the factual analysis. His approach is both critical and constructive. His first criticism is that, even if we acknowledge the existence of a number of significant differences between national legal systems, we are not obliged—as sometimes claimed by the advocates of incommensurability—to avoid comparing them because there may be some common and connecting elements beyond generic ideals, such as justice. Schlesinger's second

[28] For example, the French *Conseil d'État* held that certain acts of general applicability, such as circulars and guidelines, may not be contested judicially if they have no binding effects: judgment of 12 June 2020, n 418142, Group d'information et de soutien des immigrés.

[29] X Sun, 'China' Chapter 13 in this book.

observation is that all too often, collective surveys merely juxtapose national reports without engaging in true comparative analysis.[30]

On the constructive side, if we wish to improve our understanding of the relationship between commonality and diversity, we must ascertain whether certain problems are common to a certain group of legal systems and, if so, whether the solutions adopted are similar or not. For this purpose, the problems have to be stated in factual terms by way of hypothetical cases, hence the term 'factual analysis' adopted here.

Rejecting the majority approach of previous studies on the subject does not mean, however, that positive norms and judicial decisions are irrelevant. Quite the contrary, operational norms within each legal system and the interactions among various legal formants—in our case, this means not only legislation, regulations and judicial decisions but also constitutional conventions or custom, established government practice, and underlying theories of public law and the state—are both relevant and significant. The task of theory must be to elucidate the structures of each legal system and the assumptions implicit within such structures, not unlike the approach adopted in the field of private law.[31]

All this explains why the questionnaire is a fundamental tool for our factual analysis and why it is a collaborative effort since a hypothetical case can be included in the questionnaire if it makes sense across all the legal systems selected for our comparison. Some further remarks may be pertinent at this stage. First and foremost, given our experimentalist approach, we must seek to ascertain whether the legal formants that count in one domain of inquiry do so in others. For this reason, we have attempted to construct a set of hypothetical cases that include a sufficient range of questions concerning various aspects of public law.

Secondly, we can distinguish between the basic jurisprudential questions and more specific ones. The former pertain to some of the core principles of procedural justice, such as participation and transparency. The more specific questions can be categorized into three groups based on the constraints placed on the exercise of administrative authority. Although there is often a tendency to equate oversight of administrative action with judicial review, this is only one type of control, but there are others, including those exercised by political bodies, the ombudsman, and other institutions. Two of our hypothetical cases concern parliamentary scrutiny of administrative rules and their legitimacy in the absence of a legislative foundation. Consultation is another constraint. It may be required by either sector-specific legislation or general laws on administrative procedure. Another situation arises if the requirement is imposed by the courts, but there are jurisdictions where no such option exists, such as in the United Kingdom.[32] This brings us to the third group of hypothetical cases, where we seek to understand whether courts may be willing to impose certain standards upon administrative authorities, such as those concerning the publication of rules and the protection of legitimate expectations.

[30] See, on the same subject, RB Schlesinger, 'Introduction' in RB Schlesinger (ed), *Formation of Contracts. A Study of the Common Core of Legal Systems* (Oceana Publications 1968).

[31] For further remarks, in particular on the studies concerning the common core of European private law, see G della Cananea, Chapter 1.III.B in this book.

[32] J Morison and D Mark, 'United Kingdom' Chapter 13 in this book.

IV. Constraints on Rulemaking: Political Control

As noted above, the first two hypothetical cases concern the relationship between parliamentary and administrative institutions. In the first case, we examine parliamentary scrutiny of administrative rules, in the second we consider the absence of a legislative basis for the adoption of rules.

A. Parliamentary Scrutiny

There are some instances where one might expect the hypothetical case to reveal some common ground, or an area of agreement between the legal systems under consideration. In other cases, it can be expected that several, and significant, differences may emerge. The hypothetical case which follows falls into the latter category because, as previously observed, administrative law is inevitably shaped by the form of government.

We suppose that primary legislation (adopted by parliamentary bodies) concerning immigration confers on the Minister of Internal Affairs the power to adopt an order that defines in detail the administrative procedures concerning the treatment of asylum seekers. However, the same legislation requires the Minister to present the order before Parliament, which has 30 days to make comments or request changes, before the order comes into force. The order is laid before Parliament, but before the 30-day deadline expires, the Minister decides to enforce the order and publishes it on the Ministry's website, citing the need for immediate implementation. The main question that arises is whether this would be regarded by Parliament as a disregard of its legislation and, would thus be considered invalid. An additional question is whether the order could be contested before the courts on grounds of invalidity.

When reading the solutions envisaged by our experts, it is important to bear in mind the diversity of the institutional frameworks referred to before. Thus, in the United States, where the Constitution embraces a certain vision of the separation of powers, Congress could not require the immigration (or any other) agency to subject its orders to congressional veto or congressionally mandated changes. As a result, the order could be contested before the courts, as happened in the leading case, *INS v Chadha* (1983).[33] On the other hand, in a parliamentary democracy such as the United Kingdom, if the ministers acts outside the powers granted by Parliament, the action is *ultra vires*. Courts will therefore strike down the administrative rules.[34] In Germany and the Netherlands, too, the order would be regarded as invalid and could be annulled in court.[35] Other parliamentary democracies would opt for different solutions. In Norway, for example, the conduct of the Minister would be seen as disregarding Parliament. However, the legal validity of the order would be considered as a distinct question, with the procedural failure not necessarily entailing the invalidity of the

[33] J Lubbers and G della Cananea, 'United States of America—Case 1' Chapter 15.II.M in this book.

[34] J Morison and D Mark, 'United Kingdom—Case 1' Chapter 15.II.L in this book.

[35] L Weidemann, 'Germany—Case 1' Chapter 15.IIE; J van der Brink, L Verboeket, and V van Waarde, 'The Netherlands—Case 1' Chapter 15.IIH, both in this book.

order.[36] The underlying idea is that only few procedural infringements result in the invalidity of administrative decisions and orders.

Hungary stands apart because there is no requirement for a parliamentary opinion before a ministerial decree is adopted. This calls for a brief explanation as to our choice to keep this hypothetical case. We decided to keep it because it helps us to understand the divergence between that particular system and the other ones that are included within the EU, as well as with the EU itself, where the EU courts would most likely uphold the European Parliament's claim. In another respect, it must be noticed that there is, at least potentially, a chance to contest the decree before the Hungarian Constitutional Court, similarly to the Czech legal system.[37] Interestingly, in another form of government, namely in China, the ministerial decree would be annulled neither by Parliament nor by the courts.[38] It is within these limits and in this sense that an area of disagreement emerges. A non-democracy differs from what is common to the vast majority of democracies, though not all.

B. Standardless Adjudication?

The differing intellectual and institutional foundations for rulemaking were examined earlier. A few words will suffice, therefore, to explain why the second hypothetical case is both interesting and important from the perspective of the common core. First, until some decades ago, there were two divergent visions of the relationship between rules and discretion. One was reflected in the no-fettering rule while the other required public authorities to rigorously limit and structure their discretionary powers. However, as observed earlier, the divergence was more apparent than real. It is interesting, therefore, to ascertain how the same problem would be conceptualized and addressed today. Second, there is not only an issue concerning the existence of the power to define policy or rules. There is also a procedural side concerning how public authorities make rules, particularly from the viewpoint of consultation.

Our hypothetical case regards the rules regulating the disbursement of public money. We assume that parliamentary legislation enables public money to be granted to toy manufacturers that promote a particular social goal: greater environmental awareness in children under the age of 10. According to this legislation, the Department of the Environment can award grants to the producers of the new games. The Department decides to establish some rules of practice, including one whereby it would not award grants for any game costing more than a certain amount of money. When a producer applies for a grant for a new game, its application is rejected on the grounds that the sale price of the game exceeds the amount of money established in advance. The producer thus brings a claim before the court, claiming that, before defining its rules of practice or standards, the Department should have consulted the stakeholders, instead of acting unilaterally. The public authority objects that there is

[36] E Smith, 'Norway—Case 1' Chapter 15.II.I in this book.

[37] L Berkes and BS Gerencsér, 'Hungary—Case 1' Chapter 15.II.F; J Rajchl, D Burda, and G Blahoudková, 'Czech Republic—Case 1' Chapter 15.II.C, both in this book.

[38] X Sun, 'China—Case 1' Chapter 15.II.B in this book.

no legislative provision requiring it to consult stakeholders before adopting any rule or policy. What is at issue is, first, whether a policy or rule may legitimately be formulated; secondly, whether the court would give any weight to the claim based on the lack of consultation with stakeholders and, whether, this being the case, the court would either quash the disputed measure or require the public authority to reopen the consultation phase or stage.

As far as the first aspect is concerned, all the legal systems examined recognized the existence of legal rules that confine and structure the discretionary powers granted to public authorities. But some do so on the assumption that administrative authorities have the inherent power to do so (Portugal), others because there is a general legislative duty to adopt rules of this type (Italy), and still others because these rules can better ensure adherence to general principles, such as *Rechtsstaat* (Germany).[39] There is another distinction of prime importance. It is one thing whether administrative rules are inflexible, insofar as they leave no measure of discretion to decision-makers. Another is whether rules are conditional or flexible, for example by allowing officials to do something if a certain circumstance is fulfilled, which comes close to the idea of how discretion should be exercised 'normally' albeit not invariably. This would be accepted by the courts in Austria, Germany, and Italy.[40] It would also be accepted in the United Kingdom, where only an inflexible rule, which leaves no margin of discretion, would be quashed by the courts as *ultra vires*. Thus, for example, a minister adopting a policy such that it will refuse to hear representations from the local authorities affected by its order would amount to a breach of the principle that the parties likely to be affected by a decision should have a fair opportunity to be consulted.[41]

Some distinctions are necessary with regard to consultation before a policy or rule is adopted. First, unlike the United States, where the APA requires public participation, especially in formal rulemaking, in many parts of Europe—for instance, in Germany—there is no general norm imposing a duty to consult on public authorities. Nor is there any general requirement to consult in the EU, despite several attempts by applicants to extend the right to be heard to measures of general applicability. However, the importance of consultation is often recognized, sometimes on non-instrumental grounds, other times on instrumental grounds; that is, with a view to ascribing value to the role of social groups in public decision-making and ensuring that sound decisions are taken, respectively. Thus, for example, in the United Kingdom a ban on tobacco was deemed invalid because the company affected was not informed of the scientific basis for the ban.[42] Similarly, in its 2002 Communication on Consultation, the EU Commission set out some minimum requirements concerning the forms of consultation it may use to ensure the adequacy of the final decision. Secondly, it is for the courts to establish the consequences of failure to consult, and

[39] R Guerra da Fonseca, 'Portugal—Case 2' Chapter 15.III.J; L Parona 'Italy—Case 2' Chapter 15.III.G; L Weidemann, 'Germany—Case 2' Chapter 15.III.E, all in this book.

[40] S Storr 'Austria—Case 2' Chapter 15.III.A in this book; Weidemann 'Germany—Case 2' (n 39) and Parona 'Italy—Case 2' (n 39).

[41] See eg *R. v Secretary of State for the Environment, ex p. Brent London Borough Council* [1983] 3 All ER 321.

[42] See eg in the United Kingdom, the House of Lords ruling in *R. v Secretary of State for Health, ex parte US Tobacco International Inc* (1992).

they may act differently. In Norway, for example, the success of a legal challenge depends on whether the claimant can show that the lack of consultation could, and did, have an impact on the outcome. In the Czech legal system, however, failure to consult cannot be contested before the courts.[43] In yet other systems, such as in Sweden, a complaint could be brought before an alternative public institution, the Parliamentary Ombudsman.

The persistence of an area of disagreement between the legal systems examined should not, however, prevent an adequate understanding of the development of the law across time. It is clear that the control of discretion has not remained static. It has evolved in a way that transcends the rigid distinction between a no-fettering (inflexible) rule and the duty to predetermine criteria and standards, without which individual administrative acts are invalid. Further analysis might help to verify whether the courts are willing to embrace ideas of coherence and legal certainty.

V. Constraints on Rulemaking: Consultation

The second type of constraint on the exercise of administrative powers is based on consultation. In this context, we have imagined three related but distinct hypothetical cases; the first two focus on stakeholders and the last on users. The first distinctive element is, therefore, the nature of the persons or interests involved. A further distinctive element between the first two hypothetical cases—the *differentia specifica*—is that the first one considers all stakeholders as a whole, while the second supposes they are treated differently, thus raising an additional issue concerning the principle of equality.

A. Stakeholders

Our first hypothetical case is about policy change. We suppose that primary legislation concerning slot machine arcade licences allows regional authorities to adopt rules on the procedures for granting them, including setting a maximum number of available licences. After a recent election and a subsequent shift in policy, one of these regional authorities decides to change its policy regarding slot machine arcades. Instead of the former maximum of one licence, the authority will grant a maximum of five within the local region for a period of two years. The authority publishes its new policy in its official journal and on its website. Parties interested in a slot machine arcade licence have one month to apply for it, after which the authority will score and rank the applications according to the criteria mentioned in the policy. During the application period, the authority publishes an amendment to its policy to the effect that the applications will also be scored on the basis of a so-called prevention plan, containing the intended measures to prevent gambling addiction. Some stakeholders are unhappy with the new policy, and they challenge it before the competent court on

[43] E Smith, 'Norway—Case 2' Chapter 15.III.I; J Rajchl, D Burda, and G Blahoudková 'Czech Republic—Case 2' Chapter 15.III.C, both in this book.

two grounds. First, they argue that the authority should have consulted them before setting the licence validity period at two years, claiming that such a period does not offer enough time to recover the costs incurred to prepare the application, let alone the investments needed to purchase and maintain slot machines. Second, they assert that the authority should not have added the prevention plan to the selection criteria after the application period had already started. The authority objects that applicants have enough time to add a prevention plan to their licence application.

Not surprisingly, different legal systems have different rules concerning, for example, consultation. In Sweden, for instance, there is general discretion to consult such stakeholders as appears to be appropriate.[44] On the other hand, in a neighbouring nation, Norway, the courts would be more likely to dismiss all actions against the new policy.[45] In another administrative tradition, such as that of Portugal, public consultation would be regarded as mandatory.[46] As a result, a failure to consult would entitle stakeholders to take action before the administrative courts, challenging both the individual decision adversely affecting them and the administrative rule.[47] Moreover, when national authorities implement EU law, they are required to respect the principles of objectivity and transparency.

Outside Europe, in the United States the rule itself would be questionable on grounds of procedural fairness. At the opposite side of the spectrum, the Chinese courts would reject an argument based on the lack of consultation. However, they might endorse the other argument concerning the prevention plan and remand it to the administrative authority to correct the irregularity. This finding is interesting in itself as it confirms the necessity to articulate the conclusions about judicial review in the clearest terms. It is also interesting from a comparative perspective, as the same conclusion would be reached by various courts, using slightly differing arguments. Thus, in Portugal the emphasis would be on retroactivity, in the United States on reasonableness, in the United Kingdom on the difficulty to provide reasons are that are both 'adequate and intelligible', and in Hungary on rationality and non-contradiction.

A clearer area of agreement emerges with regard to other hypothetical cases concerning consultation. As indicated earlier, what distinguishes this case from the preceding one is the questionable differentiation in how the public authority interacts with stakeholders. Specifically, we assume that a new railway company has entered the market dominated by two incumbents for several years. Before setting new tariffs, the national regulatory authority decides to consult with all the stakeholders although it is under no obligation to do so. However, in practice, it consults only the two present incumbents, excluding the newcomer, who then challenges the new tariffs, arguing that it should have been consulted.

Both the instrumental rationale (its conduct prevented the regulator from obtaining information from all relevant sources and thus from reaching a better decision) and the non-instrumental rationale (the regulator's conduct infringed the principles of equality and procedural fairness) are invoked, while the regulator responds that,

44 P Jonason and B Forssén, 'Sweden—Case 3' Chapter 15.IV.K in this book.
45 E Smith, 'Norway—Case 3' Chapter 15.IV.I in this book.
46 R Guerra da Fonseca, 'Portugal—Case 3' Chapter 15.IV.J in this book.
47 ibid.

under the sector-specific rules governing railway transport, there was no obligation to consult all stakeholders. The questions that thus arise are whether the court would endorse the defendant's argument whereby, as there was no general duty to consult, it had general discretion to consult the stakeholders it deemed appropriate and, that not being the case, whether the court would quash the new tariffs or choose another way to protect the stakeholder that was not consulted, for example by denying that the new tariffs could be binding without proper consultation.

As observed earlier, national rules governing consultation differ in more than one respect. For example, in Sweden, the courts may be unwilling to affirm a general duty to consult stakeholders, as distinct from public authorities. However, even though there is no mandatory requirement to consult, once consultation does take place, it must satisfy certain general standards. The emphasis would be placed on slightly different concepts, including equality (Austria), procedural fairness (both in Germany and the United Kingdom), due process (in the United States), the disregard of the authority's duty to carry out an appropriate fact-finding activity (again in Germany), unreasonableness (in the Netherlands), and impartiality and good faith (in Portugal), but the outcome would not change. The notion that a public authority is at liberty to choose whom it wishes to consult at its discretion is to be ruled out. The judicial response to a grievance may nonetheless vary. Thus, for example, Dutch and Italian administrative courts, like the UK courts, would annul the regulator's new tariff. Conversely, the Czech courts would do so only if there is evidence that the interests of the stakeholder that was not consulted were adversely affected by the omission.[48]

In this case, therefore, there is more common ground than in the previous one, and the same can be said of the hypothetical case that will follow, which concerns consultation before policy change in the area of public services.

B. Users

We suppose that under national legislation local authorities are required to provide a comprehensive library service. The term 'comprehensive service' is not defined in the legislation, however. We assume it is the responsibility of local authorities to determine how to deliver public library services in the light of local needs and available funding. But there is a legislative duty to consult users, and the Ministry for culture and media can order an inquiry when there is a concern that a local authority is failing to fulfil its duties. When a local authority announces on its website that it is going to close three of its five public libraries and drastically reduce the opening hours of the remaining two libraries, a consumer association challenges this change of policy and argues that it ought to be consulted before a final decision is taken. The local authority simply asserts that its decision is due to financial difficulties and adopts the decision. The consumer association then brings a case before a court on three related but distinct grounds. First, it argues that the duty to consult users should be taken seriously,

[48] J Morison and D Mark, 'United Kingdom—Case 5' Chapter 15.VI.L; J van der Brink, L Verboeket, and V van Waarde 'Netherlands—Case 5' Chapter 15.VI.H; L Parona 'Italy—Case 5' Chapter 15.VI.G; J Rajchl, D Burda, and G Blahoudková 'Czech Republic—Case 5' Chapter 15.VI.C, all in this book.

especially when a decision adversely affecting them is likely to be taken, as is the case with a decision that will deprive them of existing benefits. Secondly, the association argues that consultation should occur in good time, when proposals are at a formative stage rather than on the point of adoption. Lastly, it claims that the local authority should consider more than one option, weighing up their advantages and disadvantages, also in the light of users' observations. Otherwise, so the argument goes, consultation would not be meaningful. As in the previous case, we seek to understand whether the court would endorse any of these arguments and, if so, whether it would be willing to quash the challenged decision.

Before considering the solutions envisaged in the national reports, some brief remarks are in order. The first is that this hypothetical case differs from the previous two as it concerns individuals as users of public services. The second, which is the consequence of the first, is that the hypothetical case calls into question not only the legal framework regarding rulemaking but also the principles that govern the delivery of public services. This is particularly important in the legal systems—in France, for instance—where there is an established range of principles, including equality of access and continuity. The third remark is that, although public authorities are bound by such principles, they exercise a considerable amount of discretion. The decision to close a school, for example, may be justified by a drop in the numbers of students in a certain area or the possibility of economies of scale. Fourth, obviously, national courts will often follow different standards concerning whether an action could be brought either by students or by their parents on their behalf.

Even a cursory glance at the national reports shows that the legal systems examined differ principally in how services must be performed, as well as whether interested individuals and groups should be given an opportunity to submit statements and produce evidence supporting or opposing the proposed policy change. Two neighbouring nations, Norway and Sweden, illustrate the importance given to consultation and, at the same time, the reluctance to give weight to the lack of consultation in the courts, opting rather for political sanctions.[49] Germany and the Netherlands, instead, place greater weight on consultation.[50] In the former, administrative procedure legislation has recently been amended by introducing what is called the duty of early public participation. In the latter, sector-specific legislation establishes a mandatory requirement to consult. Additionally, this legislation constrains the discretionary powers of local bodies concerning the closing of schools. By contrast, in the Czech and UK-wide legal systems there is no general duty to consult.[51] Accordingly, their courts would not endorse the first argument put forward by the association, namely that consultation is required.

Nevertheless, not unlike in the previous case, even though there is no mandatory requirement to consult users, if a public authority decides to do so, then some legal consequences follow on from this. Practically, in Germany the administrative court

[49] E Smith, 'Norway—Case 5' Chapter 15.VI.I; P Jonason and B Forssén, 'Sweden—Case 5' Chapter 15.VI.K, both in this book.

[50] L Weidemann, 'Case 5—Germany' Chapter 15.VI.E in this book; van der Brink, Verboeket, and van Waarde, 'The Netherlands—Case 5' (n 48).

[51] Morison and Mark, 'United Kingdom—Case 5' (n 48); Rajchl, Burda, and Blahoudková 'Czech Republic—Case 5' (n 48).

would probably deem that the users have not been provided with sufficient information, although this failure could be remedied if the local authority carries out a proper consultation before the end of the judicial process.[52] Even where there is no general duty to consult users, for instance in the United Kingdom, it is likely that the courts would hold that the duty to consult users should be taken very seriously. Moreover, they would affirm the general common law principle that consultation must take place at a formative stage, and they would thus quash the contested decree. This is not the case in Austria, where it is unlikely that the courts would affirm a duty to consult at an early stage. In other legal systems, the courts would focus on the duty to give reasons. Thus, in Austria, Hungary, and Italy, administrative courts would most probably endorse the applicant's claim that the local authority is unable to prove that the decision to severely cut services was the only possible one because of financial difficulties and would therefore annul it.[53] Austrian courts would also be likely to annul the contested decision on the grounds that the consultation period was inadequate.

Outside Europe, US courts would submit the local authority to the usual 'arbitrary and capricious' test for rulemaking and would consider whether it deviated from its own policy or rule with regard to the deadline for sending comments. In China, the courts would instead qualify the decision as an individual one and would, therefore, allow individuals to contest it on both procedural and substantive grounds.

The conclusion that emerges from this comparative survey is that the legislative and judicial formants work differently. At legislative level, there may be a general duty to consult, or such a duty may be established by sector-specific legislation. Moreover, there may be either a mandatory or a directory requirement to consult one. However, if a public authority undertakes consultation before making a policy change, as we presume in our hypothetical case, then it is required to take it seriously.

VI. Constraints on Rulemaking: General Principles

The third and final type of constraint on rulemaking is based on general principles. It was thought interesting to consider, first, whether an individual may have a protected legal interest as regards the formulation of a policy or rule. Of course, this interest may be of a different nature. An individual may wish to argue that the policy or rule should not be applied to the particular case because it is inconsistent with the legislative framework in which the public authority operates (eg it is in contrast with the stated objectives). Conversely, the individual may argue that a certain policy or rule should be applied to the particular case, while the public authority wishes to amend its policy or even abandon it because it tightens the margin of appreciation of the interests at stake. We chose to devise a hypothetical case developing this situation since the law in this area is developing in the light of the principle whereby legitimate expectations must be protected. The Court of Justice of the European Union has included it among the general principles common to the legal orders of the Member States,

[52] Weidemann, 'Case 5—Germany' (n 50).

[53] S Storr 'Austria—Case 5' Chapter 15.VI.A; L Berkes and BS Gerencsér, 'Hungary—Case 5' Chapter 15.VI.F in this book; and Parona 'Italy—Case 5' (n 48).

ensuring compliance.[54] The other hypothetical case concerns a more established general principle, whose application to rulemaking is sometimes uncertain: the principle that rules must be published because they are of interest to all.

A. Protecting Legitimate Expectations

Like the previous case, this one concerns a local authority, which defines many policies and rules affecting the daily lives of individuals and legal entities. It also concerns an area—taxi licensing—that has been recently affected by the processes of liberalization, but in various ways and to differing degrees.

We imagine a scenario where a municipality, after issuing many taxi licences over the years, provides unequivocal assurance, through a statement delivered by the city council, that it will give notice or embark upon consultation before changing its policy concerning taxi licensing. However, because of an international sailing yacht competition that is expected to take place in six months' time, the municipality changes its policy in two respects. First, white has traditionally been the most common colour for taxis, but some were blue, yellow, or green. The city council rules that all taxis had to be white to aid recognition. Secondly, it rules that, instead of the traditional working hours limits, no taxi driver may drive for more than eight hours per day. A local association of taxi drivers contests the new policy on two grounds. It argues that the new policy implies higher and unforeseen costs. It adds that, since local administrators have given clear assurance, they should be held to it. In particular, those administrators should not be allowed to effect the proposed changes without notice or consultation of affected interests. Both arguments are included in the action brought by the association before the competent court against the new policy. The questions that thus arise are whether the court would be willing to accept those arguments and, if so, whether it would deem the new policy invalid.

Before examining the solutions envisaged in the reports, three brief remarks are necessary. First, although the hypothetical case involves both procedural and substantive issues, the focus is on the former. Secondly, the case expressly refers to the 'assurance' implicit in the statement delivered by the city board and, thus, to the doctrine of legitimate expectations. This does not mean that other concepts may not be relevant, including the principle of consistency or, in less recent terminology, the maxim '*tu patere legem quam ipse fecisti*', whereby an authority is bound by its own rules, as long as such rules are not amended, abrogated, or annulled.[55] Nor does it rule out that in some legal systems, the courts may rely on other standards, such as good faith or the duty to give reasons. Lastly, the final part of the case is deliberately constructed to allow different remedies to be applied if the court concludes that the local administration erred for one reason or another.

54 See JA Usher, *General Principles of EC Law* (Longman 1998) 52, remarking that in EC law the principle of the protection of legitimate expectations was regarded as being closely related to the German concept of *Vertrauensschutz*, on which see HJ Blanke, *Vertrauensschutz Im Deutschen Und Europaischen Verwaltungsrecht* (Mohr 2000).

55 See C Perelman, *Logique juridique* (Dalloz 1976) 147 (also discussing the other maxim *venire contra factum proprium*).

It is not surprising, therefore, that some reports discuss more than one available option. Thus, for example, two options are discussed for Britain. The first is based on procedural fairness or, in an alternative wording, to the duty to act fairly. The second is based on procedural legitimate expectations, in the sense that a change of policy which would otherwise be acceptable is no longer so once the public authority has made a statement that it will not change its policy without public consultation. An obstacle may also derive from past practice. In any case, the public authority may not depart from the past policy without hearing interested parties. This does not mean, however, that their interest may not be overridden by a compelling public interest.[56] A similar line of reasoning is most likely to be followed by German administrative courts, which would apply the consolidated doctrine of *Vertrauenschutz*, implying that an individual's legitimate expectations must be protected when a public authority changes the previous administrative practice.[57] As in the United Kingdom, the court would hold that a legitimate expectation, whether arising from a representation (*antizipierte Verwaltungspraxis*) or past practice, would require the administration to provide an opportunity for consultations and to give reasons for the public interest that justifies the change in policy. In a similar vein, the Austrian, Dutch, and Italian administrative courts would most probably affirm that there has been an infringement of legitimate expectations, while the Czech legal system would emphasize a similar concept: legal certainty and good faith.[58] There is, instead, a similarity between the United Kingdom and United States in that they would both emphasize the need to respect procedural fairness and due process, respectively.

Interestingly, the same conclusion would be reached in other legal systems—in Hungary, for instance—only if the 'assurance' given by the local authority had been given by way of a regulation, as distinct from a policy statement. It is precisely on the assumption that the municipality adopted a regulation of a kind against which, in other legal systems such as Italy, Portugal, and Norway, the claim would probably succeed on grounds of equality and procedural fairness, respectively. Moreover, the Portuguese courts, like the Austrian ones, would submit the local authority's decision to the proportionality test.

A divergence emerges, instead, regarding the judicial remedy. In most jurisdictions, as noted earlier, the courts would conclude that the policy change is unlawful and would, therefore, annul it. However, in some cases, including Sweden, the courts would not do so. Conversely, in China the courts would declare the new policy unlawful and would send the authority a recommendation to address the procedural invalidity. This divergence coexists alongside the commonality concerning the crucial legal issue: both individuals and social groups are entitled, at the very least, to have an opportunity to comment before a policy change is made.

[56] J Morison and D Mark, 'United Kingdom—Case 7' Chapter 15.XIII.L in this book. See also Craig (n 1) 535–35 (same thesis).

[57] L Weidemann, 'Case 7—Germany' Chapter 15.XIII.E in this book.

[58] S Storr 'Austria—Case 7' Chapter 15.XIII.A; J van der Brink, L Verboeket, and V van Waarde 'Netherlands—Case 7' Chapter 15.XIII.H; L Parona 'Italy—Case 7' Chapter 15.XIII.G, all in this book.

B. Partially Unpublished Rules?

Our final hypothetical case concerns a traditional issue and draws on a recent experience. The traditional issue is whether a requirement for publication exists not only for primary and secondary legislation but also for administrative rules. This is an important aspect of what it means to have a government of laws, where the citizens seek to hold those who govern to the respect of rules they make because they may have acted on the basis of those rules.[59] But it is not infrequent that administrative rules are 'unpublished and hence unknown'.[60] The question that thus arises is whether a failure to publish these rules would affect either their validity or their effects, given that the public would not have the opportunity to know the rules that would be applied to them. The recent experience, with which all nations of the world have been confronted, is that of the COVID-19 pandemic. There have been sanctions and other administrative measures against professionals and corporations for contravention of new rules hastily adopted, which were not easily accessible to the public. Understanding whether those sanctions may be enforced is, therefore, both interesting and important.

We imagine a scenario where, during a pandemic, the Minister of Health sets the prices of various types of face masks through an order, also establishing pecuniary penalties if the prices are disregarded. The Minister announces that the order will be published in the official journal, as required by existing legislation. But the order is published only in part, without specifying the prices of the various types of face masks. Moreover, it is published on the Health Department's website instead of the official journal. When the order is enforced, a pharmacist is fined by the local administration for selling face masks at a different price. She contests the sanction before the competent court, arguing that if the order has not been published in full, it is either invalid or unable to produce any legal effect, because her freedom to conduct her business cannot be limited apart from in the cases and forms established by law. The Health Department responds that the order is valid, despite its failure to publish it in the official journal, because in the world in which we live, a government website can potentially reach more people than the official journal can. The questions that thus arise are, first, whether the court would endorse the claimant's arguments based on the failure to publish and, if so, whether it would deem the partially unpublished order ineffective or invalid.

Interestingly, had our hypothetical case been examined only in the legal systems of France and the United Kingdom, which in the past were deemed irreconcilably different, a sort of divide,[61] the conclusion would have been more or less the same. In

[59] See KC Davis, *Discretionary Justice. A Preliminary Inquiry* (Greenwood Press 1971) 79 (for whom regulations should be published and readily available), and PL Strauss, 'The Rulemaking Continuum' (1992) 41 Duke L J 1463. See also, for France, the report by the Conseil d'État, *Publication et entrée en vigueur des lois et de certains acts administratifs* (La documentation française 2001) 15.

[60] Craig (n 1) 374.

[61] See AV Dicey, *Introduction to the Study of the Law of the Constitution* (1884, 10th edn, MacMillan 1956) 331, but see also, for critical remarks, Wade, *Administrative Law* (n 6) 5 (observing that Dicey had fundamentally misunderstood the meaning of the rule of law in France) and Anthony and Leyland (n 9) 3 (arguing that he had given a distorted picture of English law). For further remarks, see G della Cananea, *The Common Core of European Administrative Laws: Retrospective and Prospective* (Brill 2023) 6.

France, after an attempt to eliminate circulars *en masse*, the general norm established by administrative procedure legislation is that government guidance, including circulars and instructions that interpret legislation or define administrative procedures, must be published.[62] In the absence of publication, they are abrogated. But the same legislation clarifies that unpublished circulars are not applicable, and public authorities cannot use them in their relationships with citizens. In the United Kingdom, the facts of an old case, *Sheer Metalcraft*, are very similar to those in our hypothetical one. When an act of delegated legislation was published without the annex, and a firm was charged for infringing the rules contained in it, it challenged the action due to the lack of publication. The House of Lords held that the lack of publication or only partial publication did not, in itself, invalidate the act, because the general common law rule was that only delegated legislation must be published. However, it ruled out the possibility that anyone could be held guilty of contravening an unpublished rule.[63] There is recent authority affirming that all law is subject to the requirements of accessibility and predictability.[64] This comes close to the solution adopted in the United States, where a person may not be required to resort to, or be adversely affected by, an unpublished rule, unless that person has actual knowledge of it; the courts would therefore quash the contested order.[65]

Our sample is, however, more comprehensive and, not surprisingly, provides a variety of solutions. In some legal systems (including the Czech, Dutch, Italian, and Portuguese orders),[66] where there is a general legislative requirement to publish not only regulations but also all other administrative rules, it must be expected that failure to publish would affect the validity of any such rules and, consequently, the measures for their enforcement. In other legal systems, such as Austria and Norway, where there is a general legislative prohibition on unpublished ordinances having any legal effect whatsoever, failure to publish would negate the legal basis for administrative sanctions, which would thus be annulled by the courts.[67] In still other legal systems, such as Germany, where there is neither type of general requirement, if administrative rules have direct and adverse effects on the individual, they are nonetheless subject to the requirement for publication under the rule of law (*Rechtsstaatprinzip*). Partial publication would not fulfil this requirement. Accordingly, the courts would most probably endorse the claimant's argument based on the failure to publish the order.[68] A more complex solution is envisaged for Hungary, where the Constitutional Court would have to declare that the order is invalid, and the ordinary court would then annul the sanction against the chemist. Lastly, and interestingly, in China (where a real case involved an order that could only be found on the search engine *Baidu*), our hypothetical case would probably be solved using remedies similar to those expected in the

[62] Art L 312-2 of the Code adopted in 2016.

[63] House of Lords, *Regina v Sheer Metalcraft Ltd* (1954). For further remarks, see Craig (n 1) 373.

[64] J Morison and D Mark, 'United Kingdom—Case 6' Chapter 15.VII.L in this book.

[65] US APA, § 552. For further remarks, see Strauss (n 59) 804.

[66] J Rajchl, D Burda, and G Blahoudková 'Czech Republic—Case 6' Chapter 15.VII.C; J van der Brink, L Verboeket, and V van Waarde 'Netherlands—Case 6' Chapter 15.VII.H; L Parona 'Italy—Case 6' Chapter 15.VII.G; R Guerra da Fonseca, 'Portugal—Case 6' Chapter 15.VII.J, all in this book.

[67] S Storr 'Austria—Case 6' Chapter 15.VII.A; E Smith, 'Norway—Case 6' Chapter 15.VII.I, both in this book.

[68] L Weidemann, 'Case 6—Germany' Chapter 15.VII.E in this book.

first group of legal systems. Specifically, the order would be deemed unlawful and the sanction would be annulled.[69]

This case confirms the importance of factual analysis. Comparison confined to the legislative formant would simply show that there is an area of disagreement. However, the area of disagreement is considerably narrowed if one takes into consideration the criteria established by the courts. This demonstrates that, in terms of the actual results reached in our factual analysis, the area of disagreement becomes less significant. Underlying this area of agreement is a common concern for legality and transparency not viewed as generic ideals but as principles that prevent public authorities from applying unpublished rules.

This concern is confirmed by the case law of the European Court of Human Rights since its ruling in the *Sunday Times* case.[70] The Court was called upon to clarify the interpretation of the phrase 'prescribed by law' as used in Article 9 of the European Convention on Human Rights (ECHR) with regard to freedom of the press. It observed that, for the purposes of the ECHR, the word 'law' covered 'not only statute, but also unwritten law'.[71] The Court then went on to delineate the twin requirements of accessibility and foreseeability which stem from the phrase 'prescribed by law': first of all, 'the law must be adequately accessible', so that individuals must be able to comprehend 'what is adequate in the circumstances of the legal rules applicable to a given case; secondly, a norm must be 'formulated with sufficient precision to enable the citizen to regulate his conduct' to a degree that is reasonable in the circumstances'.[72] The Court's interpretation is binding on domestic courts as a consequence of the combined effects of the entry into force of Protocol No 11 (1999) and the incorporation of the Convention into national legal systems.[73]

VII. Areas of Agreement and Disagreement

It is time now to stand back from the details of the various hypothetical cases and look more generally at the essence of our comparative enquiry; that is, not so much *whether* there is some common ground, notwithstanding the innumerable differences but *what* type of common core exists[74] in a significant part of administrative and public law: administrative procedure. We will now turn our attention to two aspects: what could be expected and what has been found.[75]

What could be expected was that, with regard to rulemaking, the area of disagreement would not only be larger but also more significant than what has emerged concerning administrative adjudication. At least two factors would justify this expectation.

[69] X Sun, 'China—Case 6' Chapter 15.VII.B in this book.
[70] ECtHR, judgment of 26 April 1979, *The Sunday Times v United Kingdom* (app No 65358/74).
[71] ibid § 47.
[72] ibid § 49.
[73] For this thesis, see A Stone Sweet and H Keller (eds), *A Europe of Rights. The Impact of the ECHR on National Legal Systems* (OUP 2008).
[74] See O Kahn-Freund, 'Review of RB Schlesinger (ed.), Formation of Contracts. A Study of the Common Core of Legal Systems' (1970) 18 Am J Comp L 429.
[75] See Schlesinger (n 30) 5.

On the one hand, as observed in the previous chapter, there is much diversity in administrative procedure legislation concerning rulemaking. On the other, as we have seen in the initial part of this chapter, other norms often diverge, such as in relation to the adoption of a policy or rule.

However, the results of our factual analysis are partially unexpected. In some instances, our findings confirm what a public lawyer sufficiently familiar with other European legal systems and the settled case law of the European Court of Human Rights would have expected, for example, with regard to consultation. This concerns, for example, the regulatory authority's failure to consult a stakeholder before setting new tariffs, which infringes the standards of procedural fairness and propriety, in addition to the principle of equality. Other findings are largely unexpected.[76] These refer, in particular, to the power to predetermine the standards of administrative conduct by adopting a policy or rule. The supposed contrast between common law and civil law systems concerning the relationship between discretion and rules was found to produce fewer differences than expected. It is everywhere accepted that administrative authorities are entitled to adopt a policy or rule allowing them to make routine their action and to make their individual decisions more predictable. The effects of those rules will not, however, be the same as those of parliamentary or delegated legislation. In some cases, those rules will have to allow administrative authorities to hear the merits of the individual applicant who wishes to obtain a different decision. In other cases, even though the court concludes that the authority unduly deviated from the policy or rule it had set out, it will distinguish any such deviation from the infringement of legislation (eg in Italy this will be regarded as a sort of abuse of power).

More generally, rather than the expected divergence between legal systems, there are overlapping areas of agreement and disagreement. To mention one further example, concerning the publication of rules, there is evident divergence among the legal systems examined as to whether there is a requirement to publish administrative rules, as well as to whether the absence of publication impinges either on the validity of rules or their effectiveness. However, all the legal systems examined adhere to the same general unwritten norm; that is, unpublished rules may not be applied to individuals and legal entities. Underlying this norm are the principles of legality, legal certainty, and transparency. The area of agreement is, therefore, qualitatively at least as important as the area of disagreement. This entails an improvement for society as a whole. 'Citizens are better off' if they can have adequate knowledge of the rules that, directly or indirectly (ie through individual administrative decisions applying those rules), impinge on their interests and can thus more easily verify whether they receive equal treatment.[77] In another example, concerning the deviation from a previously established policy or rule, the courts are not always uniform in deciding on the reason why the public body is not allowed to do so. Most of the time, they will refer either to the principle of consistency or the protection of legitimate expectations; others will concern procedural fairness (or due process), equality, and good faith. But there is an unexpectedly large area of commonality concerning the crucial legal issue; that is, the

[76] See F Moderne, 'Préface' in A Brewer-Carias, *Les principes de la procedure administrative non contentieuse* (Economica 1992) 2.

[77] Strauss (n 59) 808.

dominant solution is that the administrative authority may change its policy or rule only if the individual, or a group, has been granted an opportunity to comment upon it. Thus, it would be lawful for an authority to adopt a policy or a rule, to tell interested parties what that policy or rule is, and to apply it in individual cases after hearing those who have something to clarify or to object.

Two further remarks may usefully complete the picture. The first concerns diversity, the second commonality. While certain historical distinctions are becoming rather blurred, other differences persist, and there are new ones, for example concerning how administrative rules are published, in the light of the new technologies now available. Nonetheless, the general point to be made is that diversity does not follow the traditional boundaries. It does not reflect the dividing line between common law and civil law systems found in the field of private law. Indeed, there is diversity between the former. As early as in the mid-twentieth century, the United States introduced general legislation on administrative procedure, notably innovative in its approach to rulemaking. Moreover, while the position common to the United Kingdom and other Westminster-like democracies is that discretion must not be fettered as a matter of principle, in the United States there is a greater propensity to regulate discretion, among other things, through administrative rules. Lastly, membership of the Council of Europe is obviously another differentiating factor due to the increasingly significant case law of the European Court of Human Rights. There is diversity, too, among the legal systems of continental Europe, not only because some of them have adopted general requirements, such as consultation in rulemaking procedures and the publication of rules, while others have not done so. There is also diversity with regard to parliamentary scrutiny of executive rules, despite these systems' similar parliamentary frameworks. Hungary in particular is an outlier in this respect, echoing findings from earlier volumes in this series concerning government accountability for the exercise of police powers, for instance.[78] There is greater diversity—or much less common ground—vis-à-vis the Chinese legal system, either because of its differing cultural roots or the consequences that this particular form of government entails. Even these differences, however, concern certain, but not all, mid-level standards of administrative action.

These observations regarding diversity are helpful for a better understanding of the nature and extent of the common core. According to widespread opinion, the European constitutions adopted after the Second World War (1945) and, perhaps to a greater extent, after the fall of the Berlin Wall (1989), share both public law values and its general principles. There is also a common tendency, at least in continental Europe, to enact various forms of general legislation on administrative procedure. Both these developments are certainly important but they do not play a decisive part in setting the standards of administrative action concerning rulemaking. The decisive factor is the judicial formant, as well as the underlying theories of public law. In brief, ideas have consequences.[79] For example, as we observed earlier, some legal systems mandate a general requirement to consult stakeholders before policies or rules are

[78] G della Cananea and R Caranta (eds), *Tort Liability of Public Authorities in European Laws* (OUP 2020).

[79] RM Weaver, *Ideas Have Consequences* (University of Chicago Press 1948).

adopted, whereas others only have sector-specific requirements. The extent of the right to be consulted differs from one nation to another. However, if a public authority opts to consult citizens before adopting a policy or a rule, then it must do so conscientiously, giving plenty of notice before concluding the decision-making process and by granting stakeholders the opportunity to be heard, although, one again, there is more than one way to do so.

VIII. Summary and Looking Ahead

In an article written when there was much talk of the 'convergence' of administrative laws and European laws *tout court*, it was argued that European legal systems were not, in fact, converging.[80] The concept of convergence was considered problematic primarily because it did not clarify the direction or goal towards which these legal systems were supposedly converging. Nor did it clarify whether any significant differences still remained. In contrast, the concept of a 'common core' is more helpful because it is only the core that is common, while old and new differences exist beyond it. It is important to recognize, moreover, that this common core consists not only of public law values and general principles but also of mid-level standards, such as consultation, publication, and judicial review, the latter constrained within the forms and limitations established by the various legal systems. All this goes to show that the common core goes beyond administrative adjudication, which has already seen various areas of agreement staked out, extending also to rulemaking. Whether and to what extent it also includes planning is another question, which deserves separate treatment in the final chapter of this book.

[80] P Legrand, 'European Legal Systems are not Converging' (1996) 45 Int'l & Comp LQ 52, 53.

18
Plans
In Between Rules and Decisions

Roberto Caranta

I. Introduction: What is the Nature of Plans?

According to the online *Oxford English Dictionary*, 'plan' is synonymous with 'design' or 'proposal', while in law, 'plan' is closer to the former. In the same *Dictionary*, the first definition is 'An organized (and usually detailed) proposal according to which something is to be done; a scheme of action; a strategy; a programme, schedule. Also in a weakened sense: a method or way of proceeding; an intention or ambition for the future (usually in the *plural*)'. In law, a plan is more akin to an organized (and usually detailed) binding design, according to which something is to be done. As such, it finds itself midway between rules and decisions.

Shapiro has even argued that the law itself is 'a form of social planning'. In his view,

> legal institutions plan for the communities over which they claim authority, both by telling members what they may or may not do, and by identifying those who are entitled to affect what others may or may not do. Following this claim, legal rules are themselves generalized plans, or planlike norms, issued by those who are authorized to plan for others. And adjudication involves the application of these plans, or planlike norms, to those to whom they apply. In this way, the law organizes individual and collective behavior so that members of the community can bring about moral goods that could not have been achieved, or achieved as well, otherwise.[1]

Here, Shapiro sketches a binary system of regulation and adjudication, with plans coinciding with rules. Regulation and adjudication in fact represent the two poles of administrative action in most jurisdictions, as is seen, for instance, in the Czech Republic[2] and Sweden.[3] In the People Republic of China, however, there is no clear distinction between rulemaking and adjudication along the lines of the Western legal tradition.[4] As Ferrari Zumbini notes in her chapter, different names and notions are

[1] SJ Shapiro, *Legality* (Harvard University Press 2011) 155; see also B Celano, 'What Can Plans Do for Legal Theory?' in D Canale and G Tuzet (eds), *The Planning Theory of Law. Critical Reader* (Springer 2013) 129–52.
[2] J Rajchl, D Burda, and G Blahoudková, 'Czech Republic—Case 1' Chapter 15.11.C in this book.
[3] P Jonason and B Forssén, 'Sweden—Case 1' Chapter 15.11.K in this book.
[4] X Sun, 'China' Chapter 3.III in this book.

Roberto Caranta, *Plans* In: *Administrative Rulemaking and Planning in European Laws*. Edited by: Giacinto della Cananea and Angela Ferrari Zumbini, Oxford University Press. © Roberto Caranta 2025.
DOI: 10.1093/oso/9780198867616.003.0018

used to define rulemaking in the jurisdictions covered in this book, and this affects plans too.[5]

Still, equating plans with regulatory measures is just one of the possibilities presented in the chapters collected in this volume. The image represented in those chapters is that plans have taken precarious hold—a different one in each jurisdiction—between rulemaking and adjudication, yet they often claim their own distinctive identity.

Rulemaking, plans, and adjudication are also treated as discrete entities in some international law instruments. The 1998 UNECE Aarhus Convention on Access to Information, Public Participation in Decision-making and Access to Justice in Environmental Matters is a good case in point. Articles 6, 7, and 8 respectively concern public participation in procedures related to decisions on specific activities, plans, programmes, policies, and, lastly, executive regulations and/or generally applicable legally binding normative instruments. While the different types of legal acts are not explicitly defined, the participatory rights guaranteed under these articles progressively weaken as the Convention transitions from individual decisions or adjudication to planning and finally to rulemaking.[6]

What distinguishes plans from rules is that they are not meant for repeated application to identical situations in the future. They normally have a set period of application and are designed to address different situations according to a coordinated framework or to regulate (possibly different) situations over their duration. The first is the case of spatial, urban, or territorial plans, where different areas are treated in different ways. Some plans concern dwellings, while others regard services such as roads and schools, and others again focus on areas reserved for agriculture, forestry, and so on. The second case pertains to economic—and increasingly today—environmental (eg energy-related) planning, which involves, for example, setting different and often increasing targets to be met by certain actors, often, but not exclusively, in the public sector.

Like rules, plans must often be implemented through a succession of individual decisions, such as the issuance of building permits.[7] In Germany, legally binding plans are the basis for planning decisions (sections 72ff of the *Verwaltungsverfharengesetz 1976*).[8] This is often also true for plans concerning the environment. However, the dynamics between planning and later individual decisions, which may include expropriation, may vary widely.[9]

The situation is normally more complex when it comes to economic plans and sometimes in the case of other plans concerning the environment. Economic planning

[5] A Ferrari Zumbini, 'A Comparative Analysis of Administrative Procedure Legislation on Rulemaking' Chapter 17 in this book.

[6] See M Eliantonio, 'The Proceduralisation of EU Environmental Legislation: International Pressures, Some Victories and Some Way to Go' (2015) 8(1) Review of European Administrative Law 103; R Caranta, A Gerbrandy, and B Müller (eds), *The Making of a New European Legal Culture: the Aarhus Convention* (Europea Law Publishing 2018)

[7] See G della Cananea, Chapter 1 in this book.

[8] L Weidemann, 'Germany—Case 3' Chapter 15.IV.E in this book.

[9] Y Marique, 'Public and Private Sovereign Powers in Liberal Models of Property Protection. Belgium, Sweden and the Netherlands' in M Conticelli and T Perroud (eds), *Procedural Requirements for Administrative Limits to Property Rights* (OUP 2022) 285.

is more often than not detached from actual individual decisions in the sense that more intermediary measures need to be taken before the provisions in the plan translate into individual administrative acts. In addition to cascading plans with increasing levels of detail, targets in plans are often met through the accumulation of individual decisions and actions that do not necessarily take the form of an administrative decision. A fitting example is Directive (EU) 2023/1791 on energy efficiency (RED III). Its Article 4 concerns energy efficiency targets and provides that 'Member States shall collectively ensure a reduction of energy consumption of at least 11,7 % in 2030 compared to the projections of the 2020 EU Reference Scenario'. To this end,

> [e]ach Member State shall set an indicative national energy efficiency contribution based on final energy and shall notify those contributions to the Commission, together with an indicative trajectory for those contributions, as part of the updates of their integrated national energy and climate plans submitted pursuant to Article 14(2) of Regulation (EU) 2018/1999, and of their integrated national energy and climate plans notified pursuant to Article 3 and Articles 7 to 12 of that Regulation.

Moreover, under Article 5, which concerns the public sector's role in leading energy efficiency policy, Member States are required to reduce total final energy consumption across all public bodies. To this end, the Member States must ensure that 'regional and local authorities establish specific energy efficiency measures in their long-term planning tools, such as decarbonization or sustainable energy plans'. EU energy law relies heavily on planning and plans that do not necessarily cascade in a series of individual decisions but rather through internal organization measures (eg turning off lights at dusk) to achieve common goals.[10]

Still, even in the context of economic planning, there may be a clear series of implementing decisions—and potential contracts—as was the case in the former Soviet era. Starting from the First Five-Year Plan of the late 1920s, general plans were executed through specific orders issued to state enterprises for the production and distribution of goods and services. These orders were in turn given reciprocal binding force by contracts that state enterprises were required to enter into with one another.[11]

Because of the varying degrees of connection between different types of plans and the implementation of individual decisions, the questionnaire targets instances of spatial or environmental planning that directly raise concerns about the protection of individual rights and interests that may be affected from the outset by decisions made within the plan itself. This is particularly relevant in zoning plans that determine what is permissible in each specific area they cover. The same applies to plans affecting some general interest, such as environmental issues.

[10] As such, they are different from the EU Recovery Plan, on which see G della Cananea, Chapter 1.II.C in this book.

[11] See the translation from Russian of sections of the work by Halfina in RS, 'Plan and Contract in Transactions between Soviet State Enterprises' 5 (1953) Soviet Studies 89.

II. Regulating Plans

As the answers to the questionnaire show, the fact that plans tend to sit somewhere between rulemaking and adjudication presents the possibility of at least four very different regulatory scenarios, namely (i) the existence of general rules specific to planning in the codes and/or rules relating to administrative procedures; (ii) the application of general rules for rulemaking to plans; (iii) the application of general administrative procedure rules and/or principles to plans; or (iv) neither general procedural rules nor the provisions applicable to rulemaking are relevant for planning procedures; in this case, procedural rules for planning will only be found in ad hoc legislation.

The first situation is found in Germany, where specific procedural rules are applicable to all cases of legally binding planning procedures (sections 72ff of the *Verwaltungsverfharengesetz 1976*).[12] A similar conceptual approach to legally binding plans as measures of a general nature without normative character is seen in the Czech Republic.[13] In Portugal, guaranteed participation in matters of housing and urban planning is only laid down in Article 65/5 of the Constitution.[14] In contrast, Italy takes almost the opposite approach, where the 1990 Administrative Procedure Act (APA) excludes the application of most of its provisions to planning (and rulemaking).[15]

Assimilating plans and rulemaking is the approach generally favoured in Portugal[16] but also within the EU itself.[17] The second situation is also observed in the People's Republic of China, at least concerning urbanization plans, which are distinguished from detailed urban plans. A further consequence is that the former are not subject to review.[18] In Austria, on the other hand, regulations and plans are both subcategories of a general type of ordinance.[19]

In Norway, however, the general principles of due process, fairness, and transparency also apply to planning procedures,[20] and the application of these general (including constitutional) principles may also be assumed with reference to Sweden.[21] A variation of the third option is found in the Netherlands, where both regulations and plans, but also policy decisions, may come under the notion of 'decision' (*besluit*) if they have legal effect. In such cases, they are regulated by the General Administrative Law Act (GALA).[22]

In this situation, where neither general procedural rules nor the provisions applicable to rulemaking are relevant for planning procedures, such as in the United

[12] Weidemann, 'Germany—Case 3' (n 8).
[13] J Rajchl, D Burda, and G Blahoudková, 'Czech Republic—Case 3' Chapter 15.IV.C in this book.
[14] R Guerra da Fonseca, 'Portugal—Case 3' Chapter 15.IV.J in this book.
[15] L Parona 'Italy—Case 1' Chapter 15.II.G in this book.
[16] R Guerra da Fonseca, 'Portugal—Case 2' Chapter 15.III.J in this book.
[17] E Chiti, 'European Union' in this book.
[18] X Sun, 'China—Case 8' section IX.B of this chapter.
[19] S Storr, 'Austria—Case 1' Chapter 15.II.A in this book.
[20] E Smith, 'Norway—Case 1' Chapter 15.II.I; and 'Norway—Case 3' Chapter 15.IV.I, both in this book.
[21] P Jonason and B Forssén, 'Sweden—Case 3' Chapter 15.IV.K in this book.
[22] J van der Brink, L Verboeket, and V van Waarde 'Netherlands—Case 1' Chapter 15.II.H; 'Netherlands—Case 2' Chapter 15.III.H, all in this book.

States, specific plans are regulated under special legislation for urban development or environmental protection, for example. In such cases, the APA does not apply.[23] In Hungary, the rights guaranteed to participants depend on the specific terms of any given statute.[24]

Even when some general administrative rules or principles apply to planning, the procedures for adopting certain plans, such as urban or zoning plans, are often detailed in specific legislation.[25]

III. Plans Detrimentally Affecting Private Rights (Case 8)

Most jurisdictions require some form of due process in the adoption of plans that may be detrimental to individual rights. The best example is Portugal. Article 65/5 of the Portuguese Constitution is mirrored and supplemented by specific statutes establishing a 'complex network of participatory rights'. These include the duty to take into account and respond to observations from members of the public and even have municipal technical personnel provide clarifications when necessary.[26] Similarly, in the Czech Republic, procedures for adopting local development plans are detailed in specific statutes. The owners and the so-called agents for the public, authorized by a significant number of citizens residing in the municipality, are entitled to raise objections. Other third parties may submit comments.[27]

In the Netherlands, the application of the GALA to plans such as those concerning zoning implies the adoption of a notice and comment procedure. Moreover, Sun City will have to address objections raised by interested parties and provide reasons for adopting the plan.[28] This situation would be treated as a legally binding planning procedure in Germany, involving public consultation. Thus, Sun City will have to react to the comments submitted to ensure the best outcome possible, also considering the general interest.[29]

Consultations with interested parties are required by special zoning laws in Austria, and public authorities are expected to give reasons if they do not accept the suggestions provided.[30] In Italy, both the general public and the concerned owner have written participation rights, with the latter empowered to file what are grandly termed 'oppositions'. According to the case law, however, the administration has no duty to refute the arguments brought against its proposals in a detailed manner.[31]

[23] J Lubbers and G della Cananea, 'United States of America—Case 1' Chapter 15.II.M in this book.

[24] L Berkes and BS Gerencsér, 'Hungary—Case 1' Chapter 15.II.F in this book.

[25] For example in Storr 'Austria—Case 1' (n 19); Parona 'Italy—Case 1' (n 15); Guerra da Fonseca, 'Portugal—Case 2' (n 16), where maritime spatial planning is foreseen.

[26] R Guerra da Fonseca, 'Portugal—Case 8' section IX.J of this chapter.

[27] J Rajchl, D Burda, and G Blahoudková, 'Czech Republic—Case 8' section IX.C of this chapter.

[28] J van der Brink, L Verboeket, and V van Waarde 'Netherlands—Case 8' section IX.H of this chapter.

[29] Weidemann, 'Germany—Case 3' (n 8).

[30] S Storr 'Austria—Case 8' section IX.A of this chapter.

[31] L Parona 'Italy—Case 8' section IX.G of this chapter.

In Sweden, failure to consult relevant stakeholders results in the annulment of the plan.[32]

The EU has no jurisdiction over urban planning, but if it had, the right to good administration under Article 41 of the Charter would be applicable, including the right to be heard and the obligation to consider all relevant aspects.[33]

In Hungary, on the other hand, participation rights are subject to specific laws applicable to each planning type.[34]

In the United Kingdom, when participation is not legally mandated, it might still be required in some specific circumstances, such as a promise or established practice. Assuming this to be the case here, consultations must comply with some basic requirements, including the obligation that its 'product' be 'conscientiously taken into account'. This means that while planners maintain ample discretion, they cannot simply disregard comments without bothering to give reasons.[35]

In the United States, zoning plans are regulated by state and local governments, often following an ABA Model Statute requiring some form of notice and comment procedure, in turn implying that adverse comments are dealt with.[36] Due process will also be upheld in the People's Republic of China concerning the judicial review of detailed urban plans.[37]

On the other hand, due process rights for the adoption of plans of a 'general nature' are not guaranteed in Norway.[38] Due process requirements may also be limited *ratione personae*, like in Sweden, where only stakeholders with an 'important interest in the decision' benefit from participation rights.[39]

With the exception of the jurisdictions just mentioned, residents would normally be able to have Sun City's plan annulled as their comments and objections have been flatly ignored. This would also be the case in other states not considered in this book, such as Belgium[40] or France.[41] The conclusion is that 'the involvement of citizens in urban planning procedures is increasingly allowed or even favoured in many countries'.[42] Italy, however, stands out for its perfunctory stance on participation. The plan would be annulled if participation had not been allowed,[43] but planning authorities are not obliged to engage seriously with comments and objections.[44]

[32] P Jonason and B Forssén, 'Sweden—Case 8' section IX.K of this chapter.

[33] M Lunarderlli, 'European Union—Case 8' section IX.D of this chapter.

[34] L Berkes and BS Gerencsér, 'Hungary—Case 8' section IX.F of this chapter.

[35] J Morison and D Mark, 'United Kingdom—Case 1' Chapter 15.II.L; 'United Kingdom—Case 3' Chapter 15.IV.E; and 'United Kingdom—Case 8' section IX.L of this chapter, all in this book.

[36] J Lubbers and G della Cananea, 'United States of America—Case 8' section IX.M of this chapter.

[37] Sun, 'China—Case 8' (n 18).

[38] E Smith, 'Norway—Case 8' section IX.I of this chapter.

[39] Jonason and Forssén, 'Sweden—Case 8' (n 32).

[40] B Renders and others, 'Belgium—Case 3' in Conticelli and Perroud (n 9) 125.

[41] E Guernaoui, 'France—Case 3' in Conticelli and Perroud (n 9) 126.

[42] V Martenet, 'Comparative Perspectives on Expropriation and Other Things. England, France, Germany, and the United States' in Conticelli and Perroud (n 9) 270.

[43] S Mirate, 'Italy—Case 3' in Conticelli and Perroud (n 9) 127ff.

[44] Parona 'Italy—Case 8' (n 32).

IV. Plans Detrimentally Affecting a General Interest (Case 9)

The specific provisions in sections 72ff of the German APA will be applicable to this case. These require balancing the relevant legally protected interests, also by means of a cost-benefit analysis, to achieve an appropriate and proportionate planning decision. The consideration of private interests is also required by the Federal Building Act.[45] In Portugal too, the unwritten principle of rationality necessitates balancing the costs and benefits of different options.[46] In the Netherlands, this will qualify as a zoning plan, thus requiring a notice and comment procedure. The municipality will have to carry out a cost-benefit analysis and weigh all involved interests, including the evaluation of possible alternatives. However, standing to challenge the decision might depend on whether the association may qualify as 'public concerned' (similarly to the provisions in Article 9 of the Aarhus Convention). If not, having raised their objection during the administrative phase of the procedure (unless excused for not doing so) will be a condition precedent to standing.[47]

In the United States, the requirement of the Highway Act of 1968, limiting the use of federal funds to build roads in parks unless no other route is 'feasible and prudent', will be applied alongside the 'arbitrary and capricious' test, thus necessitating some form of cost-benefit analysis.[48] In Hungary too, planners must consider all relevant interests under the applicable sector-specific legislation, although judicial decisions might be difficult to enforce.[49]

While no specific statutory provision would be applicable in the United Kingdom, the case law indicates that planners must consider all relevant factors. Furthermore, narrowly focusing on economic aspects alone and neglecting environmental considerations would go against the principle of proportionality and lead to the decision being overturned.[50]

Even with no explicit provisions requiring a balance of interest, the decision would be found unlawful in the People's Republic of China too because of the lack of reasons.[51]

In Norway, while margins of discretion in political decisions are respected, complete omission of consideration for possible alternatives would probably render the decision unlawful.[52] In the Czech Republic, there is no requirement for a cost-benefit analysis, and a soft proportionality review will only amount to a very rough consideration of potential alternatives.[53] In Italy, no cost-benefit analysis is required unless an Environmental Impact Assessment (EIA)-type of procedure is mandated for environmental protection. Considering alternatives will be left to the discretion of the

45 Weidemann, 'Germany—Case 9' section X.E of this chapter. in this book; see also L Berkes and BS Gerencsér, 'Hungary—Case 9' section X.F of this chapter.

46 R Guerra da Fonseca, 'Portugal—Case 9' section X.J of this chapter.

47 J van der Brink, L Verboeket, and V van Waarde 'Netherlands—Case 9' section X.H of this chapter.

48 J Lubbers and G della Cananea, 'United States of America—Case 9' section X.M of this chapter.

49 Berkes and Gerencsér, 'Hungary—Case 9' (n 45).

50 Lubbers and della Cananea, 'United States of America—Case 8' (n 48).

51 X Sun, 'China—Case 9' section X.B of this chapter.

52 E Smith, 'Norway—Case 9' section X.I of this chapter.

53 J Rajchl, D , and G Blahoudková, 'Czech Republic—Case 9' section X.C of this chapter.

competent authority. Such decisions will be treated deferentially and will be overturned by courts only in cases of manifest error.[54]

In Sweden, the merits of the choice in the plan might not be reviewable, but a lack of sufficient legal basis might render it unlawful.[55] In Austria too, the feasibility of the works is considered a question of expediency, which is, in principle, unreviewable except in cases of obvious inexpediency. Even so, standing will not be recognized since the association will lack a 'subjective right'.[56]

In conclusion, several jurisdictions have positive requirements in legislation or common law, calling for some form of cost-benefit analysis or at least the consideration of possible alternatives. The case law in the People's Republic of China seems to allow for a similar outcome. In other countries, no such obligation can be derived from general administrative law principles, and any requirement to give reasons will be approached through deferential or hands-off judicial review. In these jurisdictions, the association's claims will be doomed to fail. Clearly, different traditions of more (or less) intense judicial review go hand in hand with a stronger (or weaker) development of general principles enabling judicial review.

V. EIA Requirements for Activities Significantly Affecting the Environment

In EU Member States, and for plans designed by the EU institutions themselves,[57] an EIA is required under EU law when a project is likely to have a significant impact on the environment.[58] This is the case, for instance, in Austria, Hungary, Italy, Portugal, and the Czech Republic.[59] Interestingly, this is still the case in the United Kingdom, even after Brexit.[60] The same applies in Norway, as the EU EIA directive is binding on Single European Act (SEA) countries as well.[61] In Sweden, however, exploration is not considered detrimental to the environment, and an EIA will only be required at the permission stage,[62] while Italy allows for a 'posthumous' EIA.[63]

[54] L Parona 'Italy—Case 9' section X.G; on EIA see also Parona 'Italy—Case 10' section XI.G, both in this chapter.

[55] P Jonason and B Forssén, 'Sweden—Case 9' section X.K of this chapter.

[56] S Storr and S Praniess 'Austria—Case 9' section X.A of this chapter.

[57] M Lunarderlli, 'European Union—Case 10' section XI.D of this chapter.

[58] See art 2 of Directive 2011/92/EU on the assessment of the effects of certain public and private projects on the environment as substituted by art 1(2)(a) of Directive 2014/52/EU: '1. Member States shall adopt all measures necessary to ensure that, before development consent is given, projects likely to have significant effects on the environment by virtue, inter alia, of their nature, size or location are made subject to a requirement for development consent and an assessment with regard to their effects on the environment.'

[59] S Storr and S Praniess 'Austria—Case 10' section XI.A; L Berkes and BS Gerencsér, 'Hungary—Case 10' section XI.F; L Parona 'Italy—Case 10' section XI.G; R Guerra da Fonseca, 'Portugal—Case 10' section XI.J; J Rajchl, D Burda, and G Blahoudková, 'Czech Republic—Case 10' section XI.C, all in this chapter.

[60] J Morison and D Mark, 'United Kingdom—Case 10' section XI.L of this chapter.

[61] E Smith, 'Norway—Case 10' section XI.I of this chapter.

[62] P Jonason and B Forssén, 'Sweden—Case 10' section XI.K of this chapter.

[63] Parona, 'Italy—Case 10' (n 54); this approach mirrors the one followed in the People Republic of China: see A Ferrari Zumbini, 'A Comparative Analysis of Administrative Procedure Legislation on Rulemaking' Chapter 16.IX in this book.

Even if EU law did not require an EIA in this case, in Germany, environmental considerations would number among the general interests to be balanced when reaching a decision, a duty reinforced under Article 20a of the Basic Law, which makes the state responsible towards future generations.[64] In the Netherlands, a similar conclusion might be argued based on Article 8 of the European Convention on Human Rights (ECHR), but there is no case law to support this possibility.[65] Similarly, in the United Kingdom, both legislation and case law point to the constant need to take environmental concerns into account.[66]

In the United States, an EIA is required at the federal level and in several states, but not uniformly across the country. In the states where it is not required, Terranova's actions would be considered lawful as there is no common law requirement for EIA-like procedures.[67] Likewise, in the People's Republic of China, judicial review would be permitted because an EIA is required by law. This would not be the case if such a procedural requirement were not provided for in law.[68]

In conclusion, EIA-like procedures would be required in jurisdictions where there is an explicit legal requirement to do so, and to the extent mandated by those requirements. This means that an assessment of environmental impact is not universally seen as a basic procedural requirement under due process or similar principles, with the possible exceptions of the United Kingdom, Germany, and the Netherlands.[69]

VI. Conclusions

Examining the protection of individual rights in planning procedures, Martenet concluded that,

> Considering the implications of urban planning on property owners, the involvement of the owners and other stakeholders seems to be justified. A purely top-down approach creates tensions and problems that can hinder sound urban planning. From this perspective, some bottom-up features seem recommendable, if not required by applicable constitutional or statutory provisions. This, however, is not to say that due process requirements should (fully) apply to urban planning.[70]

Table 18.1 below illustrates the area of convergence and the existing differences.

[64] L Weidemann, 'Germany—Case 10' section XI.E of this chapter.

[65] J van der Brink, L Verboeket, and V van Waarde 'Netherlands—Case 10' section XI.H of this chapter; for the reference to international law sources see also Berkes and Gerencsér, 'Hungary—Case 10' (n 59).

[66] Morison and Mark, 'United Kingdom—Case 10' (n 60).

[67] J Lubbers and G della Cananea, 'United States of America—Case 10' section XI.M of this chapter.

[68] X Sun, 'China—Case 10' section XI.B of this chapter.

[69] In Italy, this might be required under the 'sustainability principle': Parona, 'Italy—Case 10' (n 54). See also the discussion in G della Cananea, 'Judicial Oversight of Procedural Fairness and Propriety in Europe: Diversity Within Commonality' in G della Cananea and M Andenas (eds), *Judicial Review of Administration in Europe* (OUP 2021) 352ff.

[70] V Martenet, 'Comparative Perspectives on Expropriation and Other Things. England, France, Germany, and the United States' in Conticelli and Perroud (n 9) 270 f.

Table 18.1 Convergence and the existing differences

	Austria	Czech Republic	Germany	Hungary	Italy	Netherlands	Portugal	Sweden	EU	Norway	UK	US	China
Case 8: Participation	Yes	Yes	Yes	Yes	Yes	Yes	Yes	Limited	Yes	No	It depends but mostly yes	Yes	Yes
Case 8: Duty to give reasons	Yes	Yes	Yes	Yes	Not really	Yes	Yes	Limited by wide discretion	Yes	No	Yes	Yes	Yes
Case 9: Balance of interests	No	Limited	Yes	Yes according to the law books	No	Yes	Yes	No	Yes	No	Yes	Yes	Yes
Case 10: EIA	Yes	Yes	Yes	Yes	Yes	Yes	Yes	Yes	Yes	Yes	Yes	Partly	No

Demonstrating a strong similarity to the findings on rulemaking, the three cases on planning confirm the growing importance of consultations in general. The differences lie in the relevance of input from stakeholders and third parties. In many jurisdictions, the emphasis is on the wide discretion granted to planning authorities, at times linked to the important policy choices to be made when adopting plans. In other cases, the difference is due to courts not really prioritizing participation and reducing it to a mere formality. Conversely, in Germany, the Netherlands, and to a certain extent in the United Kingdom, courts take consultations seriously, requiring a cost-benefit analysis.[71]

This emphasizes the central role of the courts. In Germany and the United Kingdom, and to some extent in the Netherlands, courts are actively engaged in interpreting the law, including constitutional principles in Germany, to ensure meaningful participation. In other countries, courts choose to show deference, thus limiting—if not eroding—participation rights.[72] The central role of the courts in shaping both procedures and participation rights reinforces an old and often criticized approach that focuses heavily on judicial review in the study of administrative law, including comparative administrative law.[73]

Thus, there are few commonalities shared between different jurisdictions, especially outside the core areas of zoning and spatial/urban planning.

Supranational legal frameworks, at least in Europe, have been influential in fostering participation, with the ECHR being invoked, for example, to expand the implementation of EIA-like procedures.[74] The EIA itself, while also practised beyond Europe and is important in the United States, became mandatory under EU law, also influencing SEA countries and the United Kingdom.[75] The prominent role of EU-mandated EIAs probably explains why the provisions of the Aarhus Convention were conspicuously absent from the sections on planning in the chapters compiled in this book.

Supranational law, especially EU law, can thus be said to create a common core in plans that affect the environment, very much along the lines of the Aarhus Convention.

Lastly, the chapters collected in this volume provide further confirmation that in the field of administrative law, the key distinctions are not limited to civil law and common law jurisdictions. Civil law jurisdictions exhibit more than subtle differences, such as deference (or lack of it) towards what are perceived to be policy decisions, in their approach to procedural safeguards and judicial review.[76]

71 Concerning Germany and the Netherlands, see the convergent assessment of G della Cananea, 'Commonality and Diversity in Administrative Rulemaking' Chapter 17.V.B in this book.

72 For example Parona 'Italy—Case 8' (n 32).

73 See also della Cananea, 'Commonality and Diversity in Administrative Rulemaking' Chapter 17VII in this book.

74 Van der Brink, Verboeket, and van Waarde 'Netherlands—Case 10' (n 65); for the reference to international law sources see also Berkes and Gerencsér, 'Hungary—Case 10' (n 59); see also della Cananea, 'Commonality and Diversity in Administrative Rulemaking' Chapter 17.VII in this book.

75 See J Morison and D Mark, 'United Kingdom' in this book.

76 della Cananea, 'Commonality and Diversity in Administrative Rulemaking' Chapter 17.V and VII in this book; see already M Andenas, 'EU Countries and the UK' in della Cananea and Andenas (n 69) 295ff.

Selected Bibliography

Alves Correia F, *Manual de Direito do Urbanismo*, II (Almedina 2010)

Antoniolli W and Koja F, *Allgemeines Verwaltungsrecht* (3rd edn, Manz 1996)

Aroso de Almeida M, *Manual de Processo Administrativo* (2th edn, Almedina 2021)

Aroso de Almeida M, *Teoria Geral do Direito Administrativo* (7th edn, Almedina 2021)

Auby J-B and Dutheil de la Rochère J (eds), *Droit administratif européen* (3rd edn, Bruylant 2022)

Backes C and Eliantonio M (eds), *Cases, Materials and Text on Judicial Review of Administrative Action. Maastricht Edition* (Hart Publishing 2019)

Baldwin R, 'Governing with Rules: the Developing Agenda' in G Richardson and H Genn (eds), *Administrative Law and Government Action* (Clarendon Press 1994) 168–88

Barabás G, Rozsnyai KF, Kovács AG (eds), *Nagykommentár a közigazgatási perrendtartásról szóló 2017. évi I. törvényhez*, (Wolters Kluwer Hungary 2018)

Beatson J, 'Legislative Control of Administrative Rulemaking: Lessons from the British Experience' (1979) 12 Cornell International Law Journal 200–20

Berka W, *Verfassungsrecht* (8th edn, Verlag Österreich 2021)

Chiti E, 'La disciplina procedurale della regolazione' (2004) 3 Rivista trimestrale di diritto pubblico 679–736

Commissie Europeanisering algemeen bestuursrecht VAR, *Europa en het algemeen bestuursrecht. Burger en bestuur in de gemeenschappelijke rechtsorde* (Boom juridisch 2021)

Conticelli M and Perroud T (eds), *Procedural Requirements for Administrative Limits to Property Rights* (OUP 2022)

Craig P, *EU Administrative Law* (3rd edn, OUP 2018)

della Cananea G, *Atti amministrativi generali* (Cedam 2000)

della Cananea G, 'Administrative Rulemaking in Italy: Theories and Practice' in J-B Auby (ed), *Droit compare de la procedure administrative. Comparative Law of Administrative Procedure* (Bruylant 2016) 247–60.

della Cananea G, 'Exit or Voice? *Debat Public* Goes to Italy' (2019) 2 European Public Law 157–69

Dunlop CA and Radaelli CM (eds), *Handbook of Regulatory Impact Assessment* (Edward Elgar 2016)

Eka A, Hirschfeldt J, Jermsten H, and Svahn Starrsjö K, *Regeringsformen—med kommentarer* (Karnov Group 2018)

Garben S and Govaere I (eds), *The EU Better Regulation Agenda* (Hart 2020)

Gomes Canotilho JJ and Moreira V, *Constituição da República Portuguesa—Anotada*, I (4th edn, Coimbra Ed 2007)

Guerra da Fonseca R, 'Sobre uma hipotética harmonização europeia ao nível dos campos de aplicação da descentralização territorial' in J Miranda, AM Cordeiro, EP Ferreira, and JD Nogueira (eds), *Estudos em Homenagem ao Professor Doutor Paulo de Pitta e Cunha—Volume I— Assuntos Europeus e Integração Económica* (Almedina 2010) 1215–32

Harlow C, Leino P, and della Cananea G (eds), *Research Handbook on EU Administrative Law* (Edward Elgar 2017)

Hofmann HCH, Rowe GC, and Türk AH, *Administrative Law and Policy of the European Union* (OUP 2011)

Holmberg E and others, *Grundlagarna Regeringsformen Successionsordningen Riksdagsordningen* (3rd edn, Norstedts Juridik 2012)

Kiss L, *Önkormányzati jogalkotás, szabályozás és dereguláció. Empirikus kutatások eredményeinek felhasználásával* (Dialóg Campus Budapest 2020)

Kneihs B and Lienbacher G (ed), *Rill-Schaeffer-Kommentar zum B-VG* (1st edn, Verlag Österreich 2001)

Lavin R and Malmberg L-G 'Administrative Law' in M Bogdan (ed), *The Swedish Legal System* (Norstedts Juridik 2010) 66–94

Mattarella BG, 'Participation in Rulemaking in Italy' (2010) 2 Italian Journal of Public Law 339–51

McHarg A 'Administrative Discretion, Administrative Rule-making, and Judicial Review' (2017) 70 Current Legal Problems 267–93

Mendes J, 'Discretion, Care and Public Interests in the EU Administration: Probing the Limits of Law' (2016) 53(2) CML Rev 419–51

Öhlinger T and Eberhard H, *Verfassungsrecht* (13th edn, Facultas 2022)

Oliveira FP, *Regime Jurídico dos Instrumentos de Gestão Territorial* (Almedina 2012)

Otero P, *Legalidade e Administração Pública—O Sentido da Vinculação Administrativa à Juridicidade* (Almedina 2003)

Otero P, *Direito do Procedimento Administrativo*, I (Almedina 2016)

Page E, *Governing by Numbers* (Hart Publishing 2001)

Patyi A, *A közigazgatási működés jogi alapjai* (Dialóg Campus Kiadó 2017)

Peeters M and Eliantonio M (eds), *Research Handbook of EU Environmental Law* (Edward Elgar 2020)

Pünder H and Klafki A, 'Grounds of Review and Standard of Review' in C Backes and M Eliantonio (eds), *Cases, Materials and Text on Judicial review of administrative action* (Hart 2019) 441–553

Pywell S and West T, *Delegated Legislation: What Types Are There, and How Are They Made: A Procedural Explainer* (Hansard Society 2023)

Ramajoli M M, Tonoletti B, 'Qualificazione e regime giuridico degli atti amministrativi generali' (2013) 1 Diritto amministrativo 53–115

Scholten M and Brenninkmeijer A (eds), *Controlling EU Agencies* (Edward Elgar 2020)

Schutgens RBJ, 'Rechtsbescherming tegen algemene regels: tijd om de Awb te voltooien' in WJM Voermans, RJB Schutgens, and ACM Meuwese (eds), *Algemene regels in het bestuursrecht*, VAR-reeks no. 158 (Boom juridisch 2017) 95–145

Schwartz B and Wade W, *Legal Control of Government: Administrative Law in Britain and the United States* (Clarendon Press 1972)

Schwarze J, *European Administrative Law* (revised 1st edn, Sweet & Maxwell 2006)

Smith E and Eckhoff T, *Forvaltningsrett* [Administrative Law] (12th edn, Universitetsforlaget 2023)

Smith E, *Konstitusjonelt demokrati* [Constitutional Democracy] (6th edn, Fagbokforlaget 2024)

Storr S, 'Allgemeiner Teil' in B Raschauer, D Ennöckl, and N Raschauer (eds), Grundriss des österreichischen Wirtschaftsrechts (4th edn, Manz 2021) 1–123

Sun X, 'La notion de parti politique en Chine' (2018) 16 Cahiers de la Recherche sur les Droits Fondamentaux - Les partis politiques 59–67

Sun X, 'La réforme de la loi sur la sanction administrative de la République Populaire de Chine' in *Annuaire Européen d'Administration Publique 2020* (Presses Universitaires d'Aix-Marseille 2021) 426–41

Sun X, 'Le vivre-ensemble en Chine' in C Bouriau, A Moine, and M Rota (eds), *Le vivre ensemble saisi par le droit* (A Pedone 2021) 309–22

Sun X, 'L'adaptation des juridictions chinoises à la crise sanitaire liée à l'épidémie de COVID-19' in R Maurel, *L'éthique des procédures contentieuses en temps de pandémie. Approches de droits international et comparé*, series *Droit administratif / Administrative Law* (Bruylant 2022) 455–68

Sun X, 'Le droit souple en droit administratif chinois' in *Annuaire Européen d'Administration Publique 2021* (Presses Universitaires d'Aix-Marseille 2023) 53–67

Tamás A, 'A jogalkotási dilemmák modern demokráciában' in L Ficzere, M Molnár, and A Tamás, *Tanulmányok a közigazgatási szervezeti és jogi intézményei köréből* (Unió 1995) 127–37

Tamás A, *A közigazgatási jog elmélete* (Szent István Társulat 2005)

Vieira de Andrade JC, *A Justiça Administrativa* (19th edn, Almedina 2021)

von Bogdandy A, Huber PM, and Marcusson L, *Handbuch Ius Publicum Europaeum*, IX (CF Müller 2021)

Warnling-Nerep W, *Rättsmedel Om- & överprövning av förvaltningsbeslut* (Jure 2015)

Wenander H, 'Sweden: Non-binding Rules against the Pandemic—Formalism, Pragmatism and Some Legal Realism' (2021) 12 European Journal of Risk Regulation 127–42

Wenander H, 'Rättssäkerhet i förhållande till myndigheters föreskrifter och allmänna råd' in R Sannerholm and K Djurberg Malm (eds) *Rättsstaten i den svenska förvaltningen—en forskningsantologi* (OOS 45, Statskontoret, Rättsstaten 2022)

Index

For the benefit of digital users, indexed terms that span two pages (e.g., 52–53) may, on occasion, appear on only one of those pages.

Tables are indicated by an italic *t* following the page number.